W9-BBS-349

# THE GROWTH OF INSTRUMENTS AND INSTRUMENTAL MUSIC

# The Growth of Instruments And Instrumental Music

*by*

DAVID H. PAETKAU

*with over*
*320 illustrations*

VANTAGE PRESS

NEW YORK - WASHINGTON - HOLLYWOOD

FIRST EDITION



Published by Vantage Press, Inc.
120 West 31st Street, New York 1, N. Y.

Manufactured in the United States of America

Library of Congress Catalog Card Number :61-14645

# ACKNOWLEDGMENTS

The author is deeply indebted to many friends, musicians, instrument manufacturers, officials of museums, teachers and professors of music in schools, universities and conservatories of music, school superintendents, conductors and managers of choirs and symphony orchestras, book dealers, secretaries and officials of broadcasting concerns and research institutions who through the years of preparation of the book have not only answered countless queries by the author but have also given him new and up to date ideas in the various fields of research and, by correcting his occasionally erring concepts, have helped to steer the endeavour in the right direction.

His gratitude extends particularly to those willing assistants whose helping hands reached out beyond the expected. Among these it is a pleasure to mention specifically Miss Thelma Johannes (in private life Mrs. O'Neill), CBC pianist, E. Power Biggs, organist; Saul Goodman, first tympanist of the New York Philharmonic; Professor Dr. R. Johnston, author and musicologist, University of Toronto; Professor Rubakin, Royal Conservatory of Music, Toronto; Dr. Ernesto Vinci, Royal Conservatory of Music, Toronto; J. J. Armin, head of the Armin String Quartet, Windsor; G. Wiebe, Dean of Music of the Canadian Mennonite Bible College; L. W. Kunelius, Superintendent of High Schools, Calgary; Robert Donnell, Dominion Carillonneur, Ottawa; Dr. Alvin Harms, now Calgary; Dr. LeCaine, National Research Council, Canada; Dick H. Epp, Saskatoon, Secretary of the Alumni Association of the Exstudents of The Rosthern Junior College; Helen Dyck, teacher, librarian and President of the Music Festival of the Rosthern Educators' Association.

The names of publishing concerns, persons and museums which generously supplied the illustrations are appended to the individual pictures.

The author feels particularly obligated to his friend and colleague, S. J. Solberg, who unselfishly and unstintingly sacrificed his "leisure time" to correct the first draft of the manuscript and with his criticism and approval kept the flame burning. And for the proofreading of the final version of the manuscript a most sincere "thank you" goes forth to Miss McVeety, teacher of English.

Last but not least it is the author's pleasure to acknowledge his indebtedness to his son, Dr. E. J. Paetkau, whose enthusiasm for the work in progress in no small measure helped to bring it to its final stage.

# INTRODUCTION

For the past hundred years historians and musicians alike have shown an ardent desire to rediscover the treasures of the music of the past. The works of such masters as Bach, Handel, Palestrina, and many others have been published in authentic editions to replace unreliable versions. To do justice to these compositions, scholars started a quest for ancient instruments. Harpsichords were revived, various medieval instruments came back, the recorder appeared again—all to the enrichment of the orchestral and chamber music of our day. At the same time books by renowned scholars have appeared, advancing plausible theories concerning not only the beginnings of music and musical instruments, but the evolution of the instruments, too.

These books fall into two classes: those written for children and the lay public, and those put out for scholars. None of these are designed for the teacher engaged in teaching music. The books with popular appeal simplify things unduly or, all too often, offer inaccurate, frequently even naive, explanations. The scholarly books, on the other hand, not only presuppose an advanced knowledge of music, but abound in details which may interest the scholar but not teacher or high-school student. Furthermore, they are expensive. (Grove's latest edition of the *Dictionary* — an ideal reference work—comprises nine volumes and costs more than one hundred and twenty dollars.)

The present volume is the answer to the author's search for a suitable source book for the teaching of this phase of music to senior high-school students and the conducting of music appreciation classes. The theories presented are those of our greatest authorities: Sachs, Grove, Galpin, Geiringer, Bessaraboff, Lang, Heinitz, Jacob, and others. Footnotes and acknowledgments have as a rule not been appended, because it is felt that teachers and students are not interested in them and the scholar would find them superfluous.

The author found unsurmountable difficulty in trying to harmonize the various conflicting data and theories as expounded by the authorities. Evidently this branch of musicology is still too young to have crystallized into a definite shape. Wherever feasible, the author has sought a way out of any difficulties by advancing more than one theory, or by a plausible generalization, or simply by giving the reader the most authoritative hypotheses — generally those advanced by Dr. Sachs. Finally, views of most contradictory nature are not included in this book.

*The Growth of Instruments and Instrumental Music* attempts to give the reader a complete picture of all of our present-day instruments in their modern form, and at the same time to unfold before his eyes the beginning, growth, and evolution of each. Where possible, the story of the instrument is traced back to its origin. Since a mere recitation of facts is highly distasteful to most readers the author has attempted to illustrate the path of this evolution by delving into the causes of the changes wrought through the centuries. The human element is stressed throughout, and the many illustrations will aid the reader in his studies.

To bring to life the concepts portrayed by word and picture, the reader's attention is drawn toward modern high-fidelity phonograph recordings. Vox has just released a series of "Spotlight" records illustrating a good many historical instruments. These focus on percussion, keyboards, brass, strings, and woodwinds. Similarly, Angel has released "Bell, Drum and Cymbal . . ." on which Saul Goodman illustrates the percussion instruments, past and present. Deutsche Grammophon of Hamburg is distributing electronic music, and records made entirely from tape sounds are easily available. Unquestionably more such releases will follow.

In the last chapter of the book the author has compiled information from pamphlets, magazines, bulletins, and personal discussion with and letters from musicians, instrument manufacturers, museum directors, and others to give the reader some idea about the new music and the new instruments of our own age.

It is hoped that this book will benefit teachers as well as teachers-in-training and senior high-schol students, and that outside the school, musicians and music lovers everywhere will also find it interesting and enlightening.

David H. Paetkau

Coaldale, Alberta
Canada

# CONTENTS

PART TWO. LIP-VOICED INSTRUMENTS

# *Part One: Percussion Instruments*

*From*

*To*

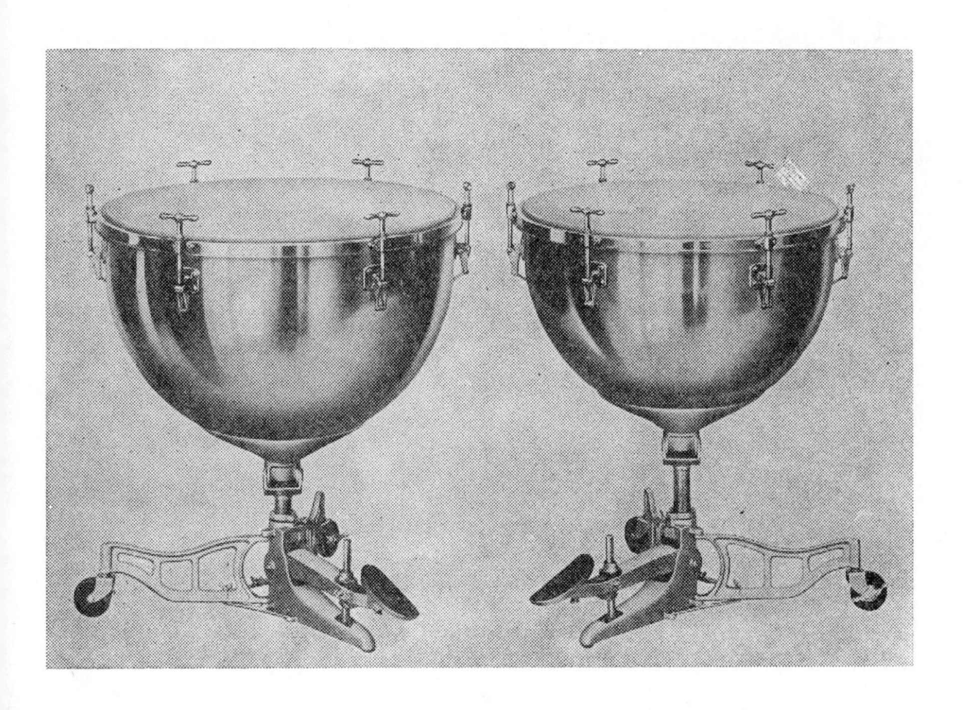

CHAPTER I

# IN THE BEGINNING

The beginning of musical instruments is veiled in obscurity and, what is more, will most likely forever remain a puzzle. Consequently, a number of conflicting theories have been advanced to solve this riddle. Let us consider some of these in order to arrive at the most plausible one.

One of the theories is based upon the following saying: "In the beginning there was rhythm, and the music was without form and void." It is easy enough to refute this. Rhythm, at least as we use the term today, took thousands of years to develop into the basis of music. If, however, we make rhythm synonymous with motor impulse, we may assume that music began with rhythm. Primitive music to this day is permeated with manifestations of the motor impulse; it does not indulge in harmony, melody, or form. Clapping of hands (later sticks), stamping of feet, jumping, running, dancing — all these may have led to the beginning of musical instruments.

Another popular theory attributes the beginning of instruments to the desire of man to imitate sounds of nature. According to this theory we adopt the following line of thinking. A man hears the song of a bird, and he fashions a simple whistle to imitate it; he hears the murmuring of a brook, the rustling of leaves, the roar of thunder, and he invents something to produce similar sounds. He hears the wind sighing over the reeds by the water, and he constructs the first reed flute. He notices the thwang of the bowstring and constructs a string instrument. And so on.

This theory has lost most of its attractiveness of late for the following reasons. In the first place, music is not an imitative art, but comes from the desire to express inner feelings and emotions. Secondly, primitive people did not indulge in music for its aesthetic values. As we shall see shortly, with primitive people music had an entirely different meaning. Whatever sounds imitative of nature there may have been—for it would be erroneous to assume that there were no imitations whatsoever—were prompted by different motives.

Both theories have certain merits, but they are not conclusive and are now supplemented by a third, more recent one. According to this theory music must be associated with symbolism.

Symbolism of sound is by no means difficult to comprehend. Any sound we utter in our language has its symbolic meaning. An infant cries out "ma-ma" not for the sake of uttering a sound but to summon the life-giving source, his mother. On seeing a dog he will respond with a "bow-wow," a sheep becomes a "bah-bah," a passing car elicits "caj-caj." Every observant parent has noticed this tendency of his offspring toward two-syllable speech: no doubt this is the primitive form of rhythm, the primary manifestation of the motor impulse. It is surprising how often primitive people in their use of instruments exhibit the same tendency by making them in pairs, giving out two-toned sounds.

Anybody listening to a foreign language fails to comprehend its meaning because the symbolism of the sounds is hidden from him. Thus, the sound itself derives its importance from the meaning attached to it. As soon as a certain sound is associated with a certain experience or idea, it becomes meaningful.

There is every reason to assume that with primitive people a musical instrument was used for a definite purpose, that is, each instrument had its symbolic meaning. With us music means organized sound, something beautiful to listen to, having melody, harmony, rhythm, form, and design. It gives vent to our innermost feelings and emotions which defy verbal expressions. We have music for its own sake, music per se. Not so prehistoric man. He employed whatever devices he could muster (one hesitates to call them musical instruments) in his struggle for daily survival.

This brings us to another vital point, which must be borne in mind throughout the study of this book: we should not attempt to measure music of the various ages with our own yardstick. Our conception of music—of marvelously efficient and beautiful instruments playing the most extraordinary compositions conceived by the greatest geniuses of all times—cannot be applied to music prior to the sixteenth century. If by some miracle we could revive representatives of the various ages, beginning with the cave man and following up through the epochs of history to the present decade of this century, and surround them with the achievements of our civilization, every one of them would be bewildered and utterly lost. They would be in no position to pass judgment and criticize their findings. Yet so many writers apply our concepts about music to prehistoric man and assume that the first noisemakers were musical instruments! If we want to understand the musical endeavors of the ages, we must penetrate the spirit of those ages. So supposing we cast a glance at the life of prehistoric man and reason out what kind of "musical" instruments were his.

We have every right to assume that the life of the primitive man was beset by fear. Natural occurrences such as sunrise and sunset, wind and rain, cloud and mist, thunder and lightning, earthquakes and volcanic eruptions, floods and storms were all mysterious to him and either evoked reverence or instilled fear—mostly fear. We also know that in an endeavor to account for natural phenomena man peopled forests with giants and dwarfs, elves and fairies, dragons and monsters. Nymphs, mermaids, witches, wizards, and what not dominated nature and controlled the lives of the people.

Numerous deities ruled over natural forces; so the poor mortals struggled to appease them. Whereas today we use lightning rods to arrest lightning, insecticides to control insects, herbicides to eradicate weeds, electricity to penetrate darkness, medicine to cure diseases, and dams to stem floods, primitive man used (among other things) "musical" instruments.

Eternal vigilance and constant battle was the price of survival. By the clapping of hands a snake could be shied away, but wouldn't a pair of sticks be more effective? Certainly. And why not use a pair of sticks in different ways, knocked or rubbed against each other or against some other hard substance so as to vary the effect against different odds? If employed in some peculiar way the same sticks in conjunction with other materials could scare away not only a wild beast, but also some demon or evil spirit. Scholars are inclined to see here the beginning of percussion instruments. At any rate, such a theory sounds logical.

The human voice could be augmented by cupping one's hand in front of the mouth. But how much more effective would a hollow tube be, for instance, an animal's horn? It could carry the voice with greater force and over longer distances. Furthermore, the voice could also be disguised to frighten enemies or even to scare away evil spirits and ghosts. By means of such "trumpets" signals could be given to distant groups. The more frightening the tone produced, the more valuable the instrument.

There is no reason why man should not have learned in the course of centuries to equip his horn with a proper mouthpiece, smooth out the bore, and gradually change its tone to something agreeable to our ears. How long this evolution took we don't know, but it is surprising to hear that even to Schubert of the nineteenth century it was a revelation that the horn could be used as a melodic instrument. It remained for the composers of the recent past to explode the wonders of the French horn. Primitive people, it is true, had horns, but let us keep in mind the kind of horns they were.

A quotation from Numbers 10:1-2, 8-10 is quite illuminating:

> And the Lord spake unto Moses, saying, Make thee two trumpets of silver; of a whole piece shalt thou make them: that thou mayest use them for the calling of the assembly, and for the

> journeying of the camps. . . . And the sons of Aaron, the priests, shall blow with the trumpets. . . . And if ye go to war in your land against the enemy that oppresseth you, then ye shall blow an alarm with the trumpets; and ye shall be remembered before the Lord your God, and ye shall be saved from your enemies. Also in the day of your gladness, and in your solemn days, and in the beginnings of your months, ye shall blow with trumpets over your burnt offerings, and over the sacrifices of your peace offerings. . . .[1]

At the time of this writing the trumpet was already two thousand years old. The primeval functions had remained: blowing the alarm against the enemy, for various festive occasions, and for being remembered before the Lord. What is more, not the common man but the priests were blowing the horns. We shall account for this fact a little later.

In later centuries trumpets and horns were extensively used by the military as well as by hunters and mail coaches. The habit of calling burghers to a meeting by sounding the trumpet survived in some countries up to the eighteenth and nineteenth centuries.

Thus, the trumpet was an outdoor instrument which owed its inception not to a desire for creating musical sound but to an urge to augment the human voice. When finally the instrument was brought into the concert hall, people were scandalized, and the musicians had to compromise with a mute. So only after some six thousand years ( not counting the days of prehistory) was the trumpet admitted into the ranks of the orchestra as a musical instrument. What a slow evolution!

Other instruments were also exclusively used in divine worship and for religious rites. Today recordings of primitive dances of natives of Haiti and other places are available. They bear out the theory that primitive instruments were used in religious ceremonies and that they did not have their present-day connotations.

"Musical" instruments were not supposed to give joy or produce beautiful effects. On the contrary, they were to instill fear, intimidate or scare demons and evil spirits, and in general assist man in his struggle for survival as a weapon against the spiritual world. By means of various instruments man could establish a connection between this world and the supernatural. Instruments were the link between man and his gods during the sacrifices; they compelled the gods to listen to him; they could exhort evil spirits to leave the body of the sick and could restore them to health. In short, the first instruments all had a definite place in human ideology.

That there is a brighter side to this picture may willingly be ad-

---

[1] See also I Maccabees 3:50-54; 4:13, 40; 5:31-33, 9:12-13.

mitted. Among the life-generating forces, those of birth, death, and rebirth were of course most important. Thus, very early certain instruments evolved which were employed as love charms. A good example may be found in the flute, which was considered the symbol of masculinity. Since love-making must have been fundamentally the same in all ages, there is no reason to object to the theory that "sweet" music could be made on the flute and similar instruments. Other instruments again became associated with funeral processions and burials, initiation of the young, wedding ceremonies, and fertility rites. Oddly enough, a funeral too could be cheerful, for the spirits of the departed must be kept happy and contented, else they would return to earth to plague the survivors. (How long do you think this dread has survived?)

There were certain occasions for imitating nature's sounds, one of which merits discussion at this point. Bird catchers must have learned to imitate the mating calls of birds, just as hunters would learn to simulate the various calls of their prey. It is not unlikely that certain tools used at such occasions gradually developed into musical instruments.

Summing up, we see (1) that musical instruments evolved gradually as an aid in man's quest to establish contact with and control of the supernatural, and as necessity warranted in his struggle for survival; (2) that the most primitive instruments are practically as old as mankind; (3) that the conversion of these instruments into real musical instruments follows a rather slow evolution; and (4) that primitive music had an altogether different meaning for its performers and listeners than for us in our day.

Two factors must be mentioned in connection with the beginning of these instruments.

First, by the time man became conscious of his instruments they had reached a certain degree of perfection and nobody could recall how they had originated. They must have by then passed through an incredibly long period of evolution. But one thing is important in this connection: the principle of producing sound had been discovered. For regardless of the diversity and number of individual instruments, they can conveniently be classified into three groups: we have the percussion group, the instruments which produce sound by striking sonorous substances together; then there are the wind instruments in which columns of air vibrate, such as the woodwinds, brasses, and organs; and finally there are the strings, which sound when rubbed with a bow—friction—or plucked with fingers or plectrum. (If you care to remember a slang expression, the methods of sound production can be summed up as "bang, blow, bow.") The introduction of the bow marks the end of the invention of sound-producing methods, nothing new in this respect having been added; any new instrument ever "invented" falls into one of these categories. (An exception is found in recent electronic instruments.)

The second factor concerns the "sacredness" of musical instruments. We don't have to overexert our intelligence to realize that nothing else could be expected of early civilizations. As we have seen, musical instruments had the function of establishing contact with or control over the gods. Consequently, they were not only sacred implements in themselves, but their origin was also divine. Numerous myths bear out this assumption. At first thought one is inclined to dismiss such myths; but when one remembers that they influenced the thinking and living of mankind for thousands of years, still exert their influence upon millions of natives, and have not yet lost their mystical properties even among the peoples of Western civilization, a brief investigation of some of them cannot lead us astray. Let us recapture some of these myths.

The Greeks attribute the invention of the lyre to the messenger of the gods, Mercury. He evidently found a dead turtle on the banks of the Nile and fashioned the dried-up sinews into strings. Another legend attributes the origin of the lyre to the infant Hermes. This crafty little fellow had stolen an ox from his brother, Apollo. Then he killed a turtle and fastened on its shell gut strings he had made from the entrails of the stolen ox. To appease his wrathful brother he presented him with the instrument. Lyre playing in Greece was actually part of the Apollo cult—not that the lyre was restricted to this cult, for it played an important role in Greek music in general.

The Panpipes originated in the following fashion. Pan was in love with a beautiful nymph whom he pursued till her flight was stopped by the river Ladon. In the nick of time a protecting deity changed the nymph into a cane. In his despair the lovesick Pan cut himself pipes out of this cane to play when longing seized him. This instrument therefore is connected with love charm.

The Indians have it that their priests fetched musical instruments directly from heaven, just as Prometheus snatched the first fire from the Olympic gods. The Germanic tribes attributed the invention of the harp to the chief of their gods, Wotan.

Similar legends could be added almost ad infinitum. The fact that the versions differ and are often contradictory need not deter from their merits. And merits these legends had, for they influenced the lives of all primitive peoples. To wit:

We all have heard about Indian medicine men. They used their "heavenly" instruments to hit the ground and make other frightening noises to drive out evil spirits which caused disease. The patient firmly believed that the priest used divine tools; hence, he would fall under the spell of the exhortations.

The ancient Hebrews had a device in which drops of water were made to fall at regular intervals upon a metal disk, the steady monotonous sound causing the patient to fall asleep and recover from his illness.

To the present day primitive peoples of the world indulge in similar treatments of their charges. "Divine" and "sacred" instruments are also used by snake charmers and monkey trainers.

This being the case, certain instruments became associated with certain deities. The sacred instrument of the Indian god Siva, for instance, was the hourglass-shaped drum, the damaru. Such drums were so sacred that throughout the year they were hidden from the public. Once a year the high priest would play them, but woe to the woman who laid her eyes on them, for she had to be put to death immediately. Furthermore, certain rites demanded the use of certain instruments.

It may be added that the practice of dedicating instruments to certain gods was not restricted to musical devices. Thus the myrtle plant was sacred to the goddess of love, Venus. (Does this explain why brides wear myrtle wreaths on their wedding day?) The egg was sacred to the spring goddess of the Teutons, Osthara. (Would that account for the origin of Easter eggs?) In a similar way mythology accounts for many musical practices among the primitives. Instruments were not only sacred but magic.

Having established the "divine" origin of the instruments and their importance in religious rites and services, we are not surprised to learn that the priest, not the common man, was the guardian of all musical instruments. It became the privilege of a selected class to play and use them. We have seen that with the Hebrews the sons of Aaron, the priests, were to blow the trumpets. The playing of instruments is the prerogative of the priests and chiefs in native tribes to the present day. In our own culture the playing of the trumpet was once the privilege of royalty and later the nobility. Thus, musical instruments were employed by the ruling classes to enhance their own importance, for certainly the one who was worthy to handle sacred tools was the favorite of the gods.

Primitive people had another conception which prompted the above views. It was held that not only was the common man barred from approaching the gods, but even the priests could not do so with their natural voices. Hence the voice had to be disguised. The most natural way of approaching a deity was, of course, by the disguised voice itself, and priests therefore trained themselves most effectively. Plain speech was unthinkable as a communication between man and god. Speaking in an unnatural voice during religious services was thus practiced widely—some ministers preach in the "voice of Canaan" to this day. "Musical" instruments consequently assumed a special symbolic meaning as an aid to the priest in approaching the gods.

Nobody can hold privileges for long without being challenged by others. To uphold their sacred rights, the priests tried to intimidate common men by threats of punishment if they impinged on these rights, and, what is more important for the development of our instruments, gave these devices increased symbolic meaning and tried to keep abreast of those who endeavored to outdo them. Nor were they above applying trickery to inspire the crowd with awe. As soon as somebody threatened to duplicate their feats or became suspicious of their doings, they had either to come forth with more important symbolism or improve the instrument so that nobody else could possibly attain their high level.

This situation, as was shown by subsequent developments, created a healthy rivalry between the more intelligent common people and the priesthood. In other words, two streams of music began to run parallel: the one dominated by the priests and royalty, which many years later was termed sacred; and the music of the people, the profane or worldly, or, to use a term more popular today, secular music.

Before continuing with the two branches of music, it should be said that even among the primitives certain norms for instruments were established. Priests were not permitted to use an instrument unless it had been tested and approved by an authority like a high priest or the chief of the tribe. The material of the instrument, its shape and size, its sound, and its maker all had to be checked before it could be employed properly. (It might be noted here that primitive man endowed matter with spiritual qualities, a most important factor in the choosing of material for making the instruments.) This helped to create law and order out of chaos, without which no coordination of instruments is possible. One is tempted to compare the oboist of our symphony orchestra to a tribal chief, for all the players have to go to him before a concert can begin to tune their instruments to his pitch; it is he who sounds the correct A-note.

The music of the people must be regarded as the more primitive force. It influenced church music, especially at times of religious laxity and stagnation. Often it proved the root-stock upon which the other music was grafted; in modern times, such composers as Tchaikovsky and Brahms as well as many others have relied greatly upon folk music. On the other hand, folk music was ennobled by church music; strong and wise rulers managed to keep the profane under check. One need only be reminded of Pope Gregory the Great and of Luther. The passage in Amos 5:23, "Take thou away from me the noise of thy songs; for I will not hear the melody of thy viols," refers to the introduction into the service of profane instruments, abominable in the context of divine worship. The early Christians fought bitterly against the music of the Roman theaters and circuses.

The interplay between sacred and secular music may be compared to a two-armed balance: the heavier (in this case the sounder or healthier) pulls the scale in its favor. There have been times when church music completely dominated, and again, there have been periods when the secular actually profaned the sacred; but often enough both branches of music benefited from each other, for after all, they originated in the same society, and people do prefer the best in the long run.

To conclude this chapter, two more factors must be mentioned.

The invention of new instruments does not make the old ones obsolete. The old and the new have often coexisted side by side for centuries. Some of the oldest instruments are still found in some places of the globe; others have been diligently revived and reconstructed, especially those of the late Middle Ages. True, many of the older instruments have been supplanted by newer ones and have fallen by the wayside; nevertheless, a surprisingly great number of primitive instruments still exist.

In this way the history of musical instruments differs from any other activity of the human race. The Red River cart was supplanted by the prairie schooner and this in turn by other vehicles and finally by the automobile, so that the cart has become a mere museum curiosity. Again, the safety match has replaced the rubbing of friction sticks, and the tractor is not used along with forked tree branches in plowing. Yet age-old instruments refuse to die.[2]

The difference in musical instruments and consequently in music between prehistoric and modern man is of such wide range that a similar evolution cannot be paralleled in other branches of human artistic endeavor. The paintings of bisons on the roof of a cave in Altamira, Spain, are still admired by our present generation, and it took years to prove that they are really some twenty-five thousand years old. The palace-style vase of some three to four thousand years ago is still a treasured article of the National Museum of Athens, just as the gold Vaphio cups or the dagger blades of Mycenae are priceless. The architecture and sculpture of the ancient Greeks re-

[2] A word of caution must be inserted here. Whenever modern musicians play old instruments, it is extremely doubtful whether their rendition of the old style of playing is authentic, for they use different scales and employ the technical skill of the twentieth-century musician, a skill which, to say the least, differs radically from the skill of the older generations. In short, even the older instruments are played in a modern fashion.

main in many respects unsurpassed. And what about the masterworks in art of the Renaissance? Or the works of Aristophanes, Plato, Aristotle, Homer, and a host of others? Such works clearly show how early the human genius soared to dazzling heights.

Not so in the field of music. Primitive music has no appeal to modern man, despite the fact that some of the primitive instruments have refused to die. Not only is its symbolic meaning incomprehensible, but its sound has no semblance of beauty to our way of thinking. Music has always exercised an influence upon peoples of all ages, but unless the spirit of those ages can be relived—an utterly preposterous thing—it has no meaning. The conversion of symbolism to sheer beauty has been so tediously slow that writers assert that even an orchestra of the Elizabethan period would make us shudder.

No matter how early the first "musical" instruments made their appearance, no matter how much they influenced the spiritual life of generations, music without ulterior motives, that is, music for its own sake, is only of recent origin. The greatest works in music are only a few centuries old, and the orchestra of today in its present form and perfection dates from scarcely a century ago. The cave man may have indulged in music—in fact, we are reasonably sure of it; but we have very little cause indeed to admire the beauty of ancient music and musical instruments, for aesthetic music belongs to a level of civilization which has been attained only in our modern period.

CHAPTER II

# SELF-VIBRATORS

Self-vibrators have the scholarly name of *idiophones*. They are instruments which are made of naturally sonorous (resonant or high-sounding) materials such as wood, metal, or glass; they do not need membranes, strings, reeds, or special tubes for air chambers. Among them we find such simple devices as sticks and clappers, castanets, and cymbals. They need not necessarily claim priority among the instruments. Indeed, it is possible that a prehistoric bone flute may have come first. But self-vibrators are still among the most primitive instruments, at least the simplest, so we may well discuss them first, especially since they had such an unauspicious beginning.

According to the method of playing we classify idiophones as those (1) struck together, (2) shaken, and (3) rubbed or scraped.

## *Idiophones Struck Together*

Striking idiophones together must have originated with the clapping of hands. It is only natural that a person use his hands and feet to relieve nervous tension, anger, or happiness. Children delight in singing action songs in which they wave their arms, clap their hands, and stamp their feet, hop, skip, jump, run, or march. A dancer performing the *hopak* emphasizes his rhythmic movements by clapping his hands, slapping his thighs and knees, and stamping his feet. If we do this to the present day, why shouldn't the primitive people have indulged in similar pastimes? So let us agree with those scholars who see in hand-clapping the origin of percussion instruments.

The development from hands to real implements must have taken place along the following lines. First the hands were clapped against some more sonorous substances, such as the top of a plank. Next the hands were equipped with sticks or a branch from a tree, which could easily be used as a sort of drumstick against another branch or the trunk of a tree. Such a stick was most likely the very first "musical instrument."

Two sticks form the first known clappers. Egyptian reliefs made before 3000 B.C. show women dancers using stick-clappers. The two sticks are bent in the form of a boomerang and held in one hand. Now, boomerangs are hunter's missiles. A hunter could therefore use such "musical" instruments to scare up water birds and then to bring down the soaring game. Such sticks are known as *concussion sticks.* They were also used for magic dances preceding a chase.

Again, other reliefs of about the same period show "musicians" using concussion sticks to accompany the tiring labor of pressing grapes in a vineyard. Figure 1 shows a file of rural workers performing a magic dance to insure a good harvest. Egyptian farmers of today use the same sticks for chasing locusts from the fields.

In ancient Greece women indulged in playing *clappers.* In Rome the chorus leader used clappers to beat time, and in the Far East they were used by temple singers. In medieval times lepers had to wear clappers or "bones" as a warning to the public of their presence. Concussion sticks, shown in Figure 3, died out.

The claves shown are simply two straight sticks of hardwood. As you can judge by the hands and cuffs of the player's sleeves, they are not used by a savage but by a member of today's society. They are used in modern orchestras, especially in bands for creating novel rhythmic effects; their musical value is next to nil.

As primitive as such an instrument is, it too underwent certain changes. Dancing sticks were by no means of uniform size or shape. Some were straight, some twisted, some large, some small. With the coming of the metal ages wooden sticks gave way to bronze sticks and then to swords, and sword and dagger dances became popular pastimes. Bones also became popular for clappers. The clown Bottom in Shakespeare's *Midsummer Night's Dream* says: "I have a reasonably good ear in music; let me have the tongs and bones." He is referring to the flat refined clappers held between the fingers and known in England as *knicky-knackers* or *nigger bones* and in France as *tablettes.* Negro minstrels of the nineteenth century used bone clappers made from the ribs of oxen cut into proper lengths.

### *Castanets*

Clappers held between the fingers gave rise to *castanets.* Castanets are of extreme antiquity, and are Asiatic in origin. At an early age they found their way into Spain, and before long they were promoted to the national instrument of the dance. The name of the square or round shell-shaped clappers itself suggests a Spanish origin, for *castanea* means chestnut, the form of the round variety.

The dancer's castanets are held in the hands, one pair in each. The two pieces, the striking faces slightly concave for fuller reso-

Figure 3
Concussion Sticks: Australian Boomerangs
From "Old World Overtones", U. of Pa.

Figure 5. Bronze Clappers

From "Old World Overtones", U. of Pa.

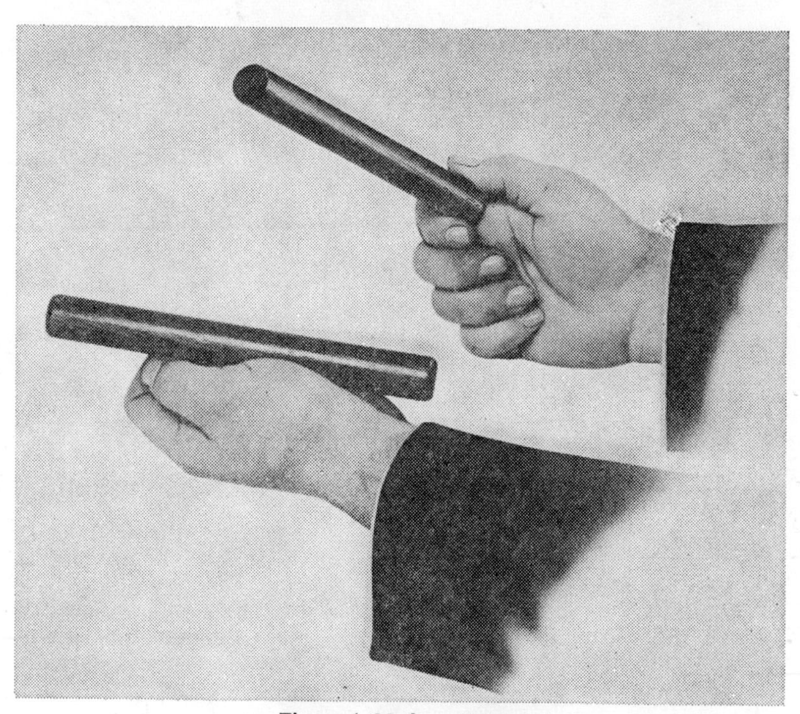

Figure 4. Modern Claves

Courtesy C. G. Conn Ltd.,Elkhart, Indiana

nance, are held together by a string in such a way that the string forms a loop at the side of each piece; both loops slide over the thumb, thus holding them in place. The castanet held in the left hand is larger in size and hence lower in tone. It is played by movements of the wrist. The right hand castanet has the higher tone and is played by the four fingers, one at a time. Since the castanets are attached to the dancer's hands, he or she uses them to emphasize the rhythmic movements of the body, the castanets being as it were part of the dancer.

Modern *orchestral castanets* are fastened to sticks for easier manipulation. Their tone is a characteristic dry click without a definite pitch.

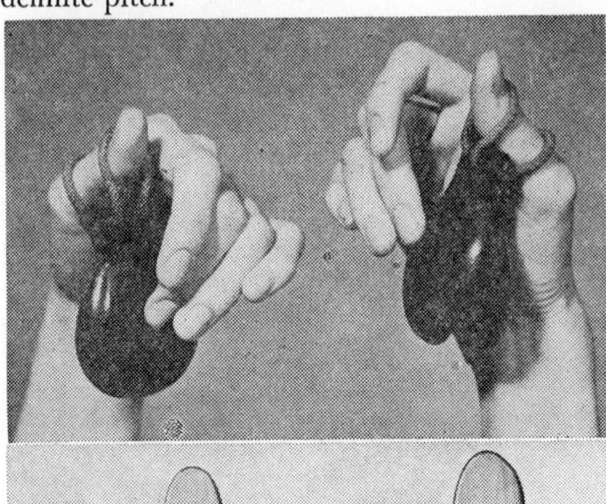

Figure 6
Hand Castanets
Courtesy Keeling Photo, Coaldale

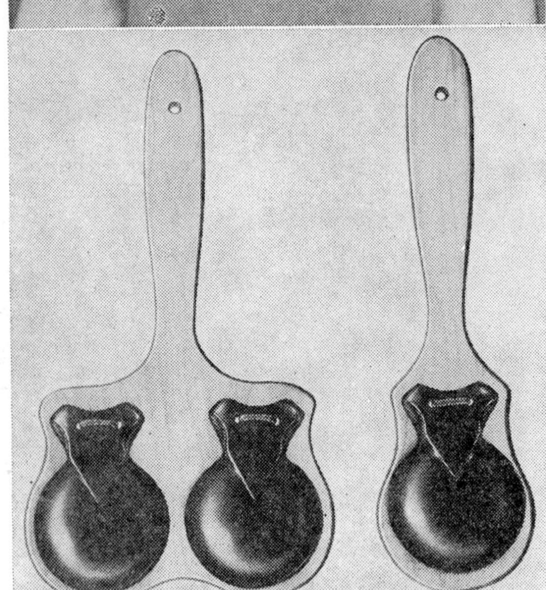

Figure 7. Orchestra Castanets
Courtesy of C. G. Conn Ltd., Elkhart, Indiana

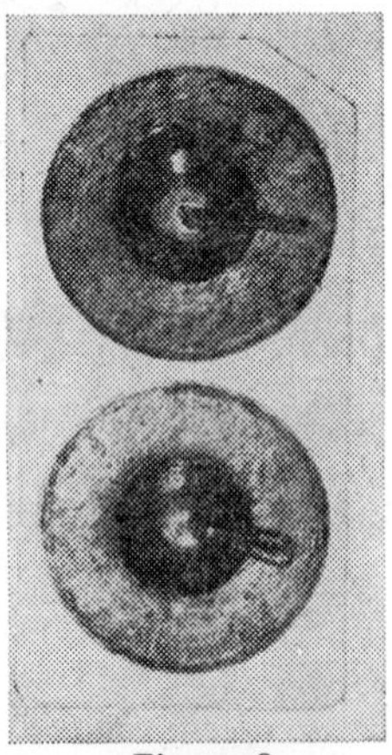

Figure 8
Small Cymbals
Courtesy Museum of Fine Arts, Boston

The long-held assumption that castanets originated in Spain has been refuted. Already the ancient Egyptians had two forms of castanets. However, the specimens preserved come from Christian tombs; they evidently had a place in the rituals of the early Coptic (native Egyptian) Church. The best castanets were those of the Greeks, and Dr. Sachs comes to the conclusion that they may have a Phoenician origin. Be that as it may, the castanets of today are the national instrument of Spain.

As Spanish dances became popular over all parts of Europe, the castanets were also adopted. The impressionists (see Chapter XIX) resorted among other things to the castanets to give their orchestration special color. No Spanish music seems to be complete without the castanets, and to give it a "Spanish" flavor a composer can hardly do without them. Thus Bizet, a French composer, employed the castanets in his opera *Carmen*. When listening to this music, one can't help marvelling how effectively this simple instrument can be used to accompany a gypsy dance.

### *Cymbals*

*Cymbals* are closely related to castanets. Fundamentally they are metal clappers inasmuch as two round plates of brass are clapped together. There is even a theory that the tiny cymbals worn on the fingers by dancers in northern Africa and Spain gave rise to castanets. Combinations of cymbals and castanets were well known in ancient Asiatic countries. Cymbal-castanets were played like castanets, held between thumb and middle finger. They are still in use in Egypt.

Cymbals on clappers, displayed on Egyptian art works, were devices in which tiny cymbals were fastened to bamboo sticks. Similarly, bamboo cymbal-clappers are still found in Burma. The Hebrews too had castanet-like cymbals, played by the thumb and middle finger or attached as cymbal-clappers to a flexible split cane.

Cymbals proper are two slightly concave plates of metal, thin and round, with a leather strap for a handle through the center of each. They are probably of Turkish origin. The Huns brought them into India, where they assumed an important role as shown by Indian mythology. They spread through the western Asiatic countries and came to Egypt and Greece. The Hebrews had them as early as 1100 B.C.; the Egyptians acquired them about a thousand years later. The Greeks considered them an effeminate instrument. The Chinese cherished them so completely that they acquired considerable skill in manufacturing them, and most cymbals of today come from that country, although the best-made cymbals still come from Turkey.

Cymbals differ in size and proportion between the rim and center piece, the boss. The boss is the heavier portion which reinforces the sound and thus makes the instrument more resounding.

The smallest cymbals were known as *acetabula,* "vinegar cups" in our language. Sometimes they too were attached to wooden rods. They were known to the ancient Greeks, and the Babylonians used them in a somewhat enlarged form. Several thousand years later Gluck, called by some writers the father of the modern opera, introduced them for his choruses in one of his operas in the classic Greek style (1779). They enjoyed a certain popularity in Europe from the eleventh to the sixteenth centuries. The large Turkish cymbals became fashionable toward the end of the eighteenth century.

Generally, there were two kinds of cymbals in vogue throughout Asia: broad-rimmed with a small central boss, and narrow-rimmed with a large boss. The former were held in a horizontal position and struck vertically, producing a soft tinkling tone used in the worship of heavenly deities. The narrow-rimmed cymbals on the other hand were held in a vertical position and vigorously struck horizontally in worship of the gods of the earth. The first cymbals of Europe, those of the early Middle Ages, were of the soft-ringing type. The Renaissance had little use for these instruments, but following 1680 they found their way into the opera and during the eighteenth century into the symphony orchestra.

The modern symphony orchestra employs cymbals about 12 inches in diameter (some cymbals in Asia measured close to 40 inches). They are played not by clashing them together but by striking their edges with a sliding motion, thus causing them to rub against each other and producing a singularly terrifying but brilliant and lasting clash. Such sound is useful in imitating storms or thunder clashes or to enhance the loudest passages in orchestral music. A familiar example is found in the well-known overture to *Tannhæuser,* in which the cymbals heighten the climax to a deafening tumult.

Yet cymbals are also used for gentle vibrations where appropriate. Wagner, for instance, uses the cymbals in his *Rheingold* to produce a mysterious ringing sound in imitation of the glitter of the gold in the river. Generally speaking, however, the clash of the cymbals produces exotic effects.

For reasons of economy and also because the cymbals are so closely associated with the bass drum, one of the cymbals is often attached to the latter instrument, or occasionally even to the snare drum. A single player is thus in a position to play the drum with one hand and use his left hand for the cymbals.

Cymbals on drums are hit directly, and thus the characteristic rubbing or sliding motion is eliminated. The result is no longer the brilliant clash, but a cheapened ersatz. The best orchestras there-

Figure 9. Cymbals on a Bass Drum
Courtesy C. G. Conn Ltd., Elkhart, Indiana

Figure 10. Cymbals on Parade
Courtesy Midwest Band Clinic

fore do not permit this practice. Bands and jazz orchestras, however, have no compunction in resorting to such devices.

There are other ways of playing the cymbals. A single plate may be struck with a drumstick which itself may be hard or soft, the plate can be suspended in midair and a drumstick roll performed on it; or the edges of the plates can be agitated against each other and thus produce a roll. In such a way the cymbal may take on the character of a gong. When short notes are required the tone is damped by pressing the cymbal against the chest of the player.

All told, no orchestra is complete without its cymbals.

### *Friction Percussions*

We have seen how sticks lend themselves for tone production through beating. Such sticks also produce tone by friction, either scraping or rubbing. Generally speaking, friction devices produced humming and squeaking noises associated with superhuman sounds. They were considered so sacred that uninitiated people dared not cast their eyes on them. Primitive friction instruments are quite numerous, but since they have never attained a place of importance among our instruments we shall mention them only in passing.

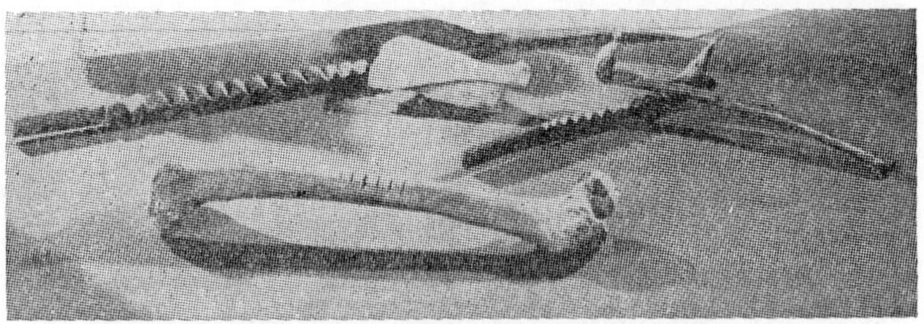

Figure 11. Scraping sticks. Human Bones and Wood
From "Old World Overtones", U. of Pa.

There are first of all the *scrapers*. Scrapers were notched tools of wood, shell, bone, or gourd. The player scraped these notches with a rigid object. The sound produced was anything but musical. Bone scrapers were associated with fertility rites and funeral services; they were regarded as life-giving and love charms. For the sake of resonance scrapers were held over a hole in the ground or else equipped with special resonating boxes (Figure 12). Hunters of the paleolithic era are known to have used simple scrapers.

An outgrowth of scrapers is *the European ratchet* (Figure 13). It consists of a toothed wheel or notched cylinder mounted on a handle which extends through a frame. At one end of the frame a thin, flexible wooden blade is attached in such a way as to reach the toothed wheel against which it scrapes when the instrument is twisted around. The ratchet is still in widespread use as it can be found in Java, India, Mesopotamia, Europe, and America. Originally it had an inherent magical meaning; later it was used as a hunting charm, and finally it became a boy's toy. (The Eskimos scrape the surface of the ice and the Indians bushes and trees.)

Whereas scrapers yielded a series of beats, *rubbed instruments* gave a continuous sound, unless the object which was rubbed was perforated or divided into segments. Central and South American Indians rubbed empty tortoise shells. Others used blocks of wood. *Friction drums,* with which the sound was not produced by drumsticks but by rubbing a stick against the drum head (leading to the German name *Brummtopf*), assumed a rather important role in connection with marriage ceremonies. Traditions featuring the friction drum are still alive in some parts of Europe.

Figure 12
Scraping Vessel from Korea
From "Old World Overtones", U. of Pa.

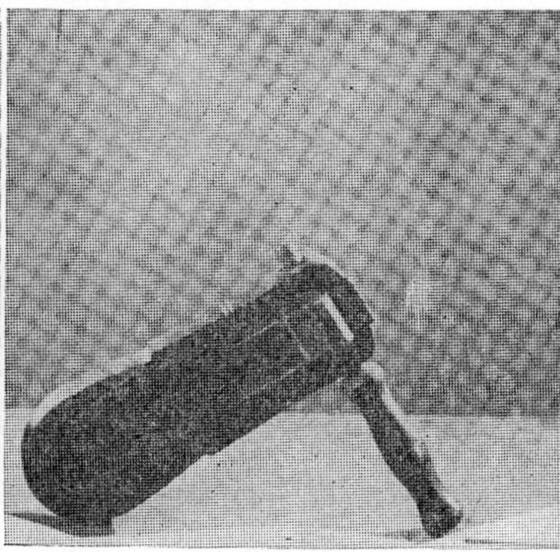

Figure 13
European Ratchet
From "Old World Overtones", U. of Pa.

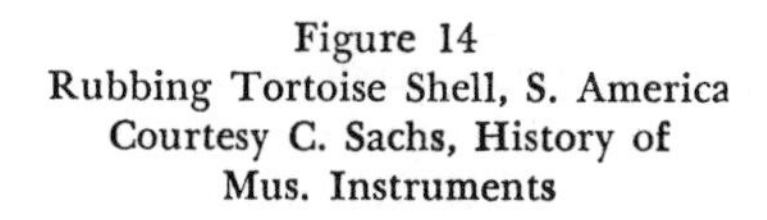

Figure 14
Rubbing Tortoise Shell, S. America
Courtesy C. Sachs, History of
Mus. Instruments

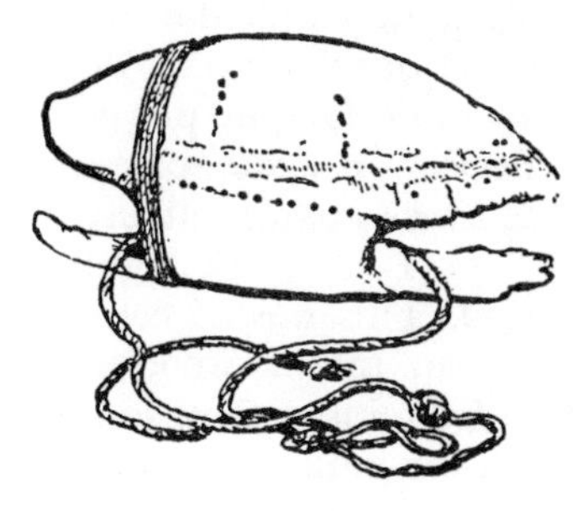

An interesting instrument of but brief significance developed from the principle of striking and rubbing sonorous substances. Toward the end of the seventeenth century some jovial fellows started to amuse themselves by rubbing the rims of their wine glasses with moistened fingers. Then somewhat later numerous friction instruments were constructed (up to 1820!). Among these the *glass harmonica* gained considerable importance.

The beginning of the glass harmonica is traced back to musical glasses. Such glasses can be easily made. Just partially fill a tumbler with water and strike it gently with the fingernail or any suitable object. You hear a melodious tinkle. Vary the depth of the water and you change the pitch. By using a whole series of glasses the complete diatonic scale can be obtained, and hence simple melodies can be played.

This sport became rather fashionable in Great Britain—witness what Oliver Goldsmith has to say in his *Vicar of Wakefield* (1761): ". . . fine ladies would talk of nothing but high life and high-lived company, pictures, taste, Shakespeare and the musical glasses." In 1746 Gluck gave a concert in London upon twenty-six drinking glasses. According to one report he performed on these glasses whatever could be done on a violin or harpsichord.

The glass harmonica followed close upon the heels of musical glasses. It is the invention of Benjamin Franklin, the American statesman, inventor, and scientist. He came to London in 1757 and later applied what he had learned about tone production on glasses. The result was the harmonica seen in Figure 15.

The basins of glass were strung on an axle which was spun by a pedal (bottom right), and their lower edges were dipped in a basin of water. The glass disks varied in size so as to produce notes of different pitches, the largest ones producing the deepest tones. Their arrangement was such that the disks—close to each other and yet isolated—could produce the usual musical scale.

The sound was produced by applying the finger to the wet edges of the rotating disks. By using more than one finger full chords could be played. The tone was soft and flute-like but of such penetrating quality that the instrument was said to be "prejudicial to the nerves of the player." Before it passed into oblivion it had given rise to some famous players, and even such composers as Mozart and Beethoven wrote some music for it.

One other attempt at inventing friction percussions merits mention here. During the eighteenth century the so-called *nail violin* emerged. This was of course no violin at all. A number of nails was driven into a wooden block, whose shape and construction varied from instrument to instrument; the length of the protruding parts of the nails determined the pitch. The nails were played with

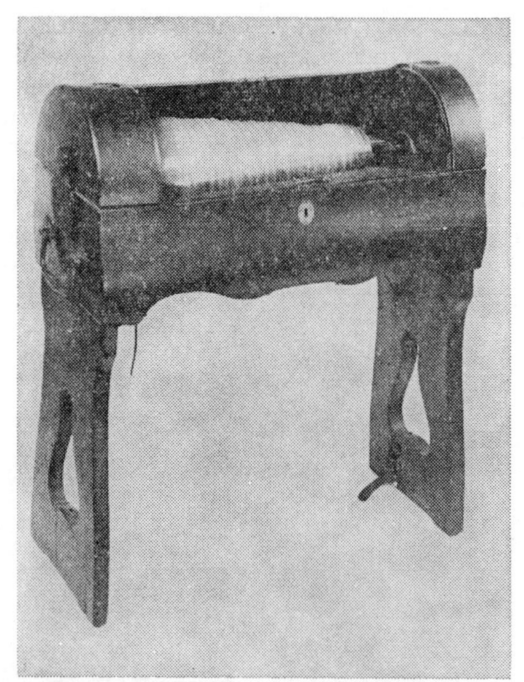

Figure 15. Glass Harmonica
Courtesy Museum of Fine Arts, Boston

Figure 16. Nail Violin
Courtesy Society of Friends of Music, Vienna

a bow in violin fashion. Although it was only a passing fancy, this instrument tempted other inventors to come forth with a great many devices constructed on the same principles (Figure 16).

Thus we see that whatever was started in friction instruments by prehistoric men at the dawn of history has occupied the minds of mankind for thousands of years. And although none of these instruments ever gained much importance, the principle of tone production by friction has remained one of the most valuable ones in the history of musical instruments. (See the section on strings.)

*Shaken Idiophones*

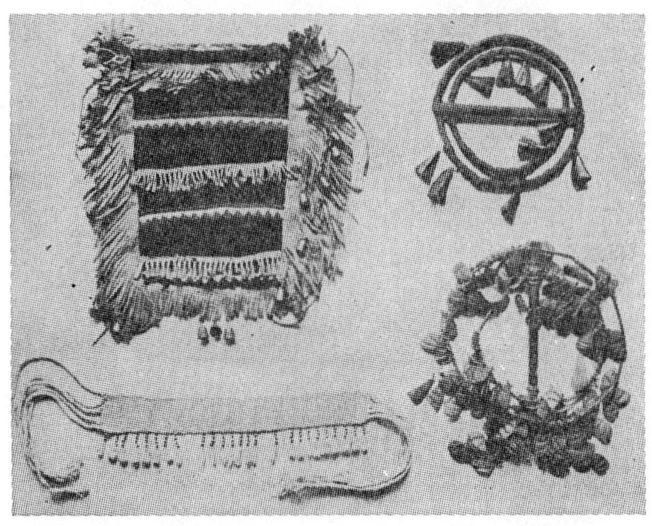

Figure 17. (lower left) Strung rattle with teeth. Mundurucu, Brazil (lower right) Strung rattle, puffin beaks on concentric rings. Tlingit (upper right) Strung rattle, deer hoofs on concentric rings. Northwest Coast (upper left) Strung rattle, metal thimbles on dance legging. Nass Indians

Shaken idiophones include all kinds of rattles, jingles, and bells. As the name implies, they are instruments played by a shaking motion of the performer.

*Rattles* are of prehistoric origin. Two varieties are known, strung and vessel rattles.

The first variety consists of hard objects such as seeds, nutshells, animal teeth, or hooves strung together. Dancers suspended strung rattles from the neck, ankles, knees, or waist to accentuate their movements. Figure 18 shows a musical bracelet rattle from Java. The underlying purpose of these "musical" instruments was to ward off evil spirits, to prevent them, as it were, from entering the

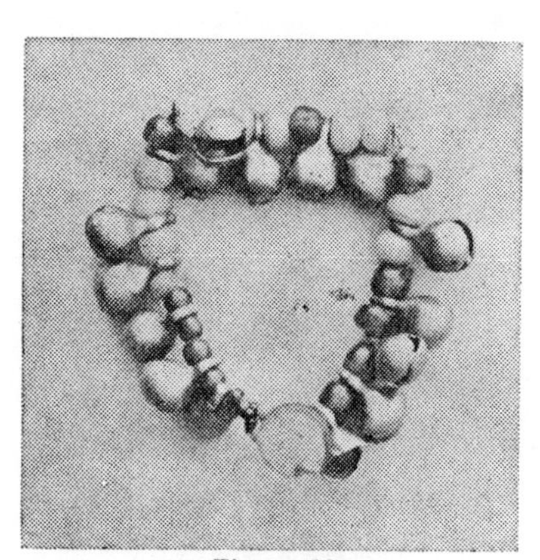

Figure 18
Bracelet Rattle, Borneo
Courtesy Metropolitan Museum of Art, New York

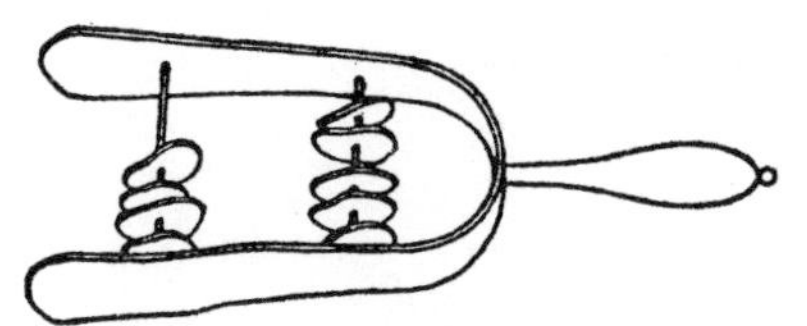

Figure 19. Sistrum, Caucasus
Courtesy C. Sachs, History of Mus. Instruments

Figure 20. Naos Sistrum, Egypt
Courtesy C. Sachs, History of Mus. Instruments

body of the player. Thus the strung rattles must be regarded as sounding amulets. In later periods the sound was detached from the amulets, and to the present day we find mute survivors in old-fashioned bracelets and watch chains with horn-shaped teeth and similar good-luck charms.

To the first class of rattles may also be added rattles on rods. They are also of extreme antiquity. Their general name is *sistra*.

The illustration above is a reproduction of a Sumerian sistrum of about 2500 B.C. The two crossbars have disks strung on them that jingle when the instrument is shaken. Such sistra still exist in the Caucasus and in the Christian Church of Ethiopia, as well as among American Indians. The sistrum is most likely of Egyptian origin, a fact which is substantiated by the second specimen above. This particular sistrum looks like the front view of a small temple. The figure represents the head of the goddess Hathor. There are holes on either side of the frame with wires strung through them; these wires jingle when the instrument is shaken. As the peoples of the Roman Empire lost faith in their old gods, Isis, the joyful maternal goddess, replaced Hathor and the sistrum became part of a joyful cult. Use of the sistrum spread as far north as France.

The second variety of rattles consisted of hollow vessels filled with stones, seeds, pellets, or similar hard objects. Natural objects, such as gourds, provided the containers for such rattles. The Indian gourd rattle was an essential implement of certain shamanic rites.

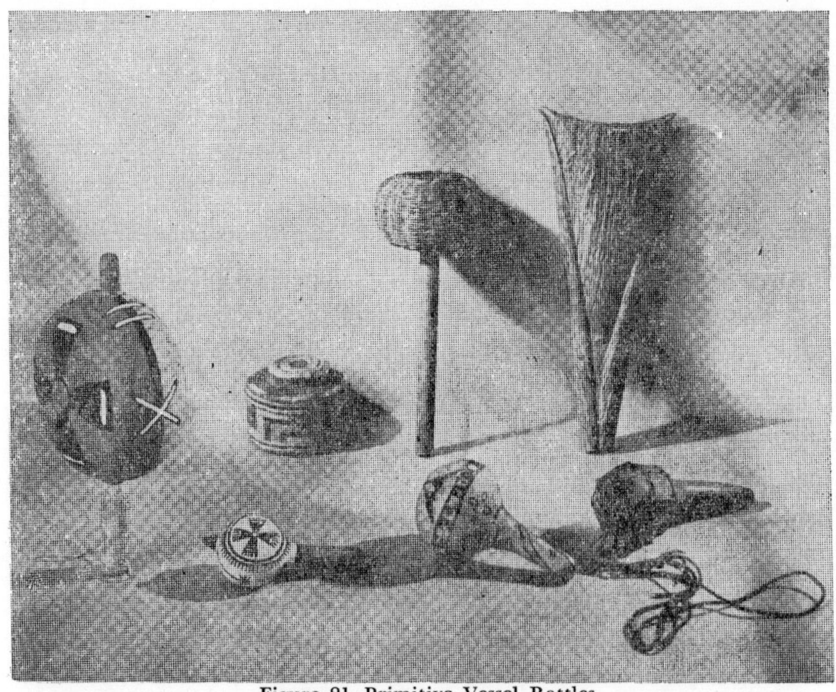

Figure 21. Primitive Vessel Rattles
From "Old World Overtones", U. of Pa.

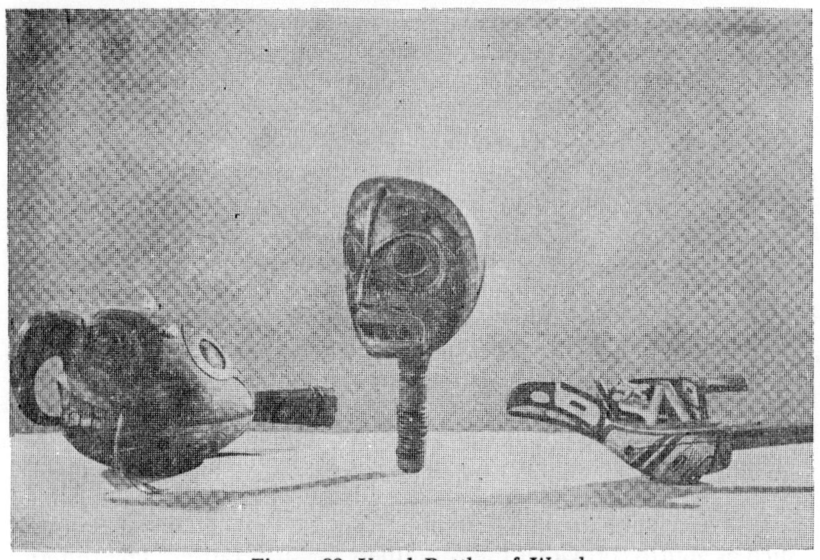

Figure 22. Vessel Rattles of Wood
From "Old World Overtones", U. of Pa.

A shaman could hold his audience spellbound for hours with such rattles. Generally, however, the rattle was played by women. As a woman's instrument it finally entered the nursery and has remained a favorite baby toy.

Where no natural containers could be found, gourds were imitated in clay, wood, basketwork, or metal. Pottery and wood rattles were made in very divergent forms, often representing deities. With the advent of the metal age, metal balls or bells supplanted the natural and artificial rattle containers (originally to be sounded before certain deities). Such rattles are seen in Figures 21 and 22.

Figure 23 is not a baby toy but an orchestral rattle known as *maracas.* It is used mostly by dance orchestras for special effects, and also for the sake of novelty. Another instance of the survival of the most primitive!

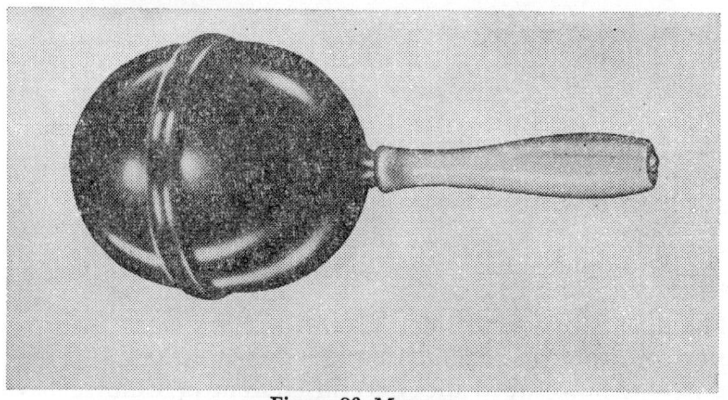

Figure 23. Maracas
Courtesy C. G. Conn Ltd., Elkhart, Indiana

Rattles filled with pebbles, and later with metal pellets, constitute the familiar *jingle* or *jingle bells.* Jingle bells are not bells strictly speaking, for they have no clappers and are not struck but shaken. An illuminating passage is found in Exodus 28:33-35. The high priest wears (jingle) bells on the hem of his robe so that they will be heard "when he goeth unto the holy place before the Lord, and cometh out, that he die not." These bells were evidently a defense against evil spirits, protecting him while entering and leaving the sanctuary and preventing them from following him.

Jingles attached to clothing were by no means restricted to Israel. In the Middle Ages dandies adorned themselves with jingles, and elegant people of the fourteenth and fifteenth centuries used them as ornaments. Later it became the custom for combatants to wear jingles on the hems or belts as amulets in battle, tournaments, or duels. Finally, jingles became the accessory of the fool's cap at courts, carnivals, and morris dances.

The habit of adorning horses' bridles and collars with jingle bells is of recent origin. Such bells have been deprived of all magic power. Our own Christmas song "Jingle Bells" seems to evoke joyful and nostalgic feelings in spite of the fact that hardly anybody has ever heard the jingles "jingle all the way." The sound even in our imagination is delicate and tinkling; the very name *jingle* suggest it. So the jingles became through thousands of years a sort of musical instrument.

Figure 24. African Jingle Bells
Courtesy Metropolitan Museum of Art, New York

The difference between rattles, jingles, and bells is not always distinct. A beautiful combination of all three is found in the *jingling johnny,* also called the Turkish crescent or Chinese pavilion. The jingling johnny is a descendant of the shaman's staff of Central Asia. It supposedly warded demons off by the tinkling of its jingles.

A similar dance staff was used in China in the twelfth century B.C. The Turks (Mohammedans) gave such a staff the crescent, and the instrument became the insignia of dignitaries. Gradually it evolved into a military musical instrument—"musical" only in a restricted sense, of course, since its pitch was of rather undetermined nature.

Our specimen, Figure 25, is of early nineteenth-century Belgian make. Contrary to expectations, it is not played by shaking. The handle is equipped with a sleeve which is moved up and down, thereby striking against a spring and causing the bells and jingles to jingle. The components of this johnny are, beginning from the top, a crescent, a small sphere, four bells, a pavilion-shaped perforated piece with twelve bells on the lower rim, and a large crescent with six bells, surrounding a large sphere adorned with stars and a perforated "skirt" with bells on the lower rim. The spring

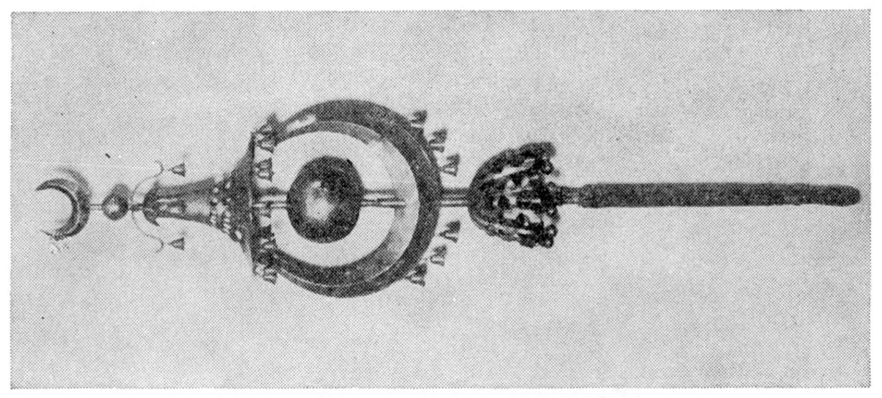

Figure 25. Jingling Johnny or Turkish Crescent
Courtesy Museum of Fine Arts, Boston

operating the whole contraption is not seen. The length of the instrument is over five feet with a diameter of about twelve inches. The lower end of the pole is therefore inserted into a leather pocket attached to a shoulder belt to facilitate holding.

Some of the Turkish crescents were adorned with horsetails and a gala array of stars. Crescents without sleeves are set in motion by shaking the pole. In military music the instrument is carried at the head of a band and assists in keeping the marching rhythm. With the beginning of the nineteenth century they became popular in Europe and are still in use in Germany.

### *Struck Idiophones*

The difference between idiophones struck together and struck idiophones is that in the former both parts are of equal importance in sound production (as for instance in the cymbals), whereas in the latter the part used for striking is the nonmusical part of the instrument (such as the clapper of a bell). Struck idiophones represent a new approach to sound production inasmuch as the sounds produced are no longer mere manifestations of the motor impulse and therefore mostly noise but are clear-cut tones of definite pitch. As there can be no real music or instrumentation without pitch, struck idiophones must be regarded as being on a higher plane than the hitherto discussed instruments, for variations in pitch lead up to scales and melodies.

The beginning of struck instruments may be credited, as with the Chinese, to the conception that sound was not something existing by itself, detached from the sound-producing medium (the concept of sound waves had not yet evolved). Sound and matter were considered as manifestations of the same phenomenon and hence inseparable just as our soul and body. Hence, to bring forth a sound from any substance was to bring its "soul" to life. This idea was especially prevalent in Eastern Asia.

It will be noted that if any sonorous substance is used as a sound producer, such an object is capable of producing but one tone. To produce a series of tones, a number of such objects is required. Hence, struck idiophones are often used in sets. Sets of bells, gongs, metal rods, or even stone slabs are known as *chimes*.

### *Chimes*

One of the earliest and certainly most durable objects used to bring forth a ringing sound was a *stone slab*. The ringing sound solicited meditation; the listener perceived the life of the substance producing the tone. Such tone requires neither rhythm nor definite length, but merits the distinction of being of definite pitch. Each stone slab was carefully wrought to the required size for a certain pitch. As seen from the illustration, the Chinese *pien king* (or pien ch'ing), in our language *lithophone,* had the stone slabs suspended in rows of eight from two rods within a metal frame, and hammers were used for striking them. They are all L-shaped, and their sizes determine the pitch. Originally, some five thousand years ago, these slabs were of stone. Our drawing, however, shows a later model with metal slabs.

Figure 26. Pien King

In September 1952 the *CBC Times* published an interesting article from the *UNESCO World Review* which stated:

> Indo-Chinese workers cutting a road through the jungle unearthed eleven large blades of stone, which when struck with a wooden mallet gave off musical sounds of extraordinary purity, resembling those of a bronze bell. . . . They had been planted vertically in the earth in a row. . . . They are prehistoric stones in a perfect state of preservation, a very old musical instrument. . . . The stones resound to the slightest touch, although some of them measure more than a yard in length and weigh twenty pounds. . . . These extremely hard stones have been turned into an instrument with a complete and perfect scale.

The "complete and perfect scale" must not be identified with our present-day diatonic scale, however. We are fully aware that ancient scales differed widely from our own.

Other specimens of the lithophone had smaller stones. Where the stones appear of the same size, they vary in thickness, thus producing tones of different pitches. Just what connotation these stones had besides meditation—for they are found in temples and were intoned to Confucius—is not quite clear, but the upper slabs represented the male and the lower the female tones. With the coming of the metal age stones were supplanted by metal, but even the metal blades retained the L shape. It is quite probable that such slabs were used as money, for the earliest coins of China had the same L form. (It is becoming increasingly clear that early "musical" instruments were not a class of things by themselves, but were closely associated with other activities of man.)

The principle embodied in the stone chimes has found wide application in other instruments even to the present day. As we have seen, stones gave way to metal, and once metal was adopted it was only a matter of time before different shapes and arrangements were devised for the sound-producing pieces of metal—or wood, for wood being easier to shape than metal, was also extensively used.

One of the most ancient of these slab- or bar-using instruments is the *xylophone*. The word is derived from the Greek *xylon*, meaning wood. The instrument is of East Asiatic origin and may be traced back to primitive men. One of the oldest form of the xylophone is the so-called leg xylophone. The player, usually a woman, sits on the ground, places two or three slabs of wood of different sizes across her legs, and strikes them alternately with two clubs.

To increase the resonance, a pit would sometimes be dug between the legs. Later logs and then a frame were used. Next, the number of slabs was increased, and finally the slabs were tuned. This made melody-playing possible, for the tones were clearly differentiated.

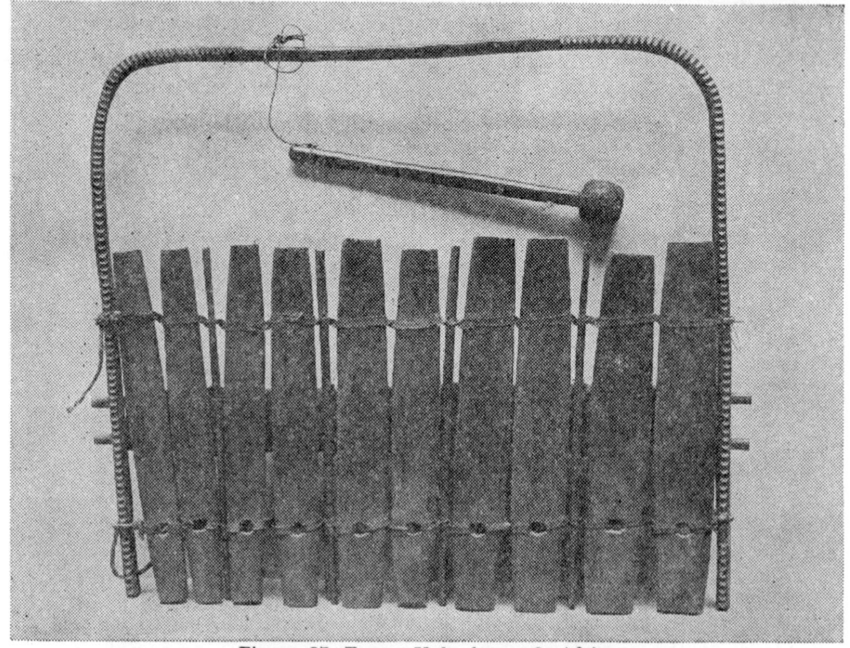

Figure 27. Frame Xylophone, S. Africa
Courtesy Museum of Fine Arts, Boston

Our illustration from South Africa shows two bars underneath the slabs, a remnant of the earlier logs. Such frame xylophones were suspended from the neck of the player. It is only natural that such instruments varied in size, shape, and number of bars. On all of them, however, some simple scales could be played.

Another very important step in the perfection of the xylophone was taken by attaching resonators to the bars. The African Negroes are said to have discovered the method of fixing gourds to the individual bars. Here we have the *gourd xylophone*. Other natives used other resonators. Thus the *saron* of Java is a xylophone in the form of a dragon carved out of wood, four feet in length and supporting on its back seven slabs of wood. Inasmuch as such an instrument represents an excessive amount of diligent labor and manual skill,

Figure 28
Saron, Java
Courtesy
Kelley Musical Instruments

it is clear that it must have meant much more to the people concerned than a mere musical instrument.

More common than the dragon type was the *trough xylophone.* Judging from reliefs found, players could produce two-part music by striking two slabs simultaneously, one with each hand.

The xylophone was introduced into Europe at the beginning of the sixteenth century. Owing to its lifeless sound it did not gain favor until the nineteenth century when the Romantic composers were in constant search for new tone color. In 1836 Mendelssohn first heard it and was greatly impressed. So finally the xylophone found its way into the symphony orchestra. Saint-Saëns employed it to imitate the rattling of bones in the dance of the skeletons in his *Danse Macabre.*

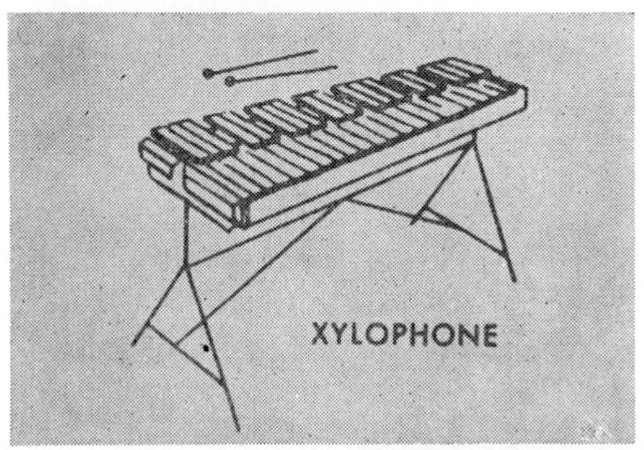


Figure 29

The modern xylophone has two rows of wooden slabs arranged like a piano keyboard, the upper row in twos and threes like the black keys and the lower row like the white keys. The slabs or bars rest upon rods made of straw—hence the name *Strohfiedel* or straw fiddle—and are isolated from each other by wood or felt. Most xylophones have twenty-seven or more bars, but some specimens are capable of playing more than three chromatic octaves (a chromatic octave has twelve tones). The tone is hard, dry, and hollow in quality. The skillful performer can execute very rapid passages, even trills, and achieve rather humorous effects. Resonators beneath the blocks of wood reinforce the sound.

Giant xylophones are now in vogue in Central and South America with large tubes for resonators. They are known as *marimbas,* a name already applied to the gourd xylophone mentioned above. This instrument was brought to America by African slaves. Its compass is from four and a half to five octaves. The bars are of rosewood. Under each bar there is a metal tube to serve as a resonator. Since two or more players perform simultaneously, chord-playing in this instrument is quite feasible.

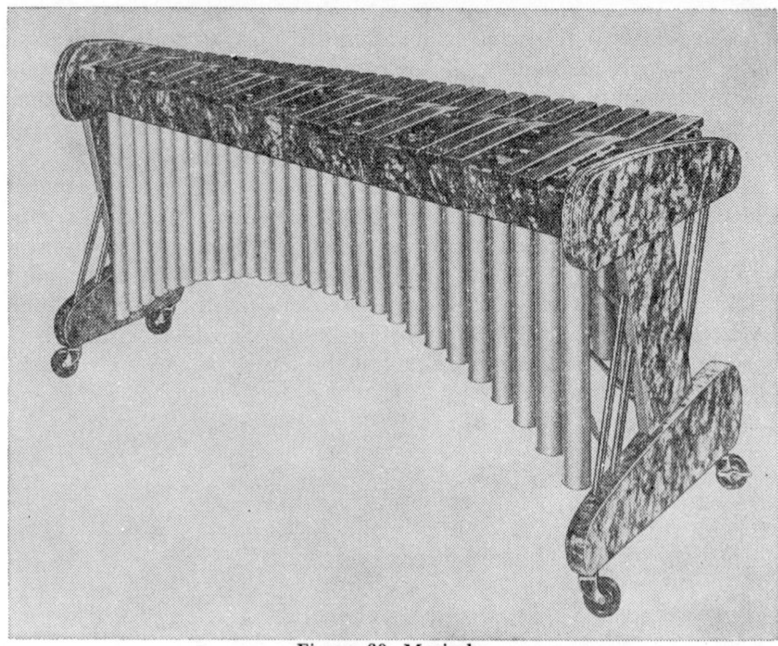

Figure 30. Marimba
Courtesy C. G. Conn Ltd., Elkhart, Indiana

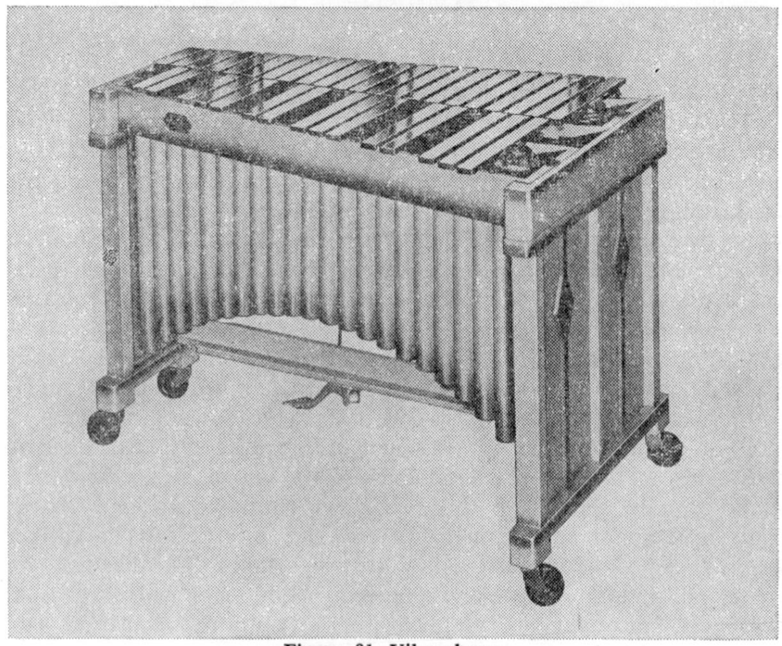

Figure 31. Vibraphone
Courtesy C. G. Conn Ltd., Elkhart, Indiana

The *vibraphone* is a recent invention. The difference between the xylophone and vibraphone lies in the resonators, which in the latter are equipped with disk-like vibrators. These impart a pleasant vibration to the tone, thus enriching its otherwise dry and hollow character. This peculiar buzzing sound has found favor with jazz bands, but the instrument is not often found in symphony orchestras.

Instruments of the xylophone type are practically as old as the metal age. They are conveniently grouped together as *metallophones.* (Incidentally, before the use of metal was firmly established, bones and turtle shells had been tried.) The difference between the bronze disks used in the later type lithophones and metal bars is actually none too great. The more elaborate Javanese saron had four rows of metal slabs (Figure 28 shows only one row of wooden bars). Other queer metallophones, too numerous to mention, also made their appearance, for the dragon had no monopoly on the design of these instruments.

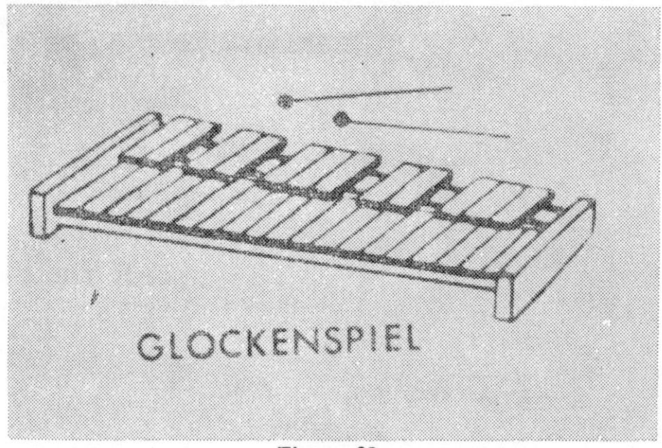


Figure 32

A modern metallophone without resonators is found in our *glockenspiel* ("play of bells"), sometimes referred to as bells or orchestra bells. It is very similar to the xylophone both in appearance and in manner of playing. It lacks resonators, however, and there is no way of damping the tone, so rapid passages are apt to sound confused. Its tone is clear like fairy bells, sparkling and brilliant, penetrating the whole orchestra.

The glockenspiel appeared in Europe in the seventeenth century. In his opera *The Magic Flute,* Mozart used a glockenspiel with a keyboard, now practically obsolete.

The name *glockenspiel* suggests that this instrument originally had bells instead of metal slabs. This is quite true, the first orches-

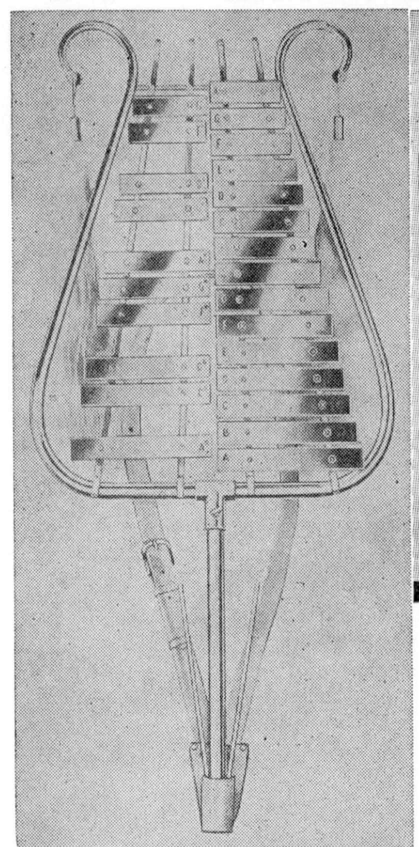

Figure 35
Clavitimbre

Figure 33. Bell-Lyre
Courtesy C. G. Conn Ltd., Elkhart, Indiana

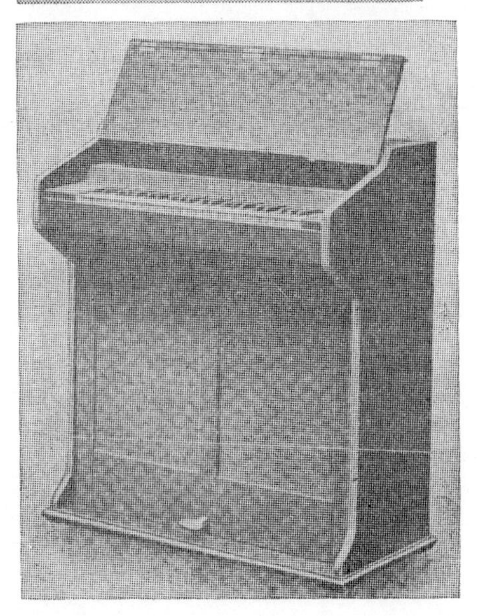

Figure 34
Celesta

tra bells being real bells. But small bells are never free from dissonant overtones and cannot be accurately tuned, so they gave way to modern steel bars. At first the glockenspiel was used only for special bell effects. Wagner featured them in the *Magic Fire Scene* in *Die Walküre* and some other works. Today the glockenspiel belongs to the standard equipment of an orchestra.

A special type of glockenspiel is the *bell lyre.* Here the metal bars are arranged on a lyre-shaped frame in two rows in a piano keyboard fashion. Such a lyre is used in bands more than in orchestras. The size varies, the larger specimens being some two feet in length; the usual compass is about two octaves.

Early attempts to mechanize the xylophone type of instruments —such as providing them with a keyboard—did not meet with notable success. However, in 1886 Auguste Mustel of Paris came forth with a metallophone resembling a piano in appearance with an almost identical keyboard and played in a similar manner. This is the *celesta.* It has certain advantages over the glockenspiel. Each steel plate is suspended over a carefully tuned resonator, which in effect suppresses the high harmonics and reinforces the fundamental note. Furthermore, there are dampers to stop the bars from ringing as soon as the key is released. In such a way the tone is more refined and less tinkling than that of the glockenspiel. Indeed, the tone is very clear and of exquisite beauty. For some time only the French composers cherished this instrument, but Tchaikovsky made it famous through his *Dance of the Sugar Plum Fairies* in *The Nutcracker Suite.* Today the celesta is found in most orchestras.

Similar in construction and appearance to the celesta is the *clavitimbre,* also manufactured by the Mustel Company of Paris. It is somewhat smaller; consequently, it does not have such a wide range. It extends a little above the celesta. The clavitimbre is the long-sought answer for those composers and conductors who wanted a glockenspiel which would be capable of executing difficult scores. To date the clavitimbre does not appear nearly so frequently in orchestras as the celesta.

Today's metallophones are by no means restricted to the xylophone type of instruments. The modern family embraces rods (straight, bent, or in spiral form), tubes, gongs, and bells. Each of these sound producers merits closer inspection.

*Rods* are used chiefly as *triangles.* As the name suggests, the instrument has the form of a triangle. It is equilateral, with one angle open. It is played with a steel beater of the same material as the triangle held in one hand, the triangle itself being suspended by a cord tied to a music stand or to a drum; the performer is thus free to play other percussion instruments, as the triangle is seldom played for any length of time. The fundamental tone of the triangle is drowned out by many high partials, not harmonics; hence, strictly speaking the tone belongs to the class of "noise" sounds, and the tone is a tinkling and clear metallic ring without a definite pitch. Single strokes can be used to mark accents in lighter forms of music. By ringing two adjacent sides a roll is produced, which is capable of coming through the fortissimo of the full orchestra.

The triangle first appeared in Europe in the fifteenth century. At that time the four-sided form resembling the shape of a stirrup was more common. The triangular shape was not mentioned before the end of the century. For three centuries the triangle was used only for irregular music. At the beginning of the eighteenth century it found its way into the opera, and then into the orchestra. Beethoven used it for tone color in the finale of his *Ninth Symphony.*

*Straight rods* find application in clocks with chimes which strike every quarter- or half-hour. Clocks striking every quarter-hour have four rods, and the little tunes they play are reminiscent of change-ringing of bells in Old England—in change-ringing a series of bells was numbered and played according to the figures given them in

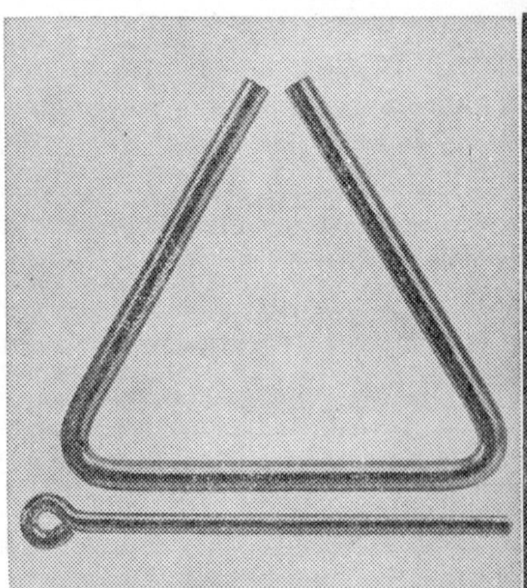

Figure 36
Triangle
Courtesy C. G. Conn, Ltd.,
Elkhart, Indiana

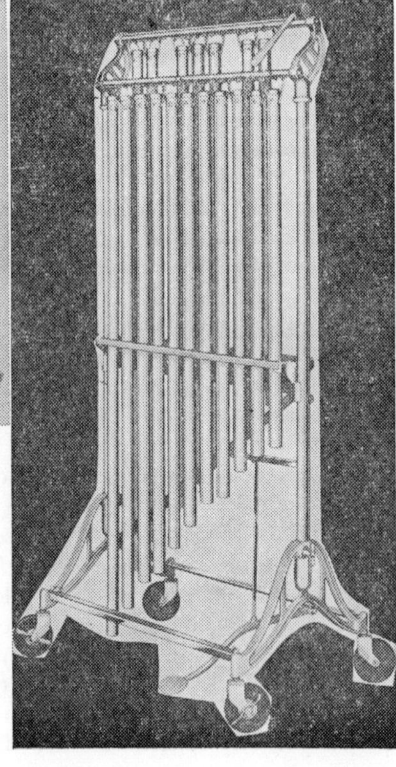

Figure 37
Chimes
Courtesy C. G. Conn Ltd.,
Elkhart, Indiana

the written score. Taking these rods from lowest to highest as
5 1 2 3
*sol, do, re, mi,* we may represent the melodies for the four quarters as 3 2 1 5, 1 2 3 1, 3 1 2 5, 5 2 3 1. At the final quarter all four melodies are repeated, followed by the deeper gong tone for the full hour.

Imitations of bamboo and gourd resonators led to metal *tubes.* Instruments with metal tubes are known collectively as *tubaphones.* The most common example is found in the *chimes* or *tubular bells* of today. These tubes are either of steel or of bell metal. They are graduated in size, the smallest giving out the highest and the largest the deepest tones, and are suspended from a suitable framework. They are struck with a wooden mallet (shown in the upper right of Figure 37) near the top end. Their tone is deep and resonant, reminiscent of cathedral chimes; hence they serve in the orchestra to create an atmosphere of solemnity, especially in works of a religious nature. They have some distinct advantages over real bells. They are easier to tune, their pitch is more exact, their harmonics are more in tune, and last but not least they are portable and cheaper. The air column inside the tubes resonates when the tube is struck and imparts to the tone a mellowness not found in the tones produced by straight rods.

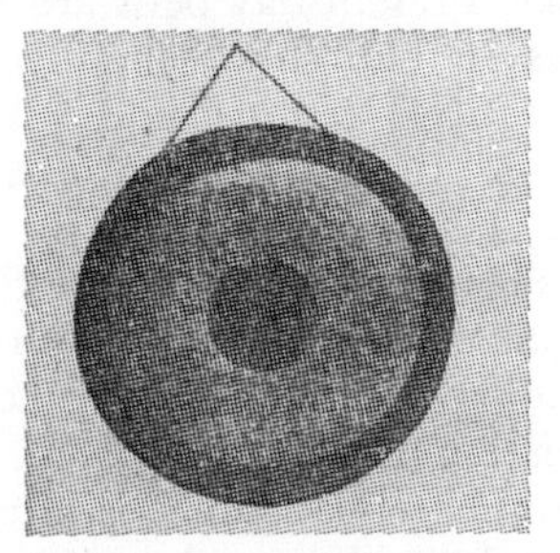

Figure 38
Gong

The *gong* is a thin round plate of bronze with the edges turned up. It comes from East Asia, although hardly from China as popularly claimed. Being of metal, it is of more recent origin than the stone chimes. Chinese sources first mention it in the sixth century A.D. It is the most important instrument in Southeast Asia and appears in many types and sizes. Thus, the edges may be narrow or wide, nearly flat or upturned; the central part—the boss, the sounding part, the edges being dead—may be large or small; the rims may also vary in width; finally, the thickness may be subject to variations. The oldest gongs were flat with shallow rims. The latest type is the deep gong with thick walls and a deep rim. The smallest gongs are but a few inches wide, while the largest known gong measures over three feet in diameter and weighs 180 pounds.

In its place of origin the gong was attributed with magic power. It was used to accompany dances, songs, religious and secular ceremonies, and when used in drum fashion, to transmit messages. Furthermore, it was employed to chase evil spirits, to heal sicknesses, and to attract the wind. Washing in a gong restored the health and drinking from it enforced an oath. No wonder the gong was a highly respected instrument. Some of the more famous gongs were even given proper names.

Since the end of the eighteenth century the gong has become standard equipment in the percussion group of the symphony orchestra. It is played with a cloth-covered drumstick. Its tone is described as pure, distinct and full, dark in color, mysterious, uncanny, crashing like thunder, creating echo effects—all of which suggests that there are different ways of playing it. But whether played softly or loudly, and no matter how it is struck, its tone is of indefinite pitch.

### *Bells*

Bells in various sizes and shapes are among the most widely distributed and universally used musical instruments not used in the orchestra or in the sense of an instrument such as a piano, violin, guitar, or the like. Present day bells are for the most part relegated to practical uses in churches, schools, homes, auditoriums, gymnasiums, traffic control centers, and what not. The most notable exception is found in the carillon (bell chimes), which will be discussed below.

With the advance of the Bronze Age the musical stones discussed earlier found their counterpart in bells and bell chimes. The origin of bells is unknown, although we are certain that modern church bells are of Christian origin. The Assyrians are credited with a cast bell dated approximately 1000 B.C., while the Peking bell in China, still in use for striking the watches of the night, is over four thousand years old.

The early bells hardly resemble our modern ones. The inverted tulip form of today was unknown to the first bellmakers. We find that some of the oldest bells were made of plates of metal bent into proper shape and then riveted together. In Iceland excavations have revealed hexagonal bells, supposedly of prehistoric origin. In the Far East, Egypt, and Ireland early bells were quadrangular, then elliptical, and finally circular, whereas in China bells were given a beehive shape. Some Egyptian handbells had handles of a sculptured ibis, their sacred bird. Figure 40 shows a queer specimen of an African bell.

Since the early bells had so many shapes, it is quite possible that there is a close connection between the gong and the bell. In the Far East, for instance, there is a so-called resting bell in the shape of a basin, made of bronze and resting on a cushion with the open side up. It is struck with a wooden mallet. Its sound is full and clear, much superior to that of suspended bells. The Greeks, Romans, and Hebrews also used small bells, but oddly enough they were forbidden by Moslem law.

Originally bells were used as amulets to chase away evil spirits and frighten demons (see page 37). Valuable animals were protected against evil forces by bells suspended from their necks, a custom that still prevails although with an entirely different purpose in view. Churches were equipped with bells to purify the place, not to call the churchgoers to worship. House doors had bells to prevent the evil spirits lurking under the threshold from entering the building. As we have seen, Jewish priests, Siberian shamans, and South American Indians wore bells on the hems of their garments. During the invasion of Europe by the Turks, the Christians used bells to frighten their enemies. The nonconformists of the Middle Ages called the bells of the Catholic Church the devil's trumpets.

It may be added that judging from various legends the bell had certain other nonmusical connotations. Bell ringing as a rain charm was common practice in China. The large Peking bell mentioned above was struck only when the emperor prayed for rain. Certain Negroes in Africa try to attract rain by filling a bell with water and sprinkling the soil. In Tyrol farmers with bells in hand march around their fields to insure a good harvest. Figure 41 shows an

Figure 39
Japanese Bell

Figure 40
African Bell

Figure 41
Libyan Bell

Courtesy Metropolitan Museum, New York

African bell with various figures and bosses or point-like projections which according to Chinese sources symbolize vital forces of nature in relation to the growing of crops and life in general. Mixing blood with the bell metal or offering human sacrifices in connection with the casting of bells was a widespread practice.

The size of bells varies greatly. Ancient bells were usually small, although the Peking bell weighed fifty-three tons. In addition to handbells, chariot bells, mule bells, curfew bells, and similar ones are known to exist. The curfew bell, for instance, only twenty-five centimeters high, was made of one piece of wrought iron two millimeters thick, welded together in a rectangular shape with rounded corners. After the periods of persecution the Christian church bells began to assume prodigious proportions. The first large bell dates from the tenth century.

The largest bell in the world is the Great Bell at the Kremlin; its weight is around two hundred tons. Cast in the eighteenth century, it was in use for three years only, for when fire damaged the bell tower the bell fell and lost a piece of its rim. To sound that bell the clapper had to be pulled backward and forward by twenty-five men on each side. The Big Ben of Westminster Abbey weighs about thirteen and a half tons, and "the Great Paul" of St. Paul's Cathedral has a weight of 33,450 pounds.

The best *material* for casting bells has been found to be an alloy of thirteen parts copper and four parts tin. Such a mixture gives an elastic, tough, hard, yet resonant metal. Early bells were also made of shells, pottery, wood, and other material. The ancient Assyrians used an alloy of ten parts copper to one of zinc. During the evolution of the bell practically every sonorous substance has been tried, even glass. Contrary to popular belief, silver and gold are unsuitable for bells; silver has less resonance than cast iron, and gold sounds like lead.

The *shape* of the bells is one of the most important features in *tuning*. Tuning must be distinguished from the tone of the bell. A bell sounds from the rim, the body being "tone-dead." The rim vibrates in sections and hence produces a number of overtones. A bell is well tuned when all the partials blend into one harmonious whole, regardless of the quality of the tone. Thus a well-cast bell will not only have the best material for a good tone but also the right shape for good tuning. It has been found that in the perfect shape there is a definite proportion between the thickness of the rim, the diameter of the mouth and shoulder, and the height of the bell. The ideal proportions have been discovered through centuries of experimentation. They are fairly standard today, although scientific proof is still wanting. Our bells are now circular, the square and elliptical forms having been discarded.

Now a word about the *tuning* of bells. As we have pointed out already, the rim is the sounding part of the bell. It sounds in four sections. If these four sections are not of perfectly uniform thickness they emit different frequencies, resulting in a throbbing tone out of tune. Furthermore, when the bell is struck it produces several tones (overtones) in addition to the fundamental tone, so that a bell may have a capacity of as many as seven tones. The object of tuning is therefore to make all four sections of the bell vibrate at a uniform rate of frequency and produce only such overtones as will blend with the fundamental and thus enrich the quality of the tone.

Primitive methods of tuning, begun in Europe in the tenth century, consisted in chipping off bits of the rim with a chisel-head hammer. Later chisels and files were used. Today's method, perfected by the firm of Taylor of Loughborough, England, employs a special tuning lathe which is capable of taking the finest shaving of metal from any part of the rim or other part of the bell. The point, however, is that the bell must have the perfect shape and approved design not merely after casting but after tuning!

The Taylor bells have five tones tuned with absolute accuracy: the fundamental (the loudest tone, of course), the hum one octave below it, the minor third, the perfect fifth, and the octave above the fundamental. (To get an idea what such a chord sounds like, play the notes, *c, c', e'-flat, g',* and *c''* on the piano, holding the pedal down and playing *c'* loudest.)

There are three ways of *sounding* bells. The "empty" bell, a bell without a clapper, is struck with a wooden hammer; bells with clappers are rung either by swinging the bell itself and making it strike the clapper or by moving the clapper in pendulum fashion to and fro to strike the rim.

Evidently bell chimes are older than single bells, for the earliest sources always refer to bells in the plural. The first chimes had only a few bells, often attached to a frame supported above the organ (Figure 42). These bells above the organ swing freely in rhythm with the working of the bellows, and it puzzles the imagination somewhat as to how they could enhance the music. One can't help wondering whether these bells are a remnant of the days when bells were used to purify the place and thus protect the organ and its player against evil forces.

Bell chimes consisting of several tuned bells were known to the ancients almost as soon as the stone chimes. In Europe sets of bells became known as the *glockenspiel* in German and the *carillon* in French. The latter name is common with us, whereas the former is given to the orchestra bells discussed above. Carillons became prominent in the Middle Ages, especially in the Netherlands, which country still leads in the art of carillon playing.

The first carillons had four bells only. The bells were small and were tapped by the performer with a suitable hammer. In the thirteenth century they were made mechanical by being connected to tower clocks and struck by a mechanism of cogwheels. Later on rotating cylinders with iron nails worked the hammers of the bells so that tunes could be played without man's interference, in a manner similar to our music boxes. Cities vied with each other for the best carillons, and so the number of bells kept increasing until it reached the number of fifty or over. The mechanical cylinders would have as many as ten thousand nails, so that not only single melodies but also chords could be played.

About 1500 the bells were no longer entirely dependent on mechanical contrivances, for they could be disconnected and played by hand. In the next century they could also be played by foot, the keys being arranged like a clavier or organ keyboard. Our illustration shows a carillon at the Antwerp Cathedral in the seventeenth century. The player is some twenty feet below the bell chamber. In the early carillons the noise of the mechanism and the ropes made the music of the chimes all but inaudible to the

Figure 42
Bells Above an Organ,
13th Century

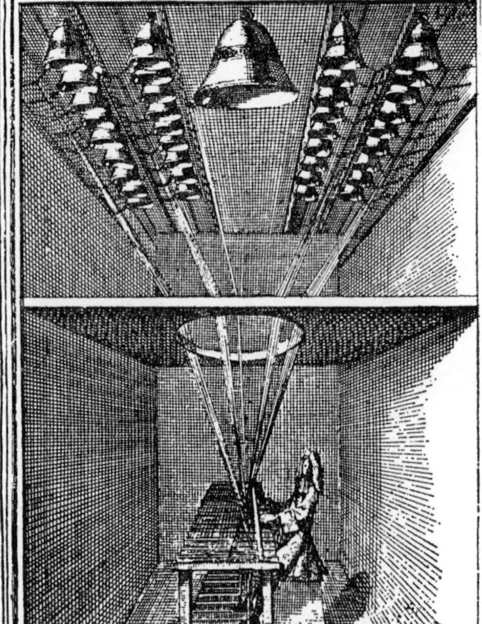

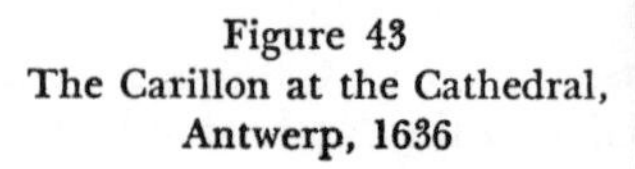

Figure 43
The Carillon at the Cathedral,
Antwerp, 1636

performer, but to the listeners outside the church in the open countryside they were a joy to hear.

Today the carillon is an elaborate piece of machinery whose development parallels that of the organ to some degree. It comprises from two to four complete octaves of bells including the chromatic notes. Belgium and Holland still have the most famous ones. The best carilloneurs (players of the carillon) also come from Holland.

The carillon of the Ottawa Peace Tower has fifty-three bells with a range of four and a half octaves. The largest bell weighs 22,400 pounds, while the smallest weighs only 10 pounds.

Figure 44
Among the Bells of the Ottawa Peace Tower

The bells of the Peace Tower at Ottawa are tuned to the intervals of the chromatic scale and struck by clappers moved by levers from outside the bells. The levers are connected with the manuals and pedals of the clavier in Figure 45.

In the U. S. too the carillons have become popular. They are found in practically all larger cities. At Riverside Church, New York City, there is a carillon of sixty-four bells, the largest one weighing

Figure 45
Robert Donnell at His Keyboard, Ottawa Peace Tower

eighteen and a quarter tons. The most famous carillon is the one at the Mountain Lake Sanctuary, Florida, called the Singing Tower.

When the carillon is played the music spreading outward seems to sing from the entire structure, hence the name. The Tower has a base 51 feet square and rises to the monumental height of 205 feet. The music blends with the natural beauty of the Sanctuary. The Tower amidst its surroundings has been called the Taj Mahal of America. Music, art, and nature combined offer here the ideal place for meditation, a "haunt of peace for the weary-hearted" and a sheer delight for the music lover.

There is a trend nowadays toward turning carillons into electric playing machines and electronic mechanisms which do not seem to have the same tones as do sweet bells.[1] Just the same, by the

[1] From a letter by H. M. Nornabell, at the time of writing director of the Mountain Lake Sanctuary.

Figure 46. The Singing Tower, Florida

summer of 1957 the Singing Tower was giving two recitals weekly on electronic bells which were installed just before the start of the summer recital series. They are played from an organ-type keyboard. Tiny electrical hammers strike bars of metal; the vibrations are amplified two million times to produce the desired volume.

The carillon is the most democratic of all musical instruments. No four-walled concert halls or auditoriums confine their music, and rich and poor alike can share it. A whole city may be its audience, for it is heard far and wide.

As for the introduction of real bells into the orchestra, we must admit that the venture has failed; for instance, Cherubini tried it unsuccessfully in 1794. Bells are too heavy and too loud and lack the necessary precision of tone. Metal bars and tubes are more satisfactory for orchestral use.

Isn't it truly marvelous how man has advanced through the ages from mere handclapping and stick beating to the various and numerous instruments described in this chapter and to wind up with that miracle of modern times, the carillon? And again, how much water has run down the hill before the primitive instruments really became musical instruments, employed for sheer enjoyment without any ulterior motives? The human spirit is indeed constantly engaged in creating better and more perfect things.

CHAPTER III

# MEMBRANOPHONES

A drum as we understand it today may be defined as a skin—the membrane—stretched on a frame or vessel of wood, metal, or earthenware. The sound—the "phone"—comes from the membrane, hence the name membranophone. Among drums the kettle-drums are the only ones producing a musical sound of a definite pitch; all the others are noisemakers used for the sake of emphasis and rhythm.

Drums, like the instruments considered so far, are of extreme antiquity. The accounts of the origin of the drum are fascinating, although somewhat contradictory. There are those theorists, whose number is still surprisingly large, who attribute the invention of the drum to chance. They take it that a native accidentally hit a hollow tree trunk, for instance, and, amazed at the sound, forthwith fashioned a small portable drum for his own amusement. Perish the thought, for a study of the habits and customs of primitive people at once reveals that drums were anything but musical instruments played for amusement! Their purpose was to assist man in his struggle for survival against the mysterious forces of nature, good and evil.

Some of the natives of Africa still use one of the most primitive drums, namely, the shield drum. This drum is simply a wicker-frame shield with an animal skin stretched tightly over the inside. It is used in war and for ceremonial purposes or military display. Is it possible that the warrior's shield is the ancestor of the drum? Some authorities do indeed accept this theory. But Dr. Curt Sachs has advanced far more plausible theories for each of which he offers acceptable proofs. Let us briefly discuss them in turn.

The forerunner of the drum is the *stamper*. Fancy a pit dug in the ground and covered with a lid of bark. Halfway down the pit there is a board fixed so that two women can stamp on it, producing a dull hollow sound to which women surrounding the pit time their dances. Such stampers still exist in the Solomon Archipelago. In time the pit was replaced by curved boards or suitable vessels, say, a pot turned upside down.

Next, implements such as sticks, gourds, or tubes were substituted for stamping feet. Thus hollow bamboos closed at one end could be pounded against the ground, producing drumlike sounds.

Stampers were widely used in connection with marriage ceremonies. By pounding rice in mortars blessings would be evoked upon newlyweds, thus insuring the continuance of the tribe. Such stamped mortars consisted of a series of holes of different shapes in a wooden log into which rice was poured. The holes were pounded with pestles by women; the sound each hole produced depended on how much rice it contained. (One might wonder whether there is any connection between this rice-pounding and the showering with rice or confetti of newlyweds.) In other places men might do the pounding and dancing, and instead of rice dried almonds or taro might be used.

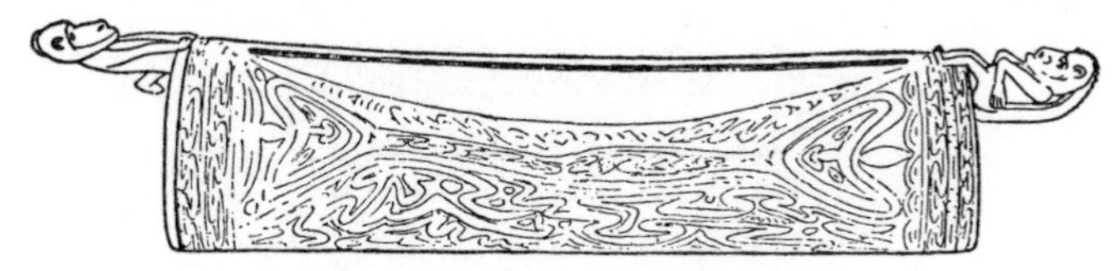

Figure 47. Slit-drum from New Guinea
Courtesy C. Sachs, Hist. of Mus. Inst.

Stamped mortars gave rise to *slit drums,* hollow vessels with a narrow opening all along the top. The original slit drums were made of tree trunks. A tree trunk hollowed out like a boat would be placed over a pit in the ground covered with planks; then men would climb into it and stamp with their feet against the bottom of the trunk, causing the trunk to strike rhythmically against the planks. Among other things, this ceremony symbolized the victory of the new moon over the old moon. One end of the drum was adorned with a woman's head, the other with an alligator's. The earliest specimens of such drums were some twenty feet long and from six to seven feet wide. Figure 47 shows such a slit drum from New Guinea. Later specimens, carved out of tree trunks with just a groove along the top, dispensed with the pit. Men used sticks for drumming against the side of the groove instead of stamping their feet.

Gradually the giant slit drums were reduced in size and became portable.

The portable slit drum shown in Figure 48 was used by Malayan watchmen. With the slit shaped into an H, two tongues were formed which, since they differed in thickness, produced two different notes.

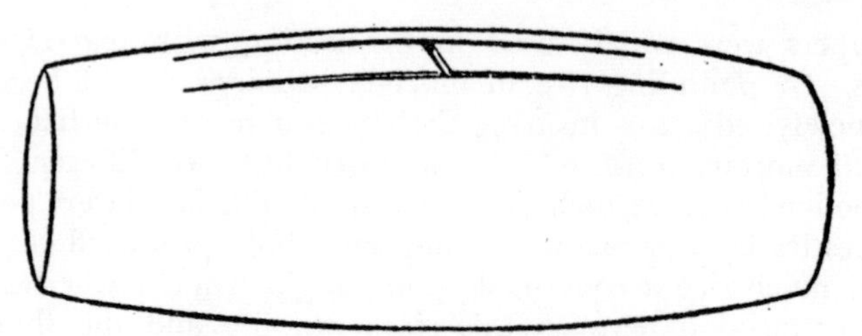

Figure 48. Portable Slit-drum, Celebes
Courtesy C. Sachs, Hist. of Mus. Inst.

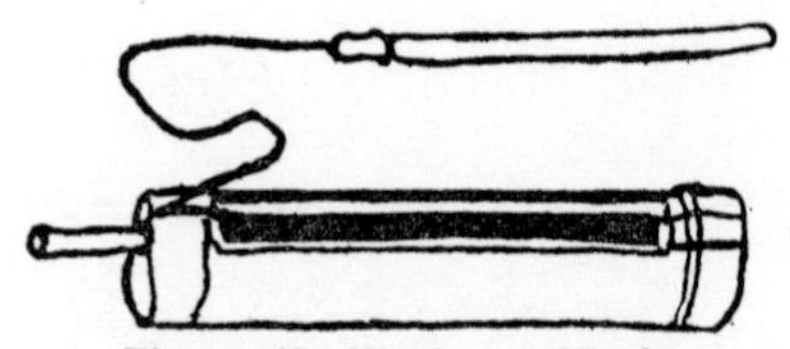

Figure 49. Slit-drum, Mexico
Courtesy C. Sachs, Hist. of Mus. Inst.

importance in religious ceremonies. In Oceania and some South American countries the origin of the slit drum is attributed to the deities of the water—there the drum is struck when the new moon rises. In East Africa a drum offers sanctuary to criminals and fleeing slaves, for once they reach the drum court they become inviolable. Often the drums are placed in huts specially built for their housing. The roofs in that case would be dome-shaped and the drums placed in special beds.

In front of the drum was placed a row of milk pots in which the daily offerings of milk were placed. The milk was left standing in the pots till the spirits had removed the essence of it. Then the guards were permitted to have the remainder for their own use. Sacred cows supplied the milk. A special woman—the Wife of the Drum—looked after the milk. Another woman kept a fire burning constantly in the house lest the spirits grow cold. Offerings of cattle or beef were made upon special occasions by the chiefs of the king, as for instance when a son was born.

Some drums were so sacred that to see them would be fatal. If anybody desecrated such a drum he would be put to death and his arm bones would be used as drumsticks. (Aren't certain bones still referred to as drumsticks?)

In the light of the facts presented above, it is hardly feasible to attribute the origin of the drum to chance.

Gradually the slit drum lost its symbolism. For a while slit drums were used for sending signals. Thus, to the present day a drum in a guardhouse in Java gives special signals for inundations, murder,

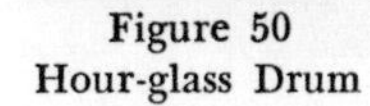

Figure 50
Hour-glass Drum

Figure 51. Drums Made of Human Skulls

theft, and fire, and is used for calling the tribe to a meeting. But the loss in symbolism involved also a loss in prestige, and the original slit drums were replaced by all kinds of other drums, such as the hourglass-shaped drum. This brings us closer to the real drum.

The *hourglass drum,* also called the waisted drum, is Western Asiatic and is some five to six thousand years old. It is a double-headed drum; it can be struck with the hands from either side. Originally it may have been a pit in the form of a tunnel, covered so as to leave both ends exposed, with a ridge of sand in the middle of the tunnel which was struck by the hands. The hourglass drum was suspended horizontally in front of the player and struck with both hands. Its voice was considered to be that of the deity enshrined within.

It must be pointed out again that primitive man had no knowledge of sound waves in air. Therefore, it was comparatively easy to account for a sound when a solid was struck, for that object had a "voice." But if a hollow vessel or what we call a resonator produced a sound without any material object being set in motion, it was accounted for as the voice of a spirit. Closed drums consequently were the abodes of deities, a theory which helps to account for the sacredness of the drum. Small wonder that the drum was used in worship. It is also quite likely that in very primitive days the crowns of two human skulls were used, as is still the custom in Tibet. Indians still use hourglass drums, although generally smaller and shorter ones; by means of lacing cords the performer is able to alter the pitch.

The hourglass drum already had membranes stretched over its heads. Thus we have arrived at the drum proper.

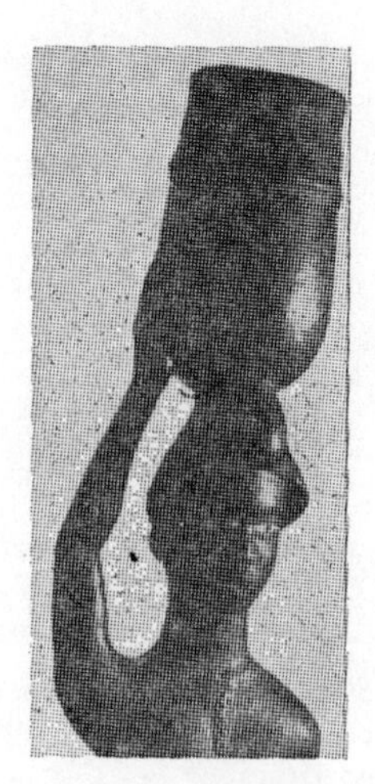

Figure 52. Vessel Drum, Pottery

Early drums unmistakably reveal their descent either from tree trunks or from kitchen utensils, such as pots and kettles. Originally pot drums were probably ten feet in length, closed at one end and covered with a skin at the lower end. They were known as *tubular drums.* Since they measured up to ten feet in length, they were played suspended form the roof of a hut. Gradually they were reduced in size. Finally, they were supplied with a foot on which to stand, and this gave rise to the *foot drum* of East Africa. Note that the lower end resembles the feet of a table.

From now on there seems to be no end to the variations in size and shape of drums. Thus we read about a *cup-handle drum,* a *goblet drum,* and others. In size they varied from the primitive twenty-feet-long ones to *hand drums* a few inches in diameter. In shape they resembled tree trunks, cylinders, barrels, or kettles. There were also *shoulder drums* which one man carried on his shoulder while another man played the head (of the drum, that is) with two sticks. As you see, the sticks are hook-shaped. Some of our modern military drums are strikingly reminiscent of the old tree-trunk form.

There is a close parallel in the evolution of drums and utility vessels. As the shape of the latter varied, so did the shape of drums, and as different materials were used in the making of hollow utensils, different materials were employed in the construction of the drums. This leads us once more to the conclusion that ancient drums had a utilitarian purpose. Indeed, they were resorted to in praying for rain, foretelling the future, and blessing newlyweds on t heir wedding night, among other ceremonies. In no case were drums owned or played by the common man, for this was the exclusive right of shamans, priests, or kings. Later it also became the preroga-

Figure 53
Footed Drum

Figure 54
Shoulder Drum, Africa

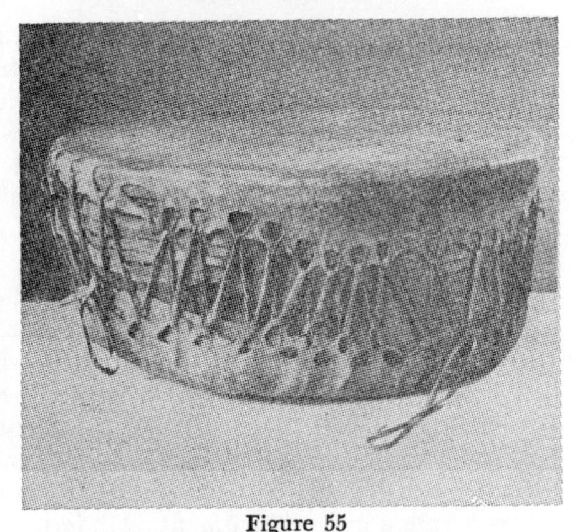
Figure 55
Frame Drum with Double Head

From "Old World Overtones", U. of Pa.

tive of the nobility. The more the drum lost its symbolism, the more it penetrated the lower strata of society.

Drums are either single-headed or double-headed, i.e., they have either one membrane for striking or two, one on either side of the frame. The double-headed are generally of a later period. Drums are further either frame drums or shallow drums, halfway between the frame and barrel.

The *frame drum* consists of a narrow frame or loop with one or two parallel skins held taut in it. The most important species of this type is the *timbrel* or *tambourine*. The frame need not be circular; for instance, the Sumerians possessed a rectangular timbrel. In the third millennium B.C. In India there are still octagonal tambourines to be found.

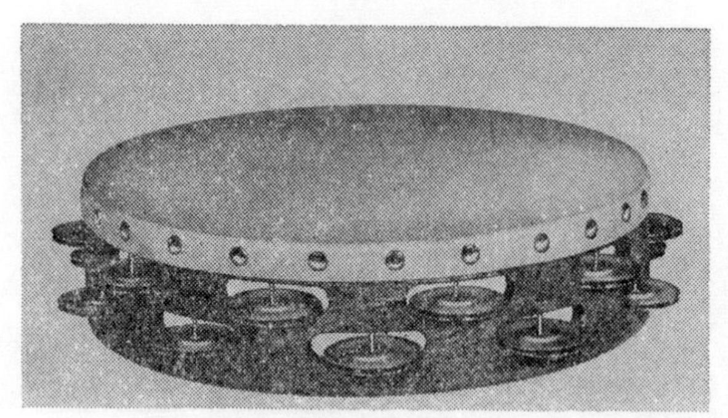

Figure 56. Tambourine
Courtesy C. G. Conn Ltd., Elkhart, Indiana

The first tambourines were without jingles. With the Old Testament Hebrews the tambourine was quite popular under the name of *tabret* (Genesis 31:27) or *timbrel* (Exodus 15:20), the old English name. The common Hebrew name, however, was *tof*. This was the instrument—still without jingles—used by Miriam and the daughters of Israel to celebrate their triumph over the Egyptians. The Gauls used it, and it was introduced into Britain in prehistoric times. In time the sides of the frame were perforated, and little jingles or metal disks were fitted into the slots. Thus, *the principle of the jingle sistrum and the rattle were applied to the drum.*

The tambourine was often used in Bacchic rites (Bacchus was the god of wine), mostly struck with the hand, occasionally thrown into the air and caught again. It is frequently depicted in ecclesiastical carvings, placed by artists in the hands of angels. The beginning of the thirteenth century saw its introduction into Europe. It was as a rule a girl's instrument. Modern composers like Weber, Bizet, and Donizetti introduced the tambourine into the symphony orchestra in their search for special effects, and during the nineteenth century it became firmly established as an orchestral instrument.

The tambourine has been in use practically unchanged for the past two thousand years. Struck by the hand, its jingles rattle and at the same time its membrane gives the drum effect. Shaken, the jingles only play. The jingles are mostly used together with other percussion instruments in music of Oriental nature, for "barbaric" effects.

Frame drums are not always of a miniature or "handy" size. In ancient Mesopotamia about 3000 B.C. there were giant frame drums six feet wide. Standing on their sides, such drums reached up to the player's face. Two men would strike the same head simultaneously from either side of the standing drum. In addition, these Sumerians possessed frame drums of all sizes as well as numerous other drums of various shapes and size.

Europe was slow to accept the drum; it was practically unknown during the early Middle Ages. The ones used during the later period were the smaller type used for delicate effects or for time beating only. The thunderous beats of our percussions were unknown at that time.

A small frame drum came into use from the twelfth century on. It was customary to play this drum together with a small pipe, as shown in Figure 57, where we see a Spanish monk of the thirteenth

Figure 57
Pipe and Tabor

century indulging in this pastime. This was the *pipe and tabor*. The tabor was suspended from the shoulder and left forearm and played with a stick by the right hand. In England this pipe—also known as the *fife*—and tabor were used by the masses of people from the fifteenth to the eighteenth centuries for the morris dance. One finds frequent references to the pipe and tabor in the literature of that period.

The *tom-tom* of the American Indians is a richly decorated small portable drum. It must not be assumed that this small specimen was the beginning of Indian percussion instruments; on the contrary, it is the outcome of years of improvement. The ornaments used to be strictly of symbolic nature, which feature has been lost

Figure 58. Tom-tom
Courtesy R. Davidson, Coaldale

to some extent by now. A marvelous illustration of the use of the tom-tom by Negroes is given by Eugene O'Neill in his drama *The Emperor Jones.*

Modern bands and orchestras employs the snare drum, the tenor drum, the bass drum, and the kettledrums, the first three of which are shown on page 69.

The *bass drum* is the largest of all percussion instruments. Until the beginning of the nineteenth century it was known as the Turkish drum, showing that it was adopted from the Turks. It used to be—and in most cases it still is—an indispensable part of the military band, although it is also used to some extent in the symphony orchestra. The Turks are known to have had it around 1500 A.D. Mozart introduced it into the symphony in his opera *Il Seraglio,* but he had it played with a sort of split birch rod or broom beating the edge, not the membrane of the drum.

The real introduction of the bass drum did not occur until 1807, when Spontini used it in one of his *Triumphal Marches.* This was considered an outrage by many, for in those days such a drum was considered a musical monstrosity. However, the attempt was successful. Soon musicians overindulged in its use, for Berlioz complained bitterly in 1830 that the boom of the bass drum was only fit to make monkeys dance. The same Berlioz refined the method of playing the drum and used it for special effects. Some of the later composers (for instance, Mahler and Richard Strauss) revived Mozart's method of playing. Modern composers use occasionally small steel brooms instead of drumsticks, as does Don Gillis in the third movement of his Symphony No. 5½. Today the bass drum is standard equipment in all bands and orchestras.

The bass drum itself is a section of a cylinder of wood about one foot wide with a diameter of two to three feet. It has a membrane—the drumhead—on either side, but it is as a rule struck with one stick on one side only. The membrane is of vellum, stretched over hoops with a cord and braces for adjustment of the tension. Some of the latest models have a brass or aluminum shell, but such drums have less resonance and are inferior in tone quality. The tone is not really a musical sound, being of indefinite pitch and used mostly to accentuate the rhythm. The proper tension is therefore sought not to adjust the pitch but to secure maximum resonance. Generally, the drum is played with a stick with a large felt-padded

Figure 59. Drums: Snare, Tenor, and Bass
Courtesy C. G. Conn Ltd., Elkhart, Indiana

knob. Occasionally, especially for the roll, a double-headed stick is used. The stick is covered with lamb's wool to secure a soft sound, and with leather to achieve a thunderous *fortissimo* effect. If played very softly, single strokes at regular intervals are most impressive, awe-inspiring, gloomy, and mysterious (a heritage from the Orient); the loud passages impart a tremendous force to the orchestra and thus help to build up climaxes. In addition, a roll is very effective, especially a soft one, which imparts to the music a shuddering effect. No "thunder" would be complete without the bass drum!

The modern orchestra also employs a *Chinese drum,* similar in size and build to the Indian tom-tom. This is a wooden hoop with painted pigskin stretched tightly on both sides. The sound is light and primitive, so it gives the hollow drum effect of the music of savage and barbaric tribes.

The *side* or *snare drum* resembles the bass drum but is much smaller. Up to the middle of the nineteenth century it had a wooden shell and cords, but the latest models of our time have brass shells equipped with screws. The drum is played horizontally, the upper head being struck with two sticks of hardwood, one in each hand, with double alternating strokes. This method of striking the membrane, the technique of which is difficult to acquire, produces a very effective roll.

As with the bass drum, the heads are of calf leather. Several cords of catgut wound with wire are stretched across the inside of the lower head. These cords are the snares and give the drum its name. When the upper head is struck the snares vibrate against the lower head and provide the characteristic dry and crisp rattle of this drum. The head of the drum is stretched so tightly that the sticks rebound automatically, which makes the drum an ideal instrument for emphasizing and giving clearness to rhythmical patterns of almost any speed, no matter how intricate. If the center of the head is struck with a kettledrum stick, an explosive sound is obtained. Furthermore, the snare drum can also be muffled, as is required for instance in funeral marches, by loosening the snares or wrapping them in cloth.

To begin with, the snare drum found its principal application in military bands, but gradually it found its way into the operatic and symphonic ensemble. One can hardly suppress a chuckle of delight, listening to Gounod's "Soldiers' March" (*Faust,* Act II), when the snare drums enter.

The *tenor drum* stands midway between the bass and the snare drum. It is slightly larger than the latter, but its proportions are altogether different. There are no snares, and its tone is duller and heavier and also of indefinite pitch. In military bands its roll replaces that of the kettledrum. Although Gluck and Wagner used it occasionally, it has not been accepted as standard equipment in the symphony orchestra. It has its place, however, in military parades, being also called the *parade drum.*

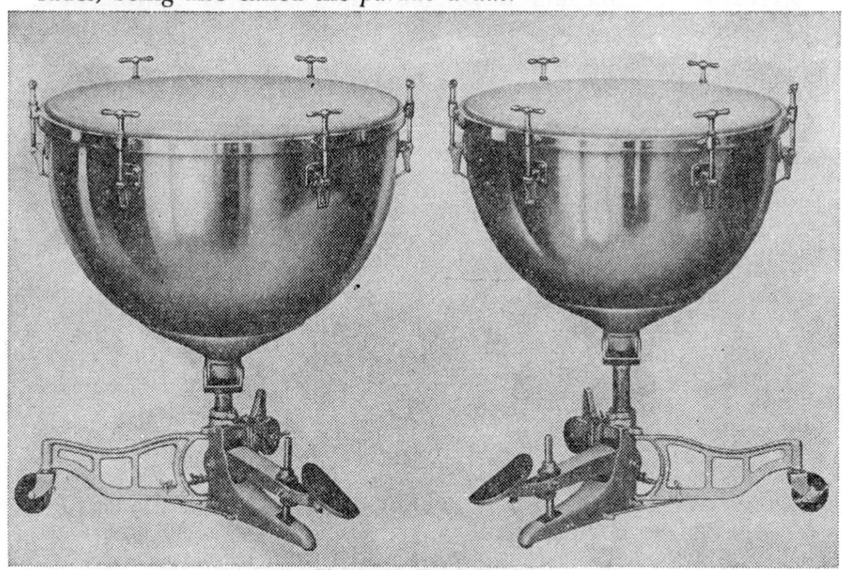

Figure 60. Kettledrums
Courtesy C. G. Conn Ltd., Elkhart, Indiana

### *Kettledrums or Timpani*

Kettledrums, also called timpani, are the only musical drums in the orchestra. Because the bowl-shaped body reinforces certain overtones, the kettledrum produces a musical note of definite pitch. The word *timpani* is derived from the Greek, meaning something that is struck or beaten.

Timpani are of Arabic origin. Their beginning may be seen in the pot drum of several thousand years ago. The pot drum had, as we have seen, a close connection with earthenware crocks for keeping food. Small kettledrums were found in Persia around 600 A.D. These were bowl-shaped. Larger kettledrums had a flat bottom and still resembled the pot drum of primitive people. Later on they assumed the shape of an egg, most likely to facilitate carrying the drum on the back of horses or camels. Originally kettledrums were employed in the cult of the dead, images of gods being deposited within them. This of course made them sacred, and the common mortal dare not use them.

In India the *main drum* is a pair of giant silver kettles five feet in diameter, weighing 450 pounds. It is still the most impressive instrument of the band officiating in State ceremonies and processions. These drums are mounted on an elephant and draped with hanging cloth ten feet long; each drum has its own drummer who perches on its rim and strikes the drumhead with a silver stick. In addition to giant drums, there are smaller ones mounted on camels with only one drummer for each set of two. Still smaller drums are made of clay in an oval form.

Kettledrums were associated with trumpets, as is shown in Figures 61 and 62. The first timpani entered Europe some time around 1300 with the Crusaders coming home from the Holy Land, or possibly via Russia and Poland into Germany, or through the Moors through Spain. They were of a rather small size. The head of the drum was about the size of the palm of the hand, and the whole drum was the size of a fist. Used in pairs, they were suspended from the performer's neck or attached to his girdle. Sometimes they were held in one hand and played with the other. It is obvious that such tiny drums had but limited use for outdoor music.

The English name for the early kettledrums was *nakers,* a word clearly derived from the Arabian *naqqara.* Chaucer refers to them in his *Knight's Tale.*

By the middle of the fifteenth century the small drums were superseded by mighty war drums. They made their way from the east via Hungary and Poland into Germany, where they were cultivated so extensively that until the middle of the seventeenth century they were known as German instruments. They were definitely the attribute of nobility and the symbol of aristocracy. No one under the rank of a baron was permitted to own them. In war they were borne with the colors of the regiment and defended to the last man. Their possession was a badge of honor, and the loss of kettledrums was considered a disgrace and could lead to the disbanding of the regiment.

Kettledrummers (as well as trumpeters) were invested with special rights and formed a "noble guild." Whoever succeeded in wresting a pair of kettledrums from the enemy would be permitted to own them and thus be admitted to the guild. The drums, as we can readily see, were instruments of cavalrymen, and were played from either side of the horse (Figure 61). In today's Abyssinia the kettledrums are still symbols of might. There the king is accompanied on his military expeditions by forty-four mounted drummers with eighty-eight drums!

Around 1650 timpani found their way into other European countries and into serious music as well, but not without some opposition. Thus Virdung, one of the great composers of that period, complained bitterly that these enormous rumbling barrels troubled honest old people, the ill and the sick, and pious who prayed and read, and he believed that the devil himself invented

Figure 61
Rider with
Kettledrums

Figure 62. Kettledrums and Trumpets

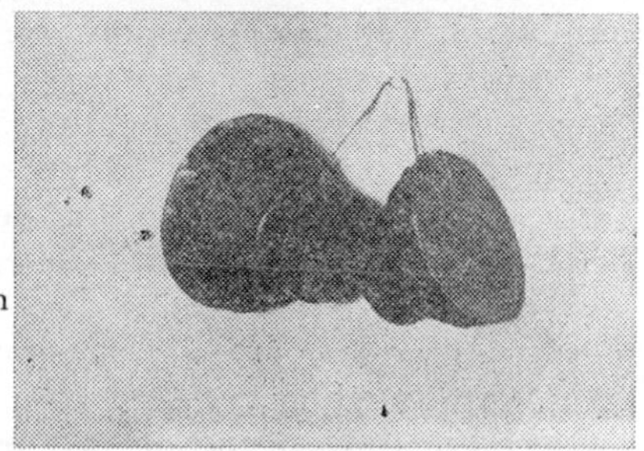

Figure 63
Small Tympani
Courtesy Museum of Fine Arts, Boston

this monstrosity for the "suppression of all sweet melodies and the whole art of music." Just the same, Lully, an early French opera composer, used kettledrums by 1670, and Bach and Handel had frequent recourse to them.

Later on, unfortunately, timpani were also used by jugglers, and for a while Negro drummers became the rage in Germany. A curious transformation, indeed: the drum started out, as we have seen, with images of deity, and then from the highest strata of society it descended into the lowest ranks of common men. In other words, we have the following chain deity-priest-king-nobility-military-juggler-Negro. Today timpani hold a respectable place in first-rate orchestras.

Today's timpani are well known under the name *kettledrums* because the body of the drums is kettle-shaped, made of copper or alloy. The membrane is similar to that of the bass drum, also made of calfskin. It is stretched across the basin-shaped opening by means of a wooden loop and held in place by a circular iron ring. Screws on this ring, usually six to eight in number, tighten or loosen the membrane. The screws insure equal tension on all parts of the skin, thus balancing the tension throughout the membrane, and they regulate the pitch. The greater the tension in the skin, that is, the tighter the screws, the higher the pitch.

Timpani are invariably played at least in pairs. This has evidently been the custom since their origin. But the pair of them are of unequal size, the larger one producing the deeper and the smaller one the higher tone. The two tones produced are, of course, reminiscent of the primitive efforts of two-syllable speech. In orchestral music the lower drum is tuned to the tonic (*do*) and the higher one to the dominant (*sol*). It is not unusual to employ three drums nowadays. In such a case the third drum is tuned to the subdominant (*fa*).

Beethoven departed from the usual procedure by tuning them in sixths (in his *Seventh Symphony*) and later in octaves (in the *Eighth* and *Ninth*). Berlioz employs eight pairs of kettledrums in his *Requiem* (1837). Since that time composers have varied the number of timpani, but the usual number in the standard orchestra has remained two or three.

One of the problems of the timpani is the *tuning*. It is clear that a composer can hardly be expected to restrict his composition to two or three bass notes for the drums. If a composition changes key, the drums become useless unless they can be tuned to the new key. Fortunately this can be done, provided the composer is considerate enough to give the drummer a few bars' rest in which to do it.

Several methods of tuning have been devised. The oldest methods used resin glue which was spread on the parchment head, making it heavier and thus lowering the pitch. Next screws were employed to vary the degree of tension. But screws made the tuning most elaborate. Consequently, musicians were looking for improvements, and we have a series of inventions. In 1812 Cramer of Munich devised a crank fitted to the side of the drum whereby all screws could be tightened simultaneously. In 1821 Stumpf, another inventor, introduced a device through which the frame of the drum could be revolved and thereby stretch or relax the skin. Then in 1837 timpani with a single central key at the side of the drum were produced which worked on the head rim by a system of pulleys.

The most satisfactory way of tuning, however, was developed in 1830 in France by the invention of a foot pedal similar to the harp pedal. By means of this pedal concentric rings are pressed against the inside of the membrane head, permitting the drummer to vary the pitch by semitones even during a performance. In this way a kettledrum may be tuned in semitones up and down the scale in a matter of seconds. The pedal arrangement is still the most often used (see Figure 60).

Figure 64
Goodman's Timpani
Courtesy S. Goodman, New York

Just recently Mr. Saul Goodman, first timpanist of the New York Philharmonic Symphony Orchestra and teacher at the Conservatoire de Musique in Montreal, has come forth with a new invention which uses chains for tuning. In forwarding an illustration to the author (Figure 64), Mr. Goodman writes: "As you see from the photo the sprocket is attached at each screw point, and the chain moves the entire ensemble in unison." In addition to New York, Goodman's drums are used in Montreal, Quebec, and several other cities. It remains to be seen whether this invention will win universal favor.

If used sparingly the timpani enrich the orchestral palette quite effectively. The drummer uses two flexible drumsticks, the ends of which are covered with felt, although for special *fortissimo* passages leather-covered sticks are used. Occasionally the drums are muffled by placing a cloth over the drumhead. (Mozart resorted to muting the drums in such a way in his *Magic Flute*.) The tone of the timpani has a velvety quality with felt-covered sticks, but wooden or leather-covered sticks produce dramatic effects, harsh and terrifying noises. To accentuate the rhythm detached notes are used, but the roll is also very impressive. The dynamic range extends all the way from the faintest tap to a thunderous *fortissimo*.

Our modern orchestras would hardly get along without this king of the drums. Once you are familiar with its sound you will find it in practically all symphonic music, for the masters, great and small, know how to enrich their music with the timpani.

What a far cry indeed from the primitive conception and use of the drum!

## *Part Two: Lip-Voiced Instruments*

*From*

*To*

CHAPTER IV

# NATURAL AND SIMPLE HORNS AND TRUMPETS

The term *lip-voiced instruments* embraces all brass instruments and their forerunners. "Natural" horns and trumpets are those man found in his natural surroundings, and "simple" horns and trumpets include the primitive instruments—man's first attempts to fashion the more elaborate instruments of our century.

Again the question arises: which was the first instrument of this type? Was it a horn or was it a trumpet? As in all such cases where the answer is evasive, various theories have been advanced, some of them rather amusing. We may discard those which attribute the origin of horns to imitation of nature. Likewise, explanations which credit primitive man with a desire to bring forth a musical instrument for his enjoyment must be dismissed. Let us recall that primitive "musical" instruments served definite purposes in man's struggle for survival, and we will agree with those musicologists who assert that lip-voiced instruments owe their origin to man's effort to augment his own voice in order to give it more power. A powerful voice assisted him in frightening evil spirits away, scaring demons, summoning help, sending out signals, intimidating an enemy, and so forth.

Originally, then, horns and trumpets were anything but musical. On the contrary, the more terrifying the sound of the horn, the more valuable it was. This means that for thousands of years trumpets, for instance, were not used for aesthetic effects. Although such masters as Bach and Handel employed certain types of trumpets for certain compositions, people were scandalized when Beethoven introduced the trumpet into the orchestra (in his *Third Symphony,* third movement). The first orchestral trumpets had to be muted to be fit for indoor use!

The first horns must have been merely megaphones used by chiefs or kings in addressing their subjects. It is evident that man would make use of the natural objects of his environment. Thus, bones with the marrow hollowed out and large spiral seashells with special openings drilled into the closed ends are known to be among the oldest lip-voiced instruments in existence. Such devices must have been very effective, for no other instrument has so many magical powers attributed to it.

The question now arises as to just when and how these megaphones were transformed into trumpets or horns; in other words, when did speaking tubes assume the role of "musical" instruments?

The discovery that a tube can be sounded in a trumpetlike fashion need not be attributed to chance. It is just as likely that in his effort to disguise his voice man finally succeeded in producing a sound by pressing his lips against the tube and then vibrating them. Again, man may have learned "lip-voicing" by experimenting with reed instruments.

The earliest record of a wooden trumpet dates back to about 3000 B.C. and is attributed to the Sumerians. This specimen was made out of a hollow branch of a tree with the lower end somewhat enlarged to augment the sound. Such primitive trumpets are still in vogue among the Asiatic Mongols, Kirghis, and Kalmucks. The Mongols, for instance, employ gigantic trumpets of wood some ten feet in length. It is worthy of note that usually these trumpets are used in pairs.

Figure 67
Mongols Playing Gigantic Trumpets

As such instruments are capable of developing a terrific thundering blast, they became rather popular among the herdsmen of mountainous regions, especially in Europe. The Swiss are still famous for their *alphorn.*

Formerly the alphorn was built of long staves of wood closely bound with bark. Today this instrument is made out of one tree. This tree must have a curve at its base. Then it is split into two halves, and each half is carefully inspected for its grain and for flaws. Next, each half is hollowed out, and the two parts are finally fastened together with bark. The result is not Tennyson's "Horns of Elfland faintly blowing," but a veritable H-bomb of a musical instrument up to ten feet in length. Even though the concert hall will never do for such a monster, it fits the valleys and mountain peaks admirably. Echo-like tones enhance the effect—the horn blasts seem to bounce from peak to peak. Recently the Swiss have begun to use the alphorn as a musical instrument. It has been equipped with a cupped mouthpiece to make the tone more musical. Naturally, the range has its limitations, since only the open harmonics can be produced (that is, mostly the *dos, mis,* and *sols*).

Figure 68. Alphorn
Courtesy Nef, Geschichte unserer Musikinstrumente

Similar instruments are found in the Himalayas and among the Indians of South America.

Animal horns, such as ox horns and elephants' and mammoths' tusks, soon provided natural horns for trumpets. Thus the Hebrews shaped the ram's horn into the familiar *shofar* used even to the

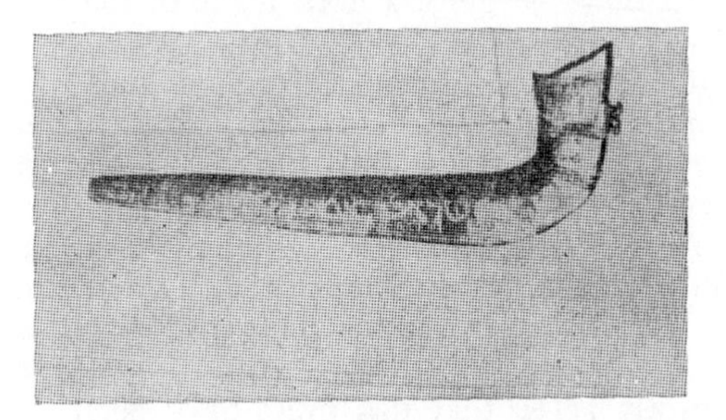

Figure 69. Shofar
Courtesy Nef, Geschichte unserer Musikinstrumente

present day in synagogue worship. This horn is actually a primitive bugle. It received its shape by being flattened in sections, the lower end being bent almost at a right angle to the stem. This process is made possible by steaming the horn before bending. Today a cup mouthpiece is formed at the small end. Present-day models are consequently easier to play than the original shofars which were without such attached mouthpieces. Being a natural horn of a small size—about a foot in length—the shofar is capable of producing but a few tones, namely, the second, the third, and sometimes the fourth partial tones. The fundamental tone can be played, but since it is hardly audible it has no practical value. If blown properly, the shofar sounds pleasant; on the other hand, if sheer force is used in blowing, the tone is rough and awe-inspiring.

The shofar has the distinction of being one of the oldest instruments in use. The Jews use it today in their synagogues on New Year's Day and the Day of Atonement in the same manner as did their ancestors in ancient Palestine. Since this instrument plays mainly *do-sol,* one is hardly tempted to call it a musical instrument.

Several forms of the shofar are known. One kind was made from the horn of the wild goat. This instrument was used for the new moon ceremonies. The mouthpiece of this horn was overlaid with gold, and that of the ram's horn with silver.

The shofar was blown intermittently with the trumpet during the month preceding the New Year's Festival as well as on both days of the Festival. It was also blown a number of times during divine service and once at the termination of the Day of Atonement. In addition, it was used in war and on other occasions. In the synagogues the shofar is covered and must not be seen by the worshippers.

In contrast to the shofar, the numerous other animal horns did not fare so well. Thus, mammoth and elephant tusks, deer horns, and so on were long ago supplanted by metal instruments. We shall discuss them presently. But before doing so we must briefly inspect a natural horn which played a most prominent part in the history of the Middle Ages, the *oliphant.*

The oliphant was, as its name suggests, a horn made of the elephant's tusk. Since Africa is the home of the elephant, it is assumed that this horn originated there. It was introduced in Byzantium in the tenth century A.D. and from there found its way into Central Europe. It flourished for several centuries, but with the decline of chivalry it lost its importance.

Our illustration features a very valuable ivory oliphant, about a yard in length, richly and exquisitely ornamented with scenes from the life of St. Hubert. The carvings are done by hand and will bear close inspection. Notice the special mouthpiece inserted into the upper end. You will readily agree that this must have been an expensive instrument to own. And so it was. Only kings and great nobles could afford such veritable works of art.

Oddly enough, the oliphant had no musical value. Its tones were those of the shofar in number, except that, being about three times the size of the shofar, all four notes were playable (*do, do′, sol, do″*). Just the same, the oliphant was a priceless treasure to its owner because it was the insignia of knighthood. Its uses therefore were restricted to signaling. In England it was given to office holders by the liege lord in lieu of a document. It found its way into medieval literature, where it is also known as the Roland horn, for this was the horn that Roland sounded to summon his friends when he was surrounded by the Saracens at Roncesvalles. Together with his sword, this horn was Roland's most precious possession.

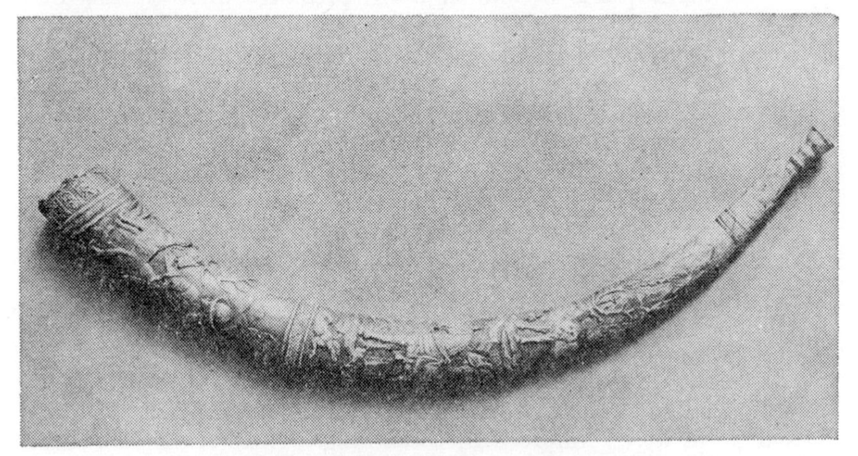

Figure 70. Oliphant, 17th cy., ca. 37 in. long
Courtesy Museum of Fine Arts, Boston

At a later period, the oliphant was extolled by the poets of the Romantic period. It was also found in works of art, for in medieval paintings we see angels pictured as blowing the oliphant on the Day of Judgment.

Specimens of the oliphant have been preserved. Figure 70 is a reproduction of the oliphant preserved at the Museum of Fine Arts in Boston. It dates from the seventeenth century. Some oliphants were wrought in solid gold or other noble metals. As they lost their dignity they penetrated lower strata of society, and cheaper, cruder forms were employed as horns by hunters, shepherds, and finally night watchmen. (In Africa the oliphant is still the royal instrument of tribal chiefs.) This slow degradation of the oliphant reminds us of the fate of kettledrums, but in contradistinction to the drum, the oliphant never found its way into the orchestra. It did, however, give rise to other modern horns, which will be discussed in Chapter VI.

We have seen how with the advance of the metal age natural percussion instruments gave way to metallic types. Animal horns were also supplanted by metallic ones. There were several reasons for this change. Let us discuss briefly the most pertinent ones.

Natural horns are somewhat brittle and hence not very permanent; metallic horns are more durable. With the extinction of the mammoth their horns were increasingly difficult to procure. Further, the bore of any natural horn was never quite satisfactory for a truly musical sound, as the interior of the horn lacked the smoothness and polish required for musical tones.

The mouthpieces of animal horns presented another difficulty. Primitive man had no way of piercing the hard tip of the horn, so he had to cut it off altogether, leaving a rough opening against which to press his lips. Such a method of playing was most unsatisfactory. Therefore, an opening cut on the side of the horn close to the tip was tried, and this proved more successful. In fact, even some of the early metal horns had such a side opening. When men finally learned to cut even the hardest horn, a portion of the hard tip would be removed and a special mouthpiece put into the hole drilled through the remaining portion. With metal tubes the mouthpiece problem was readily solved, and the size and shape could be varied at will, far more so than could be done with natural horns.

The change from natural to metal horns was most likely a gradual one. The Germanic tribes had horns in "sections," that is, animal horns were reinforced by metal rings. These rings were fitted together at the lower end in sections; in the middle they strengthened the horn. The Swiss warhorn of the sixteenth century in Figure 72 clearly shows how metal was used to strengthen a horn. Just note the metal rings at strategic places. Likewise, the eighteenth-century English watchman's horn, a twisted ox horn, shows such reinforcements (Figure 73). Partial metal horns in time gave way to metallic ones.

The fact that such reinforced animal horns have survived is no indication of recent origin. It merely proves their popularity. It has been established that pure metal horns and trumpets were known in Europe as early as 1000 B.C. This has been proved by finds in Scandinavia, Denmark, and Ireland. We also know that the Old Testament Hebrews possessed highly accurate metal trumpets, and the ancient Romans were renowned for such instruments.

Among ancient metal instruments we find the straight trumpet as well as several curved specimens. The former was common to the Hebrews, Assyrians, Greeks, and Romans.

The average length of Roman tubas was four feet, although judging by a trumpet shown on Trajan's column it may have been

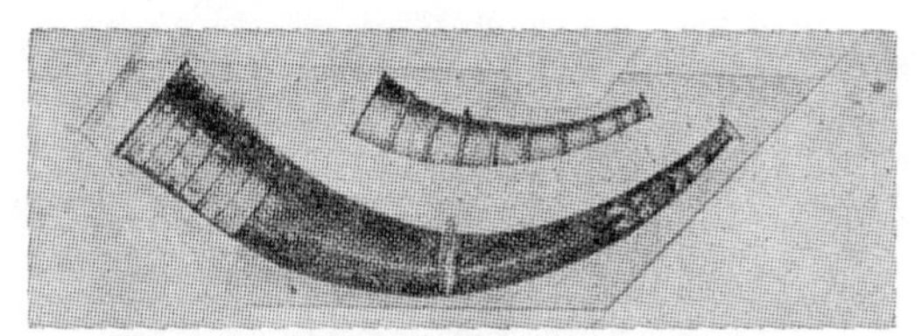

Figure 71. Animal Horns with Metal Rings
Courtesy Nef, Geschichte unserer Musikinstrumente

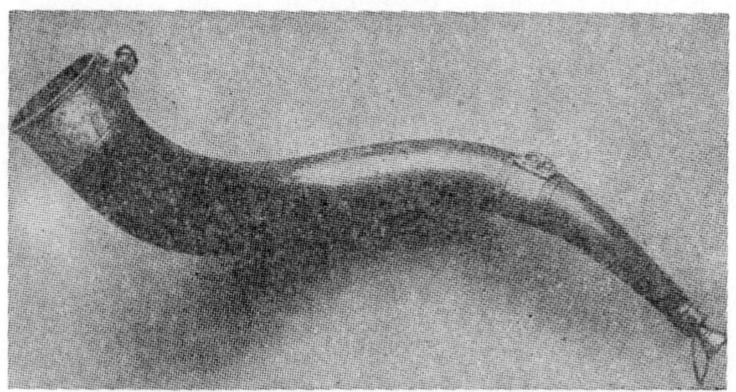

Figure 72. A Swiss Warhorn, 16th Century
Courtesy Nef, Geschichte unserer Musikinstrument

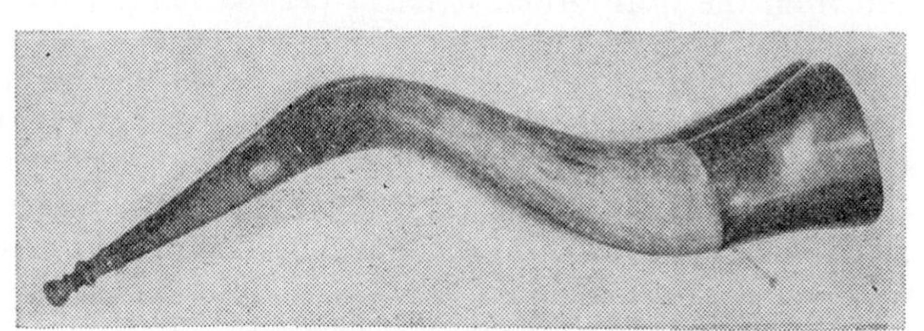

Figure 73. Watchman's Horn, England, 18th Century
Courtesy Museum of Fine Arts, Boston

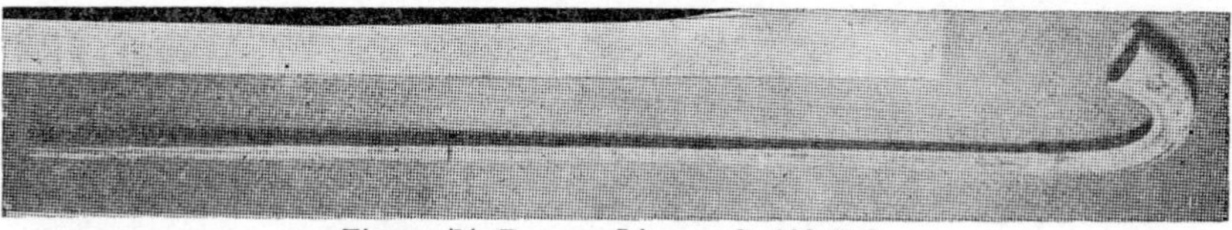

Figure 74. Roman Lituus, C. 100 B.C.

up to seven feet in length. The Roman tuba is the ancestor of our modern trumpet and indirectly of the trombone.

The Roman *lituus* was a hooked trumpet used by the cavalry. Its tube was long, slender, and cylindrical, with an upturned bell at the lower end. The shape of the instrument resembled that of the letter J or a crooked staff. The prototype of the lituus was a combination of a wooden tube with a natural horn attached to the lower end. Instruments with this combination still exist, for instance, in Ethiopia.

The Roman trumpet later received a bell of fantastic designs, such as an open-mouthed dragon head or the open jaws of some other animal. During the last two centuries B.C. such an instrument, known as the *karnyx,* was very popular with the Celts. The tone of the Roman lituus is described as shrieking and braying.

A third type of trumpet is found in the Roman *cornu* (Latin for *horn*) or *buccina.* The cornu was a curved horn of the bugle type. It had a narrow bore in the shape of the letter G. Some of these horns had wooden crossbars which rested upon the player's shoulder and were held by the left hand. The mouthpiece was pressed against the lips by the right hand. Horace, a Roman historian, refers to the sound of the cornu as a "threatening rumble." The instrument was used in infantry bands, at solemn occasions like funerals, and even in circus plays.

Surprisingly enough the Nordic tribes of Europe had developed curved trumpets a thousand years before the Romans. The Danish *lur* (plural: *lurer)* is the most amazing horn of prehistoric man. As seen from the illustration, it has a peculiar shape, resembling somewhat the letter S. The plane of the second curve is at right angles to the plane of the first. The tube is conical like a horn, and its lower end, reaching above the head of the player, has an ornamental disk for decoration. The smaller end of the tube has small pendant plates of metal to reinforce the rough, blatant, and terrifying effect of the blast given out by the lur. The lur was always used in pairs, and the two horns forming the pair were twisted in opposite directions.

The lur is almost a perfect replica of a mammoth's tusk. It is quite reasonable to assume that the original lur was the tusk of this animal and that as these animals became scarce man resorted to metal imitations. Lurer found in excavations have been tried by modern trombonists with remarkable success; the tone is unusually fine for an ancient instrument, so that its beauty has been unduly extolled. The tone is noble and solemn, reminding the listener of the French horn or the tenor trombone. However, modern players have modern mouthpieces and are skilled in their art far beyond the widest stretch of imagination of the primitive player. Thus,

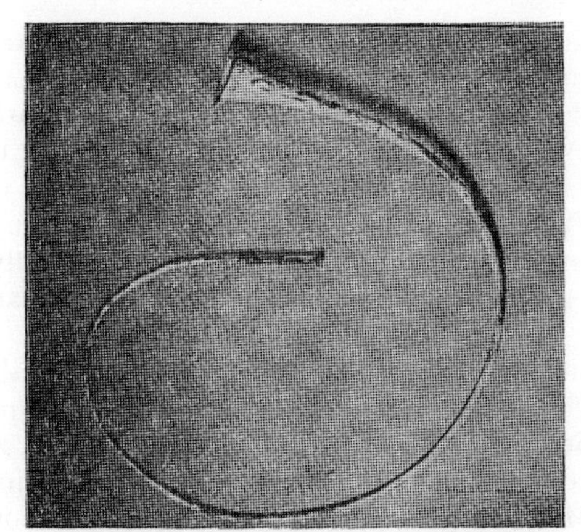

Figure 75. Roman Cornu, C 100 B.C.

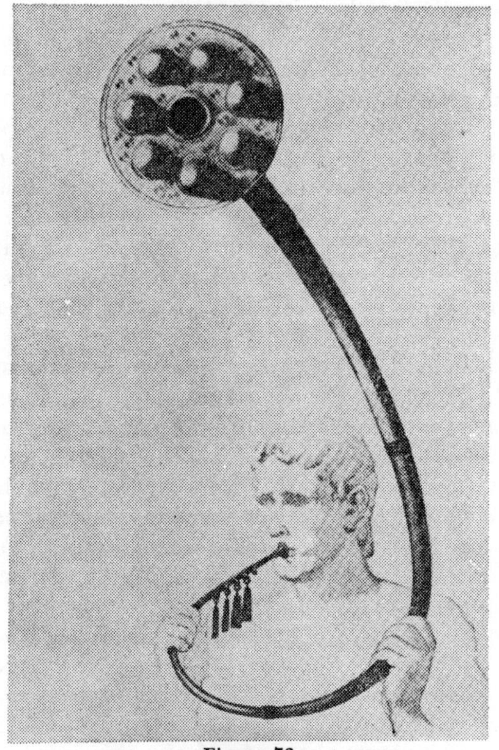

Figure 76
Danish Lur of the Bronze Age
Courtesy Geiringer, Musical Instruments

Figure 77
Buysine, 15th Century
Courtesy Museum of
Fine Arts, Boston

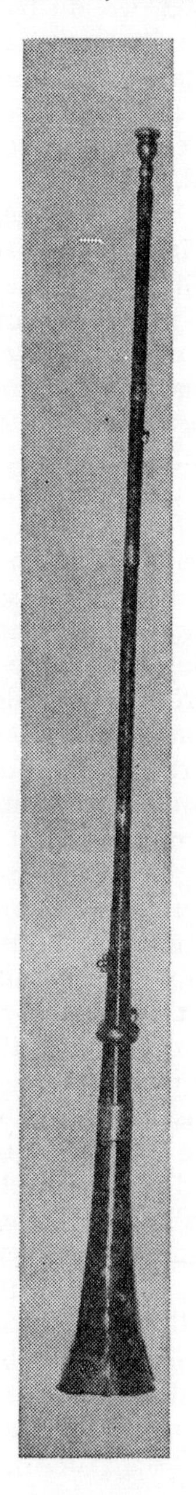

even if the lur is capable of producing in addition to the fundamental tone the eleven natural harmonics (see the next chapter), i.e., consecutive notes in the upper register and even some chromatic notes, we are by no means justified in attributing such playing to primitive hunters. Furthermore, the fact that lurer were found in pairs does not prove that they were used to play two-part harmony. In the first place, they were tuned to the same pitch, and secondly, attempts at harmony are only a little better than a thousand years old.

As we have seen, all ancient trumpets and horns served a utilitarian purpose. It is significant that all the writers of Greece, Egypt, Rome, and other countries speak of the sound of the trumpets as horrible and shrieking, comparing it, for example, to the braying of an ass. As late as the Middle Ages, carvings in architecture show angels blowing such awe-inspiring trumpets on the Day of the Last Judgment, proving that these ancient primitive natural horns and trumpets had found their way into Christian civilization. Many of them held their own well into the nineteenth century.

The invasion of Europe by the Goths in the second half of the first millennium A.D. arrested the development of the Roman trumpets and horns so that a new start had to be made. This new beginning was not made until about 1000 A.D. The most important lip-voiced instrument of the Middle Ages, the *buysine,* can therefore hardly be regarded as a direct descendant of the Roman tuba. The Roman "tuba" or Roman trumpet, also known by different writers during the Middle Ages as *buysine, buzine,* and *buzaun* (German: *posaune*), was made entirely of bronze. Its function was to give trumpet calls in the army. Thus is served the purpose of the later bugle (see Figure 77).

Irish miniatures of the eighth century depict a straight metal trumpet without a bell, but the real buysine was imported from Saracen, Sicily into Southern Italy in the eleventh century. Compared to the horns of the time, the buysine was a noble instrument inasmuch as it was the first thin-walled trumpet, and was hence capable of producing more or less musical notes. But even at that its tone was harsh and discordant. According to the popular concept of the times, this trumpet would be sounded to make the dead rise, and it is the Biblical trumpet of Judgment Day.

Figure 77 shows a famous buysine of the late Middle Ages. The mouthpiece is a later addition to the original instrument. The total length of the tube is forty-one inches, and the diameter of the bell is about three and a half inches. This makes the instrument a long slender tube with a very narrow bore. As of old, this trumpet had retained its social privileges. The ring seen in the fourth section was for affixing a banner suspended on a string.

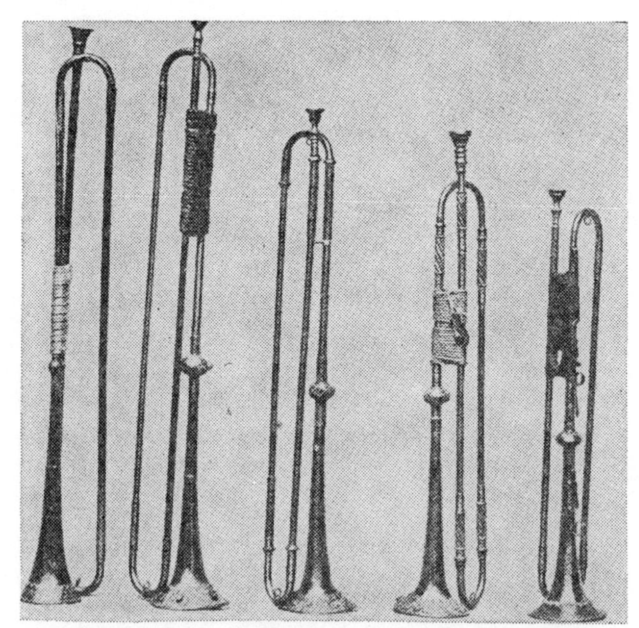

Figure 78. Bent Trumpets of the 17th and 18th Centuries
Courtesy Nef, Geschichte unserer Musikinstrumente

By the middle of the thirteenth century two types of straight trumpet had evolved, one six feet long and another shorter. The shorter type became our modern trumpet. It was restricted to military uses, while the longer one was admitted into civil functions.

Up to the seventeenth century trumpets were not made of different pitches or keys, but were all pitched in *d*. Differences in register between the higher and lower parts were obtained by variations in the bore and the proportions of the mouthpiece. Henry VIII had fourteen trumpeters in his band and Queen Elizabeth (1587) had ten.

The straight trumpet, especially the longer one, was somewhat inconvenient to handle. Unfortunately, the art of bending tubes in the manner of the ancient Danes and Romans had been lost. But in Northern Italy around 1300 the tube was folded twice in one plane, and thus the buysine became more portable. Over a century later the tube was folded a third time, the second and the third lengths being kept rigid and apart by a grooved block of wood. This was the beginning of the modern trumpet.

Above are shown five trumpets, all with two bends, each bend clearly showing the ferrules, the rings keeping the individual segments together. True to tradition, each trumpet has a special ring

Figure 79. Schnitzer's Trumpet, 16th Century
Courtesy Vienna, Society of Friends of Music

for the attachment of standards with the seignorial arms. Ferrules also served for ornamentation.

The alphorn too was occasionally made in bent sections.

The form of the medieval trumpet has remained fundamentally the same to the present day. Toward the close of the sixteenth century the smaller trumpet found its way into the orchestra.

Once the principle of bending tubes was rediscovered, trumpets began to appear in almost any shape. A good example is shown in Figure 79. This is a 1598 gold-plated trumpet by Schnitzer of Nuremberg. One can hardly imagine what purpose such a fancy form could have served. Today such instruments are museum pieces, this particular model being the property of the Society of Friends of Music, Vienna.

The Middle Ages also saw the development of various natural

horns. The three principal types of horns evolved were the bugle, the post horn, and the horn.

Since the days of old, *bugles* have been the signal horns of the infantry. During the Middle Ages most bugles had a wide, tapered, cone-shaped bore and produced a tone of good quality, brilliant and pure. Scale playing, however, was impossible, since only the natural harmonics could be produced. Hence the typical calls for signals. Although the bugle of our day has undergone some significant changes in structure, it has retained its role as a signaling instrument.

The English bugle in Figure 80 seems a rather dark picture. The reason for this is that the instrument was actually lacquered black. The total length of the air column was a little over five feet.

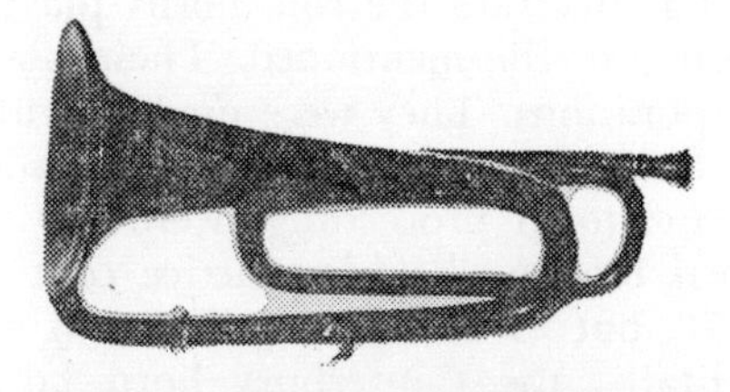

Figure 80
English Bugle,
Early 19th Century
Courtesy Museum of Fine Arts, Boston

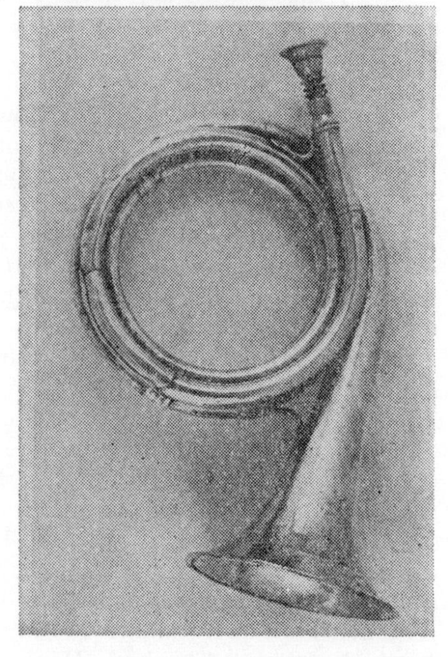

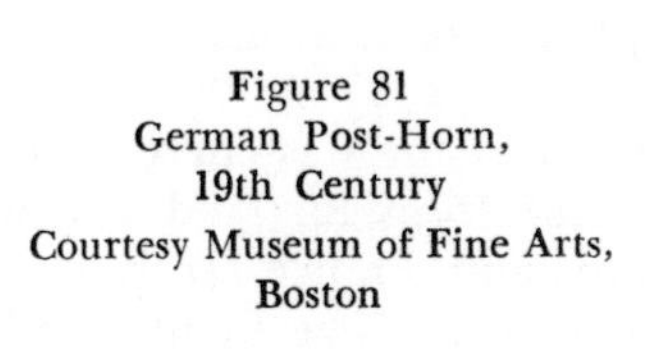

Figure 81
German Post-Horn,
19th Century
Courtesy Museum of Fine Arts, Boston

The *post horn,* intended as a signal for stage coaches carrying mail, was a short instrument with a wide bore and a narrow bell until about the middle of the seventeenth century. There was an English model with a double-bent tube and an air column of slightly over two feet. The original ones were still smaller. Figure 81, on the other hand, shows a later German model with an air column of six feet nine inches. There is considerable difference in the structure of these two horns. The bell of the second is much wider, and its whole tube is more conical. Surprisingly, if this latter horn is played with a trumpet mouthpiece, its tone is remarkably like that of the trumpet.

The post horn used to be a great favorite with the romantic poets. It cast its spell on the imagination of lovers for some four hundred years, into the beginning of our century. Today it is obsolete, but it has given rise to the cornet family of instruments to be discussed later.

To illustrate the role horns played in signaling, the Burgmote horns may be mentioned. These horns were the property of town corporations. They were used for calling together the corporations of Dover and Canterbury at the order of the mayor. The minutes of the town proceedings were constantly headed, "At a common horn blowing." This practice continued in Dover until the year 1670, but in Canterbury it was in vogue from 1376 to 1835! Incidentally, the Canterbury horn bore the inscription, "Thou art mighty for ever, O Lord!" It is still blown on the occasion of certain municipal ceremonies.

By far the most important member of the horn family is the one descendant of the buysine known as the *horn,* the latest offspring being the modern French horn.

The first horns of the buysine type still retained certain characteristics of the trumpet. We have seen that the trumpeters of the Middle Ages enjoyed an enviable position in society. This fact probably accounts for the structure of the first horns. For one thing, they did not have a true horn mouthpiece; nor was their bore conducive to a true horn tone.

In the fourteenth century the straight buysine was curved into a semicircular shape. This innovation came from England and was adopted shortly afterward in Germany and France. It is rather amusing to trace the naming of the instrument. The English called it the French horn, for presumably this noble instrument had originated in France; the French called it the German horn, for it was rare in France. We still call it the French horn, but in Germany, France, and Italy it is just a simple *horn* without any adjectives.

Be that as it may, the horn was rather important in Germany. The first horns were known as hunter's horns, for they were used by the hunters on horseback. Hence the horn was made to encircle the hunter's body. A typical hunter's horn is shown in Figure 82.

Figure 82. Hunter with Horn

It is a fine-toned instrument of German make of the middle-eighteenth century. Its total air column is some eleven and a half feet.

During the hundred years following 1636, the hunter's horn was perfected and became such a noble instrument that composers only reluctantly saw it replaced by the modern form of the French horn. Brahms, for instance, wrote a famous *Horn Trio* for the natural horn, not for the later models of valve horns, although at his time these had been accepted by orchestras. The perfected natural horn was known as the forester's horn (*waldhorn*). The nobility used it also when hunting. Special hunting calls and fanfares in four to five distinct parts played by the huntsmen of the German princes were extant well into our century.

Figure 83 is just an oddity of a horn with a dragon head for the opening.

With the advance of the modern technical age, natural horns underwent certain changes and finally emerged as today's orchestral instruments. The story of this interesting transformation is told in the next chapter.

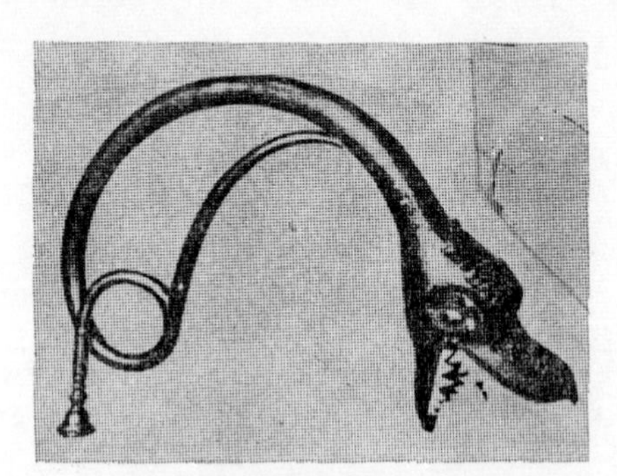

Figure 83
Horn with Dragon Head
Courtesy Nef, Geschichte unserer Musikinstrumente

## CHAPTER V

# CHARACTERISTICS OF HORNS AND TRUMPETS

The natural horns and trumpets discussed in the previous chapter all had a rather limited range in scale production. One of the major problems of instrument makers, therefore, was to equip their instruments with devices which would permit the production of complete chromatic scales, that is, not only every note of our common scale but also the customary sharps and flats between the whole tones. This was a difficult process, and even with the best of equipment considerable skill is required to play modern horns and trumpets satisfactorily.

To understand the evolution of lip-voiced instruments from natural horns and trumpets to the complicated instruments of today, a study of the former must first be made. Some of the typical characteristics were discovered at the dawn of history. The lur makers already knew that a large horn was capable of producing more tones than a small one; they also knew the difference between the tone production of a wide- and a narrow-bore tube, but they hardly knew the reason for it. The intricacies of horns and trumpets were only gradually explored. Fortunately, scientists have come to the aid of musicians so that today certain theories and explanations are common knowledge among instrument makers. Let us therefore consider the basic principles of these instruments.

### *Method of Sound Production*

The term *lip-voiced* is highly suggestive. (The common term of our day, however, is *brass instruments.*) A lip-voiced instrument is basically a tube whose upper end is applied to the lips of the player, the lower end being somewhat wider in dimension.[1] In order for the tube to produce a sound, the air in it must vibrate, for here, as in all sound-producing devices, sound is caused by sound waves.

---

[1] To avoid any possible confusion along this line, the word upper, even in the woodwinds, always means the playing end of the instrument, the *lower* end being away from the mouth, regardless of whether it is lower than the mouth of the performer or elevated above his head.

The sound waves are produced in the following manner. The player presses his lips tightly against the mouthpiece of the tube and uses them as a set of reeds. By compressing his lips and then blowing against them, he makes them vibrate and emit tiny puffs of air into the tube. These tiny puffs of air set up the vibrations in the tube itself. Thus, the player has control of the number of pulses or the frequency of the tone, and his lips are directly responsible for the "voice" of the tube. The higher the pitch is to be, the faster the player must vibrate his lips. The sound, therefore, is not produced by blowing air into the instrument.

We come now to an interesting question. If the player determines the number of puffs with his lips, where does the size of the instrument come in? The answer is found in the fact that a sound wave must have certain dimensions which must correspond to the length and width (bore) of the tube. The longer the tube the longer the air wave will be, for in each case the sound wave must fill out the whole tube. Long waves naturally move slower than short ones, and consequently a longer tube will generate fewer sound waves. In other words, the larger the tube, the lower the frequency of the tone, that is, the lower the pitch of the note produced. It is technically impossible for a bass player to duplicate on his instrument the high frequencies of a bugle, for the pulses created by the lips must correspond to the capacity of the tube.

### *Overtones*

And now we come to a musical concept of such paramount importance that a study of it at this place will benefit us greatly, especially as most music lovers have only vague ideas about this all-important matter. I am referring to overtones, often also called partials or harmonics.[2]

As we have just seen, the size of the instrument determines the pitch of the tone. Size alone, however, does not determine the *quality* of the tone produced. In a tone we do not look for pitch only. If a musician sounds the same note, say *a* of 440 vibrations per second, on different instruments—a trumpet, horn, or trombone, or, to make it more drastic, a piano, violin, clarinet, etc.—we immediately perceive the difference, although each instrument has played exactly the same note. It is comparatively easy to identify instruments by their peculiar qualities of tone, because they are by nature part and parcel of the instrument itself. This character-

[2] For some reason, the term overtones is usually applied to string instruments; and harmonics to brasses; the word partials may be used for either overtones or harmonics.

istic (or quality) of tone is known as *timbre* or *tone color*. Timbre is caused by overtones, without which a tone becomes lifeless and dull.

What then are overtones? Briefly stated, overtones are sectional vibrations. When a string is plucked or rubbed, it vibrates first of all from end to end, setting up the *fundamental* tone. Thus the length of a string (or a tube) is responsible for the fundamental tone.

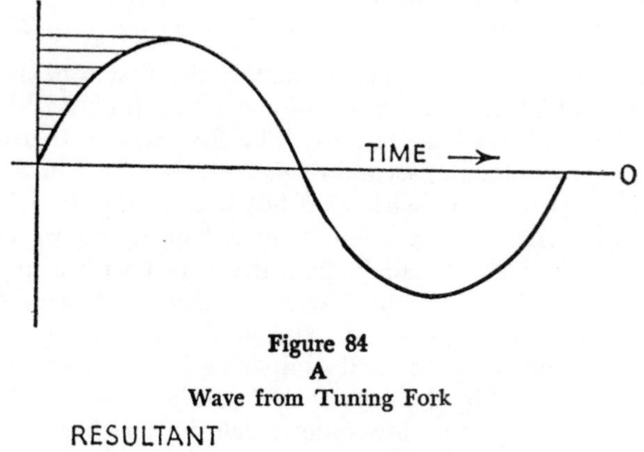


**Figure 84**
**A**
**Wave from Tuning Fork**

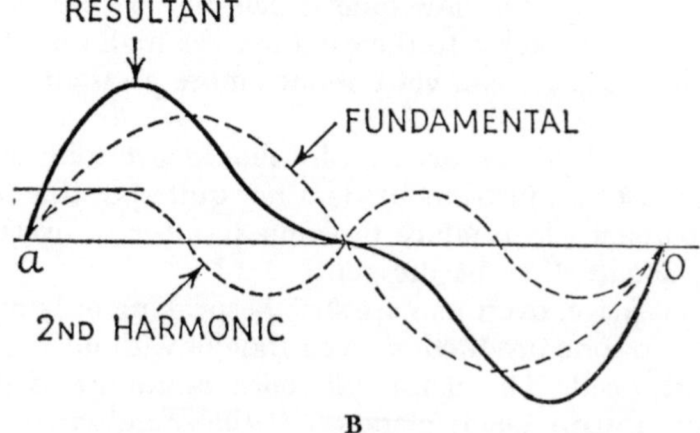


**B**
**Addition of Second Harmonic Plus Resultant**
**Courtesy, Douglas, The Electronic Musical Instrument Manual, Pitman**

Other tones are produced simultaneously, for a string or air column also vibrates in sections. Each half of the string will vibrate by itself, producing a tone an octave higher than the fundamental one, for half a string has twice the frequency of a whole one. This second tone will be heard along with the fundamental and is known as the *overtone* or *second harmonic*. As a rule it is not so loud as the fundamental. Note that in musical terminology *second* harmonic actually means the *first* overtone, third harmonic the second overtone, and so forth.

Next we find that each half of the half-string vibrates by itself, setting up vibrations twice as high as the second harmonic and producing the fourth harmonic. Harmonics are produced as multiples of the fundamental.

The following table will serve as an illustration.

If the fundamental has 55 vibrations per second (vps):

| | | |
|---|---|---|
| — the second | harmonic will have 55 x 2 vps | 110 |
| — the third | harmonic will have 55 x 3 vps | 165 |
| — the fourth | harmonic will have 55 x 4 vps | 220 |
| — the fifth | harmonic will have 55 x 5 vps | 275 |

In plain language, this means that if the first tone is *do,* then the second is high *do;* the third, *sol* above that high *do;* then comes the third *do* followed by *mi,* etc. The first octave, therefore, consists of one *do* only; the second of *do, sol;* the third of *do, mi, sol;* the fourth again begins with a *do* but it can play the whole scale. If we begin with a large trumpet or a bass string we can consequently obtain more overtones than if we start with a small instrument. (We realize now why larger trumpets had preference over smaller ones in the days of old.) You may verify this by sounding a very low tone on the piano and comparing it with a very high note; you will be amazed by the difference if you hold the key down until the sound dies out. The low tone is definitely richer in overtones, and hence more pleasant to the ear than the high one. Here is the reason why a deep human voice sounds more pleasant than a high, squeaky one.

Another question now arises: why should overtones account for the tone color of an instrument? Is it not quite possible for two different instruments to produce the same number of overtones? And if so, why should they be different?

In the first place, overtones are strictly speaking only of secondary importance in tone production, even though without them the tone seems to be dead. The main difference in timbre is due to the material the instrument is made of. If the sounds were purely air-produced, the material would not make any difference. But actually the material of an instrument does vibrate, and at a frequency of its own, even though the instrument is not an idiophone. Naturally, such vibrations combine with the overtones of the string or air-column either favorably or adversely. This property, found in the human voice as well as in instruments, is known as a *formant.* Formants are chiefly responsible for the difference in quality between the voices of singers, or between cheap and expensive pianos, or between a Stradivarius and a kitchen fiddle.

Secondly, timbre depends not only on the number of overtones, but also on the kind of overtones it carries and emphasizes. In other words, it becomes a matter of selection of overtones. Not every instrument produces every overtone, and whatever overtones are there seem to receive different treatment by different instruments, a particular one being more emphasized than others. The clarinet, for instance, eliminates all even overtones, reproducing only the odd ones, so naturally its tone color is different from an instrument which has the whole series. It is another question as to which of the overtones produced will be emphasized by a particular instrument and to what degree, and which ones will be suppressed, for not every overtone is agreeable to harmony. A good instrument can produce over a dozen overtones. Which of them will be conspicuous?

So far it has been assumed that any sound-producing medium will be decent enough to vibrate in sectional frequencies of simple multiples of the fundamental. As long as this is the case, we have a sound made up of partials bearing a clear-cut simple ratio to each other. Such a sound is referred to as a *musical* sound. However, a sound made up of partials in a haphazard way, that is, in such a way that no ratio between them can be determined, is known as *noise.* Into the noise category we put rattles, primitive drums, bass and snare drums, the banging of doors, hammering of nails, and so forth. The popular concept that musical sound is caused by regular and noise by irregular sound waves is somewhat misleading, for noise waves may be just as regular as musical sound waves. A drummer, for instance, may produce quite regular sound waves; still, the sound remains a noise. In such a case one could speak of a series of regular irregular waves, the regularity itself imparting to the sound a somewhat musical quality.

Just as color is due to a mixture of light waves of different length, so sound is characterized by a conglomeration of tones added to the fundamental, which commonly predominates. In fact, in many instances overtones are barely perceptible. On the other hand, we will encounter lip-voiced instruments which do not produce the fundamental tone!

Some instruments (voices, too) are definitely richer in overtones than others. Sometimes overtones are not exactly to our liking, and then we are at a loss to deal with the tone. Is it still a musical sound or is it a noise? Large church bells, you may recall, must be very accurately tuned before they can lay claim to the production of musical sound. An instrument which does not produce any overtones out of proportion probably does not exist. It is the life-long ambition of all musicians to produce the richest combination of overtones with the least amount of noise. Still, our ears are so used to a mixture of tone and noise that any attempt to eliminate all traces of noise whatsoever—as some electronic instruments do—is woefully disillusioning.

It is also a known fact that overtones in nice proportion to the fundamental linger longer in the air than those out of proportion to it. The seventh and the eleventh overtones, as an example, are not in strict harmony with the series and are therefore not so prominent. If you listen to a loud, fairly harsh bell sound, you will notice how mellow and pleasant the tone becomes as it gradually fades away. The most agreeable overtones sound longest with the fundamental.

Instruments producing a rich tone by the proper mixture of overtones are indeed priceless treasures. A good piano costs well over a thousand dollars. Similarly, the cost of a good violin or cello may run into the five-figure bracket. Why? Because the expensive instrument has had finer workmanship and is of better material, sounding more overtones.

Having discussed overtones (or harmonics) in general, we are now ready to investigate what exactly determines the nature of the harmonics and the tone characteristics of horns and trumpets. The answer may be given briefly as follows: in ad:dition to the material of the instrument, it is its mouthpiece and the size and proportion of the tube.

### *The Mouthpiece*

The mouthpiece is that part of the tube which is applied to the player's lips. Although the mouthpiece is not an indispensable part of the instrument, it has become one of the most important parts. The original natural horn of primitive men had no special mouthpiece. The solid tip of the horn would be cut off to form a natural opening for the lips. But such an opening was hard on the lips, and man learned to shape it in such a way as to facilitate sound production and ease the tension on the lips of the performer.

Gradually, specially designed mouthpieces were attached to the upper end of the tube, and it was found that the tone quality varied with the shape and size of the mouthpiece. Moreover, it was discovered that mouthpieces of certain shapes would fit certain types of tubes. Today each brass instrument has its own characteristic mouthpiece, precision-made, for any variation in size—diameter, depth, rim, relation between the throat (the diameter of the opening) and the tube of the instrument itself—has its bearing upon the tone quality. All mouthpieces are divided into three general types in accordance with their shapes and the tubes they have to serve.

The horn generally has a *funnel-shaped mouthpiece,* whereas that of the trumpet is *cup-shaped. This is an important distinction between horn and trumpet.* The third type of mouthpiece (Figure

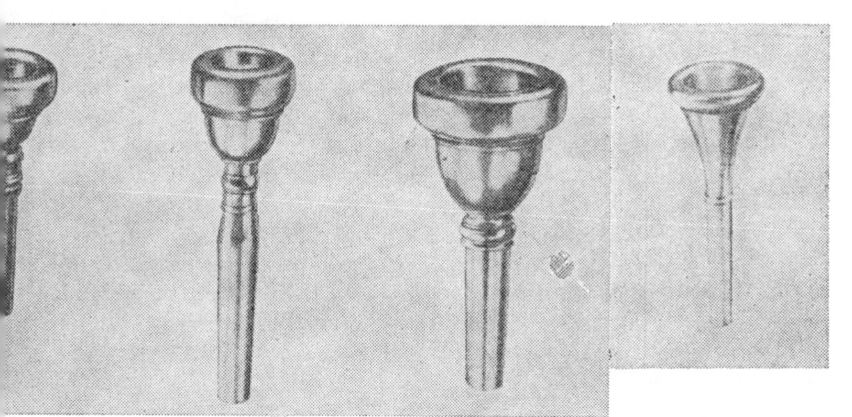

Figure 85. Mouthpieces
(a) Cornet, (b) Trumpet, (c) Trombone, (d) French Horn

85a) combines both types, for it is an elongated cup. It is intermediate in character between that of the horn and the trumpet. Cornets, bugles, and saxhorns have this type of mouthpiece.

It is usual to provide the mouthpiece with a rounded, cushion-shaped edge for accurate and painless pressure of the lips.

The first mouthpieces were most likely simply carved cup-shaped cavities in the natural horn or the wooden strips of which the tube was made. We find an illustration of the latter type in some of the alpine horns to the present day. In the Middle Ages mouthpieces of ivory were prevalent. Modern mouthpieces are turned out of brass, ivory, aluminum, silver, or even glass or India rubber. (One wonders how soon plastics will make their appearance.) An examination of the instruments illustrated in Part Two of this book will reveal that each instrument has its particular mouthpiece, but you should not find it too difficult to classify them into the horn, trumpet, or intermediary groups.

### *The Tube*

Variations in the size and shape of the tube are so numerous that to the present day no standard horn or trumpet has evolved. This of course does not exclude a general classification of these instruments. Before discussing this classification it must be said that the form of the instrument, whether straight or curved or bent back upon itself, coiled, plain, or fancy, has no appreciable bearing upon the tone production or the tone quality and therefore does not warrant further discussion. The classification of the tube is based upon its proportions. A tube may be *conical* (*or conoidal*) or *cylindrical*. This is a second distinction between horn and trumpet: *a horn has the shape of a cone while a trumpet is cylindrical.*

It may help you to remember this important distinction to recall that animal horns narrow down from a broad base to a narrow tip ending. Straighten them out and they will form a cone. Compare, for instance, the oliphant (Figure 70) with the lituus (Figure 74). You note that the oliphant, a natural born, is narrow at the upper end and gradually widens out just like a cone. The lituus, however, is a straight tube, that is, the tube forms a cylinder up to the bent bell-shaped end.

Things become slightly more complicated when we compare the lur (Figure 76), the buccina (Figure 77), and the alphorn (Figure 68) with the bugle (Figure 80), the trumpet (Figure 99), and the trombone (Figure 111). Each trumpet ends in a cone-shaped bell. Some of these bells are fairly long, as in the bugle, and one wonders whether the instrument is still a trumpet or already a horn. Where, to be exact, should the conoidal lower end of a trumpet begin, or what portion of the total tube should be cylindrical and which part should be conoidal? There is no exactness about it; the question is answered by the ingenuity of the instrument maker.

Despite the lack of standards in the make of the tube, the number of different tubes is surprisingly small today. Certain proportions between length and form in the make-up of the tube are most conducive toward certain types of instruments, and thus we find that instead of having countless horns and trumpets originated at the whim of instrument makers, we have only a limited number in our orchestra today. Musicians just pass on their experiences from generation to generation, and today's instrument makers profit from the accumulated wisdom of their forebears.

As far as horns are concerned, there is no ambiguity in their form; they are invariably well-defined cones. Trumpets, on the other hand, may be partly cones, partly cylinders. As long as the cylindrical portion predominates, it is clearly a trumpet; otherwise it may be the intermediate type of instrument, such as the saxhorn or bugle. Trumpets, therefore, are somewhat difficult to classify from this point of view. But this much should be clear by now: a horn is always a horn, whereas a "trumpet" may be a horn *or* a trumpet.[3]

At this point a third distinction between the horn and the trumpet must be mentioned, which for practical purposes is the most important one—the tone quality of each. This quality is determined by both the mouthpiece and the form of the tube. *A trumpet has a sharp and brilliant tone quality,* whereas *a horn*

[3] We may consider here the following analogy: it is correct to say that a human being is an animal, but we never term an animal a human being. We speak of animals and human beings, but not of animals or humans.

*has a less brilliant but broader and more vocal tone.* These tone qualities may be varied by shades, but generally speaking they are as characterized here.

### *The Bore of Horns and Trumpets*

The term *bore* refers to the inside of the tube. One of the first essentials of this bore is perfect regularity. In a horn the widening of the tube must be gradual and smooth; in a trumpet the diameter must be uniform. Any irregularity interferes with the production of the harmonics. This is one of the reasons why metal horns so readily supplanted animal horns. It is hardly conceivable that the latter would ever have a perfect bore, which means that the tone produced would lack the musical qualities obtained from artificial horns. It is further readily seen that a natural horn in the majority of cases would defy efforts to smooth out its interior.

A perfectly regular and smooth bore eases the *intonation* of the instrument. The tone produced will be of the right "constituency" of harmonics, and all the vibrations making up the tone total will blend properly and produce the desired beauty. Thus, in selecting a horn or a trumpet a musician will invariably inspect the instrument for its intonation. It is further noticeable that the better the intonation of a horn, the greater is the ease of blowing and the greater the carrying power.

The *proportion* of the bore to the length of the tube is also of vital importance. Whether the tube be of a wide bore with a short length or of a narrow bore with a greater length, or whether the tube be narrow and short or wide and long—all such factors must be considered in the manufacture of the instrument. For the question remains: which type will produce the desired harmonics for a given purpose? In general, long tubes require wider bores than short ones. A certain bore/length ratio is required for certain harmonics, and some harmonics cannot be produced at all with a certain bore/length ratio. The harmonics of a cylindrical tube add brilliance and a certain crispness to the tone, hence the differing tone qualities in trumpets and horns.

The *length* of the tube is also of extreme importance in tone production. A horn three to four feet in length can produce the first six harmonics only. Evidently, the longer the horn, the more harmonics can be obtained. Thus, on a horn twelve feet long sixteen harmonics can be played. A true trumpet must have considerable length. However, no instrument more than four feet long can be handled conveniently, so the tube is bent in various ways, either doubled upon itself or coiled. The art of bending tubes, as we have seen, is by no means of recent origin. The modern orchestral trumpet, for instance, acquired the form in which we use it today during the sixteenth century.

Here is an illustration just to show how exact instrument makers have come to be: for each unit in the bore of a tube its length must be exactly 153 centimeters, no more or less. This is why catalogue listings of instruments will give you all measurements—the size of the mouthpiece, its length, its diameter, the diameter of the bore, length of the bell, and so forth.

It may be added here that a tube with a narrow bore almost never produces the fundamental tone. There is hardly a horn or trumpet on which it is easily produced. Therefore, for all practical purposes the fundamental tone, also known as the *pedal* tone, is of minor importance. The reason for this is that the production of the pedal tone requires an undue relaxation of the lips!

### *Scale Playing*

A scale is a ladder (*scala* in Latin), or in musical terminology a series of tones following each other in a certain succession, that is, with certain distances or ratios between the notes. Our most common scale, the diatonic, contains the notes *do, re, mi, fa, sol, la, si* and *do.* It has taken thousands of years for it to become accepted as the standard. Primitive people and natives of different continents still have altogether different scales, and modern musicians, in addition to the so-called major and minor scales, employ several others.

When man first began to use horns and trumpets, he had no notion of scale playing. He was satisfied with these instruments as implements to reinforce his voice. But with the passing of time he learned to play more than one note on the same horn. Which ones? We do not know, of course. We do know, however, that a natural horn produces the second, third, and fourth harmonics, most easily, in other words, low *do,* middle *do, sol,* and high *do.* As we have seen, the pedal tone was for all practical purposes useless. This left the natural horn with but three notes, a highly unsatisfactory state.

Long before man had any concept of scientific principles of tone production, he learned to play a number of notes on the same horn by a method which musicians call *overblowing.* When a wave is set up in a tube, it vibrates back and forth (they call it *transverse* wave in contrast to the *longitudinal* wave set up by a string). Now, if the original fundamental wave in its backward vibration, that is, in its motion toward the mouth, is stopped by a new puff of air before it reaches the end of the tube it bounces back before it has vibrated its full length and thus creates a shorter wave. But shorter waves mean higher frequencies, and consequently a new note of a higher pitch is produced. This new note is the second harmonic, but this time it will be as prominent as formerly was the fundamental tone. By further overblowing, other harmonics may be converted into the predominant notes. (It should be kept in mind that overblowing does not mean harder blowing.) The net results of overblowing on a sufficiently long tube are four octaves, the fourth of which will be a complete scale and the first hardly existent.

Now, fancy a piano with a three-octave keyboard half of whose keys are out of order and all of whose black keys are missing. This is what a natural horn or trumpet represents. Naturally, for musical purposes such instruments had rather limited uses, especially in orchestral music. At the time of Bach and Handel, the players were proficient enough to play the upper scale satisfactorily, and we find that these masters wrote for horns and trumpets in the high registers.

Modern instruments produce complete scales, including semitones. How did musicians and instrument makers learn to do this?

Thus far we have seen that tone production depends on the lips, the mouthpiece, and the tube. Musicians learned to produce new and clearer sounds by improved lip-technique and by more refined mouthpieces. But the greatest improvement in scale playing was made with the tube. Briefly, scale playing involves the following: *stopping, side holes, keys, crooks, slides,* and *valves.*

### *Stopping*

Stopping consists in shortening the tube by inserting the hand into the lower, bell-shaped end. If the hand (not the closed fist) is thrust into the bell, the tube is shortened. This would lead you to conclude that the pitch of a given note would be raised, because shorter tubes have shorter waves and shorter waves vibrate faster. Actually this is not the case, because when one closes a tube, one lowers its tone. Of two identical tubes, the one open at the lower end will produce a tone an octave higher than the one with its lower end closed.

The art of stopping consists in introducing the hand in such a way as to close the tube enough to lower a given tone either by a semitone or a whole tone. Now, don't read this next point if you are afraid of becoming confused—but there are certain cases where it is actually possible to raise a tone somewhat by stopping. If the tone is lowered a semitone, we have a *half-stop;* if the difference is a whole tone, we have the *whole-stop.*

Supposing the player has his lips in position to play a *g.* By a half-stop he can change the *g* to *f#* and by a whole stop to *f.* Similarly, he can produce from *a* a *g#* or a *g,* and so forth.

As we will show presently, stopping is only a limited help in scale playing. In the first place, mere stopping just lowers the already obtainable notes; it does not produce entirely new notes where they are missing, let us say in the first three octaves. But what is just as important, stopping produces new harmonics. Unfortunately, these new harmonics are quite distorted, for which reason they are referred to as *inharmonics*. Consequently, stopped notes compared to open notes are not so sonorous. A skillful player may nearly suppress this unevenness in tone quality by blowing the open notes softly, but in rapid passages this alternation of stopped and open notes remains disagreeable.

Some writers will tell you that the art of stopping was already known to medieval horn players, but credit for this method of playing is given to Hampel of Dresden, Germany, who introduced it around the middle of the eighteenth century. Following his innovation, instruments were specially designed with a view to permitting stopping and even bugles would be constructed with large bells, so that the player's hand could be inserted into it. Other inventions, which we will discuss below, made stopping less important, but the player of the French horn still relies to great extent on this technique.

### *Side Holes*

A hole drilled into the side of a horn will permit the air to escape before it reaches the end of the tube, thus in effect shortening the air wave and raising the pitch of the tone produced. By closing and opening such a hole with the finger, an extra note can be produced. A second hole can be used to produce still another note, and a third and fourth hole come still closer to a complete scale. You can easily verify this if you have access to a tonette or an old-fashioned whistle flute.

Side holes were originally placed in such positions that the player could easily operate them with his fingers, even though such placement meant a violation of the wave length principle. A hole placed in a spot most convenient for the player does not necessarily make allowance for correctly tuned notes. Neither does a symmetrical distribution contribute to proper tuning. (We are going to encounter such holes in our discussion of the early woodwind instruments, Chapter VII.) So generally the first side holes created but indifferent harmony.

Side holes were applied to small horns, but they were unsuitable for trumpets. The reason for this is not so difficult to find. As has been stated before, a trumpet is for its major part cylindrical, the lower part being enlarged into a conical bell. Its harmonics are therefore determined by the cylinder plus the bell. If now a side hole permits the escape of the air before it reaches the bell, naturally the overall sound wave will have a different pattern and hence a different tone quality.

### *Keyed Horns*

Key horns work on the same principle as horns with side holes, the holes being operated by keys instead of with fingers. The advantage lies in the mechanization of the system, for keys make the holes easier to manipulate and hence the placement of holes can be in conformity with true pitch production. This system proved most satisfactory with bugles, although it had its limitations. Keys were first introduced by Koelbel in Germany in the second half of the eighteenth century. The beginning of the nineteenth century saw the innovation of four- and five-keyed trumpets, but none of these instruments became popular. They held their own only till the valve mechanism (see below) was perfected. The keyed bugle was prominent from 1820 to 1835, the ophicleide (see next chapter) somewhat longer.

### *Crooks*

A crook is a short coiled tube of uniform bore, open at both ends which can be inserted between the mouthpiece and the tube proper, thereby lengthening the original tube. In this way the length of the fundamental wave can be altered and the range of the instrument extended a degree or more into the lower register. In other words, the player is in position to change the original key of the instrument to a lower one and thus obtain additional tones. If, let us say, a player using a C-horn inserts a crook, he can transform it into a B-horn, etc.

At the time of Mozart crooks were standard equipment for players. The composer made allowance for the insertion of crooks by giving the player a few bars of rest before he was asked to play in the new key.

In the second half of the eighteenth century curved U-shaped crooks were inserted in the middle of the horn (at a bend) to facilitate more rapid changes and also better tone production. Incidentally, this technique was developed by the same Hampel mentioned above in connection with stopping. A further advantage of this system was the fact that more than one crook could be inserted whenever the horn or trumpet had more than one bend in its construction, and thus a single horn could be supplied with several crooks for almost any desired additional key or tone. But even so this did not permit of rapid changes.

Just in case you wonder why all this fuss about changing keys, let me tell you that we do it constantly even in singing. Any sharps or flats introduced into a song demand a change of key. For instance, sing a song in the key of C, and as soon as you come across an *f#*, you have modulated into the key of G. So a player must be in position to play in different keys.

### *Slides*

Slides are rather lengthy U-shaped crooks which slide over the two sections of the original tube. The best current illustration of a slide is found in the modern trombone (Figure 111). A slide enables the trumpeter (horns could not possibly employ slides) to vary the length of the tube freely. In contrast to hand-stopping, the slide does not change the nature of the harmonics, and consequently it does produce a uniform series of tones. Thus, the slide makes a lip-voiced instrument completely chromatic.

It must not be supposed that each note of the scale requires a different position of the slide. When the slide is shifted "home" as far as it can go, the tube is shortest and produces the highest notes. This is the first position of the slide. In this position the player, by various degrees of overblowing, can produce seven tones extending over three octaves. By shifting the slide into the second position, that is, by pulling it out a certain distance, the whole series of the first position is lowered by a semitone. And so on. All told, there are seven positions for producing the complete range of the trombone.

In spite of all its advantages, the slide has some serious disadvantages. In the first place it is not applicable to horns proper. A slide is necessarily cylindrical, so it could not possibly fit into a conical horn tube. Secondly, there is always a break between notes obtained from different positions. Consequently, smooth *(legato)* passages are difficult to play. Even the ordinary C major scale on a C-trombone is a challenge to the player, for the following positions are required: 1, 6, 4, 3, 1, 4, 2, 1. Thus the simple interval *do-re* is not really simple to play, at least not in a truly *legato* fashion.

Slides are found to be most satisfactory for trombones. Musicians composing for this instrument bear its deficiencies in mind and obtain truly astonishing effects. Listen, for instance, to the overture to *Tannhäuser* by Wagner, where the trombones enter into the *Pilgrim's Chorus.*

### *Valves*

A valve is a mechanical device for diverting the passage of gases or fluids through pipes. Its underlying principle was applied to primitive instruments like the Panpipes (see Figure 116). The natural pad of the fingertip working from the joint of the finger can be regarded as the first valve in musical instruments. It follows that side-holed horns and keyed instruments are also in a certain sense valve instruments.

The modern valve of brass instruments may be regarded as a means of instantaneously adding a cross or a piece of tubing of the length required to lower the pitch of the tube by one or more semitones.

The introduction of the valve was by no means sudden or revolutionary; it took a surprisingly long time before instrument makers began to embody valves in their instruments. The first noteworthy attempt is attributed to the Irishman Clagget of London. In 1788 he patented a double horn constructed in such a way that either horn could be played with the same mouthpiece. One horn was tuned to D, the other to E-flat. In addition, it had one valve which could lower the pitch of either horn by one tone. This made the instrument completely chromatic, the first with this potential. Its appearance created a sensation, and although it did not hold its own very long, it had set music makers on a new track—the operation of crooks fitted to the tube itself by valves. The early valves, which now sprang up almost like mushrooms after a rain, were soon outdated and do not therefore merit a description here.

The invention of the immediate precurser of the modern valve is credited to Blühmel (1813) and Stölzel (1815), both of Germany. Stölzel purchased the invention from Blühmel and had it patented in 1818. The Blühmel-Stölzel valves are a two-way system; they are similar to our present-day tubular pistons. Of course, they were not yet perfect, as a matter of fact, they were somewhat cumbersome. The passages through them were either constricted in diameter or so placed as to introduce sharp angles instead of gently flowing curves which impaired the resonance of the sound. Further efforts to improve valves resulted in the invention of the rotary valve action (Blühmel, 1828). But the real progress in perfecting the valve mechanism is largely due to the work of the famous firms of Sax of Brussels and Paris (1845).

Figure 86 illustrates both piston and the cylindrical valves. By following the arrowheads it will be seen that the depression of the valve—in each case shown to the right side of the drawing—diverts the air current into an additional piece of tubing, thus lengthening the air wave and lowering the pitch. (Since any additional tubing

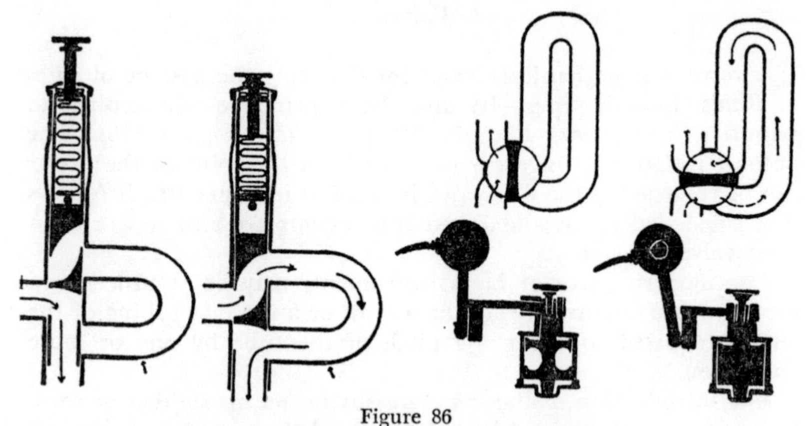

Figure 86
Piston and Rotary Valve, Both in Rest and Action
Courtesy Sachs, The History of Musical Instruments

always adds to the original length of the tube, valves always lower the pitch; they cannot therefore be used to raise a tone.)

Three valves are sufficient to produce the complete chromatic scale. True, some tubas have a fourth valve, but this valve is used to lower the fundamental tone of the instrument. Of the standard three valves, the first lowers the original tone by two semitones, the second by one, and the third by three. By working these valves in combination, any gap between the harmonics can be bridged. Thus, the first and second valve in combination lower the tone by three semitones, the first and third by five, the second and third by four, and all three together by six.

And now I suppose you are ready to accept the valve system as *the* solution to the problem of scales. But are valves the perfect mechanism for scale playing? Well, no, they aren't. And here is why they must be used sparingly and why they do not offer faultless tone production.

An extra piece of tubing operated by a valve is naturally made in such proportions that it bears a precise, clear-cut ratio in length to the fundamental tube. If the crook lowers the pitch one tone, its length must be 1/x of the original tube. The second piece of tubing too has its own ratio to the original tube. Likewise, the third crook has been made with the proper length ratio.

Now, what happens when two valves are used at the same time? Immediately complications arise, because even though each crook has its proper length ratio, the proportion is disturbed when two of them are in operation, for no longer is the combined length of the two in correct proportion to the original tube. When all three valves are used, the distortion is even more noticeable. As a result the pitch obtained by using more than one valve is slightly sharp. To correct such defects, especially in the lower register of the large brass instruments, "compensatory" pistons were designed (around 1875). Today, however, correct intonation is achieved by "lipping," a special lip-action (not to be confused with ordinary vibrations or overblowing).

Summing up, we may say that scale playing is accomplished in the following way: (1) for each note the player must know the extent of overblowing; (2) if the instrument is provided with a slide, he must also know the positions for each note; (3) if the instrument is equipped with valves, he must further know, in addition to overblowing, which valve or valves to depress; (4) at any given moment he must know how to correct a silghtly off-pitch note by either lipping or hand-stopping. No wonder only expert players can delight the discerning music lover. Even the best players are occasionally out of tune on certain notes, and the flow of the notes suffers from unevenness.

### *Transposing Instruments*

To complete our discussion of the characteristics of brass instruments, we must discuss transposing.

We have learned already that the size of a tube determines its pitch, that is, that the larger the tube, the larger the sound wave set up. We also know that the larger the sound wave, the slower it moves; therefore the larger the tube, the lower the pitch. Suppose we now consider a tube of such dimensions that its lowest note is a *c*. Such an instrument would be a C-trumpet (or horn, as the case may be). A player sounding the notes from his printed sheet of music or a C-horn obtains the correct notes and no transposing occurs.

But horns and trumpets come in various sizes. Consider therefore a horn which is a little larger than the C-horn so that its primary note is a *b-flat,* a tone lower than the C-horn. Again, a player has his printed sheet of music to play from. Since, however, his horn is no longer a C-horn, he does not render the notes at their face value, as it were. If he plays a *c,* the B-flat horn will not sound the *c* but the *b-flat*. So if the composer writes a line for the B-flat horn and wants him to sound a *c* on his score he will write a *d;* i.e., he transposes the *c* to a *d,* so that when the musician plays *d* it will sound the desired *c,* the note required for the melody or harmony. In this way the composer writes the whole piece for the B-flat horn: every note is transposed a note higher, because this particular horn sounds the notes one tone lower than the score indicates. Thus, the B-flat horn is a transposing instrument.

There are also horns and trumpets (as well as some woodwinds) which transpose more than one tone. Thus, an A-horn transposes a tone and a half, sounding every note written that much lower; an F-horn transposes five tones, and so on. In fact, horns in ten different keys exist, or at least they did exist until recently. We still refer to certain brass instruments as *alto horn, tenor trombone,* and *bass tuba,* among others.

For instance

Horns in D

whereas the same passage for horns in E♭ would sound

Figure 87
Diagram of Transposing Notes

A skilled musician must be able to transpose at sight where the composer has failed to transpose.

Transposing instruments originated before the invention of valves, when instruments had only a narrow range and had to come in different keys. Today this complication would seem unnecessary. However, we still have the transposing instruments, though their number has been greatly reduced. It is true that with modern valves and slides any horn could play accurately any note desired, and theoretically there is no longer any need for transposing instruments. Why then do musicians uphold all this confusion with transposing? Here is the reason.

The size of the instrument determines not only its pitch but also the nature of the harmonics produced, thus influencing its tone color. This means that each instrument has its own characteristic tone quality. A trumpet in B-flat for instance, is a "nobler" instrument than the C-trumpet. For certain effects the composer will therefore call for instruments in certain keys, thereby enriching the total orchestral tone color. It may be added that an A-horn is easier to play than a C-horn if the music is written in three sharps, the key of A. The standard horn today is in F, and the standard trumpet in B-flat.

The contention that the transposing instruments exist only by force of habit need not be taken too seriously. Why should musicians insist on transposing—which does mean extra work—if there were no need for it? Composers are a hard-working lot, but do they cherish endless hours of futile labor? It hardly makes sense. This much, however, cannot be disputed: composers, musicians, and instrument makers will go to any length of trouble, research, and work if thereby they can improve their music. So we may rest assured that there are certain advantages even in transposing instruments.

The above discussions of the principles of lip-voiced instruments and of the evolution of mechanical devices which gave us modern horns and trumpets show clearly how man is forever employing his intellect in search of newer and better things. It is amazing how much the human genius has already accomplished in the production of musical instruments. What has tomorrow in store for us?

CHAPTER VI

# MODERN HORNS AND TRUMPETS

The term *modern* in the above title includes all non-natural horns and trumpets, that is, instruments with mechanical devices for scale production. This chapter is therefore a direct continuation of Chapter IV. Inasmuch as a thorough description of these complicated instruments must include fundamental technical definitions, however, Chapter V has been interpolated for ready reference.

Chapter V has probably led the reader to the conclusion that modern devices are of rather recent date. This is only partly so, for some of the improvements date back as far as the early Middle Ages.

With the advance of the eleventh century, the creative spirit of Western man began again to assert itself, and musicians devoted themselves to the production of instruments the primary object of which no longer was to cause fear and fright. To be sure, war horns and signaling trumpets retained their importance for centuries; in fact, they are not yet obsolete. However, as human society became more civilized the urge to play melodies, no matter how primitive, even on lip-voiced instruments resulted in numerous improvements of the simple horns and trumpets. These improvements have given us the brilliant array of horns and trumpets of a modern orchestra. But of course Rome was not built in one day. The evolution of our instruments of today makes a fascinating chapter of history, and naturally we must begin with their most important forerunners. We shall soon realize that the outcome of this evolution is truly a case of the survival of the fittest.

So let us begin with the oldest "modern" horn.

## *The Cornett or Zink*

The primitive shepherd's animal horn is the ancestor of the *cornett* or *zink*. (*Zink* is the German word for the smallest branch of a stag's antlers.) A short animal horn with several fingerholes was known to the Persians as early as 700 A.D. Similar horns with from two to five holes are still in use not only in Africa but also in the Scandinavian countries and Jugoslavia.

The medieval cornett achieved great popularity. From the standpoint of classification it was a queer instrument. It stood somewhere between the woodwinds and brasses and was neither horn nor trumpet. In its outer form it resembled a horn, being of a conical bore, but its mouthpiece was cup-shaped like that of a trumpet. For simplicity's sake we shall regard this hybrid as a horn.

The cornett was the first lip-voiced instrument capable of playing the scale between the fundamental and second and third harmonics, hence its importance. It has also given rise to several other instruments which will be discussed in their proper places.

The tube of the cornett is comparatively short and of a wide bore. This means that it is capable of producing the lower harmonics, beginning the scale with the pedal tone, but incapable of playing the higher harmonics. Since, however, cornetts were rather little, especially the "small" cornetts, they were not bass instruments, the highest range of the smallest cornett being *e'''*,[1] the lowest of the larger instruments beginning with *c* an octave below middle *c*. The total range of a family of cornetts was thus slightly over three octaves. The highest notes were obtained by lipping. The following illustration shows the common types of cornetts.

[1] For abbreviations for staff notations, see page 381.

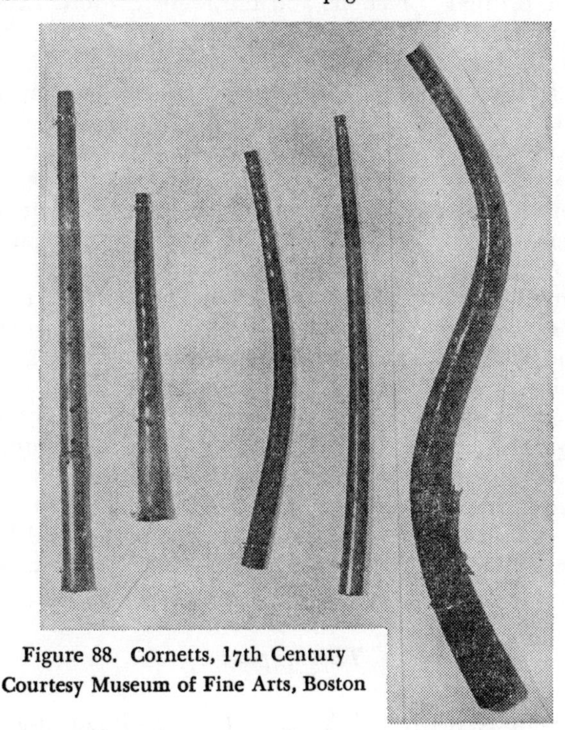

Figure 88. Cornetts, 17th Century
Courtesy Museum of Fine Arts, Boston

The smallest specimen shown measures about twenty inches in length; the upper opening of the tube is only fifteen millimeters in diameter. It is made of an antelope's horn and has no detachable mouthpiece. When attacked with the proper force, its tone is very clear, but it is deficient in the higher harmonics and thus lacking in brilliance. The latter characteristic was present in all cornetts.

The curved cornett, about two feet long, was of an irregular octagonal shape, made of two pieces of wood in the alphorn fashion and sheathed in black leather. It was commonly known as the tenor *zink.* Its mouthpiece was detachable and is not shown in the illustration.

The straight cornett, first to the right, made of pearwood, had no special mouthpiece. Due to its soft tone it was known as the *mute cornett.* It has eight fingerholes in the front and a thumbhole in the rear. Smaller specimens of the mute cornett had only six fingerholes.

The *great cornett* is nearly a yard long. Its tube is bent twice in the form of the letter S, and is also sheathed in black leather. Note that there is a key for the lowest hole.

The curved cornett later developed into three sizes: the high or descant, the ordinary or choir, and the tenor cornett. Each instrument had a range of two octaves. The straight cornett being the hardest to play, due no doubt to the absence of a special mouthpiece, fell into oblivion first, barely reaching the beginning of the seventeenth century. Curved cornetts, also somewhat difficult to play, lost their significance when the old-style polyphony gave way to newer types of composition after 1600. Due to the peculiar lack of high harmonics, which rendered the tone less brilliant than that of the trumpet, it was well adapted to supplement the human voice and to provide the treble part of the trombone choir.

A seventeenth-century writer compares the tone of the cornett to a ray of sunshine piercing the darkness, and an eighteenth-century musician admires the excellence with which the cornett imitates the human voice. Bach employed cornettists to accompany the boys' choir in some of his cantatas. Some town bands played cornetts even at the beginning of the last century. The most surprising item is that in Russia cornetts were heard as late as 1923!

What finally happened to the cornett? Well, the violin replaced it as a treble part, and the valved trumpet gave it the final knockout. But before dying, the cornett gave birth to the serpent, which instrument in its turn paved the way for others.

### *The Serpent*

The serpent is really a bass cornett. The elegant form of the tenor cornett could not possibly be prolonged without unduly

Figure 89. Serpent, Early 19th Century
Courtesy Nef, Geschichte unserer Musikinstrumente

inconveniencing the player. In order to make the six fingerholes reachable on larger tubes, the tube was bent as shown in the accompanying figure.

The name *serpent* may have been derived from the shape of the instrument, although even before the appearance of the serpent proper some of the cornetts had serpent's heads for their lower ends by way of adornment, as did some early models of the instrument so named.

Serpents were made of chestnut or pear-tree wood covered with black leather. The holes were spaced to facilitate handling and could not possibly be used to produce our diatonic scale. However, a skillful player could produce some chromatic intervals in the lower register with the help of overblowing. The fingerholes were rather narrow; hence, the tone was poor in quality. The range embraced two to three octaves. The mouthpiece, often of ivory, was not directly fitted into the tube but connected or joined to it by means of a brass crook.

The origin of the serpent is usually accredited to France (sixteenth century), where it achieved great popularity. It was also popular in England, and was distributed throughout Europe. In the hands of a skillful player its tone was soft and woody, similar to certain pipe-organ stops. Composers prescribed it even for serious music. Thus Handel used it in his *Water Music* (1717) and *Firework Music* (1749); Bach employed it as the bass support in his choirs, and Mendelssohn in his *Meeresstille Overture* and in *St. Paul* (1836). In Catholic churches the serpent was used to accompany the plainsong until the nineteenth century. It also supplied the bass in band music.

The serpent was also featured in literature. We find it, for instance, in Hardy's *The Three Strangers,* where Elijah New accompanies the "weedle-dee" of the fiddler by the booming ground-bass of the serpent (in the 1820s).

At the height of its popularity the serpent began to undergo certain transformations. More holes—fitted with keys—were added, the shape was altered, and in some cases the instrument assumed monstrous proportions. In general it began to resemble the present-day bassoon. A common later type equipped with holes and keys is shown.

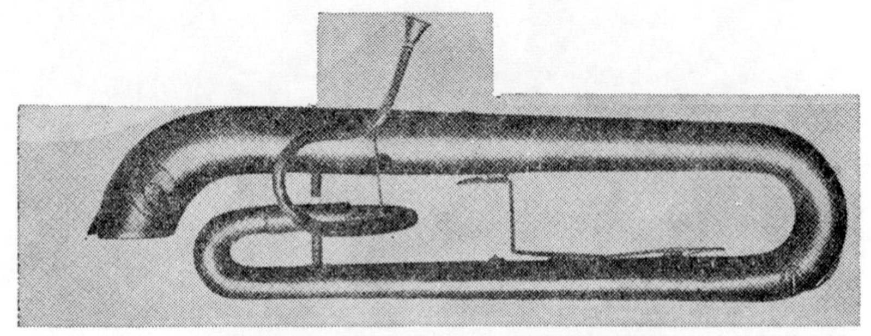

Figure 90. Keyed Serpent, 19th Century
Courtesy Nef, Geschichte unserer Musikinstrumente

By the middle of the nineteenth century the art of serpent playing had suffered considerably, due probably to the introduction of more refined instruments. Its tone no longer appealed to the progressive composer. There need be no contradiction in the fact that Mendelssohn, Beethoven, and even Wagner accepted it, whereas Berlioz heaped abuse upon it. The only justification Berlioz found for use of the poor serpent was in masses for the dead, and hence he prescribes it for the *Dies Irae* (*Day of Wrath*) in his *Fantastic Symphony*. Here, he claims, its "cold and abominable howling" is in its place.

The improvements in form and size of the serpent generated two new models of instruments, the bass horn and the ophicleide. In giving rise to these new instruments the serpent quietly passed out of existence.

### *The Bass-Horn*

The *bass-horn* was a transitional instrument between the serpent and the ophicleide. Its chief use was confined to military bands. It made its appearance in London around 1800 and was commonly known as the English bass-horn, even though one of the inventors, Frichot, was a Frenchman. The other was Astor, an Englishman, but both lived in London.

A study of our illustration reveals the chief characteristics. The two sections of the conical tube and the short butt were made of pear wood. The modern bassoon form—a tube bent back upon itself—is already apparent. The six fingerholes are bushed with ivory, the two keys reinforced with brass. A lengthy curved crook with an ivory mouthpiece forms the upper end of the horn; the lower end has an oval brass bell. The height of the instrument is about thirty-three inches, and its air column is over six feet. Note the position of the fingerholes—do they suggest convenience of handling or true intonation? Consequently, it seldom found its way into serious music. Mendelssohn had it in his *Funeral March* and Spohr in his *Ninth Symphony* (1849).

The lifespan of the bass-horn was about four or five decades, after which its place was taken by the ophicleide.

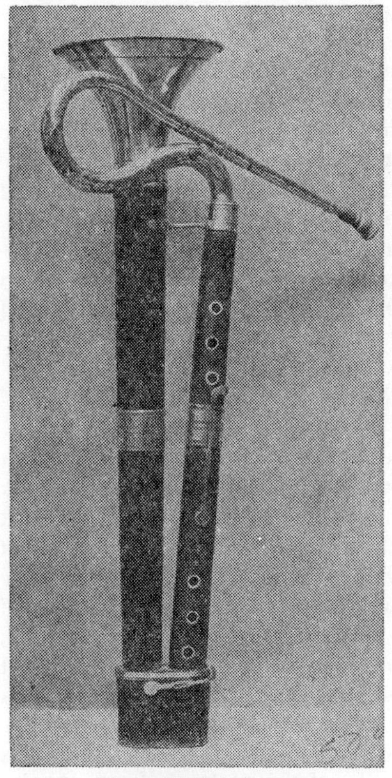

Figure 91. Bass-horn,
England, ca 1800
Courtesy Museum of Fine Arts, Boston

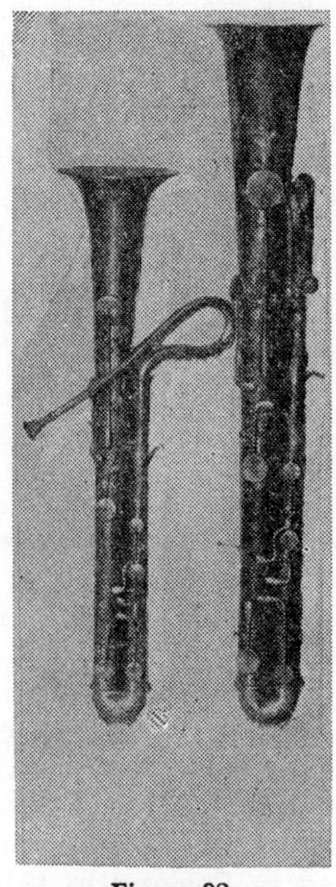

Figure 92
Ophecleides, 19th Century
Alto and Baritone
Courtesy Museum of Fine Arts, Boston

### *The Ophicleide*

A rather free translation of the word *ophicleide* would give us something like a "snake with a door key." So let us say that the ophicleide is a keyed serpent, or at least a derivative of the serpent. But even the most superficial look at this instrument will show its close relation to the bass-horn.

In 1817 Halary of Paris applied keys to the fingerholes of the serpent and thus remedied the faulty intonation caused by the symmetrical disposition of the holes. Not only were the holes now in their correct positions for scale production, but they were also enlarged, thus improving the tone quality. The number of keys varied from nine to eleven and sometimes twelve, with a range of over three complete octaves. Due to the wide bore of the tube, the ophicleide was almost exclusively a bass instrument, although our first specimen was the alto horn. The long curved crook was used for tuning and adjusting the position.

The tone of the ophicleide, though somewhat hollow and raw, was more precise and even, but less tender than that of the serpent. Worst of all, it did not blend with the other instruments. Hence, it found only brief popularity with musicians. Moreover, it made its appearance at a time when the other brass instruments were being greatly improved by valve mechanisms with simpler and more convenient fingering, but above all with richer tone qualities. Such masters as Mendelssohn, Wagner, and Berlioz used it to simulate special sounds like a wild barbaric tone or the braying of an ass. After 1850 it fell into disuse and by 1875 it had been supplanted by the modern tuba.

### *The Bugle*

The *bugle,* as we have seen, is essentially a signal horn. The first attempts to improve on the range of the natural harmonics may look somewhat primitive to us, as for instance those four holes seen in the Northern European goat horn, the *bukkehorn,* Figure 93. But we are entering the age of rapid improvements; around the middle of the eighteenth century a horn with one or two keys was produced for use by coachmen. Some thirty years later more keys were added, generally from four to six, although without much success. But these attempts paved the way for the keyed bugle proper. This bugle, several examples of which are shown to the right, was invented in England in 1810 by Joseph Halliday. It was known as the *Kent Bugle,* in honor of the Duke of Kent, then commander-in-chief of the British Army.

The Kent bugle had from five to seven keys, although for experi-

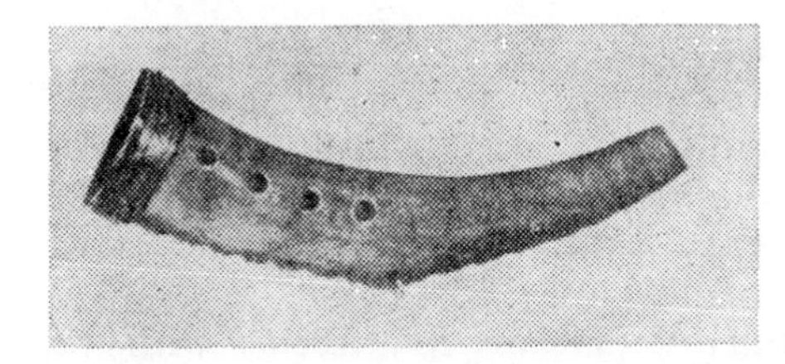

Figure 93
Bukkehorn Made of Goat's Horn, 19th Century

Courtesy Museum of Fine Arts, Boston

Figure 94. Keyed Bugles
Courtesy Museum of Fine Arts, Boston

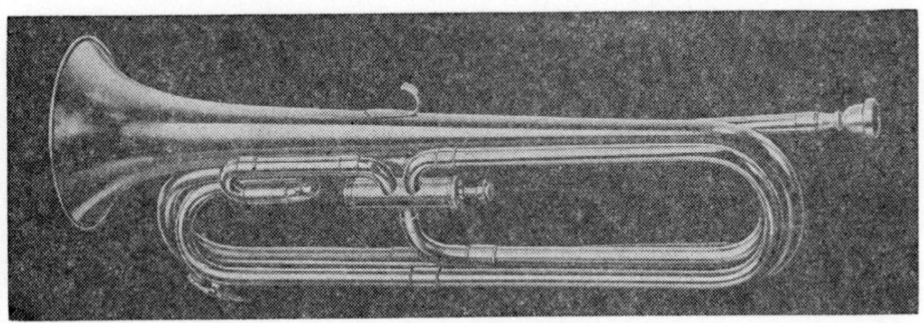

Figure 95. Modern Bugle
Courtesy C. G. Conn Ltd., Elkhart, Indiana

mentation this number was later increased. In addition to signaling, this bugle was used for playing soprano parts in military bands and was extremely popular up to 1835. By that time the valve mechanism for brasses began to claim attention, and so the keyed bugle had to make room for the valved bugle and the cornet à pistons (not to be confused with the cornett just discussed).

It was pointed out in Chapter V that any interference with the natural tube by holes, keys, crooks, or valves impedes the clarity of its tone. For this reason the simple bugle without valves or keys has not yet fallen into oblivion and still finds application for certain special effects. The bugle with one valve, however, is more frequently used. This one valve still leaves the bugle in the class of signal instruments.

*Three Modern Successors to the Bugle*

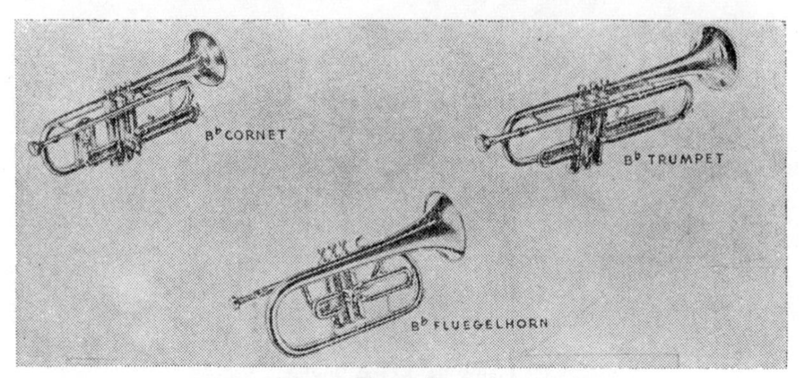


Figure 96
Three Modern Successors to the Bugle
Courtesy C. G. Conn Ltd., Elkhart, Indiana

### *The Flügelhorn*

The *flügelhorn* is the immediate successor to the valved bugle. Its name is derived either from the fact that in military bands the player marched on the right wing (*Flügel* in German means *wing*) of the column, or from the huntsmen's habit of using this bugle to watch in the paths (*Flügeln*) cut through the woods and give a signal on the approach of game. Its tone is peculiarly sweet and of a clear and beautiful quality. European orchestras still view it with favor, but on our continent it finds but a restricted use, much to the consternation of ardent musicians. Its place is taken by the trumpet.

### *The Trumpet*

The *trumpet* often has to pose as the present-day military bugle. However, there is a clear distinction between these two instruments. The trumpet is longer and more cylindrical than the bugle and has a larger bell, and the mouthpiece is deeper and not so cup-shaped; in addition, it is used by the cavalry.

The trumpet is the soprano of the brass choir. Its range is about two and a half chromatic octaves. Its great-grandparent is the Roman lituus (Figure 74). In the age of Bach and Handel, before the modern mechanism had evolved, the trumpet was shrill and high-pitched. The tone of today's trumpet, on the other hand, is noble, triumphant and very effective in flourishes and fanfares. You can easily verify this by listening to the trumpet fanfare at the beginning of the fourth part of Rossini's *William Tell Overture*; you will find it electrifying, especially if you have listened to the preceding quiet passage. But even the softer accents of the trumpet are clear, for the trumpet is an agile instrument.

By means of single, double, and triple tonguing, that is, by interrupting the breath with the tongue once, twice, or three times, rapid and clear staccato notes can be produced, even on one and the same note. Listen for instance to the *Grand March in* Wagner's *Tannhäuser*. On the other hand, long, sustained trumpet passages never fail to express a certain nobility of tone. This is well illustrated by Beethoven (who incidentally gave the trumpet its present individual character) in the third movement of his *Seventh Symphony*.

Furthermore, once produced the tone seems to be well under the control of the player from beginning to end. To clarify this statement let us consider a piano player. As soon as he strikes a key the tone is practically out of control; it simply fades away. The trumpeter, however, can not only hold his tone for quite a while, but he can vary the loudness while holding it. Wagner, for instance, in his *Rienzi Overture* gives us a thrilling trumpet crescendo and diminuendo on one long, sustained tone! (This is admittedly the most difficult passage ever written for the trumpet.)

A trumpet can also be muted. The mute is a pear-shaped contraption inserted into the bell of the instrument. They used to be made of papier-mâché or cardboard, but today aluminum and copper are in favor. When the muted trumpet is blown softly, it produces a beautiful and intriguing far-away effect. When blown loudly, however, a grotesque and bizarre sound results, so often heard in modern jazz bands and dance orchestras. Mutes come also for cornets and trombones. Figure 97 shows a group of mutes for cornet and trumpet and for trombone. These mutes are made of

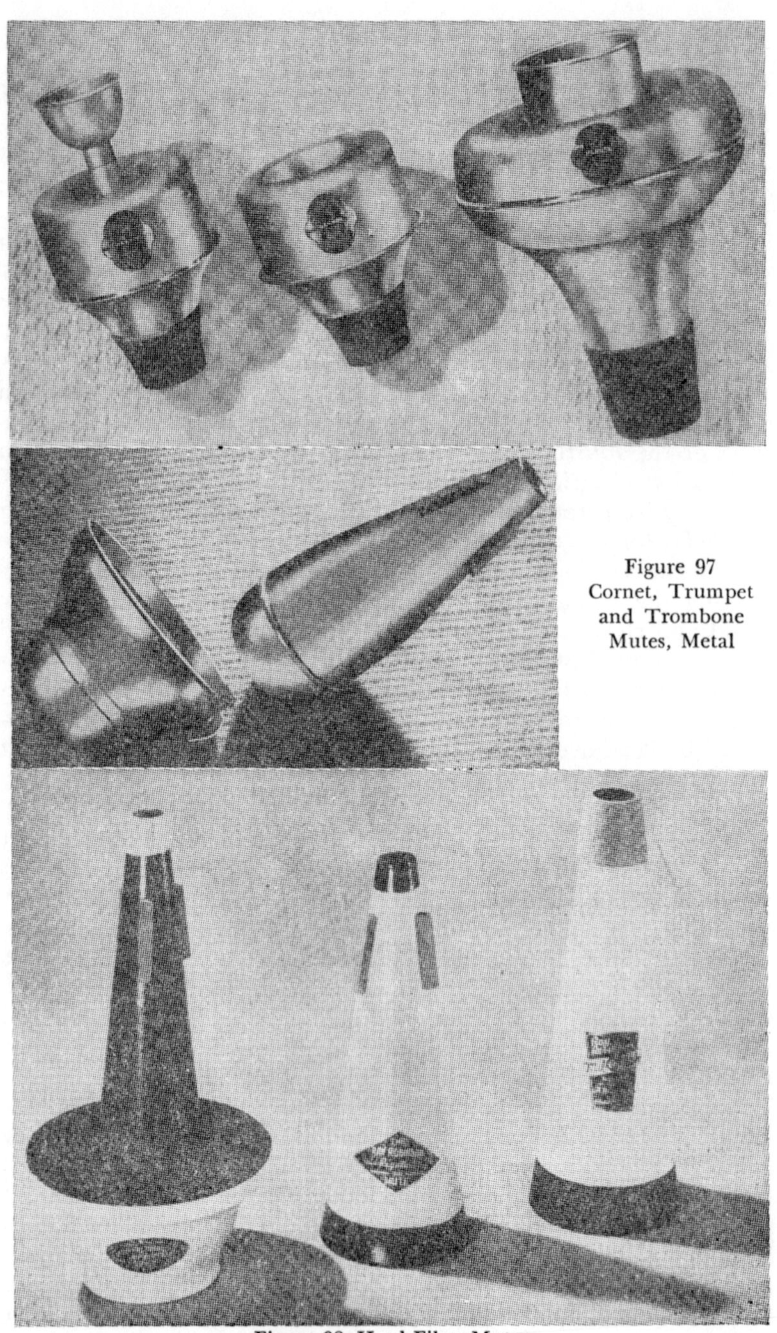

Figure 97
Cornet, Trumpet
and Trombone
Mutes, Metal

Figure 98. Hard Fibre Mutes

metal. On the other hand, Figure 107 shows mutes for the same instruments made of hard fiber.

The modern symphony orchestra employs two trumpets, meaning that one trumpet can hold its own against some thirty violins! For special effects extra trumpets may be called for. The most common trumpet of today is the B-flat trumpet.

## *The Cornet*

The *cornet* is a hybrid instrument. It resembles the trumpet but is shorter and broader; the tubing is more tapered and the mouthpiece is cup-shaped. The contrast may be studied from Figure 99.

The cornet is intermediate in character and proportions between the trumpet and the bugle. Its tone is therefore less brilliant and not so noble and dignified as that of the trumpet, but it is superior to the keyed bugle, its nearest relation. Since its bore begins to widen close to the mouthpiece, it is easier to play than the trumpet. In the hands of the skillful player it has some justification in the orchestra, but composers hesitate to prescribe it. In Germany and Austria the flügelhorn is justly more popular. Other countries use

Figure 99
Trumpet and Cornet, Contrast Study

the cornet more freely, although Berlioz complained that it cheapened the musical production. Hence, the cornet is more at home in military bands and dance orchestras. Unfortunately, it is all too often vulgarized, notably by modern jazz players.

Like the trumpet, the cornet can be muted without interference with tone production. There is also an echo attachment, known as the "coffee-pot effect." An independent bell attached to it is brought into action by a special valve, thereby creating a distant-sounding quality of tone.

The cornet was first encountered around 1828, when the French equipped the smaller, straight type of post horn with two and later with three valves. Just like the other brasses, it underwent some alterations. Today it is frequently made with a more cylindrical bore approaching more and more the features of the trumpet, so that these two instruments are not always clearly distinguishable.

### *The Slide Trumpet*

Toward the close of the eighteenth century the *slide trumpet* came to England. It became very popular during the nineteenth century, especially in the performance of classical trumpet music, notably that of Bach and Handel. The instrument can be traced back to the fifteenth century, when trumpeters started to use detachable mouthpieces with long throats.

The ordinary throat of a mouthpiece is about one inch in length, but at that time, prior to the introduction of proper slides and

Figure 100
English Slide Trumpet, ca. 1810
Courtesy Museum of Fine Arts, Boston

valves, musicians began to use a ten-inch mouthpiece. By inserting this extra tubing into the main tube, the pitch of the instrument could be adjusted to the right key to fill out certain gaps between the harmonics and thus to produce the diatonic scale. Such a "to-be-pulled-out" trumpet dates from the middle of the seventeenth century. It was known to Bach, who used it in several of his cantatas.

The player had to press the mouthpiece against his lips with two fingers and draw the body of the trumpet in and out in a trombone fashion. After 1810 the slide assumed the U-shaped form, thereby becoming twice as effective in altering the length of the tube. Our drawing shows also a center rod. This rod contained a spring which would pull the slide back to its original position after use.

The slide trumpet remained restricted to England, and even there it was soon supplanted by the valve trumpet.

### *Saxhorns*

Viewing the first half of the nineteenth century in perspective, we find that brass instruments were so varied and numerous that they formed a motley array indeed. Music is a universal language; yet the means of expressing it were far from universal. Practically none of the instruments was standardized. A horn in one country might mean a different thing in effect in another country. So consider the plight of the composer. Was he ever sure that his music would be rendered properly outside the limits of his circle? Or what was the musician to do with "foreign" specifications concerning certain instruments?

Here is just a partial list of the most common brass instruments: cornetts, serpents, bass-horns, ophicleides, keyed bugles, slide trumpets, valved bugles, flügelhorns, althorns, baritones, euphoniums, tubas, cornets, and trumpets. Furthermore, a number of natural horns like post horns were still fighting for survival, and all the instruments mentioned were making their appearance almost simultaneously in different countries in different shapes and guises. Consequently, an instrument parading under the same name in different countries was not necessarily the same instrument as far as tone quality was concerned.

The cry went out for more uniform and standardized instruments. Taking up the challenge, Adolphe Sax of Belgium succeeded in 1843 in uniting cornets, flügelhorns, althorns, baritones, euphoniums, and bass and contrabass tubas into one homogeneous family. All these horns are of the bugle type, i.e., they are midway between the horn and trumpet, and taken together they provide a range of about five octaves of more or less similar tone color. The instru-

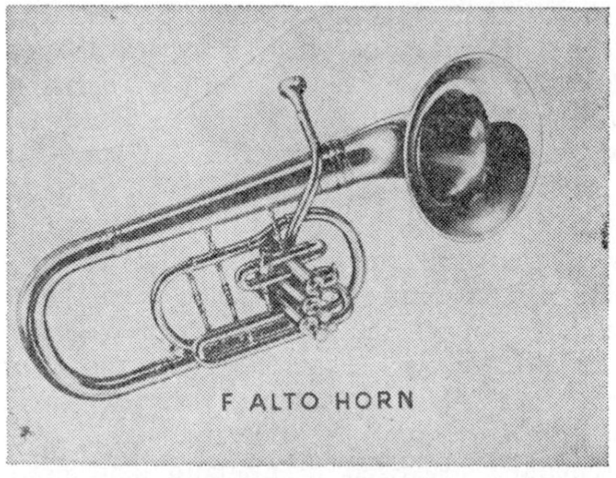


Figure 101
Alt-horn, a Typical Saxhorn
Courtesy C. G. Conn Ltd., Elkhart, Indiana

ments perfected by Sax are known in his honor as *saxhorns* (not to be confused with saxophones).

Our illustration shows an althorn, a typical saxhorn. It is played in an upright position, that is, the bell rises above the head of the player giving the lower end, the end with the bell, a higher position than the upper or mouthpiece end. The mouthpiece is perpendicular to the tube, held horizontally, and the piston valves stand on top of the horizontal part of the tube. If you will look back at Figure 96, the difference between ordinary instruments and saxhorns will at once become apparent.

The althorn is the connecting link between the cornet and the baritone. Its tone resembles that of the French horn, although it is not so round and mellow. Consequently, it replaces the French horn only in military bands and amateur orchestras. It is equally useful as a solo instrument and for accompaniment. Sometimes the althorn is shaped in the form of a French horn which gives it the name of *mellophone.*

The *baritone* saxhorn, too, has a full, sonorous tone. It operates like the cornet but sounds an octave lower.

The *euphonium,* another saxhorn, is identical with the baritone, but has an extra valve to extend its normal compass downward five semitones.

The euphonium and baritone are so closely akin, that some writers make no distinction between the two. Its technical facility makes it equally valuable as a solo and an orchestral instrument. There is also a type of euphonium with two bells, the second smaller. By a special valve the air vibrations can be diverted into this smaller bell, and a different tone quality, akin to that of the trombone, is obtained. The euphonium comes nearest the tuba, the bass of the brasses. Its range is such, however, that it figures as a tenor tuba.

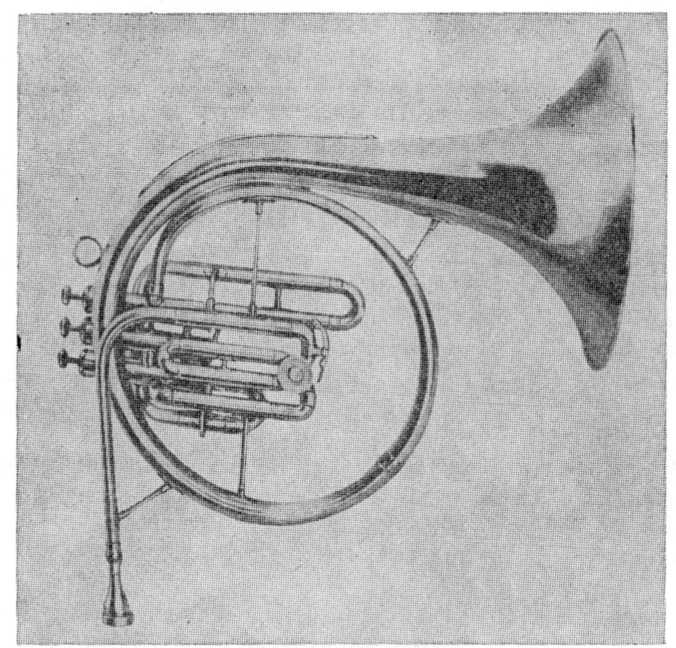

Figure 102. Mellophone

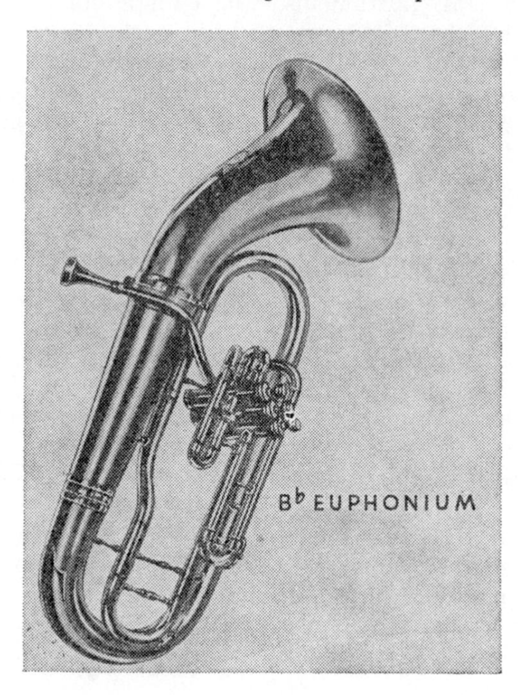


Figure 103
Courtesy
C. G. Conn Ltd.
Elkhart, Indiana

The whole family of saxhorns comprises seven members divided into two groups. The soprano and alto horns form the first, and the tenor, baritone, bass, and contrabass horns the second. The alto and baritone are still much in use in military bands.

Sax's contributions may be summed up as follows: (1) Up to his time the valve mechanism had been a rather clumsy contraption. Sax simplified it and applied scientific principles of acoustics so that his instruments became truly musical. It has been said that trumpets and horns preserved their medieval qualities up to the 1830s when Sax began his experiments. (2) His instruments, constituting a whole family, provided the means to play in any key without the addition of special crooks. (3) He attacked and solved remarkably well the problem of true intonation; his instruments contributed greatly toward the solution of the problem of faultless tone production.

We will have the pleasure of meeting this distinguished instrument maker again when we discuss another of his inventions, the saxophone.

### *The Tuba*

Originally the name *tuba* signified a short, straight horn or trumpet corresponding to the coach horn. Today *tuba* is applied to the deeper-toned valved brass instruments. The euphonium is often classified as a tuba, but the chief instrument here is the bombardon in its two forms: the bass tuba and the contrabass tuba.

The ordinary *bass tuba* has three valves, whereas the *contrabass* has four valves. The fourth valve is necessary to produce the pedal octave, i.e., the scale between the fundamental note and the second harmonic. It also corrects the sharpness in tone which results from the combined use of several valves.

The tone of the tuba is broad and round. It forms a solid bass to trombone harmony; hence the instrument is used not only in bands but also in symphony orchestras. It blends well with the bass strings, producing the very low notes with clarity and definiteness. Contrary to appearance, this huge instrument is quite flexible and agile, rendering it all the more useful for the orchestra. It is conical like a horn, but it has a cup-shaped mouthpiece like a trumpet.

The inventor of the tuba is Wieprecht (1835). The first tuba was, as may be expected, quite different in appearance and shape from the modern one which is fashioned after the saxhorns. Several forms of the tuba exist. For marching and horse riding the tuba is made in circular form so that it can be carried around the shoulder. Such a tuba is known as the *helicon.* A helicon with a gigantic movable bell is known as the *sousaphone,* in honor of John Philip Sousa, the "march king".

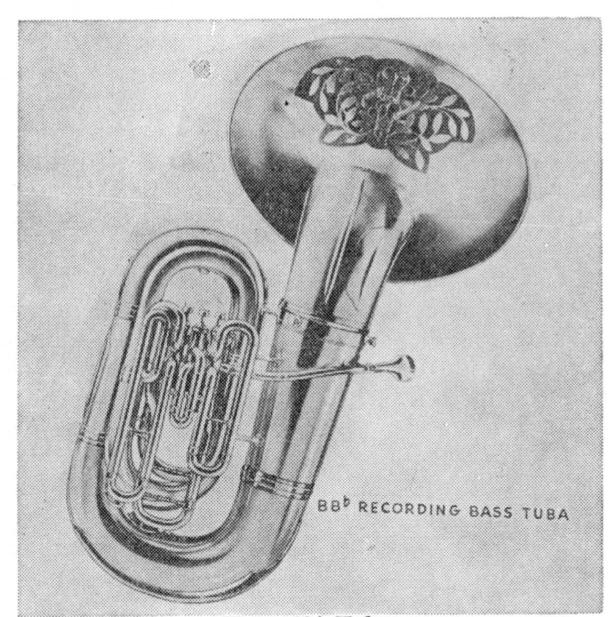


Figure 104. Tuba
Courtesy C. G. Conn Ltd., Elkhart, Indiana

Figure 105
Sousaphone

Figure 106
Wagner Tuba

The contrabass tuba is not so useful as it appears on the surface. In America some specimens of this instrument are of gigantic proportions, the tube having an air column of some thirty-six feet in length and its bell measuring thirty inches or more in diameter. Such an instrument cannot fail to impress the audience, but it is mostly showmanship, since the human lungs and lips are too limited to do it justice and the deep rumbling bass notes are actually too low for the ear to appreciate.

For the sake of completeness we must mention the *Wagner tuba.* Wagner was so exacting in his demands that nothing already existing seemed to be good enough for him. (Recall the building of his theater at Bayreuth.) When he wrote his four-opera *Ring* he envisioned special brass instruments, which were made to his specifications (1870). These tubas were midway between ordinary tubas and French horns; they were narrower in bore than the former but wider than the latter. Their tone was of a majestic quality. Some modern composers—Bruckner and Richard Strauss, for instance—still call for Wagner tubas, but they are no longer in common use.

### *The French Horn*

The French horn is the present-day orchestral form of that family of instruments. Prior to the emergence of its modern guise, several other forms were in vogue during the nineteenth century. Some of these are shown on page 133. They all antedate the saxhorns.

The first horn shown is a typical German hunting horn. It is the prototype of the horn. The second horn, an English make (shown just below the hunting horn), is about half a century older, and is already known as a French horn. Instead of valves it has a tuning slide. The third horn (upper right) is the German *Inventionshorn,* "invention" being applied for a crook of a special design, a combination crook as it were. The fourth horn is a Belgian make, called *cor omnitonique.* It has a straight cylindrical tube in the middle to which are attached eight oval-shaped branches. These branches are controlled by a sliding piston with a knob worked with the index finger. By sliding the piston up and down, the eight branches can be brought into play progressively. Needless to say, none of these models was the long-sought solution to the scale-playing horn.

Around 1843 there appeared in London a French horn shown in Figure 108. Its main features are the two valves and the combination crooks. The first valve was a semitone, the second a whole-tone valve. The combination crooks had the effect of lengthening the main tube to the equivalent of seventy-four feet nine inches. This sounds extraordinary, but of course they were never all used at the same time. The net result was an instrument that could play in various keys. What is more, it was really a fine musical instrument.

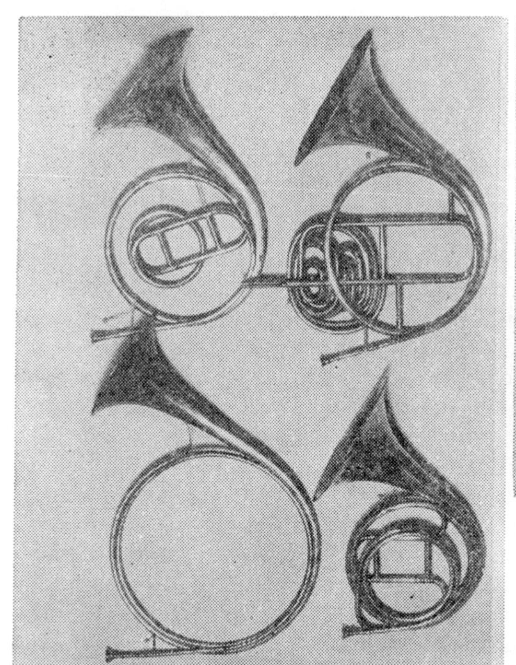

Figure 107. Forerunners of the Modern French Horn
Courtesy Museum of Fine Arts, Boston

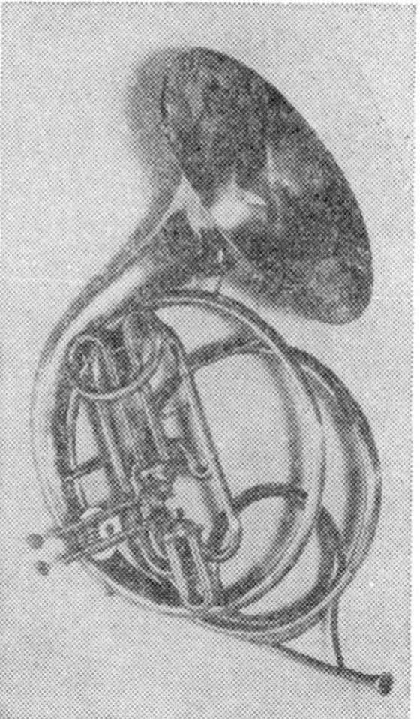

Figure 108
French Horn of 1833, Belgium
Courtesy Museum of Fine Arts, Boston

Figure 109
BBC Symphony Orchestra Horn Players
Courtesy BBC, Broadcasting House

The final answer is seen above, showing the five horn players of the BBC Symphony Orchestra. The manner of playing the French horn has been explained in Chapter V. Some French horns had three valves after 1820, but it took several more decades to give us the final form of the present-day horn.

The French horn with its funnel-shaped mouthpiece is conoidal throughout and is therefore a true horn. As has been shown, the valve-operated crooks interfere with the cone of the tube and remedial steps in tone production have to be employed. The range of the horn is three and a half octaves. There is no pedal tone. The bell is about eleven inches across; the air column of the usual F-horn is twelve feet, although larger horns are occasionally used with a sixteen-foot air column. The horn is the alto of the brass.

The tone quality of the French horn lies midway between the woodwinds and brasses, which means that it blends equally well with either. It also sounds good by contrast with the strings. Its voice is pure and noble, lovely and mellow, even and resonant. *Fortissimo* passages, if played by the usual four horns, cut through the entire orchestral mass, and when played softly they still have a pervading quality. If it is muted, there is no other instrument that creates such realistic romantic and mysterious echo effects. It makes you think of distant hills and dales, hunting and forests. In short, the French horn is a profoundly expressive instrument.

The French horn is the most difficult of the brass instruments to play. Even the most skillful player is likely to make an occasional slip. Indeed, it is not unusual to hear a sour note over the radio. Loud passages especially are apt to become blatant and nasal, producing an evil, sinister effect. Only in the hands of experts are the loud passages still agreeable. This is probably the reason why the French horn is not used in bands or school orchestras.

The horn lacks the agility of the trumpet, and hence it is used more often for slow, sustained melodies of a pastoral nature. Have you ever heard the exquisitely lovely melody of Mendelssohn's *Midsummer Night's Dream Nocturne* or the muted horns in Beethoven's *Leonore Overture No. 3*? Or *Siegfried's Horn Call* by Wagner? Or Weber's horn passage in his *Freischuetz Overture*? It will be worth your while to give some such music your attention.

All told, the French horn is the aristocrat among the brass instruments. But believe it or not, it had to overcome some fierce opposition on the part of the best musicians for whom even the best is hardly good enough. The resentment, of course, was caused by faulty tone production, and it must have taken a long time for the players to overcome the deficiencies of the valve horn. Some musicians consider it a pity that the French horn has so completely supplanted the "real" horn.

## *The Trombone*

The word *trombone* means *big trumpet.* Some writers claim that the trombone is of great antiquity and attribute its origin to the ancient Romans. This theory is no longer considered valid. It has been established, however, that the ancients did occasionally use a slide as a means of slightly altering the pitch, but there is nothing to suggest that this primitive use led to the development of the trombone.

The earliest undisputed evidence of the existence of the trombone dates from the fifteenth century. The Spanish apparently had a kind of trombone after 1300, calling it *sachabuche,* meaning *pull-push* or *draw trumpet. Sackbut* is a familiar name in the Old Testament, being used for the old Hebrew trumpet, which of course was no trombone at all, nor a *sachabuche.* But the sackbut of the fifteenth century is the first trombone. It clearly resembled the modern trombone, except that its walls were thicker and the bell was less expanded. Its tone was softer and more suited for smaller groups. Generally speaking, the trombone has undergone the least change of all brass instruments in its quest for perfection.

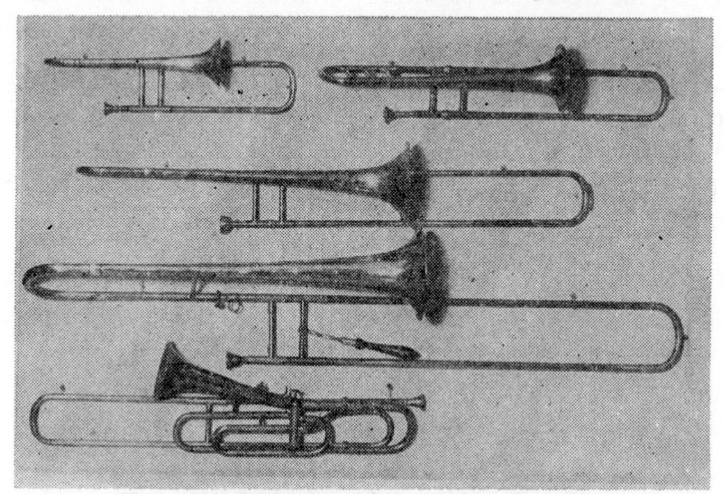

Figure 110. Forerunners of the Modern Trombone
Courtesy Museum of Fine Arts, Boston

The illustration shows a few evolutionary changes the trombone did undergo. The two top specimens are the soprano (1781) and the alto trombone (late nineteenth century) respectively. We have seen that the brass player must resort to lip-corrections for true intonation; the shorter the tube, the more difficult the corrections are. Since stopping in the right places was also a problem, and since both the soprano and the alto trombone are rather short, they never achieved any degree of popularity, and thus never became full-fledged members of the trombone family. Had their tone been pleasant, musicians no doubt would have tried to improve them. But when the valved cornets and trumpets appeared they took the place of the high trombones.

The old classical scores employed the alto trombone. The tenor trombone—third in the above illustration—differs from the modern specimen only in its mouthpiece. The bass trombone has a special extension handle for shifting the slide in the lower positions. The valved trombone is one of the many attempts to improve the trombone. Since no practical advantage was derived thereby, this instrument did not survive.

During the eighteenth century the bells were sometimes made in the shape of dragons, especially in military bands, evidently to intimidate the enemy; but since such a procedure impaired the tone quality, it was soon forgotten.

The two common trombones today are the tenor and the bass, with air columns of nine and twelve feet respectively. The manner of playing the trombone has already been discussed (Chapter V). It may surprise you that even trombones must be tuned. Look closely at the right end of either trombone above and note the U-bent section in segments. They are for adjusting the length of the trombone so that the player will get the correct results from the desired position.

Contrabass trombones exerted too severe a strain on the player and therefore never assumed any importance.

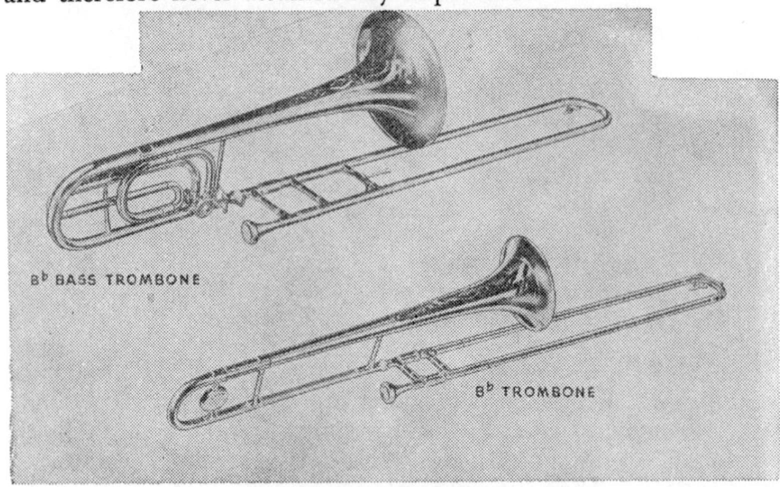


Figure 111. Trombones
Courtesy C. G. Conn Ltd., Elkhart, Indiana

Since the trombone has no valves and is bent only in two places, it has a look of dignified simplicity. The tube is cylindrical with the exception of the lower third, which gradually expands into the bell. Hence, the trombone is classified as a trumpet. The mouthpiece, however, differs from that of the true trumpet; it is more cup-shaped, no doubt to facilitate the production of the lower notes. The trombone is the bass of the trumpet section of the orchestra.

The tone of the trombone is remarkably pure and noble, one of exaltation and solemnity; it is calm and dignified, and yet manly and powerful. Because *fortissimo* passages produce the effect of blazing brilliance, trombones can be employed for making overwhelming noise. When muted and blown hard, the trumpet produces an extravagantly nasal and metallic sound. Furthermore, the trombone permits of a true *glissando* (a gliding scale), so expertly used by modern dance orchestras. But such deficiencies are not the fault of the instrument. In the hands of a true musician the trombone remains an aristocratic instrument.

One of the imperfections of the trombone is found in the fact that the sleeve is slightly wider than the main tube, causing a disturbance in wave formation. This disturbance is particularly noticeable when the slide is completely drawn out; certain notes then are likely to crack if not corrected by lipping. Another imperfection is the lack of agility. Rapid passages are almost impossible on the trombone. Likewise, a trombone is happiest in its own company, since it does not blend too well with the other instruments. A trombone choir by itself, however, is indeed very impressive, creating a solemn and reverent atmosphere. Wagner knew how to employ trombones with telling effects. Listen, for instance, to his *Pilgrim's Chorus* from *Tannhäuser*. Humperdinck's prelude to *Hansel and Gretel* begins with a delightful melody for trombones in the children's prayer theme.

Incidentally, the trombone was never the prerogative of royalty, for since its very beginnings it has been the people's instrument.

### *Summary*

We have traced the evolution of modern brass instruments from primitive animal horns and shells to the present day. Thousands of years passed by before men learned to employ the first fear-inspiring devices as musical instruments. During the last century or two lip-voiced instruments have become truly musical, musicians have learned to use them for the creation of beauty.

The question now arises whether men really appreciate such a change. After all, it is almost impossible to eradicate customs of several thousand years' standing. Modern dance orchestras and jazz bands seem to excel in creating all sorts of disagreeable and bizarre effects with their cornets and trombones (they seldom use trumpets or the French horn). Yet they are more popular than the symphonic orchestra, and their members certainly receive better pay than the expert player whose sole endeavor is to create aesthetic effects.

Finally, we give here the normal specifications of the brass department of the full symphony orchestra. Deviations from the norm are, of course, quite frequent.

4 French horns
2 trumpets
2 tenor trombones
1 bass trombone
1 tuba

In addition to the above, the brass band uses cornet, flügelhorn, bugle, alto horn, mellophone, euphonium, baritone, and possibly other instruments of less importance.

Figure 112
BBC Symphony Orchestra Trombone Players
Courtesy BBC Broadcasting House

# *Part Three: Woodwinds*

*From*

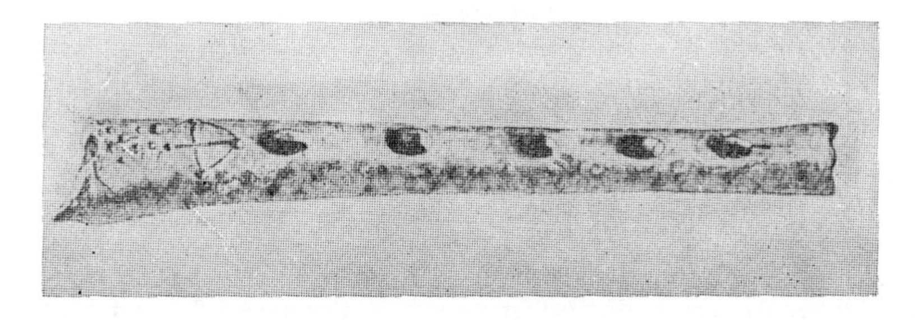

***To***

## WOODWINDS

The name *woodwind* is highly suggestive, for woodwinds include a group of instruments made generally of wood which depend for their tone production on the vibrating column of air inside the tubular part of the instrument. The sound is therefore made by a vibrating column of air, and such instruments are thus given the name of *aerophones.*

There are three distinct methods of sound production with aerophones:

1. the breaking of a wind passage against an open hole;
2. causing air vibrations by means of a single reed; and
3. causing air vibrations by means of a double reed.

Group 1 includes all kinds of tubes, whistles, flutes, and recorders; group 2 deals with clarinets and their forerunners; and group 3 embraces oboes, English horns, and bassoons and their prototypes. It is assumed that group 1 antedates the horns, but that the reeds are of a later origin.

CHAPTER VII

# FLUTES

The prototype of all woodwinds is found in the flue-blown tube provided by nature. According to popular theory, man was taught to construct his first flute by the whistling of the wind over hollow river reeds. This belief is several thousand years old but modern musicologists discredit it. The assumption that man invented musical instruments by imitating nature and then used such instruments for his own edification is, as we have seen, no longer thought valid. Practically everything which primitive man did in the direction of the finer arts was first associated with some supernatural notion, and only later attained some definite practical use. We have seen how this theory is upheld in the case of percussions and lip-voiced instruments; we shall presently find it substantiated by the woodwinds.

Historians trace the flute back twenty-five to thirty thousand years, although it did not assume any importance until some six thousand years ago. Without going into details, it has been proved that the flute was a charm of life, rebirth, and love. It was strictly a masculine instrument; women would not touch it. A flute had special influence over girls. Young men used them in their courtships, especially if a medicine man or the like would exercise his power over them. In some parts of Europe men are still forbidden to play the flute when serenading a girl, for admittedly it is bad for girls to hear the flute at night. (One wonders why a "wolf" will whistle at an attractive girl and where and when this custom originated.)

Among the reasons for associating the flute with rebirth is the fact that archeologists often find flutes at the sides of skeletons in ancient tombs. Until recently their explanation was that they had uncovered bodies of musicians, whereas the truth of the matter is that the flutes were placed there as life charms to aid in the resurrection of the bodies. Slaves and boys to be sacrificed played bone flutes, not to amuse themselves by lovely music but because the flutes were associated with the mystery of rebirth.

Another striking example of the supernatural role of the flute is found in the nose flute, which was played by breath from the nose. Nose breath, according to primitive man, contains the soul, and hence has more magic power than mouth breath.[1]

### *Primitive Flutes*

The oldest of all flutes is the primitive whistle pipe of prehistoric cave men. The sound was produced in the same manner as that a boy uses when he blows across the top of an empty bottle: by directing a thin stream of air against the sharp edges of a hollow cane, thereby making the air inside the tube vibrate.

Curiously enough, the simple reed or cane flute was not the oldest of these pipe instruments. All evidence bears out the fact that bone whistles made of reindeer joints, swan or goose bones, or occasionally even of a lion's tooth antedate the simpler instrument. The reason for such materials is easily conjectured. Since the flute was a charm of rebirth, it had to be made from something living, a bone, for instance, and not a lifeless reed. Bone flutes are twenty-five thousand years old.

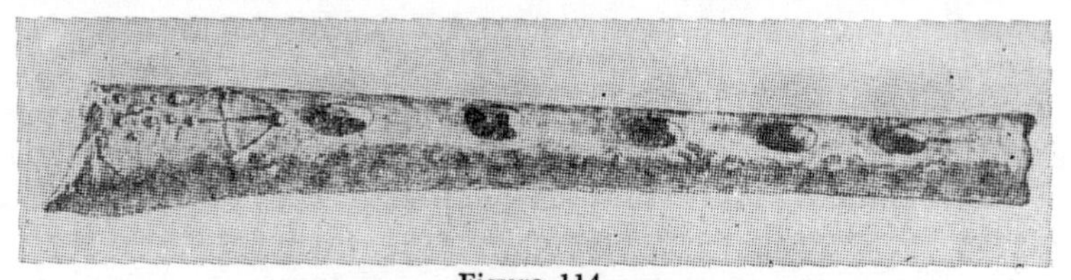

Figure 114
Bone Flute from the Stone Age
Courtesy Geiringer, Musical Instruments

Figure 114 shows a bone flute some five thousand years old. The surprising feature of this bone flute is the side holes. Since this flute must already have a long ancestry, one cannot help wondering why man took ages to provide trumpets with side holes, when the caveman had such holes in his flute!

To fashion bones into flutes was a laborious process, so it is only natural that almost any object whose natural shape would lend itself to such purposes would be substituted. Hollow reeds became the favorite medium. But almost any kind of hollow vessel could be used. Kaffir children of South Africa would sing into hollow

[1] Among German peoples it is still customary to wish a person good health after sneezing — they say *"Gesundheit"* — for fear that such a breath explosion might have damaged the soul. An amusing anecdote comes to the mind of the author, who as a young conductor was instructed to teach his singers to inhale through their noses while singing!

fruit shells. The same shells were later used for whistling. Thus originated the globular flute, known today as the *ocarina*. There may not have been too great a difference between such flutes and the globular trumpets or shells. The original fruit shell may have been the coconut. Bones were also used. Later, however, clay became the principal material for ocarinas.

As you notice in Figure 115, ocarinas have fingerholes. The mouth hole is on the top edge. Due to their large internal cavity and the absence of any bell, their tone is hollow, but not disagreeable; overtones are lacking.

In addition to ocarinas there were also so-called *bird whistles*, used for imitating bird calls.

Globular flutes never gained any importance, whereas the simple whistle pipe laid the foundation for our modern woodwinds.

The whistle pipe was held vertically, that is downward from the mouth. This mode of playing has given rise to the term *vertical*

Figure 115. Ocarinas
Courtesy Museum of Fine Arts, Boston

Figure 116
Panpipes

*flute*. It is the earliest form of musical pipe. It is still in vogue in Arabia, India, Japan, Africa, Greece, and Bulgaria. Different materials are used in its manufacture, such as clay and pottery, ivory being fairly common in Africa.

The ancient Greeks combined several such whistle pipes into one instrument, which regardless of its primitiveness has stood godfather to our modern organ. (Now, that is a long story, and will be dealt with later on.) From three to nine pipes of different lengths—the usual number being seven—were tied together in the form of a raft or a bundle so that the upper ends were on a level, permitting the player to blow at will into each of them, and thus forming a kind of mouth organ. Such pipes were known as ***Panpipes, Pandean pipes,*** or the ***syrinx.***

Panpipes derive their name from the legend of the Greek god Pan (see page 18), the same one who causes "panics." Once more we find substantiation for the theory that the flute was a lover's instrument. Actually these Panpipes were used only by shepherds, and no musical value was attached to them. Wood, bronze, clay, or a similar material was used in their manufacture.

The syrinx is considered one of the oldest instruments. The Chinese had twelve pipes in their syrinxes, which number was later increased to sixteen. The "organ" mentioned in Genesis 4:21 was actually a syrinx. The syrinx held its own well into the Middle Ages as a herdsman's instrument, but again, musically it was of no appreciable value.

Returning to the simple flute, let us now trace the improvements. The first step was a notch cut on the edge of the pipe. Into this notch

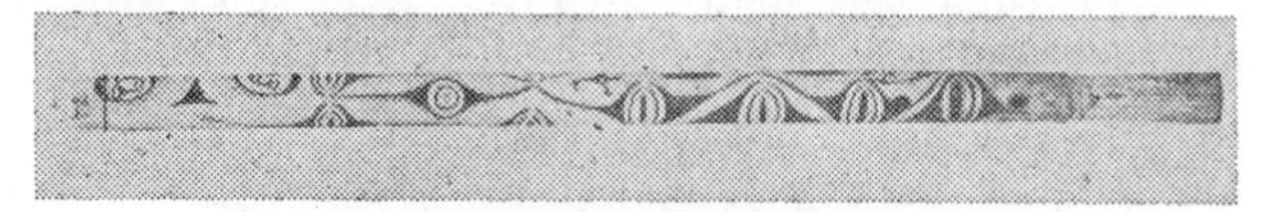

Figure 117. African Flute with Notch
Courtesy Metropolitan Museum of Art, New York

the player placed his lower lip. If you look closely, you will see a notch in the upper end of the African flute shown in Figure 117.

Next, the upper end of the tube was almost entirely closed, the little notch only remaining, thus leading up to the proper whistle head. Further improvements led to the development of the flageolet-type whistle head from a special mouthpiece, usually the prolongation of the cane from the septum (the natural knot between the sections of a reed); a leaf or rag tied tightly over the orifice directed the air stream against the lower edge of the notch. The flageolet whistle head is important enough to merit a diagram (Figure 118), since it was used prominently in many instruments of the flute type and is far from being obsolete even today.

Fingerholes enabled the player to produce tones of different pitch on the same pipe. As we have seen, flutes with fingerholes are of much earlier origin than trumpets with holes. Early flutes had three equidistant holes, and later models up to eight and nine. To what extent these fingerholes are responsible for the development of concepts of a scale is a controversial issue. It has been shown that even in cornetts and serpents the disposition of the fingerholes was governed by expediency and not by musical principles. Only since 1832 have side holes in the flute been placed with a view to obtaining the correct intervals of our scale.

Primitive vertical flutes are recorded in Egyptian history as early as the fourth millennium B.C. They were also common to many other

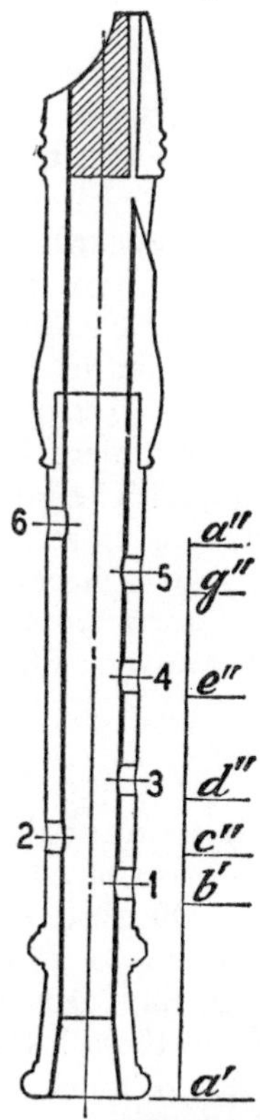


Figure 118
Section of the Flageolet
with Whistle Head
Courtesy Museum of
Fine Arts, Boston

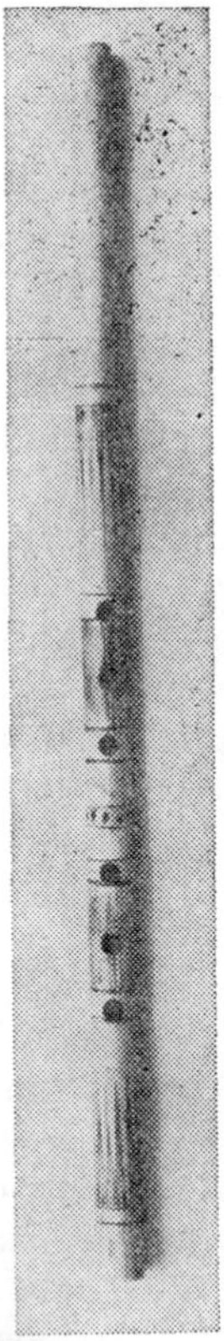

Figure 119
Vertical Flute,
Javanese
Courtesy Metropolitan
Museum of Art, New York

Figure 120. Primitive Egyptian Flute

countries, among them Java and Peru. Egyptian flutes measured approximately a yard in length and were half an inch wide. They were made of cane, had no mouthpiece, and had from two to six fingerholes at the lower end.

Larger flutes were equipped with whistle heads. These whistle-head flutes, although more complicated, are of older origin than the simpler vertical flutes. (No, this is not a paradox for simplification often follows original complex inventions.) But let us note carefully an important difference in tone production between these two types of flutes: vertical flutes without any mouthpiece had greater musical possibilities than the whistle-head pipes. The latter are more mechanical, whereas in the former type the player, by varying the angle of blowing against the edge, can give more expression to the tone and produce sustained notes and warm *vibratos*. We will find this difference again in recorders and transverse flutes.

### *Fipple Flutes*

A *fipple flute* is a vertical flute with the whistle head modified into a mouthpiece (Figure 118). The mouthpiece consists of a tube leading into a cavity containing a block which directs the air stream against an opposite sharp lip. The block was known as a *fipple,* hence the name of this group of instruments. It included the recorder, the flageolet, and the pipe and tabor. All of these instruments have been supplanted by the tranverse flute, although the recorder is again claiming some attention today.

The *recorder* made its first appearance in France during the eleventh century. The first recorders were made of one piece and had the shape of a smooth, simple staff as shown particularly by the fourth recorder from the right in the above illustration. Note that the tubes are reversed cones, that is, they taper off toward the lower end in contrast to the regular cones of the horns. This peculiarity plus the absence of a true bell at the lower end gave the recorder a pale tone, deficient in dynamics. The method of playing was mechanical; the player had practically no control over the way in which the air stream entered the tube, and consequently the recorder lacked subjective expression and tonal contrasts.

The size of the recorders in the above family of seven varies from about eighteen to twenty-four inches. The larger the tube the lower the pitch, of course; hence the thinnest one is the tenor. The above typical recorders came from various countries. A common French recorder is shown in Figure 122. It is included because it so clearly reveals all its parts. The French called it a "gentle flute" (*flûte douce*), because notwithstanding its hollowness, the tone was sweet and gentle. The more decorative models are of a later date.

The word *recorder* was derived from a now obsolete meaning of the word *record,* comparing the sound to the warbling of a singing bird. During the Middle Ages the recorder became the most popular wind instrument, especially in England, where it was also known as the English flute in contrast to the German, a transverse flute. Recorders were commonly used in sets of four, corresponding to the four parts of a mixed choir. Bass recorders were not too popular, but some of them reached prodigious proportions, one form being known in the shape of a small pillar with a capital and base.

An ensemble of recorders—seven or eight of them—made delightful chamber music. Such writers as Bacon, Milton, and Shakespeare extolled the recorder in their poetry. Henry VIII had seventy-seven recorders in his collection of musical instruments! Bach used the recorder (usually called "flute" at that time) in six of his cantatas, *St. Matthew Passion,* and other works. Handel, Mozart, and Gluck also featured it in their compositions.

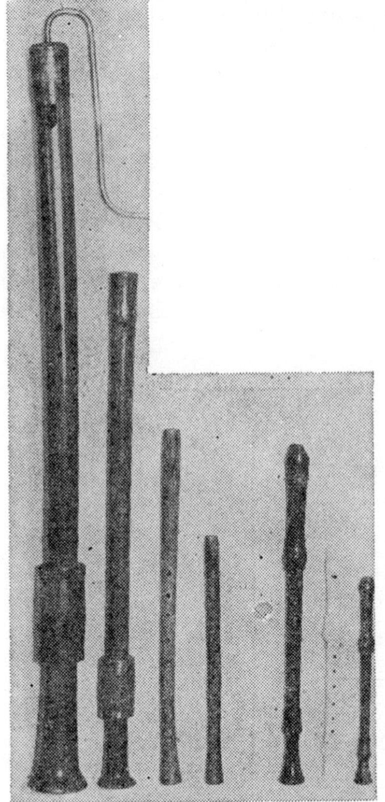

Figure 121. Recorders
Courtesy Museum of Fine Arts, Boston

Figure 122
French Recorder, 18th Century
Courtesy Museum of Fine Arts, Boston

With the growth of the orchestra and the demand for brighter orchestral colors, the recorder had to give way to the transverse flute. During the past quarter-century, however, interest in the recorder has revived, and efficient makers and players are to be found again. Even special compositions are being written nowadays for this instrument, either as a solo or in combination with other members of the group. If you listen, let us say, to a CBC broadcast of a recorder program, you will find that the music is indeed gentle and sweet; but being unused to such quiet music you will probably feel as if you were enjoying nature all by yourself remote from civilization. You might find its steady, unvaried flow of tones somewhat monotonous.

### *Flageolets*

Certain types of flutes were known as flageolets. English flageolets, not nearly so common as the French instruments, had the holes in recorder fashion; hence, there is some confusion among writers whether to call them flutes or recorders. The latest tendency leans toward the former. In appearance flageolets resemble more the recorder, but in tone quality the flute. The important feature of the flageolets is their small size. Single flageolets vary in size from about seven or eight inches to about fifteen inches. They all have four fingerholes in front and two for the thumbs at the back. The last specimen shown is a later model, already equipped with keys.

Double and triple flageolets are more curiosities than musical instruments. The two tubes of the double flageolets were played from one mouthpiece, constructed in such a way that the tubes

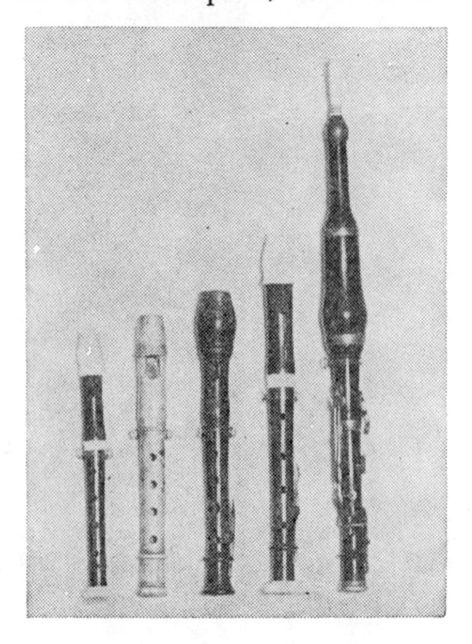

Figure 123
Flageolets, 19th Century
Courtesy Museum of Fine Arts, Boston

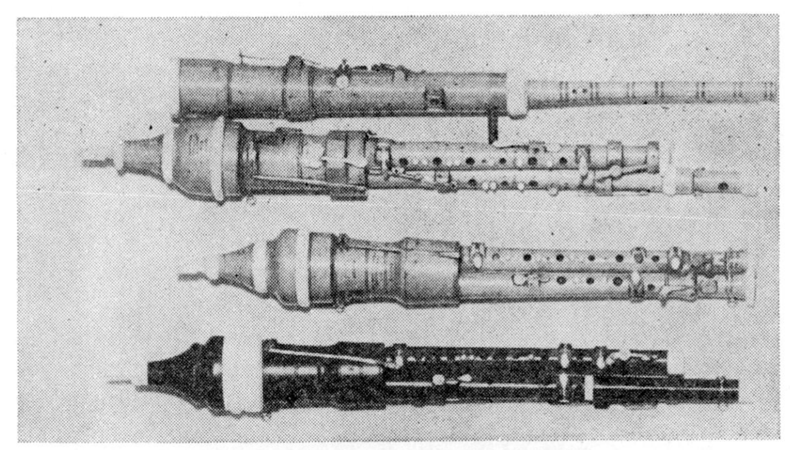

Figure 124. Double and Triple Flageolets
Courtesy Museum of Fine Arts, Boston

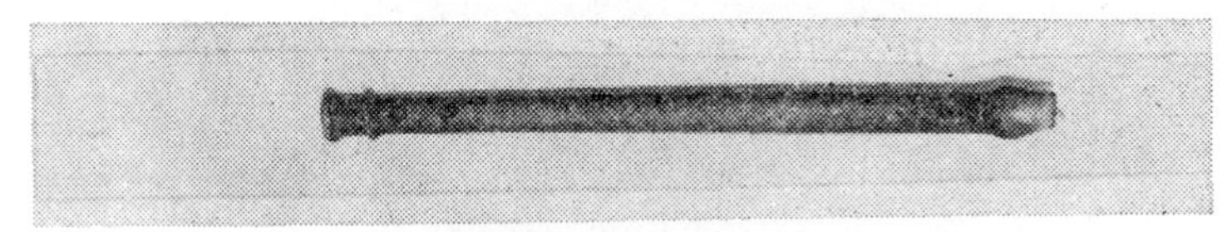

Figure 125. Tabor Pipe
Courtesy Museum of Fine Arts, Boston

could be played separately or simultaneously. The top or nozzle also contained a sponge to absorb the saliva from the player's mouth. The triple flageolet was rather rare. Its third tube extended only to the ivory ring seen close to the middle, the rest being just an ornamental tailpiece, so that it actually was more like a receptacle of an ocarina than a flute tube.

In spite of its few merits, the flageolet survived from the end of the sixteenth century until the second quarter of the nineteenth. At one time it even enjoyed the status of an art instrument, for Handel, Mozart, and Gluck wrote music for it. It was finally replaced by the piccolo and flute.

The bird flageolet was a small instrument of delicate quality used for the training of singing birds.

The pipe in the *pipe and tabor* was a miniature recorder or fipple flute. The one illustrated here is only a little over a foot long, the maximum inner bore being less than half an inch. Such a pipe was held and played with the left hand only and had therefore only three holes, two in front and one at the back, instead of the usual six. It was used for dances, especially the morris dance, where the player used it in conjunction with the tabor, a small, shallow, one-handed drum, which was tapped with a small drumstick in the right hand. The tabor had no snares and was held in position by a string attached either to the left arm or to the waist. The pipe and tabor is often associated with the Elizabethan jester. We find it mentioned in Shakespeare's *Tempest.* A form of it is still used in certain parts of France, where the pipe is accompanied by the tambourine.

### *The Modern Flute*

Here we see the mouth-hole of the modern flute, called the *embouchure,* contrasted to the whistle head of the recorder. Note that the upper end of the flute is closed. The embouchure, however, offsets this effect somewhat so that the flute acts as an open tube. To produce the tone, the flutist places his lower lip partly over the embouchure and blows across, not into the hole. The air

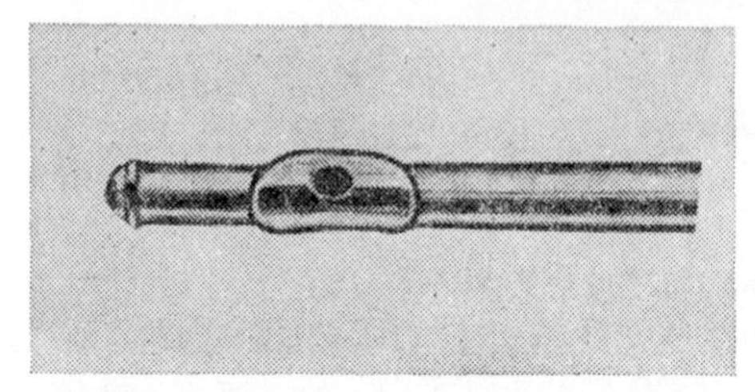

Figure 126
The Embouchure of the Modern Flute

stream is cut by the opposite sharp edge, and vibrations are set up inside the tube, giving rise to sound waves. From the manner of playing, the instrument has become known as a *cross-blown* or *transverse* flute in contradistinction to the vertical flute. The playing position is at right angles to the face of the player, the lower end extending in a horizontal or nearly horizontal position to the right.

Several centuries elapsed before the present-day flute emerged in all its brilliance. Its evolution makes a rather interesting page in history. Here are some of the highlights of the course it ran.

There is evidence that the transverse flute was known to the Greeks around 800 A.D. It had made its entry from Asia via Byzantium, probably from Arabia. By the end of the twelfth century it had reached Germany, and during the thirteenth century France made its acquaintance. The first flute was of necessity a primitive instrument. Note for instance the absence of keys and the equal distribution of the fingerholes—placed as in all primitive instruments with a view of accommodating the player and making no allowance for true intonation. The tube was slightly cylindrical, made in one piece, rather small in size, and of narrow bore.

Such a flute became immensely popular with the Swiss infantry and soon was designated as the Swiss pipe, the *Schweizer Pfeife.*

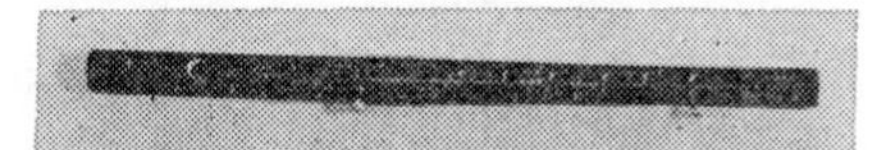

Figure 127. Swiss Pipe, a Transverse Flute
Courtesy Museum of Fine Arts, Boston

When this instrument reached England the name was conveniently modified into *fife.* The usual Swiss flute was about twenty seven inches long, but there were as yet no standardized sizes. The fife shown in Figure 128 is only about fourteen inches long. It assumed a leading role in the drum and fife band.

Figure 128. English Fife
Courtesy Museum of Fine Arts, Boston

The tone of the fife must have been anything but agreeable, for Shakespeare refers to it as the "wry-necked" fife and is shocked by its ear-piercing tone quality. No wonder musicians were looking for improvements.

The road to perfection was by no means straight and well-defined. Just as with vertical flutes, all kinds of curiosities and monstrosities made brief appearances. One such oddity is shown at left, a flute in the form of a walking stick. This "walking-stick flute" is not so old as one might be inclined to assume, for this model is a late nineteenth-century specimen. It as nearly a yard long and made in three parts.

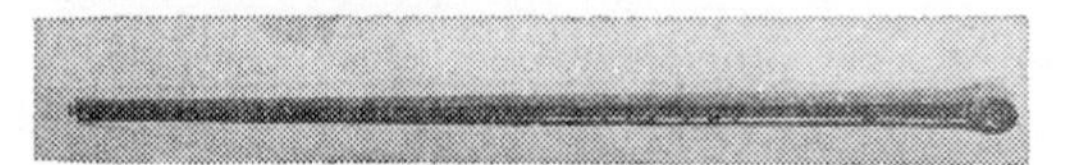

Figure 129. Walking-stick Flute
Courtesy Museum of Fine Arts, Boston

During the late Middle Ages Germany became the production center of the improved flute. From here it spread over the world under the name of *German flute.* For one thing, it was larger than the fife and had a wider bore. Still, it was chiefly a military instrument, not suited to the requirements of serious music. As before, it was constructed in one piece and could not be tuned; its size determined its pitch. To obtain the full range, flutes of various sizes had to be used. One inventory of the Stuttgart Orchestra of the sixteenth century lists thirty-five flutes, whereas the usual number in a modern symphony orchestra is four! The French evidently learned to play the flute in a more musical way than any other nation and resented the name "German" flute.

The improvements leading up to our present-day concert flute will now be taken up step by step.

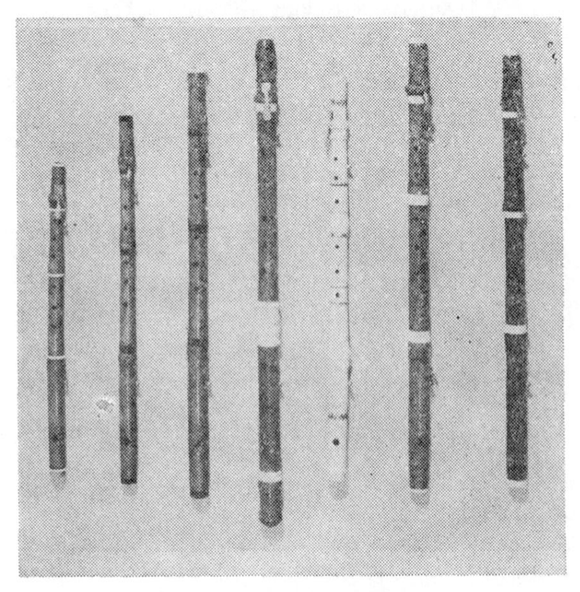

Figure 130. One-keyed Flutes
Courtesy Museum of Fine Arts, Boston

The above flutes show the first modern innovation—the key. This key, appended to the flute about 1660, added a note to the chromatic scale.

Some twenty years later the cylindrical bore was abandoned in favor of the inverted conical one similar to that of the recorder. This innovation gave the flute a softer, mellower, and smoother tone.

Next, the one-piece tube was discarded in favor of a sectional tube, so that the flute could now be tuned similarly to stringed instruments. The first sectional flutes were made of two pieces, and the six fingerholes were placed in different sections. Soon three- and four-part flutes became common. You can clearly see these sections in the above illustration.

Further experimentation resulted in a shaping of the upper part cylindrical and a conoidal shaping of the lower, whereby the tube could be shortened to produce higher notes more correctly. The three sections of the flute now were the head joint, the body, and the foot or tail. After 1700 the body was further subdivided, thus improving the intonation, and a few decades later the foot joint also received subsections.

Thus, we have come to the famous flute of the first half of the eighteenth century. It enjoyed great popularity and was considered a noble instrument. King Frederick the Great of Prussia was one of

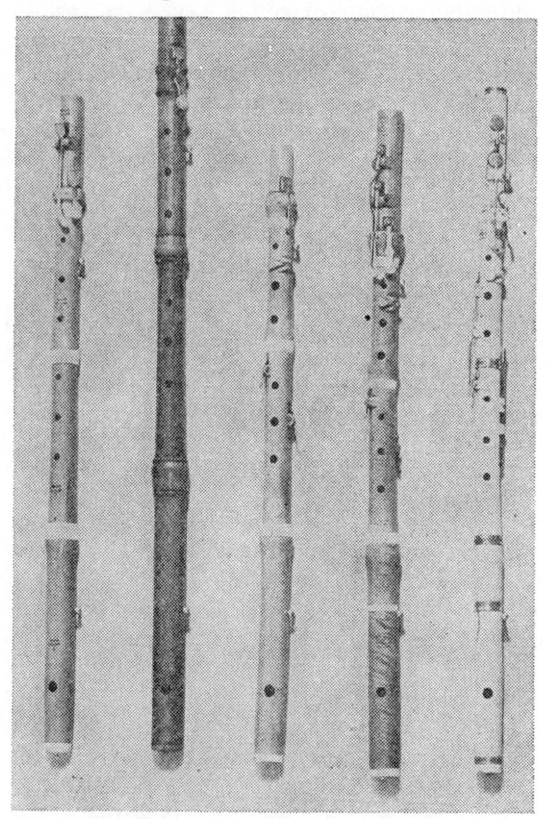

Figure 131. 2, 4, 6 and 8 Keyed Flutes
Courtesy Museum of Fine Arts, Boston

its most enthusiastic players and admirers. Still, there was room for improvement. So let us resume our march.

Just look for a moment at the flutes in Figure 131. What do you notice concerning the number of keys? They increase from two to four, then to six, and finally to eight. The thing for you to notice is the still regular spacing of the holes. Consequently the players had no end of trouble in correcting faulty pitches. (Just recall our discussion on true intonation in Chapter V).

A few attempts to correct faulty intonation are of interest. For instance, one instrument maker, in his efforts to produce the perfect flute, invented a special key to correct the difference between D# and E-flat! This was of course before Bach's "equal temperament." [2] Turning slides made their appearance. The first ones were added to the head joint, the later ones to the foot joint. Also, screw buttons were added, again for the purpose of correcting faulty intonation. Finally, special correction keys were installed.

The final answer, however, did not come until physicists had done extensive research on sound and by analyzing wave lengths and harmonics had established true frequency ratios. The German flutist, Theobald Böhm, was the first to apply these principles, and he thus revolutionized the art of flute making. Böhm created the prototype of the real concert flute. His invention embodied the following innovations, as shown in his first flute of 1832:

1. He enlarged the hitherto small fingerholes (not altogether his own conception).
2. He spaced the fingerholes with a view to obtaining correct intonation, i.e., he based the distribution of the holes on acoustical principles regardless of the player's convenience.
3. He perfected the key mechanism to such an extent that more holes could be operated than the human hand had fingers.
4. Finally, in 1846, he restored the cylindrical bore, but with a parabolic head, thereby improving the third octave.

Regarding the size of the fingerholes, it may be said that if each hole were of the same size as the bore of the tube, then the opening of one particular hole would eliminate the lower end of the tube, the distance from the embouchure to the open hole providing the complete vibrating air column. Such holes are impossible, of course, not only because they are impractical, but also because they would prevent the formation of any new tones obtained by using several holes simultaneously. In other words, there would have to be a separate hole for each semitone or thirty-six holes for the complete scale of three octaves. Böhm, however, made the holes as large as possible.

Böhm's model of 1846 (1847?) was remarkable not only for the pure and even tone of all its notes, but also for much fuller and

---

[2] Anyone looking at the piano keyboad finds that there are no special keys for flats and sharps, a sharp note equaling the corresponding higher flat note—*c# = d-flat, f# = g-flat,* etc. Theoretically there is a difference between such notes, however. Now, Bach conceived the idea to eliminate these triffling differences. To do this, he composed forty-eight preludes which he called *The Well-Tempered Clavier,* in which he made a sharp equal to the flat of the upper adjacent key. Musicians accepted such scales, and ever since the use of the well-tempered scale, the one we have in our pianos, has remained the universal practice.

more powerful quality of tone. Naturally, some flute players resented Böhm's invention, preferring the thinner but more delicate and sweet tone of the older flute. German flutists especially were reluctant to adopt the new instrument. But the large orchestras of this new era could not do without the brilliant Böhm flute. Our latest models are fundamentally Böhm's design.

Efforts to produce the perfect flute resulted in still newer forms. Flutes with a conical bore and Böhm's mechanism appeared, such as the reform flute of 1895. This particular flute was further improved in 1912. Today's models, however, are back to the cylindrical

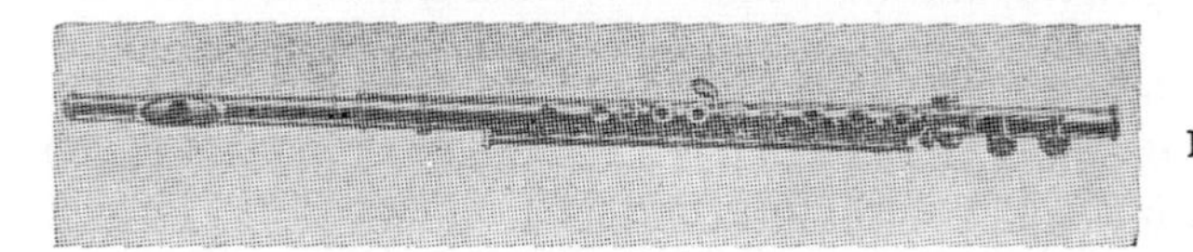

Figure 132
Reform Flute of 1895

form. As was stated before, they are fundamentally the Böhm flute, although strictly speaking they are Heckel-Kalaphon-Böhm instruments.

The *concert flute,* an indispensable member of all orchestras, has a compass of three chromatic octaves. All notes are produced and are remarkably pure. The flute is the most agile wood instrument—it is a "quick" instrument, capable of rapid runs, trills, embellishments, and so forth. It is equally effective in *legato* and *staccato* passages. Furthermore, repeated notes may be rapidly executed by "double-tonguing." In addition, the flute is a highly personal instrument, allowing the player to express his personality through his playing, for it responds readily to the slightest variations in blowing. Marked crescendos and diminuendos, however, are not readily obtained, and great variations in dynamics are generally not expected of the flute. Incidentally, the flute is by no means a dramatic instrument. Just the same, it is a melodious instrument of unsurpassed beauty.

The tone quality of the flute varies with its range. In this connection it is customary to speak of three registers. The lower register, including the notes from *c'* to *a',* is very rich and beautiful; when played loudly these tones may even support the string quality of tone, depending upon the skill of the player, producing as many as six to eight harmonics, or they may be made to resemble distant trumpets. Since, however, these lower notes are easily obscured by other instruments, the accompaniment, if any, must be very light.

The middle register, extending from *a'* to *a",* is best suited to quiet melodic work, especially lyric passages. Again, the accompaniment must be light.

The upper register possesses a clear, bright tone, brilliant, bird-like, with considerable penetrating power.

Theoretically the flute is capable of producing all the ordinary harmonics. In practice very few overtones are produced. When played very softly, overtones are scarcely perceptible. Even in loud passages there are only traces of a few overtones. Consequently, the tone of the flute is simple and clear.

We may regard the flute as the coloratura of the orchestra. As an accompaniment to the coloratura voice it is unsurpassed. Listen to such selections as *Lo, Here the Gentle Lark* by Bishop, *Caro Nome* from Verdi's *Rigoletto,* and the *Mad Scene* from Donizetti's *Lucia*—just to mention a few excerpts—and you will be astonished and delighted at the interplay of flute and voice.

Played solo the flute likewise has a prominent place among the instruments. Bizet's *Minuetto* from his *L'Arlésienne Suite No. 2* is as good an example as any.

The flute in the orchestra is a must. No composer ever dared or wanted to ignore it. Flute cadenzas are quite the thing. The flute is found in practically every symphonic composition of any length.[3]

### *The Piccolo*

The piccolo is a miniature flute taking its name from the Italian *piccolo flauto,* a little flute. It is just about half the size of the regular flute and sounds therefore an octave higher. Its compass of three chromatic octaves extends far above the human voice, suggesting a kind of supernatural force. Like the flute, the piccolo is extremely agile.

The tone of the piccolo is shrill and piercing. This tone quality makes it a suitable instrument to increase the brightness of the woodwind section. Because the lower register is weak and of little effect, its tones are replaced as a rule by the second octave of the flute. The second register imparts brilliancy to *fortissimo* orchestral passages, extending the range of the flute. But the real characteristics of the piccolo are revealed by its third octave. These high notes are so shrill and piercing that one single piccolo can hold its own against the full orchestra. Music of a stormy or terrifying nature are well within the scope of this little flute. Generally, however, the piccolo is used to increase the brightness of the woodwind section of the orchestra.

---

[3] Bach's and Handel's sonatas for flute and harpsichord feature probably the recorder, not the flute. Mozart's flute, of course, did not measure up to our own, so it is the more amazing how these masters managed to get along so well.

For the sake of completeness it must be stated that in addition to the concert flute and the piccolo other flutes are occasionally still used. Thus, there still exists the *alto flute,* known also as *flute d'amour* (love flute); the *voice flute,* which uses a thin membrane for causing vibrations; the *bass flute,* and the *Giorgi flute.* None of these flutes are of much importance.

Figure 133
BBC Symphony Orchestra Flute Players
Courtesy BBC Broadcasting House

CHAPTER VIII

# REED INSTRUMENTS

Reed instruments are pipes equipped with reeds in their mouthpieces. The term *reed* in this case is derived from the material out of which the thin, elastic tongue is made. Various materials have been used in the construction of this vibrator, among them cane, wood, or metal, but the reed made out of certain species of cane growing in southern Europe on the shores of the Mediterranean is most satisfactory and generally in use in the modern reed instruments.

There are several forms of reed instruments, of which the following three are important: (1) the single-reed, (2) the double-

**Figure 134. Reeds Cut from Cane**

reed, and (3) the free-reed. The free reed vibrates in a frame without beating against it; it is found in the reed and pipe organs. The other two types of reeds are found in the woodwinds, the single beating reed in clarinets and the double reed in oboes and bassoons.

### *Ancient Oboes*

Both single- and double-reed instruments are of great antiquity. They are indeed almost as ancient as the primitive flute. There is good evidence that the double-reeds are the older of the two. A blade of grass held between the tips and base of both thumbs may have served as the prototype of the later reeds, inasmuch as stiff and sharp blades did find certain applications in the older pipes. Not much is known about the very first of such instruments, although it is known that they are of Semitic origin. Since their tone is more resonant, fuller and richer in quality, reed instruments always have had precedence over the open-mouth flute. The numerous pipes mentioned in the Bible are usually reed pipes, even though they have been translated as flutes.

The significance of the reed instruments is not so clear as that of the flute. With the Hebrews reeds had the power to induce a state of trance. The Syrians employed them in orgiastic rites of Cybele, the mother-goddess. Reed pipes were also used during festive occasions, as well as during mourning ceremonies such as funerals. The Moslems used them in their armies as an incentive to victory. All these facts once more bear out the theory that early musical instruments were not invented for aesthetic effects but rather for some immediate practical use.

Ancient reed pipes were made of cane; they had no special mouthpieces and were played in a downward position. Up to the second century A.D. they were cylindrical. Later models assumed the conoidal shape. The question now arises whether they were oboes or clarinets. As far as is known they were either double-or single-reeds, but generally known as oboes. However, the name should not mislead us, for they were by no means identical with our modern instruments of that name.

The earliest definite mention of the oboe is found in Mesopotamian scriptures of 2000 B.C. Thirteen hundred years later we find the oboe in Egypt, where it evidently had replaced the flute. After 1000 B.C. the oboe dominated the ancient world.

It is a curious but significant fact that reed pipes were used in pairs. Two pipes of slightly different size were played by the same player (the flute was always single). Efforts to account for this method of pipe playing have not yielded satisfactory results, but

Figure 135
Double Reed Pipes

certain it is that one of the pipes played a monotonous drone while the other chanted a sort of melody. The principle of the drone was later embodied in the bagpipes, but one hestitates to see in it a conscious effort at creating harmony.

It is further assumed that the divergent pipes were double-reeds, and the parallel running pipes, tied together, single-reed instruments. The Greeks called their double pipes *aulos,* the Romans *tibias.* Both terms are frequently but erroneously translated as flutes. These pipes must have been hard to blow.

A close inspection of the middle illustration in Figure 135 reveals a leather tongue tied over the mouth of the player. This leather strip was perforated in the middle allowing the pipe to be inserted into the mouth and at the same time affording protection to lips and cheeks. No wonder the ancient Greeks and Romans relegated oboe playing to their slaves.

The tone of ancient oboes is described as sharp and clear, exciting, harsh sounding, and (mainly according to the poets) as sweet, high-pitched, and plaintive. Such contrasting attributes can only be explained by the assumption that those oboes were far from being standardized and must have been made in various sizes of length and bore. Early attempts to improve and perfect the instrument were frequent. Up to the fifth century B.C. oboes had from three to four fingerholes; later more were added until special contrivances, such as collars, were installed to stop and half-stop the holes so that the player could operate as many as fifteen finger-holes!

The student of ancient history will find many references to pipes. They were used not only during religious ceremonies, but also for festive occasions, amusements, and entertainments. They were used as well for stimulating laborers; in Egypt, for instance, it was not uncommon to find a pipe player chanting the pipe for toiling field workers.

### *The Shawm Family*

During the twelfth and thirteenth centuries (according to some authorities the fourteenth), the "oboe" made its entrance into Europe via Sicily due to Arabic and Saracenic influences. The prototype of the above is the Arabian *zamr,* shown in Figure 136. The zamr had a large conical bore and a wide bell; its double reed was wholly inserted into the mouth of the player, so that control over the tone color was lost. The zamr consequently lacked personal expression.

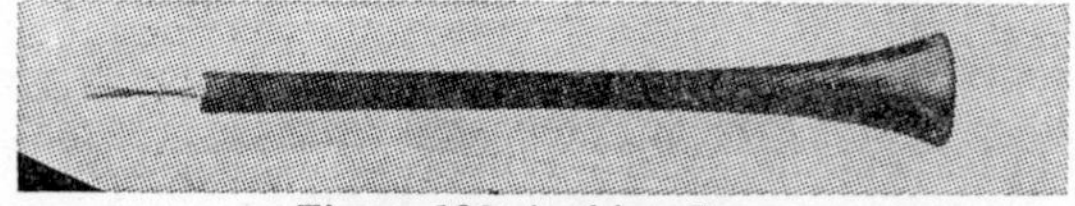

Figure 136. Arabian Zamr

There seems to be some confusion in the naming of the *shawms.* Historically they are important since several instruments have developed from them. The modern oboe and the English horn are derived from them; some writers also attribute the origin of the clarinet to this source, although this seems farfetched. The bassoon's origin, contrary to popular assumption, is not attributable to shawms, for it developed parallel to the bass shawms.

Here we see four typical shawms of the seventeenth century type:

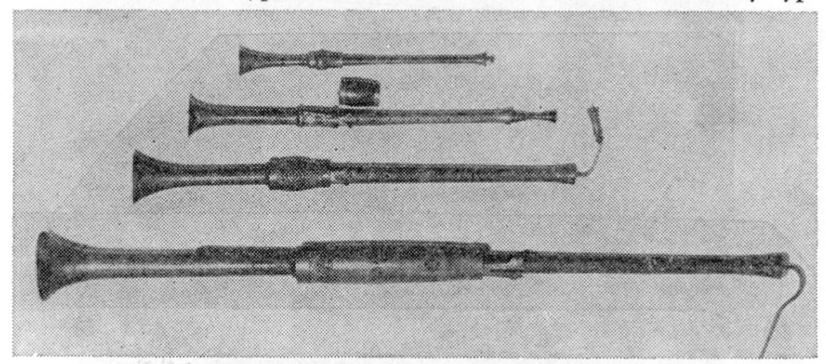

Figure 137. 17th Century Type Shawms
Courtesy Museum of Fine Arts, Boston

the treble, alto, tenor, and bass shawms. The bass shawm was also known as the *bombarde,* this name appearing as *pommer* or *bomhart* as well. Some of the characteristic features of shawms are the following:

(1) There are seven fingerholes in the front. The lowest hole is operated by a key mechanism and covered with a sort of sleeve, known as a *fontanelle.* The alto shawm in the above illustration has its fontanelle removed and shows the key mechanism.

(2) The reed was affixed to the tube by means of a brass extension which had the shape of an inverted cone; it is clearly marked by a white line in the tenor and bass shawms above.

(3) A turned piece of wood (known as *pirouette)* partly surrounds the reed and permits the player to take into his mouth only a portion of the reed. In the smaller specimens the wooden tube seems to enclose the reed completely, while in the bass shawn it is lacking altogether. Pirouettes were discarded in Western countries, but they are still in use in the Orient.

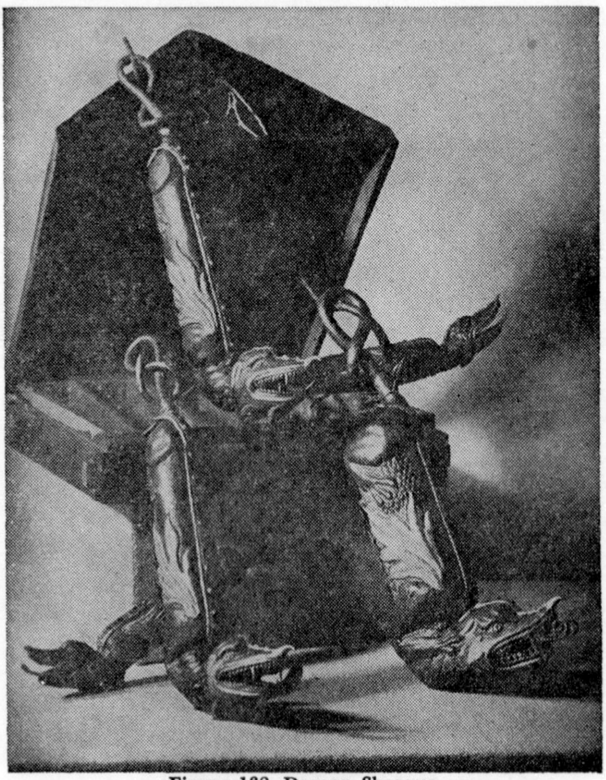

Figure 138. Dragon Shawms
Courtesy Kunsthistorisches Museum, Vienna

The tone of the shawm has been described as shrill and bleating, suitable with trumpets and percussion instruments, and comparable with the voice of a cackling goose! Shakespeare frequently refers to the *hautbois,* the French name for the oboe. These Shakespearean hautbois must have been shawms, as the real oboes are of a later date. Shawms were mostly pastoral instruments. By the nineteenth century shawms had nine keys and were no longer heavy-built, but had acquired graceful lines and rounded bells.

### *Double-Reed Oddities*

The real oboe did not emerge from thes hawn overnight. As always, musicians experimented. Some of their results must be mentioned here. First of all, there are the rare and unique instruments preserved in the Kunsthistorisches Museum of Vienna. These fanciful double-reeds formed a so-called family. They were known as *tartoelds.* The body of a tartoeld was of yellow brass and painted in green, red, and gold. The dragon's twisted tail contained the reed. The main tube was concealed inside the dragon's belly and was cylindrical, coiled like a tube in a gas heater. Evidently in this case not all was gold that glittered, for these dragon shawms never gained any importance and their musical value was questionable.

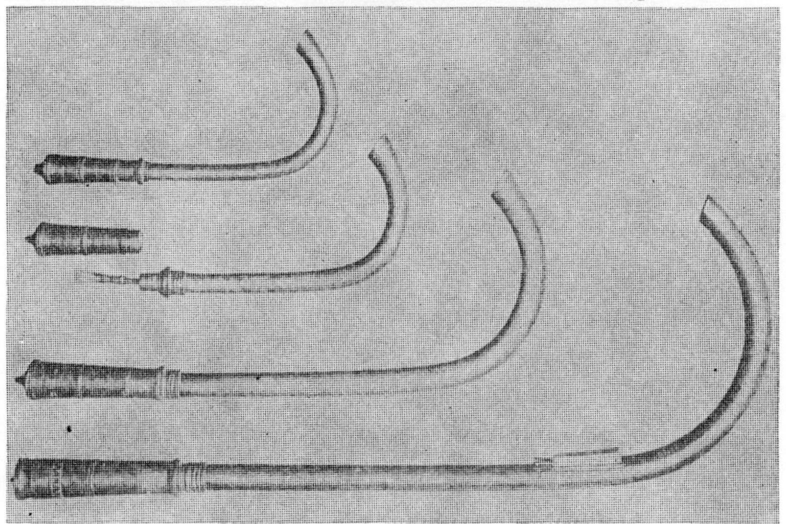

Figure 139. Cromornes, Early 17th Century
Courtesy Nef, Geschichte unserer Musikinstrumente

The *cromorne* and the *rackett* come next. The cromornes came in families. The shape of the instrument is curved, for which reason the Germans called it *Krummhorn,* meaning a curved or crooked horn. *Krummhorn* was later changed to *cromorne* by the English and French. One of the instruments illustrated in Figure 139 shows the double reed with the wooden cap removed. This wooden wind cap was a characteristic feature of the cromorne. It concealed the reeds entirely, and the player never touched them while playing. Hence again we encounter a purely mechanical instrument.

Incidentally, the cromorne is the oldest European reed instrument with such a wind chest, going back to the fourteenth and fifteenth centuries. You may note from the illustrations that the largest specimen also has a fontanelle like the shawms. But the tone color of the cromorne was softer and darker than that of the shawm. Cromornes were in use in Europe up to the seventeenth century.

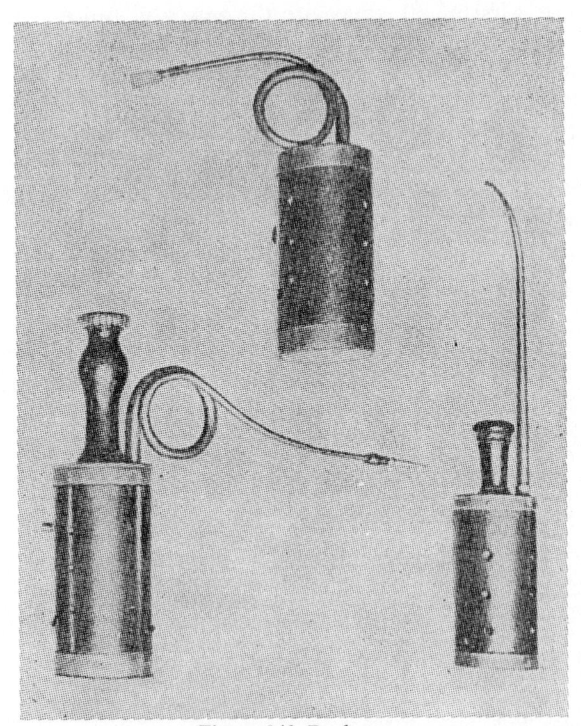

Figure 140. Racketts
Courtesy Nef, Geschichte unserer Musikinstrumente

The *rackett* (also *rankett*) was a freakish instrument. Despite its shortness it had a deep tone. In the first place, it was a closed cylinder; hence, its pitch was an octave lower than that of the corresponding open pipe. Secondly, the cylinder consisted of many channels, for it was pierced lengthwise in such a way that all the channels, usually nine or ten of them, were connected at top and bottom and formed one continuous channel for unbroken air passage. This explains why the French called the rackett a *sausage* and the English a *sausage bassoon.* The mouthpiece protruded above the block, thereby adding to the length of the air column. The center piece on top was the lower end of the air pipe, i.e., the exit. The tone of the rackett was somewhat thin, reedy, and muffled.

Figure 141. Courtaud
Courtesy Museum of Fine Arts, Boston

Finally, one more curious specimen of an oboelike instrument merits mention here, the *courtaud.* It is worthy of note because it had a U-shaped air column formed by two long bores which were joined at the bottom by a cross-bore. The extra holes were stoppered by wooden plugs, seen protruding from the sides of the tubes. The length of the total air column in this instrument was nearly four feet.

### *The Oboe*

During the seventeenth century the French developed the prototype of the modern oboe out of the older shawms. The present-day form of the oboe is rather recent, for it was not until 1880 that Böhm's mechanism for the flute was adapted to the oboe.

Compared to the shawm, the tube of the modern oboe is narrower and is conoidal, and the lower end has a small bell not like a

Figure 142
BBC Symphony Orchestra Oboe Players
Courtesy BBC Broadcasting House

trumpet's. The mechanism is so complex that certain notes can be produced in different ways. In spite of this complexity, the oboe is a fairly agile instrument. Its pitch is stable, and it takes a very delicate adjustment to change it. Hence this instrument has the privilege of tuning the standard A for the other instruments of the orchestra. It is made of cocus, rosewood, or ebony. For the convenience of the player it is made in three sections and can readily be taken apart and reassembled.

The oboe has a penetrating and nasal tone, yet it is capable of great musical expression. It can produce up to twelve or more overtones. When the high harmonics become too prominent, it acquires a piercing quality, and is best substituted by the flute. The lower notes again can be rich and admirable when played *mf*. Between these two extremes the oboe plays a noble role in the orchestra. It is essentially a melodic instrument. Dialogues between flute and oboe or clarinet and oboe are delightful, and no music of pastoral nature can dispense with such woodwinds. Symphonic music abounds in beautiful passages for oboe, and no special reference to particular selections need be made here. If the flute is the coloratura, the oboe is the lyric soprano of the woodwind section. It certainly adds considerable color to the orchestral tone.

The oboe is a fatiguing instrument to play, since only very light

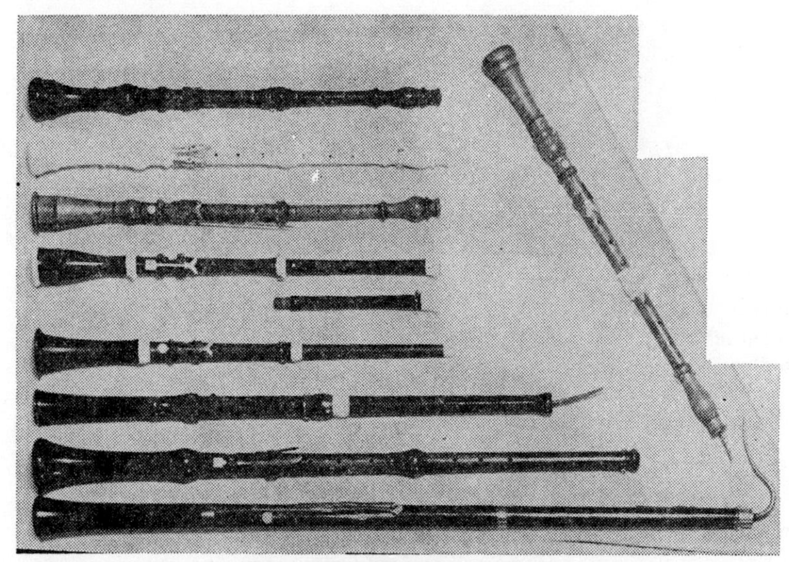

Figure 143. 18th Century Oboes
Courtesy Museum of Fine Arts, Boston

breath pressure is required to set the air column in vibration. Consequently, the player must hold his breath and take frequent breathing spells. Yet we do not ask for slaves to play it; on the contrary, oboe players are highly esteemed members of the orchestra.

Eighteenth- and nineteenth-century oboes still bear a close resemblance to shawms. Most of them still have their reeds concealed, and the seventh hole is operated by a key without the fontanelle. Pear wood, boxwood, maple, and ebony were used in their construction. The range varied with size from high treble to an octave below middle *c*. These were the oboes of Mozart and his colleagues. One wonders what they would have achieved with our modern oboes, clarinets, horns, and other instruments.

Bach's favorite oboe was the *oboe d'amore,* the alto oboe. In pitch it was a third lower than the common oboe, and hence somewhat larger in size. It enjoyed great popularity until the middle of the eighteenth century. Today it has been revived to some extent.

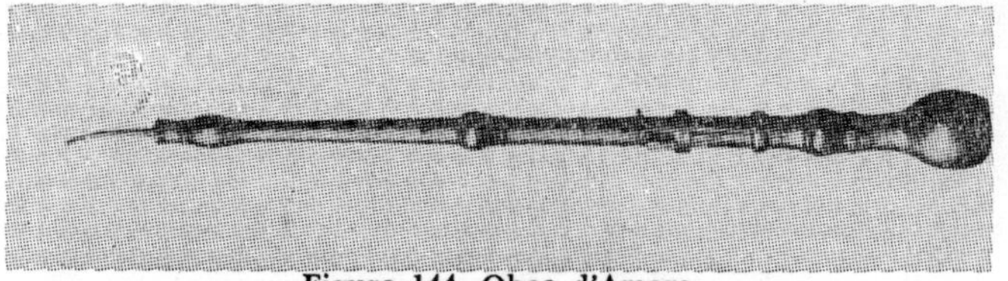

Figure 144. Oboe d'Amore

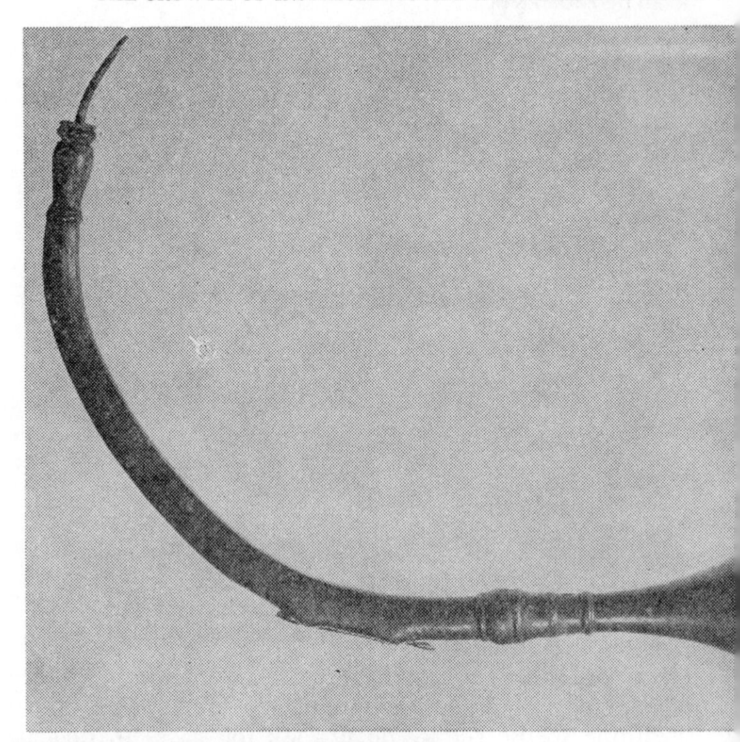

Figure 145
Oboe da Caccia,
18th Century
Courtesy Museum of
Fine Arts, Boston

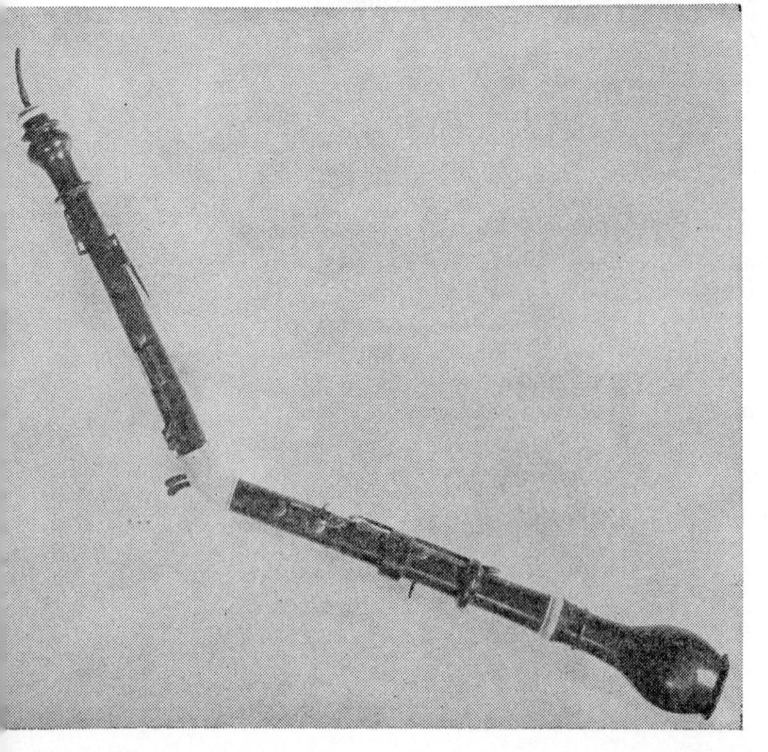

Figure 146
English Horn, Vienna,
ca. 1835
Courtesy Museum of
Fine Arts, Boston

In the performance of Bach's *Mass in B Minor,* for instance, this oboe is still used. Its tone is of soft quality, beautiful and warm, accounting probably for the name of the instrument, the "love oboe" or, in German, the "oboe with the love-foot" (*Liebesfuss*). The oboe d'amore is the link between the present-day oboe and the English horn.

In Italy the oboe d'amore assumed a curved form and was known as the *oboe da caccia* (Fig. 145). It had a strident, heavy tone. The oboe da caccia is the direct forerunner of the *English horn,* more properly called *cor anglais* (Fig. 146). "English horn" is just a misnomer, for the instrument is neither English nor a horn. It is a double-reed, just like the oboe. Judging from its appearance as shown in Figure 146, "cor anglais" must have meant "angled horn." Others derive its name from the popularity the instrument enjoyed in England.

The cor anglais is pitched a fifth lower than the oboe and is really just an enlarged oboe. It lacks the gaiety of the oboe, but is nobler and richer in tone quality. It blends well with the other members of the woodwind family; it also doubles violas and cellos

Figure 147. Modern Cor Anglais

effectively. It is chiefly used for solo work in melancholy and expressive passages. One needs only to listen to the shepherd's call in Wagner's *Tristan and Isolde,* where the dying Tristan is longing for his Isolde, to realize the almost heavenly beauty of this instrument. The *Largo* from Dvorak's *The New World Symphony* is equally famous. (You may have heard this passage sung as "Goin' Home. . . .") The third oboe player of the symphony orchestra is usually also the English horn player. (See Figure 142.)

Since the bells, the lower ends of the reed instruments, are partially responsible for the tone quality, the above diagram is included to point out the difference in their shapes. You can see that the modern oboe and the English horn differ not only in size but also in the shape of the bell. Similarly, the difference between the oboe d'amore and the oboe da caccia are shown.

Attempts to construct a bass or baritone oboe have resulted in the production of the *sarrusophone,* named after the inventor Sarrus, who designed it in 1863 for the French army. Sarrus was anticipated by some Viennese instrument makers, but he created a

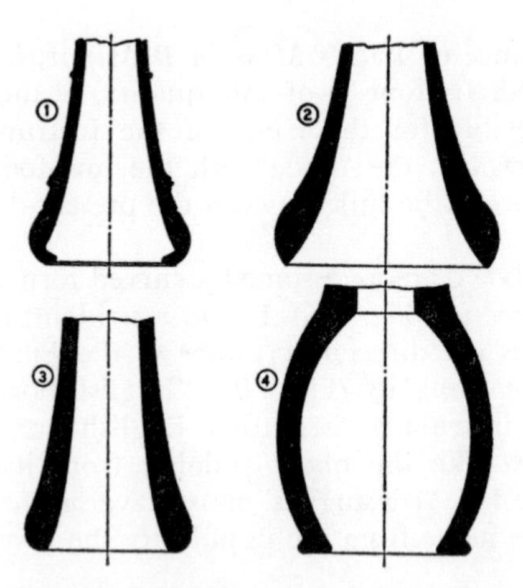


Figure 148. Bells of Double Reed Instruments
1. Oboe bell, old type. 2. Oboe da caccia bell. 3. Oboe bell, modern.
4. Pear-shaped bell (*Liebesfuss*) used on the *obove d'amore,* English horn, and the 'hautbois baryton'
Courtesy Museum of Fine Arts, Boston

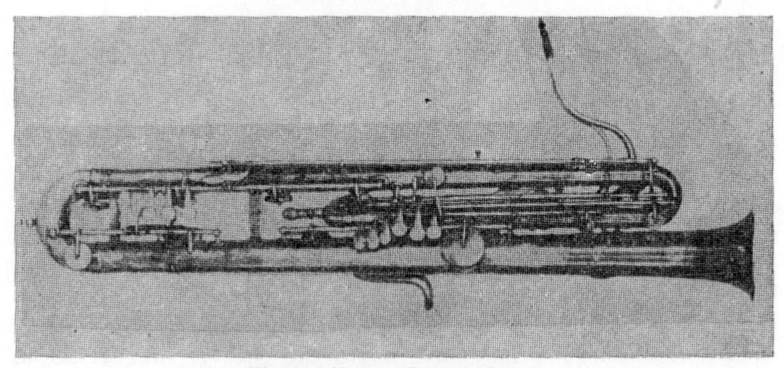

Figure 149. Bass Sarrusophone

whole family of such instruments, beginning with a sopranino and winding up with a contrabassoon. They were supposed to take the place of oboes and bassoons, but with the exception of the bass oboe, they remained mere experiments. The tone of the sarrusophone lacks the delicateness of the wooden double-reed instruments.

The sarrusophone of our illustration has survived, although it is but rarely used. It is a brass instrument with a double reed mouthpiece. Saint-Saëns thought highly of it and used it in several works. Other composers have followed his example.

Figure 150. Bassoon Players of the BBC Symphony Orchestra
Courtesy BBC Broadcasting House

*Bassoons*

The *bassoon* is the bass of the oboe family. As we have it today, it is a slightly conical tube bent upon itself to facilitate handling. The straight tube would require all of eight feet in length. Whose brilliant idea it was to double the tube and thus make it more compact is unknown. It is also uncertain whether there is any connection between the rackett and bassoon, although the name *sausage bassoon* would lead us to believe so.

As was mentioned before, and contrary to popular belief, the bassoon did not even develop from the shawms but evolved parallel to them. So the direct forerunner of the bassoon is hard to find. The assumption that the *phagotus* was partly responsible for the birth of the bassoon, however, merits some credit, and a short discussion of the phagotus is therefore now in order.

The first phagotus is credited to the Italian Afranio, who invented it at the beginning of the sixteenth century. As seen from the illustration, this "bassoon" consists of three wooden cylinders. The middle one was purely ornamental, which of course means that it had no function musically and could easily be left out in later models. Each of the other cylinders is divided into an upper and lower chamber, the upper one containing two parallel air passages

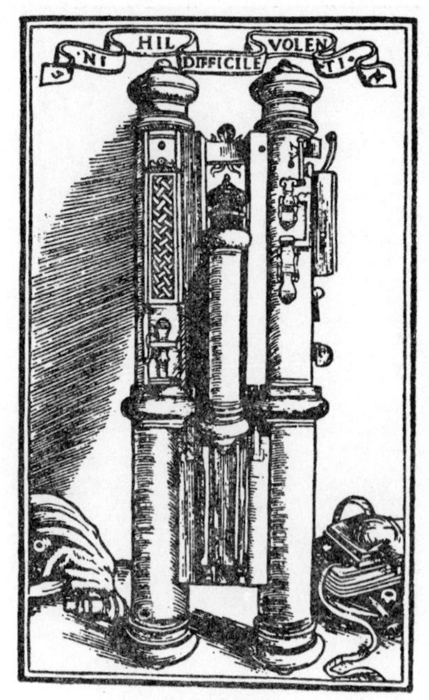


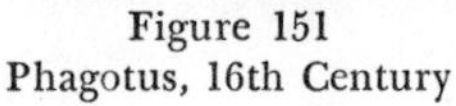
Figure 151
Phagotus, 16th Century

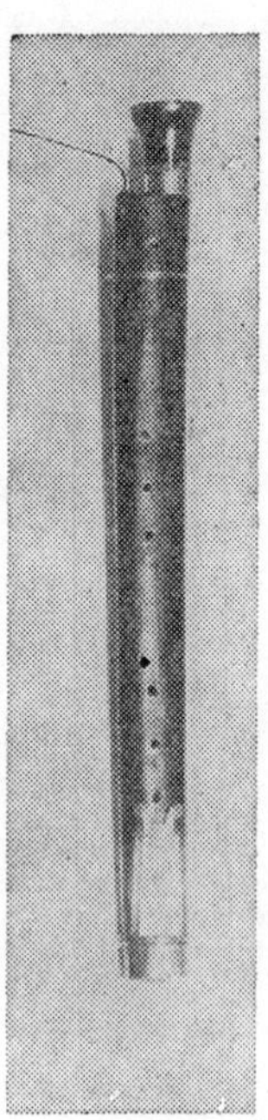
Figure 152. Curtall, Early 17th Century
Courtesy Museum of Fine Arts, Boston

joined at the top. The lower half contained one single reed in each chamber.

The phagotus was actually an attempt to improve a certain type of bagpipe. It was played by means of bellows held under the right arm and an air reservoir held under the left arm. Both the bellows and the air reservoir are shown in the illustration. The instrument itself was held on the knee for playing. The meaning of the word *phagotus* is somewhat obscure, but the most plausible explanation is found in "a bundle of tubes or sticks." The Germans still call their bassoons *Fagott*. Thus even though the phagotus was only remotely similar to the bassoon, instrument makers may have been stimulated by it to evolve the true bassoon.

The first bassoon (sixteenth century), known also as the *dulcian* (or dulzian), was made of one block of wood. It had two longitudinal channels which were joined at the lower end to form a continuous tube for the air passage. The mouthpiece as well as the bell of the lower end protruded from the upper end. Such a construction makes the bassoon a unique instrument, for no other instrument brings both ends so close together. The English called this bassoon *curtall,* a word derived from the Low German *Kortholt,* meaning *short wood,* apparently signifying that the tube was shortened.

During the seventeenth century the bassoon assumed its present-day shape. If you compare the curtall above with the first bassoon shown in Figure 153 you will note the transformation. The long single block of wood was shortened and two additional tubes were inserted into it. Thus the original double-cylinder block became the *butt* (see Figure 91), the tube connecting the butt with the mouthpiece the *wing*, and the other tube the *long joint*. All three parts are clearly discernible in the first example of our illustration.

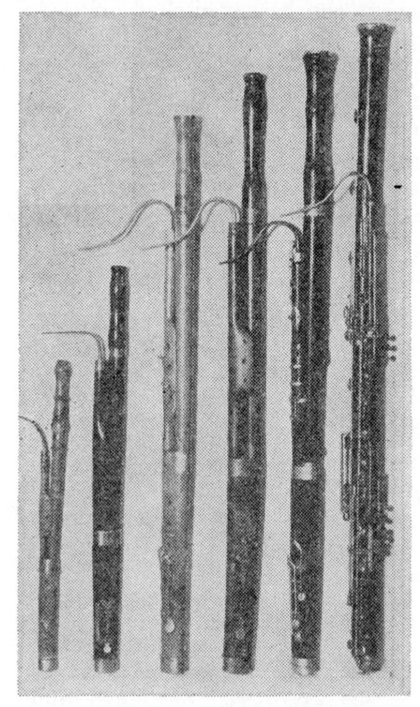

Figure 153. 18th and 19th Century Bassoons
Courtesy Museum of Fine Arts, Boston

In addition to these three parts there is the so-called *crook*, a metal tube which connects the double reed and the wing. The lower opening has a certain constriction, which reduces the bore and thus makes the size of the tube available for the air passage conform with the opening of the fingerholes. Without this constriction there would be a pronounced difference in quality between the tone produced by the fingerholes and the one produced by the open lower end.

The bassoon has remained an imperfect instrument. Attempts to improve it resulted, for instance, in the model shown at the right in Figure 153. This particular bassoon is equipped with a Böhm mechanism and certain other innovations. Its mechanics are now perfect, but the characteristic bassoon tone is lost; it has become more of a sarrusophone. History has taught musicians that the substance of the bassoon cannot be altered without sacrificing its beauty of tone, so they are reconciled to the price they have to pay: the high degree of musicianship demanded for proper playing. Instrument makers are still attempting to improve some details in the make-up of the bassoon.

Following the fashion of the times, bassoons were made in complete families. We see such a family in the first four models of Figure 153. The first two of these are the higher-pitched ones, the *baritone* and the *tenoroon*. The others are *contrabasses*. The former were built up to the middle of the nineteenth century, afterwards falling into oblivion. Rossini may have written his famous cor anglais solo of the *William Tell Overture* for the tenoroon.

The original bassoons were unwieldy and ill-proportioned. The fingerholes were too close together for the size of the instrument. The bassoon was therefore used only to reinforce the bass in the orchestra. With later perfections, seen in Figure 150, the bassoon obtained an independent position. Mozart wrote melodious passages for the bassoon with the flute at two octaves' distance. Beethoven also wrote passages for it. Today the bassoon has gained considerable importance as a solo instrument.

The natural function of the bassoon is, of course, to provide the bass of the woodwind group. Its tone is somewhat narrow and compressed—now nasal, now penetrating, capable of a dry cracking humor. So you need not be surprised if you find somebody calling the bassoon the clown of the orchestra. One need only to listen to the *do', sol, do* and *do', sol, sol, do* of the bassoon in the third movement of Beethoven's *Pastoral Symphony* to have this verified with a chuckle. But why not tolerate a joker?

The bassoon blends well with the oboes, clarinets, and horns. Two bassoons and two horns played softly together are a good substitute for four horns; two bassoons and two calarinets blend admirably in four-part harmony. In short, the bassoon is a splendid complement to the other members of the woodwind family. (Always keep in mind that it is a bass instrument.) In spite of its size, the bassoon is quite agile and rivals the flute in the rendition of staccato passages. As with the other woodwinds, the tone is not even throughout its compass, but varies with the upper, lower, and middle registers.

### *The Double Bassoon*

The double bassoon or contrabassoon is exactly what its name implies: a *double* bassoon; it has double the length of the ordinary bassoon. Its air column is some sixteen feet in length, and the tube is folded upon itself not twice but four times. (Some of the latest models are folded even six times.) The pitch of the double bassoon is an octave lower than that of the ordinary bassoon, which makes it the deepest-toned instrument of the orchestra.

The first double bassoon made its appearance in 1618. As its intonation was rather faulty, it was but sparingly used. In his *Creation* Haydn prescribed a single note for it to create the impression of a heavy and crushing burden. Even today its function is to add weight to the bass rather than to carry melody. It is neither wieldy nor agile, and the parts given to it must be simple to execute. Passages below the *mf* range are practically impossible to play; for louder passages, however, the instrument is an excellent strengthener.

The double bassoon is to the bassoon as the contrabass is to the cello. Before its time, the serpent provided the deep bass of the orchestra.

### *Single-Reeds*

As has been shown already, single-reeds are very old. Here we are concerned with single-reeds as they emerged before the evolution of the clarinets. Although practically obsolete today, covered single-reeds used to be quite important. We have met such covered-up reeds in the krummhorn (Figure 151). Among the covered-up

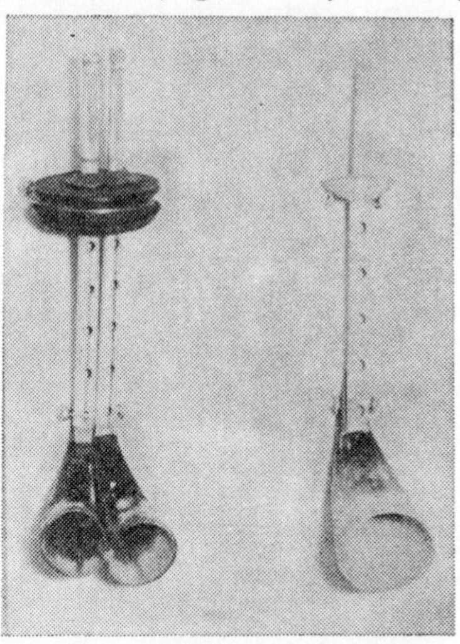

**Figure 154**
**Single and Double Hornpipes**
**Courtesy Museum of Fine Arts, Boston**

single-reed instruments we find first of all the single and double *hornpipes.* The single hornpipe consisted of a reed tube with five equally spaced fingerholes. The bell added to the tube was made of the tip of a cow's horn. The double hornpipe was similar in construction, but, as the name indicates, had two pipes with two separate bells. (Double pipes, as will be recalled, also date from early times.) Both these horns were rather small, the overall length being about ten inches only.

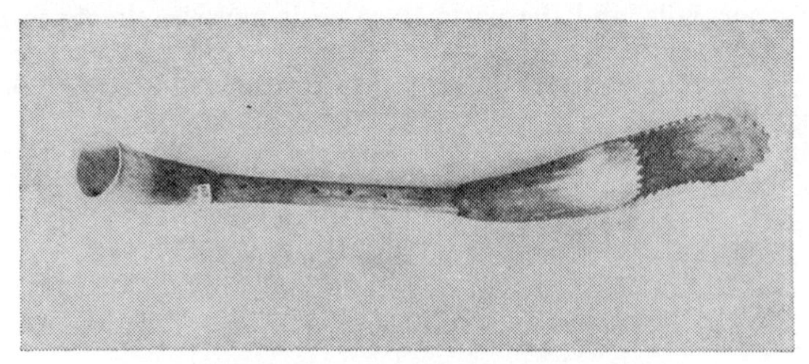

Figure 155. Pibgorn, a Horn Pipe, Welsh, 18th Century
Courtesy Metropolitan Museum of Art, New York

The Welsh *pibgorn* is a larger type of a hornpipe, being some sixteen inches long. The resemblance to a clarinet is not too obvious, but there is a distinct connection between the ancient Chinese clarinet (which had its reed covered with a cap of oxhorn) and the pibgorn. The pibgorn had a small straw beating reed but no special mouthpiece. The large circular opening at the top was pressed firmly against the lips and thus formed the air chamber. Note the serrated edges of the two unequal lips of the bell. The tone of the pibgorn was very pleasant.

Scotland came forth with yet another hornpipe, the *stock-horn.* A close inspection will show you that the holes are pairs instead of single. The reason is that the tube had a double bore. You will also note that the front of the tube is partly flattened and nicely em-

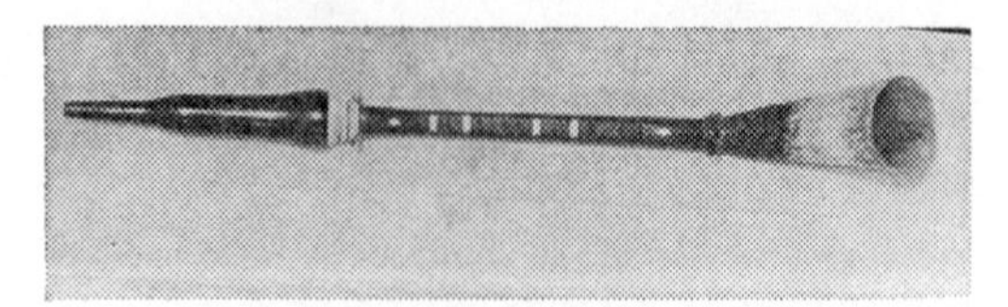

Figure 156. Stock-and-horn, Scotland, 19th Century
Courtesy Museum of Fine Arts, Boston

bellished with inlaid bars and diamonds. The back was also partially flattened. There are seven pairs of holes in the front and two thumbholes in the back. The bell is also a cowhorn. The mouthpiece, covered with a wooden cap, has two single straw reeds. The total length of the stock-horn is about twenty-two inches.

Hornpipes were peasants' and shepherds' instruments. Their musical value is questionable. At the end of the eighteenth century they were already rare. Thus the poet Robert Burns had great difficulty in obtaining a "stock-and-horn," but finally in 1794 he was successful. In a letter to a friend of his he rejoices over his fortune in obtaining the instrument, but at the same time complains "that we can make little of it." It may have been the workmanship. But small wonder, for the covered reeds make the hornpipe a mechanical instrument (see the krummhorn), and what can one expect of the spacing of the fingerholes? We may say, however, that the germ of the clarinet was hidden in the hornpipes, although it would be too farfetched to see in them the direct forerunners.

Another application of the single reed is found in the *signal horn* of Argentina. Made of a cow's horn, the tip was faced off so as to provide a small cavity similar to the clarinet mouthpiece. The reed

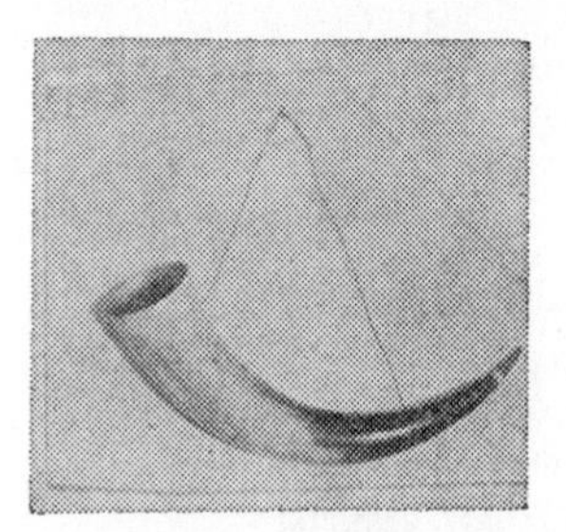

Figure 157
Signal Horn with One Reed, Argentina
Courtesy Museum of Fine Arts, Boston

was of very thin bone, tied by a silk thread. The cap covering is not shown. As the name implies it was not a musical instrument at all, for it found its use merely as a horn for signaling.

## *The Clarinets*

The primitive clarinet, like the oboe and flute, is of great antiquity. The early Egyptians had their clarinets made of cane. These one-reed pipes had neither special mouthpieces nor extra reeds, the upper end simply providing both by a three-sided slit with the fourth or lower side providing the vibrating part.

The origin of the clarinet is unknown. When it first entered higher civilization it appeared as a double instrument. The "double" in such a clarinet must not be given the same connotation as "double" in a double bassoon or in aulos, for the double clarinet was a short double tube about one foot in length. It was a two-in-one clarinet, as it were, the two tubes being glued and tied together alongside each other. Each pipe had from four to six equidistant fingerholes arranged symmetrically, and consequently the intonation left much to be desired.

Such a double clarinet is still to be found in India but with the mouthpiece concealed in a calabash similar to the later cromorne. The early Egyptian model of the double clarinet has survived five thousand years without the slightest modification (cf. the shofar).

The modern clarinet is the youngest member of the orchestra. It was never really invented, although some authorities are willing to concede this feat to the Denners of Nuremberg. We may say that

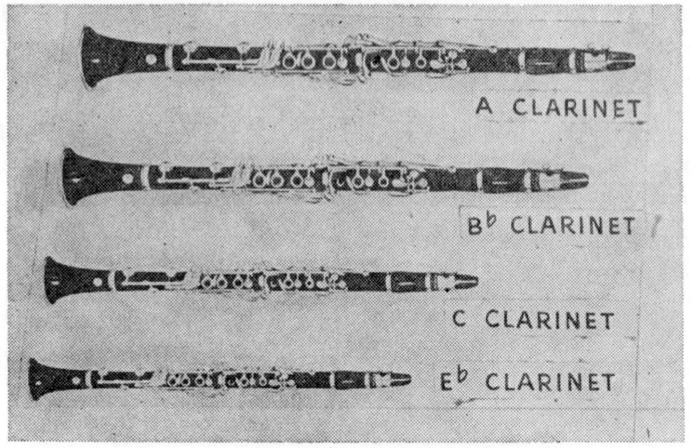


Figure 158, Clarinets
Courtesy C. G. Conn Ltd., Elkhart, Indiana

the clarinet just evolved from other instruments. Its precursor is found in the one-reed seventeenth-century shawm with a cylindrical tube.

The name *clarinet* appeared first in 1732. This early clarinet had a smaller reed than the present-day instrument, and its tone was lighter, more penetrating, and shriller, resembling that of the oboe; from a distance it was comparable to a trumpet. The name itself suggests trumpet-like, for *clarion* means "rousing sound," and the Italian *clarino* signifies "little trumpet" or "high-pitched trumpet."

Around the middle of the eighteenth century this clarinet found its way into the orchestra, and by 1770 Mozart had adopted it. The contention that Haydn introduced the clarinet into the orchestra can no longer be upheld as valid. Beethoven made the clarinet an indispensable member of the orchestra. In Weber we meet the real master of the clarinet.

**Figure 159**
**Clarinet Players of the BBC Symphony Orchestra**
**Courtesy BBC Broadcasting House**

About a century ago Böhm's mechanism was applied to the clarinet, rendering it all the more useful.

The modern clarinet has a cylindrical bore with a lower conical end. It is usually made of hardwood—ebony or cocus—in four parts and measures about two feet in length. The lower end terminates in a narrow bell. The mouthpiece is chisel-shaped with one side flattened so as to support the single reed which is fastened to it by a metal band. The vibration of this reed is produced by the breath of the player and the pressure of the lower lip.

The tube itself is constructed in such a way that it has the effect of a closed pipe, a fact which interests us inasmuch as such a pipe eliminates the even overtones, or at least makes them faint and extremely difficult to produce. The prominent overtones therefore are the third, fifth, and seventh series. This, coupled with the manner of producing the sound, gives the clarinet its characteristic tone quality. At the same time, it makes the clarinet a difficult instrument to play.

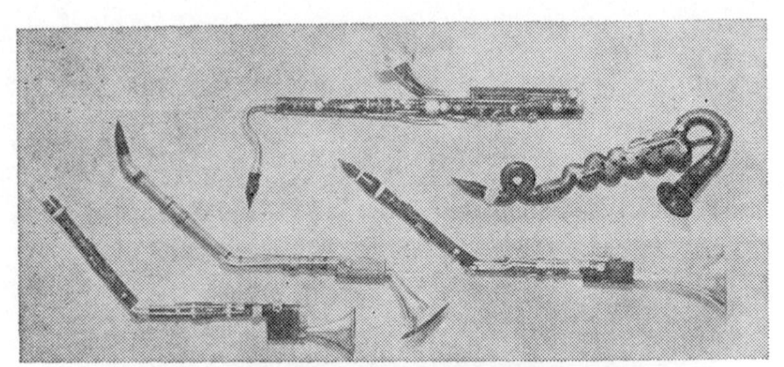

Figure 160. 3 Basset Horns and 2 Bass Clarinets
Courtesy Museum of Fine Arts, Boston

It has been stated already that the clarinet never was invented, in the proper sense of the word, and that the tone of the early clarinets was only remotely akin to that of the present-day instrument. Figure 160 shows some odd-shaped specimens of the clarinet.

Such instruments clearly reveal a similarity with other instruments. Evidently the clarinet grew by imitation until it finally emerged in its present form. The three models on the left side of the illustration are known as *basset horns,* and the other two as *bass clarinets.* We see that clarinets, too, came in families. Just what other instruments do these clarinets remind you of?

Since the basset horn is historically of some importance, we must take a closer look at it. It owes its existence to a German clarinet maker by the name of Horn (1770), and the name signifies a little bass clarinet made by Horn. People unaware of the name of the inventor took it to be a horn, making *basset horn* a misnomer, of course.

However, this bass clarinet was tonally a beautiful instrument. Its tone was fuller and more reedy than that of the ordinary clarinet. Mozart appreciated it and wrote much for it. Later models of the basset horn were very similar to the ordinary clarinet, the shape having been straightened out. This straight form found favor with Mendelssohn. Why this "horn" has fallen into oblivion is hard to conjecture. However, it has begun to attract the attention of orchestral composers again.

The *bass clarinet* is an octave lower in pitch than the soprano. It has a piece of curved metal tubing as a link between the mouthpiece and the tube proper, and it ends in a wide bell pointing outwards and upwards. In tone quality it resembles the ordinary clarinet, but it sounds more hollow. As its name suggests, it is the bass instrument of the clarinet family.

The *alto clarinet* is another member of the clarinet group. Figure 162 shows an early nineteenth-century model, while the next illus-

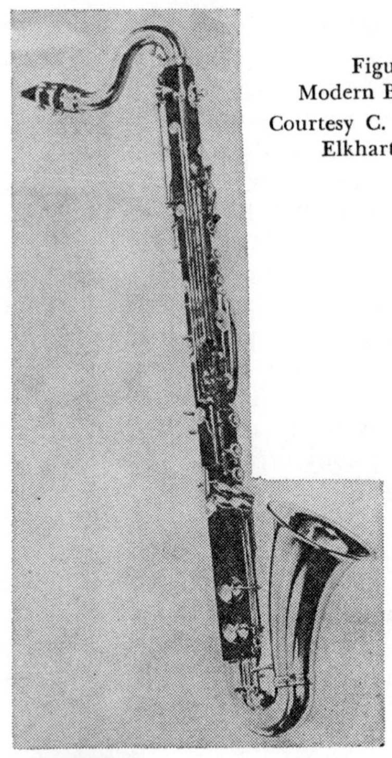

Figure 161
Modern Bass Clarinet
Courtesy C. G. Conn Ltd.,
Elkhart, Indiana

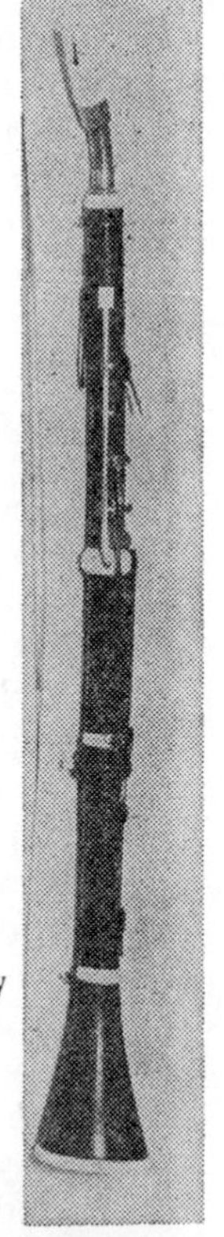

Figure 162
Alto Clarinet, 19th Century
Courtesy Museum of
Fine Arts, Boston

Figure 163
Modern Alto Clarinet
Courtesy C. G. Conn Ltd.,
Elkhart, Indian

Figure 164
Saxophone, 1850
Courtesy Museum of
Fine Arts, Boston

tration gives us the modern instrument. The tone of the alto clarinet differs from that of the basset horn in that it is more open and vigorous; but is also beautiful, rich, and sonorous.

*Soprano clarinets* (see Figure 158) are still made in several keys, the most common one today being those in B-flat and A. Both are therefore transposing instruments (see Chapter V) and may be used interchangeably. If a piece of music is written in flat keys, the B-flat clarinet is used, and if in sharps the A-clarinet is more practical.

The least important of all clarinets is the *pedal clarinet,* which has a range an octave below the bass clarinet. It is said to be a marvelous instrument, but its price is out of proportion to its usefulness and it is therefore only seldom heard.

When speaking of clarinets we have the soprano in mind. Its role in the orchestra is that of the lyric soprano voice, and in the band that of the strings in the symphony orchestra. It is the most useful and also the most beautiful of the woodwind instruments. It possesses great agility, which means that it can produce rapid arpeggios and runs; it can be played *legato* as well as *staccato.* Further, it is capable of wider leaps and rapid changes from piano to *forte*—it can swell a tone and decrease it—thus making it capable of varied and subtle shades of tone (nuances) and relating it to the human voice in dynamic power and tone quality. No other woodwind has such dynamic range.

As with the flute and oboe, a clarinet's tone quality varies with the registers. Its lowest register, the bottom octave of its compass, is unlike any sound produced by other instruments—rich and oily, hollow and rather sinister. Tchaikovsky loved to exploit this register, as is seen for instance in the introduction to the *Fifth Symphony.* The cat in Prokofiev's *Peter and the Wolf* is also represented by the clarinet in the lowest register. The second register of the clarinet has a lifeless and dull tone and is usually not called for in performance. The third register, up to about *a‴*, is clear and uniform and much featured in solo work. The very highest notes are shrill and often screechy.

All great composers have written abundantly for the clarinet. Once you are familiar with its tone, you will find it well represented in all symphonic works. Concertos for clarinet and either orchestra or other instruments offer the music lover some of the greatest delights imaginable.

## *The Saxophone*

The *saxophone* holds a unique position among orchestral instruments. It is neither a woodwind nor a brass. In shape it resembles a tobacco pipe. The mouthpiece is taken from the clarinet,

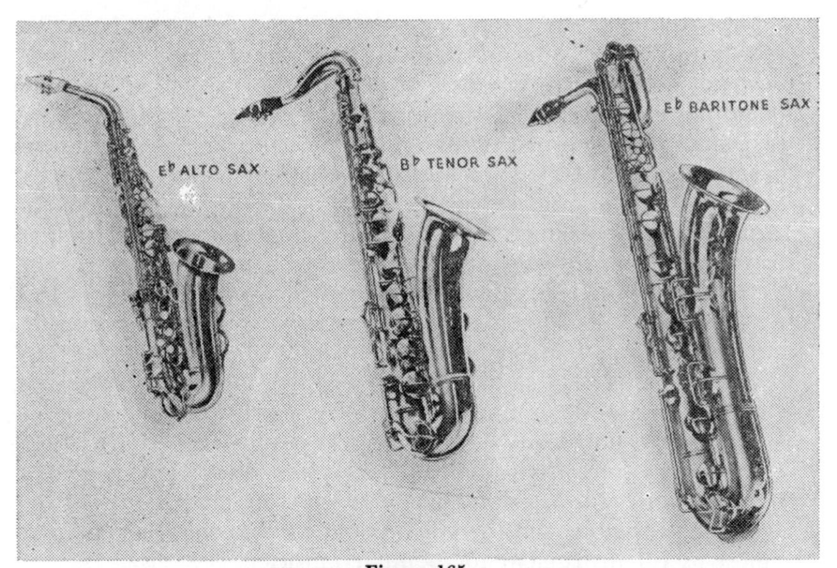


Figure 165
Modern Saxophones in Different Keys
Courtesy C. G. Conn Ltd., Elkhart, Indiana

the mechanism borrowed from the oboe, and the ball is wide and tapering but parabolic rather than conical. The tone has the ready quality of the clarinet, but is more powerful; in addition, it has the metallic strength of some of the brasses, at the same time being capable of the softness of the flute and the mellowness of the cello.

When Alice visited Orchestralia (see Bibliography) she found that the saxophone had to dwell all by itself on the outskirts of the other villages, for Fiddladelphia, Panopolis, and Brassydale would not grant it asylum. Thus LaPrade humorously hits the nail on the head. The saxophone with its peculiar tone does not blend with the other instruments of the orchestra and thus is not a member of it. We may call it a musical hybrid. Military bands, dance orchestras, and in particular jazz bands have frequent recourse to it; in fact, the saxophone has become *the* instrument of jazz. Some modern composers do employ it well even in their symphonic works, but mostly, however, for novel effects.

Saxophones originally comprised a family of seven members, ranging from a high sopranino to a low bass. The latest (American) addition is the contrasaxophone, a veritable monster in size, produced by C. G. Conn. The alto and tenor saxophones are the most frequently used, for they are tonally superior to the others. Since there is no saxophone in C, all the saxophones in use are transposing instruments.

The inventor of the saxophone is Adolphe Sax, whom we have met already while discussing his saxhorns and whose name it bears. It must not be assumed, however, that Sax all of a sudden invented something entirely new. Even primitive people are known to have used small signal horns with one reed. In 1807 a French instrument maker experimented with a similar instrument which resembled a bassoon in shape and was played with a clarinet mouthpiece. In 1820 a Scottish bandmaster, Meikle, invented a somewhat similar instrument. This instrument was referred to by one authority as the "saxophone before Sax." It shows the clarinet mouthpiece attached to a bassoon. A great deal of controvery was aroused by its appearance and various names were given to it. We include it here just to show once more that when it comes to musical instruments it is more a case of evolution than clear-cut inventions, and that the road to perfection leads through a great deal of experimentation.

It remains somewhat doubtful, to say the least, to what extent the saxophone was Sax's original idea. But his models proved immediately workable, and there is no denying that they have become a most useful instrument for popular music.

Figure 166
Alto Fagotto, England, ca. 1830
Courtesy Museum of Fine Arts, Boston

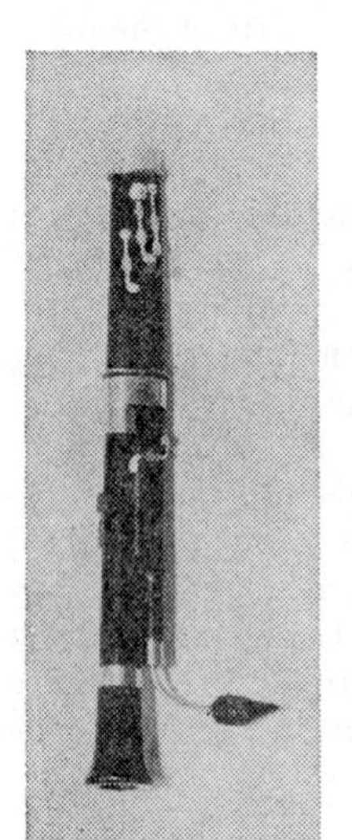

Figure 167. Clarinets, 2 Centuries of Growth (17-19th)
Courtesy Museum of Fine Arts, Boston

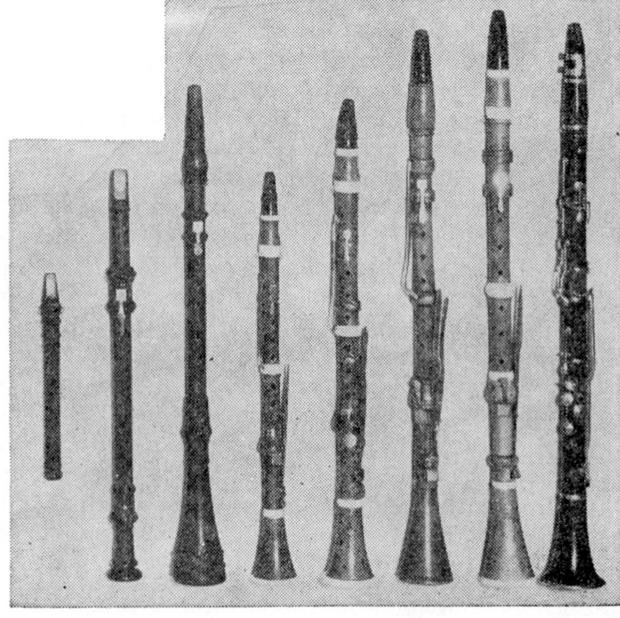

# *Part Four: Strings*

*From*

*To*

CHAPTER IX

# CLASSIFICATION AND ORIGIN OF STRING INSTRUMENTS

To avoid any confusion later on it is advisable to begin our discussion of string instruments by introducing some fundamental concepts related to their structure, the materials used in their construction, and other aspects, even at the risk of becoming somewhat technical.

## *Strings*

There are three types of strings used:

1. *Open strings.* Open strings are strings of constant length and produce one tone only. They can be plucked, struck, or bowed. As a rule, they provide the "drone" and are often referred to as *bourdons.* Three typical examples, according to the three manners of playing, are the psaltery, the dulcimer, and the crwth, respectively, each of which shall be discussed in its place. Then there are the strings of the keyed instruments, such as those of the spinet, virginal, or harpsichord, but that is, as it were, a story by itself.

2. *Stopped strings.* The vibrating length of stopped strings can be temporarily altered at will by various methods of stopping. Examples will be found in the zither, guitar, violin, and others—in short, in those instruments which are equipped with a neck and fingerboard. Again, the method of stopping the strings in clavichords is a story in itself.

3. *Sympathetic strings.* These are free strings and not played at all. They resound in "sympathy" with certain fundamental notes, thereby adding tone coloring to the tones produced. To see how such strings work, soundlessly depress, let us say, the key of middle *c* on the piano and strike the *c* an octave below it; after a second or two release the lower key while still holding middle *c* down, and you will find that middle *c* will now be playing (provided your

piano is in tune). Other notes may also be excited in this way. Strike a low bass note while pressing the loud or sustaining pedal down; listen carefully and you should hear quite a number of strings in action. Or simply open the front panel of your piano, depress the pedal and sing a note against the open strings. The more resonant your own voice, the greater the echo that will come out of the piano. Other examples could be cited. Sympathetic strings reinforce the fundamental tone first of all, but then the overtones are brought out, the number of overtones being determined by the quality of the instruments, loudness of original tone, etc. If you are curious to see an instrument with sympathetic strings, you may turn to Figure 227 right now.

### *Material of Strings*

Primitive strings were made of vegetable fiber or hemp. Later on gut, silk, or wire became common. The term *catgut* is misleading, for the gut is taken from sheep or sometimes goats. Gut was the musical string of the Egyptians, Greeks, and Romans. Silk was in vogue in the East. Wire became practical in the fourteenth century after wire-drawing was invented (about 1350). Since then gut, wire, and gut overspun with wire (silver, copper, or mixed metal) have become equally important. The wire around the gut adds weight to the string, thereby slowing down the vibrations. Hence, overspun strings, invented in France about 1675, are used in the bass section of the instruments. The advent of wire made it possible to construct keyed instruments with strings, such as the clavichord, the virginal, the harpsichord, and their latest offspring, the piano.

The origin of the term *catgut* has not yet been traced. The best and strongest intestines for strings are those of lambs of a certain age. According to an old saying, September is the month for fiddle-string making. In Biblical times the Israelites were instructed to make the strings of "sons" of sheepgut. This term probably refers to the small intestine directly under the stomach, in pigs called chitterlings today.

Today only the soft, fine, submucous membrane of sheepgut is used, 1/25 inch in diameter. In this way even the smallest string of the violin is given considerable tensile strength. (The total tension of the four violin strings on the instrument is over sixty pounds.)

To equip the violin with its four strings, the guts of from two to three lambs are required. For the deeper-tone strings the gut is overlapped with metal. According to Grove (see Bibliography): "the best Italian strings are those made of English gut by German makers"!

### *Resonators*

Resonators reinforce the sound, giving it beauty and volume. To prove the point, strike a tuning fork and hold it up in midair; the sound will be feeble and will not carry. Now, repeat the performance, but this time set the solid end of the vibrating tuning fork on the top of a desk. You will be surprised at the difference it will make. Or to take another illustration, stretch a violin string between supports in midair and try to play it. You certainly don't expect to get a violin tone out of it. Similarly, a radio loudspeaker detached from its cabinet will sound tinny. In short, a sound-producing medium depends to a great extent on a suitable resonator for its tone.

To construct a resonator, the instrument maker must consider the size, shape, length, width, depth, and number of openings as well as the material which is to be used in its construction, for all these factors determine the characteristics or tone quality of the sound to be produced. Of equal importance are the proportions of the various parts in relation to each other, to the thickness, etc. Wherein for instance lay the value of the famous Cremona violins? And just why is a good instrument so expensive? Their price is not determined by the strings they use, for all violins use the same kind of strings; they are inexpensive in themselves. In each case the important factor is the resonator.

Just what does a resonator do to the tone? In the first place, it strengthens the tone by resonating in sympathy with the vibrations produced. That is to say, when you set the vibrating tuning fork on the table, the whole top of the table begins to vibrate with the same frequency as the original tone. A resonator box does more than that; it also makes the air enclosed in it vibrate.

Secondly, a resonator emphasizes the overtones; without it they are practically lost. But we know by now that the beauty of the tone is determined by its overtones. A resonator can also bring out more overtones than a mere vibrating body. Thus, a resonator not only strengthens the overtones but increases their number. The better the resonator, the more overtones. Thirdly, a resonator will also suppress the disagreeable overtones. The ideal resonator, therefore, is the one that reinforces the tone without harshness, augments the number of agreeable overtones, and suppresses the undesirable ones. In this respect resonators differ widely. This difference, of course, is very fortunate, for it has given rise to the great variety of string instruments we have.

The prototype of the resonator, that is, the oldest and most primitive one on record, dates back to prehistoric times and was provided by nature by hollow fruits with hard rinds, such as gourds

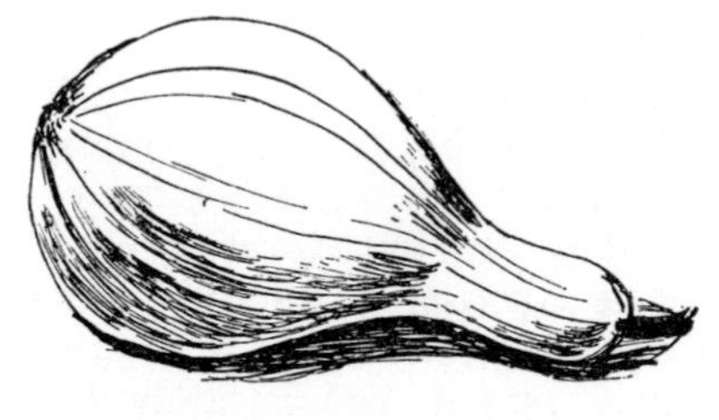

Figure 170
A Gourd, the Prototype of Resonators

or calabashes. Even a superficial examination of our present-day string instruments reveals certain similarities between their bodies and gourds. (The piano has a flat, solid sound board, but we will deal with the piano later.) As we shall see later, the first string instrument actually consisted of a string with an attached gourd (Figure 168). It was only with the progress of civilization that man learned to fashion handmade resonator boxes. Naturally, these boxes would show enormous variations in size, shape, volume, and material. But man soon learned to experiment with resonators, thus beginning the era of musical instruments unlimited.

There are two categories of resonators: the one group includes flat-bottomed instruments, the second those with round bottoms. Curved backs are variations between the two extremes. We find them in the violin family.

*String Fasteners and Supports*

Strings are fastened to the body in such a way that it is possible not only to secure a certain tension for a desired pitch but also to vary the tension for tuning. As a rule one end, let us say the lower end, is fastened permanently, while the other end is attached to a peg or tuning pin. Rather than give you all the technical names for the different types of fastenings, page through the following section and compare the peg boxes of the instruments illustrated and you will find some startling differences. Note the ways in which the lower ends of the strings are fastened directly: to the sound board or to the lower end of the body by pins, a tail piece, or a loop. The supports are of paramount importance.

At the upper end of the string there is the *nut.* The nut is a notched piece of hardwood or ivory placed at the top end of the fingerboard just below the tuning pegs. It holds the strings a definite distance above the fingerboard and keeps them the desired distance from each other, and it aids the pegs in holding the strings.

The counterpart to the nut is the *bridge* at the lower end. The bridge is a wedge-shaped, notched piece of hardwood with a broad base and a narrow top. In addition to fixing the string to its place, it transmits the vibrations of the strings to the body. The vibrating part of the strings is thus confined to the section between the nut and the bridge.

The *neck* connects the resonating body with the peg box.

The *finger board* is for stopping the strings at various places for pitch variation. It covers the neck and often extends close to the sound hole.

The *belly* is the face of the box or upper side of the resonator.

The *sound post* transmits the vibrations from the belly to the back; in addition, it synchronizes the vibrations of belly and back, making them uniform. The French call the sound post the soul of the instrument, so it must be important.

The *bass bar* is a long piece of wood glued to the inside surface of the belly. It modifies the tone produced by the belly and distributes the vibrations over it. It also stiffens the belly structurally.

### *The Origin of String Instruments*

Several theories concerning early string instruments merit an introduction here. The first, which attributed the invention to pagan deities, was held for thousands of years. Interesting as these myths may be, they lead us to conclude that man was completely ignorant of the origin of stringed instruments, but held them in such esteem that he gave them a divine beginning.

As musicologists started to apply scientific reasoning, they advanced a second theory which, however, is not strictly based upon scientific principles. This theory you will find expounded in practically every history book on musical instruments. According to this theory, man learned to fashion a string instrument from his hunting bow. As he noted the twang or snap of the released bowstring, he conceived the idea of constructing a musical bow, from which originated the harp and other string instruments. Such a theory sounds plausible, but in the light of latest research must be disqualified.

By far the best account of the origin of string instruments is again given by Dr. Sachs. He traces these instruments to the ground harp, the ground zither, and the musical bow respectively.

It will be helpful at this point to recall that primitive people were at a loss to account for natural phenomena which are commonplace today. Thus, though it was clear even to a native of the jungles that a sound could be produced by beating sticks, on the other hand he did not see that a hollow substance, that is, a resonator, should intensify a sound. The only explanation he had to offer was that such a substance harbored a spirit. So whoever could use a hollow object properly could make a spirit talk, or else he could trap a spirit or even communicate with the outer world. It is therefore quite conceivable that the ground instruments we are about to consider served certain ritual functions.

The *ground harp,* still found in some parts of Central Africa, consisted of a pit dug in the ground and covered with a layer of bark. Beside it was a flexible vertical rod which provided a support for a string. The string was strung between the upper end of the rod and the opposite end of the bark lid, forming a sort of triangle. The lid of bark thus provided the sound board and the pit the resonator. (Just what kind of spirit inhabited it is not recorded.) By the player's striking or plucking the string, the spirit would talk. The tension of the string could easily be altered by tying it lower or higher on the rod. Likewise, the length of the string could be changed. Thus, the pitch of the "harp" could be varied.

The *ground zither* was similar to the harp. It also consisted of a pit covered with bark, but had two rods, one at either side of the pit, instead of one. A string was stretched horizontally between the tops of the poles above the pit. From this top string another string stretched to the bark, dividing the upper string into two parts of unequal length. If the longer section were struck, a lower sound was produced; the tone of the shorter section would then be the higher-pitched one. The top string measured from thirteen to

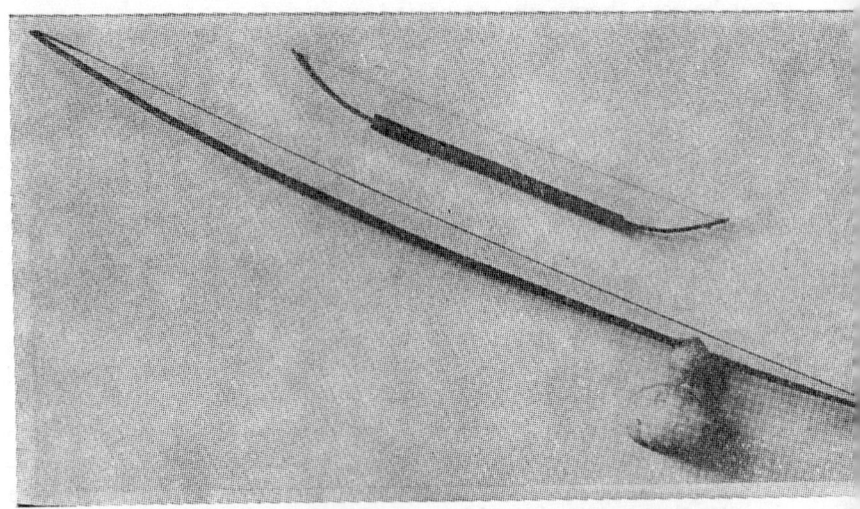

Figure 171. Musical Bows, with and Without Resonator
From "Old World Overtones", U. of Pa.

fourteen feet, thus representing a gigantic primitive instrument. In Java there still exists a ground zither of several strings with a separate pit for each string.

The principles of sound production embodied in Figure 171 ground instruments apply also to the *musical bow*. As stated before, popular belief has it that this bow evolved from the hunter's bow. Dr. Sachs refutes this theory in the following manner: (1) the musical bow was up to ten feet long, and therefore had nothing to do with hunting; (2) string and bow were made of the same piece of cane, the string being split off from one side of the cane and supported by bridges so as to be raised off the bow; (3) it had a special resonator; and (4) it was not associated with hunting at all. In Mexico such a bow was the sacred emblem of the goddess of earth and moon.

The musical bow is one of the rare primitive instruments man used to induce gentler feelings. Its tone was sweet and muffled, ideally suited to contact gentler spirits and induce meditation.

The evolution of the above three primitive instruments can easily be conjectured. As far as the ground instruments are concerned, the first step would be to substitute a wooden box for the pit, thus freeing the instrument from the ground. The second step must have been the gradual reduction of the size of the resonators, making the instruments portable. The musical bow would not have been too difficult to improve. Bigger and better resonators were devised, different methods of fastening the strings invented—in short, all the factors mentioned at the beginning of this section were altered to suit the occasion, giving rise to literally hundreds of different string instruments. (It is said that India today still has some five hundred different string instruments!) We will discuss only those that played their part in bringing the modern strings into existence.

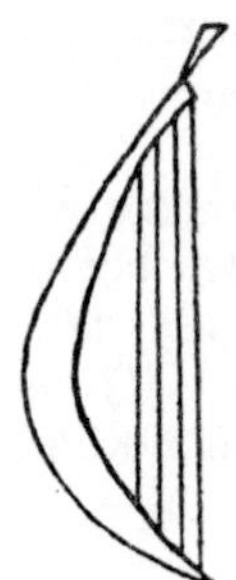

Figure 172
Arched Harp, Babylonia, ca. 2700 B.C.

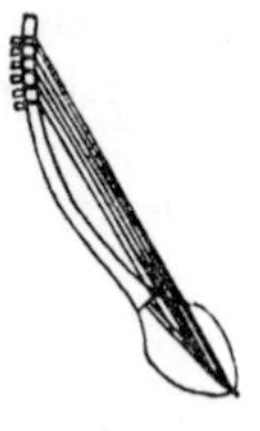

Figure 173
Egyptian Harp, ca. 2500 B.C.

Figure 174
Egyptian Harp, ca. 2000 B.C.

CHAPTER X

# PLUCKED STRING INSTRUMENTS

## *The Harp*

The first harps bear such a close resemblance to the musical bow that their direct descent from it is now conceded. The land of the Pharaohs is generally considered to have had the oldest harps, but this view is erroneous, since the Sumerian harp shown (Figure 172) is older than any Egyptian harp. It was an *arched harp* and is approximately five thousand years old. It is assumed that the original harps had one arch or bow for each string, just as in the ground zither there was one pit for each string. We can readily see that such harps were somewhat clumsy contraptions.

The Egyptian harp was very similar to the Sumerian, but the strings were attached by means of special knobs. The harp was *the* instrument of Egypt and seems to belong to that country. However, it was most popular throughout Asia, and the number of shapes and sizes it assumed was legion.

Figure 173 shows a primitive arched harp with a resonator at the lower end. Characteristic is the absence of the pillar and the shape of the bow. It would be difficult to classify or name all the harps of the ancient world. By 2000 B.C., however, harps had assumed an angular shape. Angular harps are shown in the illustration below.

Figure 175
Angular Harps
2nd Mill. B.C.

The tendency to decorate musical instruments with ornaments is already evident. To us these embellishments may seem without significance, but taking the psychological background into account one wonders whether to the people of those times these decorations were really meaningless. At any rate, we may conclude that the music produced by such instruments had some nonmusical purpose.

Two other types of harps are worth mentioning: the shoulder harp and the horizontal harp, illustrated on page 197.

All these harps consisted of two integral parts: the sound board (or the body) and the neck. Later on the so-called frame harps appeared, harps in which the outer end of the neck was connected to the body, thus lending support to the neck and enabling it not only to sustain greater tension but to anchor more strings. From these harps evolved the *pillar* harp, which is generally considered the European type.

Before turning to a discussion of the European harp, let us mention King David's. I Samuel 16:23 reads: "And it came to pass, when the evil spirit from God was upon Saul, that David took an harp, and played with his hand: so Saul was refreshed, and was well, and the evil spirit departed from him." It appears that this "harp" is a translator's error. The instrument played by David was not a harp but a lyre, known as a *kinnor* in Hebrew and a *kithara* in Greek (see Figure 186). Evidently David plucked the kinnor with his fingers, whereas the lyres were usually played with plectra.

When the harp appeared in Europe about the eighth century, it had already assumed its three-part form of body, neck, and pillar. From what country the Europeans obtained it—whether from Persia, Syria, Egypt or somewhere else—cannot be determined. The first European harp resembled the ancient angular harp of the Egyptians. It is sometimes claimed that northern Europe is the place of origin of the harp. Ancient Britain and notably Ireland seem to be its home. The name *harp* at any rate, denoting something to pluck, is of northern origin.

The *Irish harp* was so popular that it soon became symbolic of that country and figured in its coat of arms; Irish minstrels during the Middle Ages spread the harp throughout Europe. The first Irish harps were portables. One of the early specimens preserved, the lude-harp, is described as being thirty-six inches high and sixteen wide with thirty-two strings. The longest string of our illustration is about forty-four inches.

It is noticeable that the later harps did not fundamentally differ from the early models. They did, however, become more ornamental and considerably larger. Welsh and minstrel harps often had straight pillars. The straight pillar, necessitated by the mechanism of tuning the strings, has remained a feature of the modern harp. The

Figure 176. Boat-shaped Harp, S. East Asia

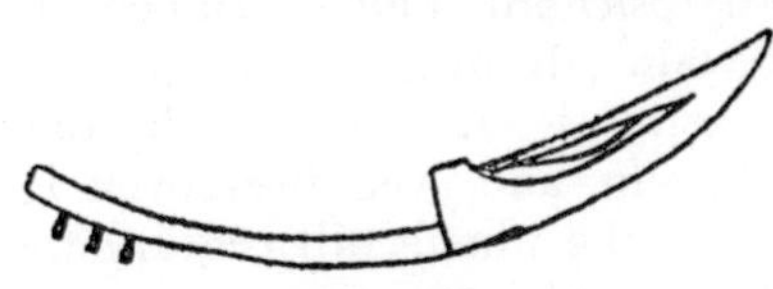

Figure 177
Egyptian Shoulder Harp, ca. 1400 B.C.

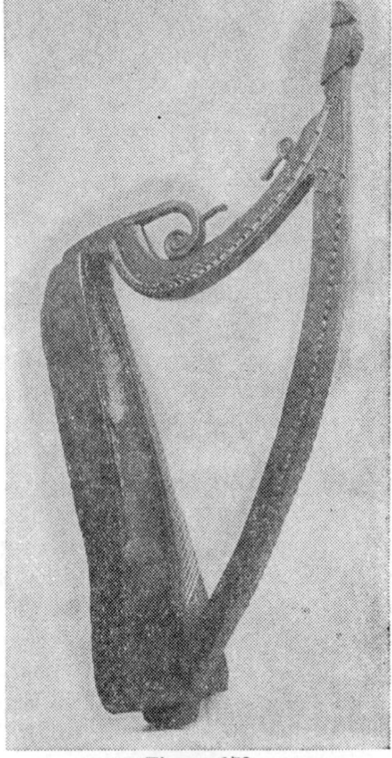

Figure 179
Large Minstrel Harp, Ireland, 1734
Courtesy Museum of Fine Arts, Boston

Figure 178
Assyrian Horizontal Harps, ca. 600 B.C.

transition from the curved or Romanesque type to the straight pillar or the Gothic harp occurred during the fifteenth century—not that the latter type supplanted the former abruptly, for the curved pillar was found as late as the eighteenth century.

It is interesting to note that in entering the continent the harp encountered competition from the lyre. But since the lyre had all strings of equal length, its compass was restricted to the middle registers, whereas the unequal length of the harp strings enlarged the range in a natural way. Thus the harp, in tone quality very much like the lyre, gained preference over it and became the favorite indoor instrument of the Middle Ages. Members of royal households and the nobility and aristocracy played the harp. Murals depicted angels playing it, for the harp had powers to ban evil spirits, yea, even stop the flow of rivers and make cattle leave off grazing. (Greek mythology?) Later the harp became the instrument of wandering minstrels and beggar girls.

Why should the harp have fallen into disfavor? The answer is provided by the appearance of the harpsichord. This instrument, to be described in due course, had certain advantages over the harp that made it more suitable for domestic use. It is noteworthy that such composers as Handel, Bach, Haydn, and even Beethoven ignored the harp almost completely. By the nineteenth century the piano had superseded the harpsichord, and interest once more returned to the harp. Composers began to employ the harp for special effects. The restoration of the harp to a place of honor among instruments is mainly due to the French composers, Berlioz, Meyerbeer, Debussy, and others.

One can hardly blame the classic composers for scorning the harp. Not only was the mechanism of the harp of that time crude and imperfect, but, what was of even greater consequence, the instrument lacked semitones. In other words, a harp was something like a piano without black keys.

As we have seen, early Irish harps had but a small compass. The tendency to increase the range of the harp resulted in larger sound boards and longer pillars, making room for strings of lower tone. The harp of the fifteenth century was already taller and more slender, with the three parts distinctly marked off against each other. These harps still had no semitones. The first attempts to introduce chromatic tones were made around 1600. A separate string for each note of the chromatic scale produced the *chromatic harp*. Now, a complete chromatic scale requires twelve strings, one for each semitone, so it is natural that the chromatic harp found but little favor with musicians. In the first place it was a cumbersome thing. The strings, to be manipulated, had to be placed so close together that there was interference in the vibrations. Various attempts at improvement, such as placing the strings in parallel rows or crosswise, resulted in little satisfaction. Finally, as late as the middle of the nineteenth century, the chromatic harp was abandoned altogether.

The *hooked harp* of the second half of the seventeenth century was more successful than the above-mentioned chromatic harp. You will note from the illustration that close to the pegs which hold the strings, that is, in the neck of the harp, there are iron hooks. When a hook is pressed against the string in the way a violinist depresses a string on the neck of the violin, the vibrating part of the string is shortened and the tone is consequently raised, in this case by a semitone. Thus, sharps could be introduced and the music could be played in different keys. Adjusting these hooks, however, always involved interruptions in the performance, and therefore even the hooked harp found little favor.

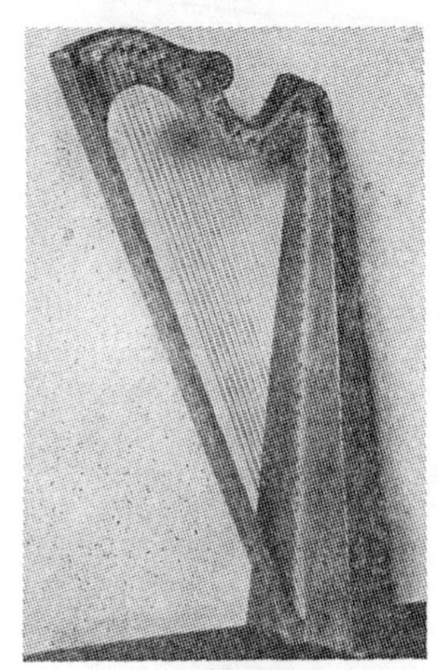

Figure 180
Hooked Harp
Courtesy Society of Friends of Music, Vienna

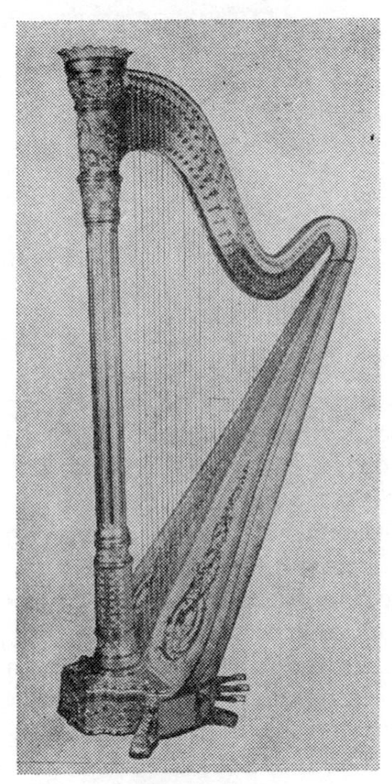

Figure 181
The Modern Pedal Harp

The next step on the road to the modern harp was the *pedal harp*. Around 1720 a German music maker conceived the idea of operating the hooks with the feet by means of foot-levers, the pedals. The weakness of this system was that strings could only be sharped, not flatted. Thus, one could play *a#*, but not *a-flat*. Then in the 1820s a Frenchman finally perfected the idea of the *double-pedal harp*. The double-pedal harp is our modern harp.

The double pedal works on the following principle: The mechanism is concealed within the neck. There are separate levers connecting the same strings, i.e., one lever operates all the *c* strings, another all the *d* strings, etc. The levers are operated by means of pedals at the base of the harp; the pedals in their turn are connected by rods concealed in the pillar. In all there are seven pedals for the seven

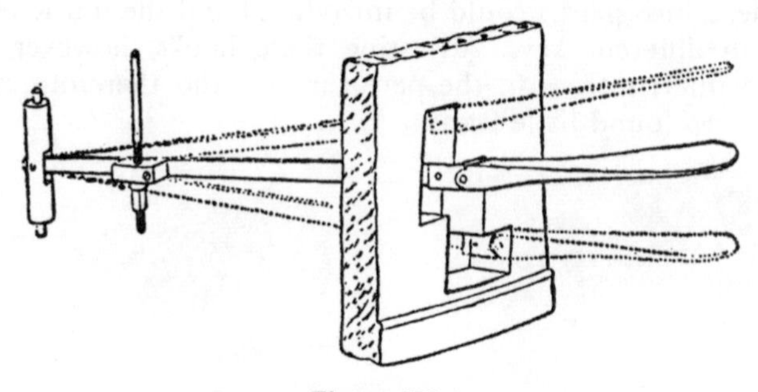

Figure 182
The Double Pedal Action
Courtesy Sachs, History of Mus. Inst.

strings of the scale. As seen from the diagram above, a pedal in neutral position rests in the upper notch; depressed to the middle position it raises the pitch of a string by one semitone; in the lowest position the string is shortened by two semitones.

Now, a harp is tuned to *c-flat*. If the *c* pedal is worked, the second position will change all the *c-flat* strings to *c-natural;* in the third position the pedal changes all the *c* strings to *c#*. This change is accomplished by means of two disks in the frame close to the upper part of each string. In the first position the pegs of the disk do not touch the string; in the second position the upper disk makes a turn for a semitone raise; in the third position the second disk completes the shortening to a whole tone.

The modern harp has nearly the range of a piano, six and a half octaves. It can produce any desired note, natural, sharp or flat, within this range. It is a graceful, ornamental instrument, and is more or less a lady's instrument, although some of the most famous harpists are men. One is tempted to add that the lady in question must be a lady of leisure. Today's harps are rather expensive and their use is restricted. This is partly because of the "monochordic" feature of

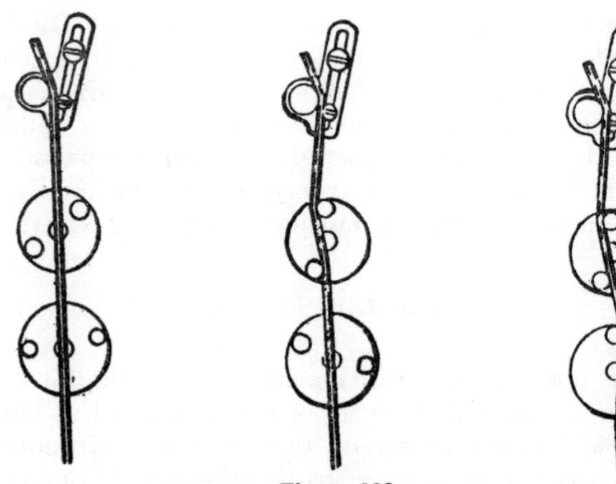

**Figure 183**
**The Double Action of the Disks**
**Courtesy Sachs, History of Mus. Inst.**

the harp—chord playing is out of the question. Orchestras like to use them where prescribed but can do without them. Finally, one fancies that harp teachers must be a rare commodity. One almost has to go to a large city to learn to play the harp properly.

There are forty-seven strings on the harp; the eleven bass strings are of wire, the others of gut. To guide the player's eye, the *c* strings are colored red and the *f* strings blue. The pedal mechanism naturally excludes the rapid playing of chromatic passages, and the composer must bear this limitation in mind when writing for the harp; he must arrange his score in such a way as to simplify pedaling as much as possible. Still, broken chord effects (arpeggios), gliding passages produced by quickly sweeping the hand over all the strings, harmonics played by pressing the hand lightly against the middle of the string and then plucking it with the thumb of the same hand —all these effects are within the reach of the skillful performer. There being no damper to stop the strings, the left hand is used for deadening the sound.

Modern composers delight in the harp. They use it for interludes or for accompaniments in music of a quiet nature. Delightful compositions for the harp are found in Tchaikovsky's *Waltz of the Flowers,* Ponchielli's *Dance of the Hours,* Bizet's *Minuet No. 2* from the *L'Arlésienne Suite No. 2,* the Bach-Gounod *Ave Maria* and others too numerous to mention.

Harp and flute combinations are very popular; likewise, harp and clarinet duets please the listener. Generally the voice of the harp is not loud enough to mix with a full orchestra. Most instruments therefore maintain a respectful silence while the harp takes over.

For certain effects composers use more than one harp. Thus, Wagner in his *Ring der Nibelungen* calls for six harps. (Just to give you an idea how much work is entailed in writing for six harps, fancy composing over three hundred notes for one single bar of the written music! This is just what Wagner did for certain passages!) Each harp is made to play different arpeggios, and the total effect is a very real imitation of the murmuring of rippling waters.

### *The Lyre Family*

The lyre is not a familiar instrument today. We find it well represented in the literature and poetry of the past, which is not surprising, as it held its own for several thousand years. In addition the lyre has given rise to so many instruments—directly or indirectly—that we cannot refrain from including it in our discussion.

The lyre, of Asiatic origin, is probably as old as the harp. The archaic lyre had open strings just like the harp. But whereas in the harp the strings were set perpendicularly to the sound box, the lyre had its strings above and parallel to it. It had a yoke-shaped frame made up of two arms and a crossbar which connected the two arms and also lent support to the strings. The sound box was either a tortoise shell (see the Greek lyre, page 203) or a wooden bowl with a piece of skin for a belly. The arms were occasionally made from the horns of an antelope. Page 203 shows some archaic lyres, four to five thousand years old.

The first lyres were large and heavy, resting on the floor. Later models, after 2000 B.C., were smaller and so light that they could be held in the arms. The two arms of the Egyptian lyre shown above were of unequal length. The crossbar was slightly slanted in relation to the sound box. Such a position permitted the player to adjust the strings by shifting them along the bar and so vary the tension of the strings. As we have seen, Sumerian harps were tuned the same way. Note that the player has a plectrum in her right hand for scratching all the strings at once. The left hand was used to deaden the strings which were not to be heard. The strings of the lyre were tuned to the pentatonic scale.[1]. Lyres which had more than five strings either duplicated some strings or extended the scale somewhat.

The lyre never gained a strong foothold in Egypt. With the Israelites, on the other hand, it was so popular that it was regarded as their national instrument and emblem. Genesis 4:21 should read:

---

[1] A scale of five tones; for instance, "Auld Lang Syne" has a melody based upon such a scale. Play this tune on the black keys of the piano and you will know what is meant by a five-tone scale.

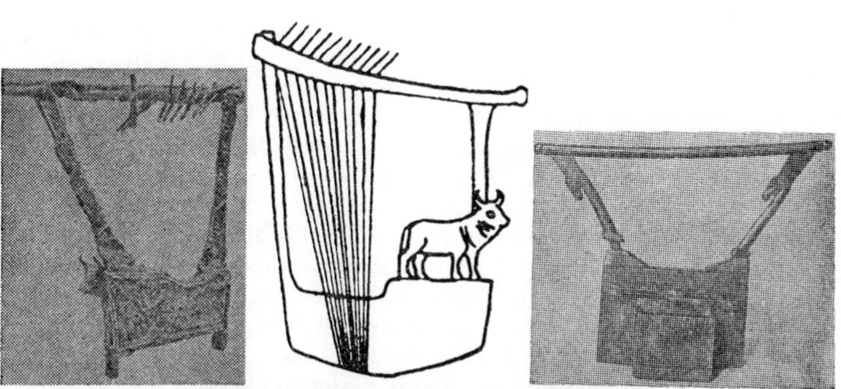

Figure 184. Archaic Lyres, Sumerian, Egyptian

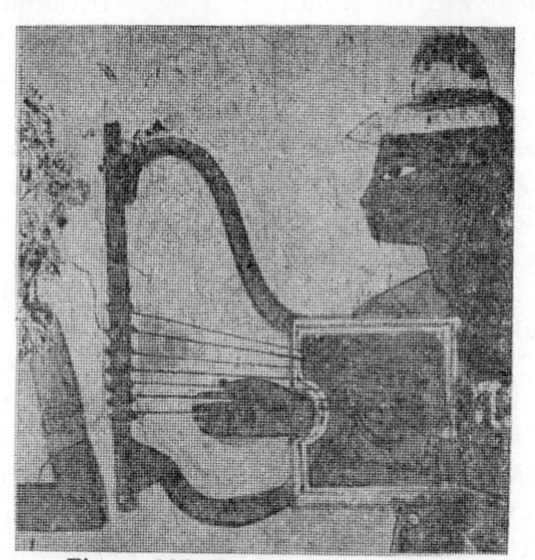

Figure 185. Egyptian Lyre Player

Figure 186
Greek Harp, Kithara and Lyre, 5th Century B.C.
Courtesy Historisches Bildarchiv, Handke-Bad Berneck

"Jubal . . . was the father of all such as handle the [kinnor] [not the harp] and [ugab] [most likely a flute, but certainly not an organ]."

The *kinnor* was a lyre, made of wood, sometimes ornamented with precious metal or amber, the strings being of gut. King David's use of the "harp" (already mentioned above) illustrates what power the Jews attributed to this instrument. The kinnor also found application in the temple during divine services.

In Greece the lyre also became a national instrument, particularly during the classical period. Most writers even today consider Greece the home of the lyre. Unjustly so, for according to Dr. Sachs no instrument originated with the ancient Greeks (nor the Egyptians either, for that matter). The Greeks had two types of lyres: the lyre proper and the *kithara.* Both the lyre and the kithara had flat bottoms. The former was the smaller type used by amateurs for smaller circles. It was the instrument of the Apollonian cult. Our illustration (Figure 186) shows all the characteristics of the lyre, even the tortoise shell. The kithara was more solidly built and had a much heavier resonator. It was used by professionals, not only for the accompaniment of singing (as was the lyre) but also for instrumental solos, often on public occasions like the Delphic games. The kithara was the implement of the Dionysian cult. Bards rendered their songs in praise of heroes and the gods to the strains of the kithara.

The lyre was one of the first instruments to reach Europe. We first find it in Northern Europe in pre-Christian times. Celtic bards accompanied their songs upon a lyrelike instrument which the Britons called *crot.* Around 500 A.D. the crot was known as the *rotte* or *rotta.* Chaucer spelled it *rote* in his time. You may note from the illustration that the strings are fastened by pegs and that the arms are not added to the sound box but cut from the same piece of wood as the instrument, thus forming an integral part of it. Both these features distinguish European lyres from the Asiatic. The rotte was considered the kithara of the Teutons and was prominent from the eighth to the eleventh centuries. It varied in size from small to very large, some forms having as many as seventeen strings.

Another type of lyre is the *crwth.* In the ninth century a bowed instrument, the *fiedel* or *fiddle,* made its appearance and gradually supplanted the lyre. The crwth, favored particularly by Welsh bards, combines the yoke of the lyre with the neck of the fiddle and is also played by bowing.

Now, take a careful look at the bridge. It is straight on top, so how is one to play a single string? It was practically impossible. Next, note that the right foot of the bridge rests upon the belly, whereas the left foot goes right into the sound box and rests on the back. This part of the bridge therefore acts as the sound post, connecting the top of the resonator with the back.

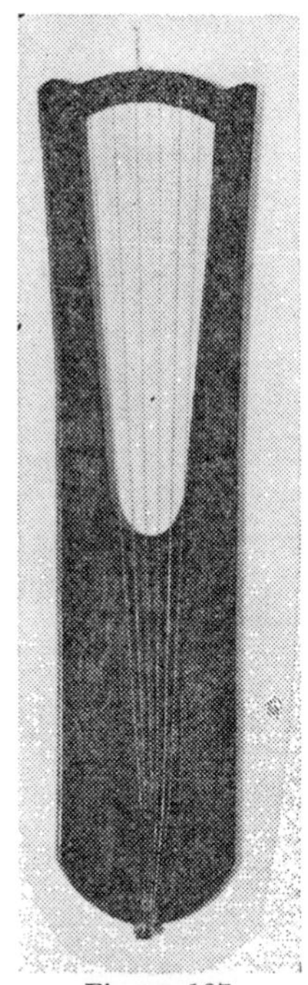

Figure 187
Rotta, European Type of Lyre, 5th-7th Century
Courtesy Museum of Fine Arts, Boston

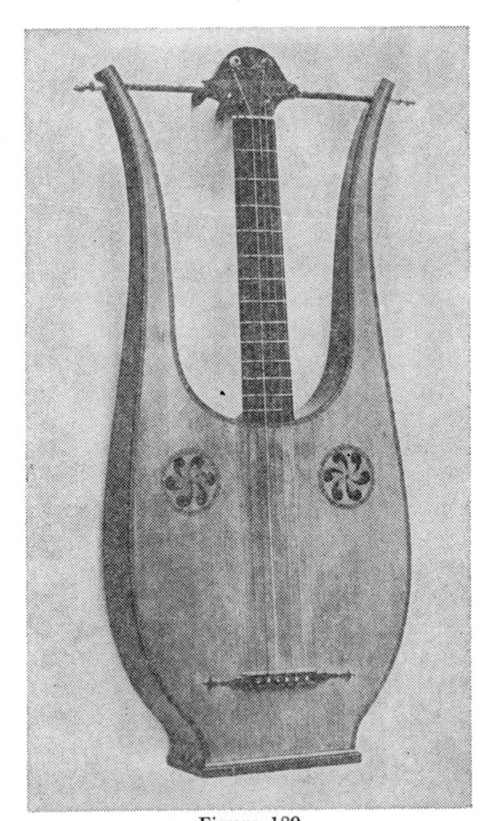

Figure 189
Lyre-Guitar, Paris, ca. 1800
Courtesy Museum of Fine Arts, Boston

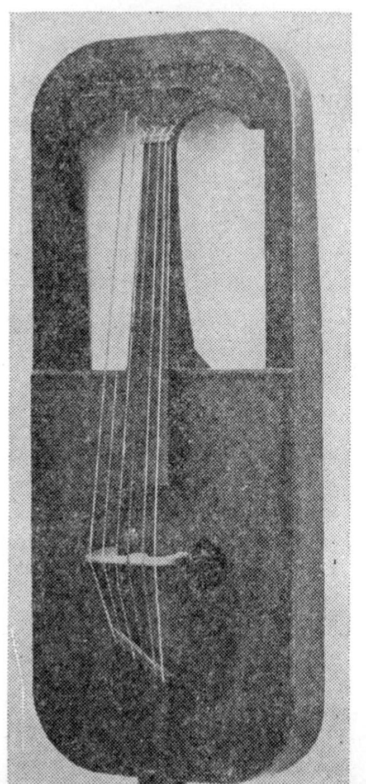

Figure 188. Crwth, Wales
Courtesy Museum of Fine Arts, Boston

Finally, do not overlook the two strings off the neck. They are the drones, for they are open and never vary their pitch, emitting a constant, monotonous tone as accompaniment to the melody. (Such drones will later be found in several viol-type instruments, as well as in bagpipes.) The strings are of gut, attached to metal tuning pegs at the top. As yet there is no special peg box. The whole instrument, with the exception of the belly, which is glued on, is made of one solid piece of wood.

Up to the end of the eighteenth century there were still skilled players of the crwth, but since then the violin has taken its place. The assumption that the crwth was the forerunner of the violin is altogether wrong; on the contrary, the latest crwth models were influenced by the violin in their shape and structure. The crwth in no way determined the evolution of the violin; it just illustrates what happened to certain types of lyres before they died out.

Another offspring of the lyre that struggled unsuccessfully for survival was the eighteenth-century *lyre-guitar.* This instrument was a product of the French Empire period, and represented an effort to revive the form of the classical kithara. Some of these guitars were rather ornamental. They were the instruments of fashionable, classic-minded ladies (see Figure 189).

It is clear such guitars could not possibly have served a useful musical purpose. Apart from their being graceful and charming, the two arms merely incommoded the player; the fingerboard made them superfluous. Lovers of beautiful antique forms welcomed them. Their tone is described as dull and muffled. No wonder it barely survived the first quarter of the nineteenth century. But while it was fashionable, it came in different forms. The English had a similar lyre-guitar, known as the Apollo lyre. (Incidentally, have you ever wondered why a particular Australian bird is called the lyre bird? I hope you see the connection now.)

### *Citterns and Guitars*

Both names, *cittern* and *guitar,* are derived from *kithara.* The resemblance between these instruments is, however, so remote that there is no direct proof of any derivation.

The *cittern* probably originated in southern Europe on the shore of the Mediterranean Sea as a plucked instrument. It was known under such names as *cither, cistre, cister,* or *citole.* These names may well have stood for variations of the same instrument, making a whole family of citterns. One of these became known as the *English guitar.*

During the late Middle Ages, that is, the sixteenth and seventeenth centuries, the cittern enjoyed great favor in England and on the

Figure 190. A Cittern
Courtesy Kunsthistorisches Museum, Vienna

Figure 191. English Guitar, 18th Century
Courtesy Museum of Fine Arts, Boston

Continent. It had a flat-backed body and was usually adorned with engravings. Indeed, it was the custom to decorate the top of the peg box with a carved head. A term of abuse, for instance, was the expression "cittern head."

The cittern in our illustration was made in 1574 for Archduke Ferdinand of Tyrol. The head represents the death of Lucretia. She is holding a dagger ready to plunge into her breast—a rather gruesome embellishment for a musical instrument, don't you think? What other figures can you find on it?

Note that the strings are arranged in pairs, each pair, of course, being tuned in unison. The strings were of wire and played with a plectrum. There seems to be no set rule for the number of strings; some had only four, while others had as many as fourteen.

The cittern shown is the famous *English guitar* by Lucas (Figure 191).

During the middle of the eighteenth century it was so popular that it supplanted other wire-strung instruments as accompaniment to the voice. Spinet and harpsichord makers saw in it a serious rival to their business. Although it was known as a guitar, its circular body strongly resembles older citterns. One noteworthy characteristic of this cittern is the absence of pegs; instead the strings are fastened to metal hooks which are tuned by keys.

The workmanship is exquisite. There is much inlaid ivory, and the sound hole in the form of a stamped gilt rose represents a star with musical instruments. Unfortunately, one almost needs a magnifying lens to see all the trumpets, horns, violins and other details. The elaborate and costly adornments of the cittern made it an instrument especially prized by the nobility.

The *guitar proper* is not a direct descendant of the cittern; it ran a parallel course. While some authorities claim that it developed from the fiedel, others assert that the lute was its parent. It came to Europe not long after the lute and was known as early as the eleventh century. The *Moorish guitar* was introduced into Spain by the Moors. This guitar had a long neck and a lutelike pear-shaped body.

The *Spanish guitar* is the most generally known modern representative of a large family. The back is nearly flat and curved like a bow, and the sides curve inwards after the pattern of bow instruments. The name *Spanish* was adopted when it began regularly to be made with six single strings rather than pairs of strings. At the close of the eighteenth century it became a fashionable instrument on the Continent and finally displaced the English guitar at the beginning of the nineteenth century.

Popular composers wrote music for the guitar, even such giants as Berlioz, Weber, and Paganini. Today the guitar is the most important as well as the most popular wire-strung instrument, probably because of its simplicity and cheapness. Some guitarists have attained almost world-wide fame.

An older type, the Italian struck, was played with a plectrum. The body was unusually deep, and was composed of many panels of extremely thin wood separated by lines of light color. The whole body was backed with parchment. The sound board slopes away at the bottom. The sound hole with a deep-sunken gilt paper rose was outlined with black pearl inlay. The nut and the top of the bridge were also of ivory.

Another specimen had even more ivory adornments. The sound board, as in the previous example, extended slightly into the neck. The frets (divisions on the fingerboard) were of gut. The manner of fastening the strings at the lower end differ somewhat between the two models.

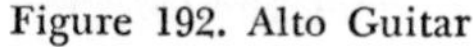

Figure 192. Alto Guitar

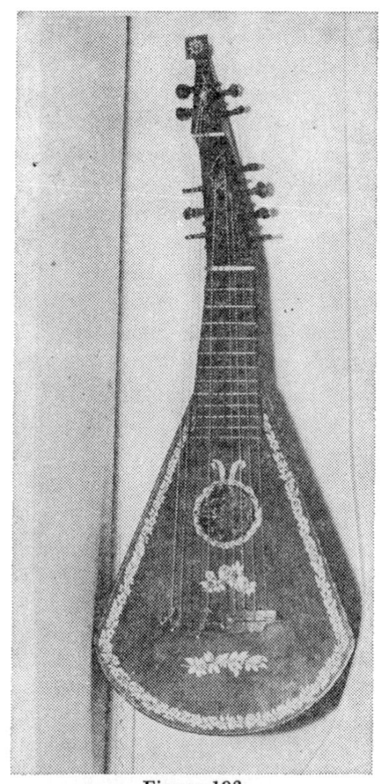

Figure 193
Harp-Lute-Guitar, Early 19th Century, England

The *alto guitar* has all the characteristics of the ordinary guitar. As its name implies, it was a deeper-toned instrument.

Combinations of guitars and lyres or harps were fashionable, for a time, at least. As seen from the illustration, the instrument has free strings vibrating in sympathy. The overtones thus created enrich the tone and give the guitar more resonance.

The Portuguese had a small guitar with the body measuring only some eight inches and the vibrating section of the string about twelve. In 1877 they introduced this dwarf of a guitar into the Sandwich Islands. From there it was exported in the twentieth century into the United States as an original invention named the *ukulele,* and finally reached Europe again. The ukulele is very common in Hawaii.

The *Hawaiian guitar* is a large instrument strung with steel strings and with a special bridge. A metal pressure bar is used on the strings. When this bar is pressed against the finger board, the strings are shortened and the pitch altered. The bar enables the player to produce excessive *vibrato* and *glissando* effects, gliding amorously from note to note, resulting in ready-made sentimentality and exaggerated emotionalism. Most Hawaiian guitars nowadays are equipped with electric amplifiers and differ in shape from the conventional prototypes. We will encounter an illustration when dealing with electronic instruments.

The *banjo,* also an instrument of the guitar type, is an American instrument of African origin. It differs from the true guitar in that it has a longer neck and a drumlike body of parchment. The parchment is stretched upon a hoop to the required degree of stiffness for resonance. There is no back to it. Banjos have from five to nine gut strings, although at present there is a tendency toward tenor banjos with four or five metal strings.

A peculiar feature of the banjo is the placement of the strings: the melody string is played with the thumb and is therefore placed on the bass side of the lowest-tuned string. What is more, its tuning peg is inserted midway up the neck instead of in the head. This string is known as the thumbstring. Its length is given as sixteen inches as compared to twenty-four inches for the other strings.

It is assumed that the African Negro adapted the pandora, a medieval cittern, into the banjo, for the Africans still have a primitive stringed instrument consisting of a shallow tray over which the strings are stretched, the *bandju.* The conjecture is that American Negroes coming from Africa have given us this name and instrument. Today the banjo is one of the principal instruments of jazz music. Played with a plectrum, it has a hard, metallic tone well-fitted to accentuate rhythmic effects.

Figure 194. Banjo

### *Psalteries, Dulcimers, and Zithers*

Psalteries, dulcimers, and zithers form a special group of instruments similar to lyres. But they have neither arms nor necks, and their strings are fastened to either end of the sound box itself. The most primitive psaltery was merely a plain board with the strings stretched over its entire length. For a resonator the board had a gourd just underneath it. Such psalteries still exist among some primitive peoples. Gradually a boxlike chest was substituted for the board and gourd, thus combining resonator and frame.

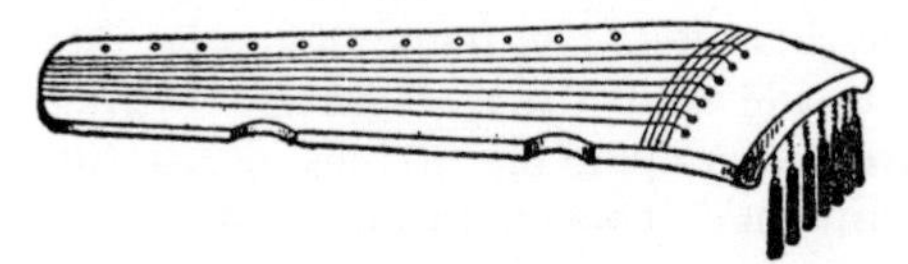

Figure 195. Chinese Ch'in

The oldest psaltery is the thousands-of-years-old Chinese *ch'in,* or *koto* in Japanese. Confucius played such a psaltery, except that his was of the larger type, the *cheng*. The sounding board was slightly convex, forming a slight cavity below it which was closed by a flat board, thus forming a hollow resonator. The ch'in and cheng were played in a horizontal position, the instrument either being held on the knees or resting on the table or even the ground. Not that the ch'in you see in the illustration is the oldest form of the psaltery, for it is already a refined instrument to a certain extent. The resemblance between it and the horizontal harp, however, is rather striking.

The European psaltery evolved in Asia Minor during the first millennium A.D. During the eleventh and twelfth centuries it reached Europe. It carried the name *cythara barbarica,* which need not imply its direct origin from the Greek kithara.

The most common shape of the psaltery was a trapezoid. However, it also appeared in the quadrangular form, sometimes in fan-

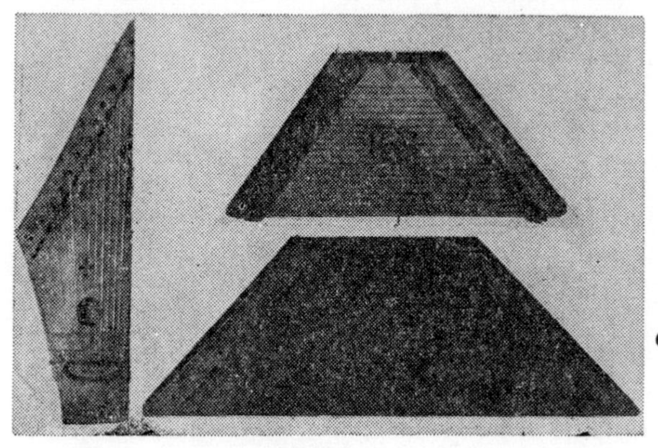

Figure 196
Psalteries
Courtesy Museum of
Fine Arts, Boston

tastic shapes, with a boar's head adorning it, for example. But it must have been a respectable instrument, for angels are frequently depicted playing it. One type, played by suspending it from the neck, was known as *Schweinskopf* or pig's head. Ordinarily psalteries looked like the specimens, on preceding page:

Here we see a Finnish, a German, and an English psaltery. The last was also known as the shepherd's harp, and the strings were plucked, not struck.

It was only natural for musicians to experiment with the psaltery too. A double psaltery is shown (see Figure 197), an instrument which had playing strings on either side. The name of it was *Spitzharp* or *pointed harp*. On one side were thirty-six melody strings, and on the other seventy-three accompanying strings. Both sides were profusely decorated by paintings. It was not so unusual to refer to the psaltery as a harp, since the word merely indicated an instrument to be plucked. The plucking was done either by hand or with a plectrum. In Chaucer's time it was known as *sautrie* or *sawtrie,* and in the *Canterbury Tales* Chaucer lets the "poor scholar" of *The Miller's Tale* delight in it in the following manner:

> And al obove ther lay a gay sawtrie
> On which he made a-nyghtes melodie
> So swetely, that all the chambre rong
> And "Angelus ad Virginem" he song.

The psaltery is the parent of the harpsichord, the spinet, and virginal.

Very similar to the psaltery was the *dulcimer*. The main difference was in the manner of playing: whereas the psaltery was plucked, the dulcimer was struck with a hammer (or hammers). Thus the dulcimer together with the monochord became the parent of the piano. The first dulcimer above shows a padded hammer, the second a pair of smaller ones.

Having given birth as it were to keyed string instruments, both the psaltery and the dulcimer gradually and quietly fell into oblivion. Still, they survived well into the nineteenth century. In one form they were nevertheless to be immortalized, namly in that of the zither.

The *zither* is a psaltery with a finger board for the first four or five strings, the "violin strings." It is still the national instrument of Bavaria, Styria (Austria), and Tyrol. Here it is played by all classes of people; music and dancing are unthinkable without the zither. It is the ideal instrument for folk-song singing. (Today the lute is being revived for this purpose.) Some zither players have international reputations.

Figure 198. Dulcimer
Courtesy Museum of Fine Arts, Boston

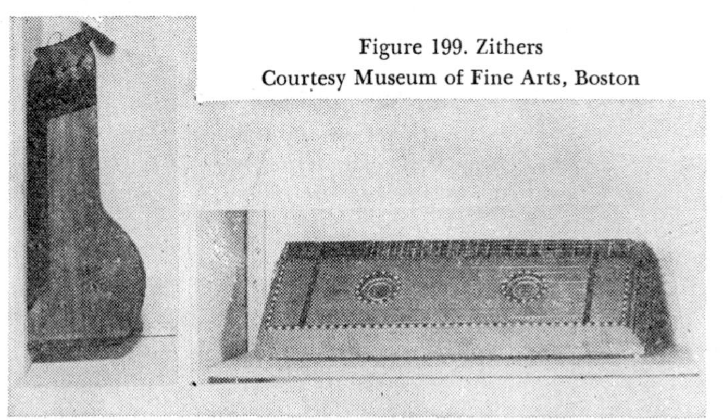

Figure 199. Zithers
Courtesy Museum of Fine Arts, Boston

Figure 197
Pointed Harp — "Spitzharfe"
Courtesy Museum of Fine Arts, Boston

It would be too hasty to assume that the zither made its appearance after psalteries and dulcimers. Indeed, both the psaltery and the dulcimer are regarded by some authorities as zithers, for they all seem to form one family, and the zither is probably the head of it.

The first form of the zither evidently was the *Scheitholtz,* that is, a log of wood. You can easily recognize in it the features of the later zither. You find several sound holes, and the right side reveals about a dozen frets for the melody strings. In addition to Germany, the scheitholtz was found in parts of France and the Scandinavian

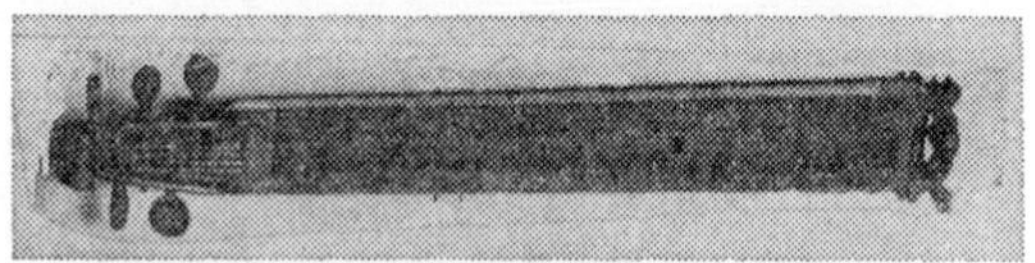

Figure 200
Scheitholtz — a "Log of Wood"
Courtesy Museum of Fine Arts, Boston

countries. Interestingly enough, these instruments were played in the manner of Hawaiian guitars, the melody strings being pressed down by a small rod. The strings, made of wire, were less than twenty inches in length. In some places the scheitholtz survived into the nineteenth century.

Zither strings have a naturally plaintive tone which is enhanced by the romantic setting in which it is usually heard. The accompaniment is a harplike tone, and the sympathetic vibrations of the free strings greatly increase the resonance. On certain occasions even orchestras make use of the zither.

As most other instruments, the zither has appeared in many varieties. The *autoharp* is more or less a children's toy. Here the mechanism eliminates the fingering of the zither which is necessary for chord playing. Some zithers are bowed, but they have been modified with a "waist-line" and so forth.

Lately the zither has found entry even into the symphony. Thus, the Minneapolis Symphony Orchestra under Antal Dorati embodies a zither solo into its rendition of *Tales from the Vienna Woods* by Johann Strauss.

Figure 201. A Lute Player
Courtesy Museum of Fine Arts, Boston

CHAPTER XI

# LUTES

Once upon a time—in fact, until the eighteenth century—lutes belonged to the most respected, popular, and important musical instruments. Historically they are also important, for they hold a vital place in the development of European music. Their peak was reached, it must be said, before keyboard and bowed instruments came into general use. Up to that time the lute was regarded as the most perfect instrument. No musician's education was considered complete unless he knew the art of lute playing.

The lute is the ancestor of most modern string instruments, including the violin. It has a long and romantic history. The European lute can be traced back to the early Middle Ages. It was derived from Arabia and introduced by the Saracens and Moors. But none of these people had invented it, for the origin of the lute lies with the Cappadocians in Asia Minor or the Assyrians—and not the Egyptians, as is still held by some writers.

The oldest lutes appear on Mesopotamian reliefs of the third millennium B.C. But the lute must have existed long before it could have been depicted in art. So we see that the lute is one of the oldest string instruments.

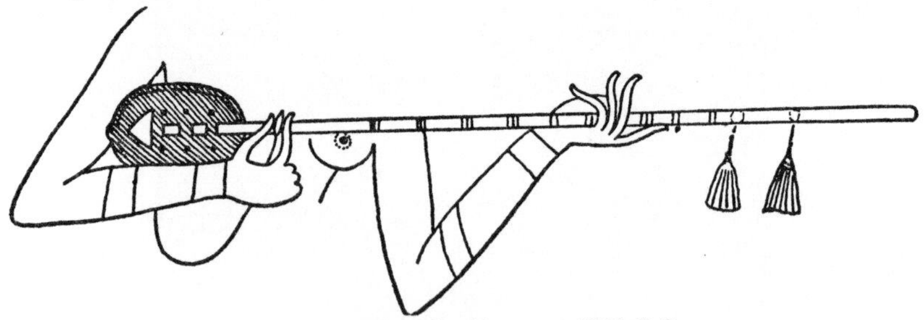

Figure 202. Egyptian Lute, ca. 1200 B.C.
Courtesy Sachs, Hist. of Mus. Inst.

The Egyptians used the lute extensively, whereas the ancient Greeks and Romans did not generally cherish it. The ancient Hebrews likewise did not employ it, for there is no reference to it in the Old Testament.

Our sketch of an early Egyptian lute is quite instructive. The body of this lute is small and of oval shape; it is made of wood. The skin covering acts as the sound board. The sound hole is cut in the form of a triangle, although the opening could also be round. The neck is really a long handle. It pierces the body lengthwise, being held in place by wooden crosspieces inside the body. There are no pegs, so the strings, usually two in number, were merely wound around the end of the neck. The two tassels show early attempts at decoration.

Next we note that this lute is played by a woman. This is not a mere coincidence, for the ancient lute was a woman's instrument. Furthermore, the lady in question shows the manner of playing the lute; note the plectrum she is holding between her right thumb and index finger. She uses her left hand for stopping the strings so as to alter the pitch, a principle already discovered in prehistoric times.

Lutes like the one in Figure 202 may still be found among the natives of Northwest Africa.

It is obvious that such a lute evolved from the musical bow. The flexible bow was exchanged for a rigid rod and the resonator fastened to one end of it. Some of the early lutes were rather heavy contraptions with troughlike bodies.

The Arabs adopted the lute in the seventh century A.D., and some time later it reached Europe. The first European lutes were of two kinds, the long and the short lute. The long lute (ninth century) had a slender neck two to three times as long as the body and a peg disk, several pegs, and six frets. The short lute (tenth century) was a heavy instrument carved out of one piece of wood, reminiscent of the ancient Egyptian lute. Slowly it gained more ground, and when an instrument was required that could cope with the demands of polyphonic (many-toned) music and chord playing, i.e., after 1400, the lute was the answer. By 1500 the classical form had emerged.

The classical lute had a pear-shaped body. The back was round or vaulted in contrast to the flat-bottomed lyres and guitars. The body was built up of separate ribs, the usual number being nine. The rib joints were reinforced on the inside with parchment. This structure greatly increased the resonance. The belly, made of a thin piece of fir wood, was reinforced from the inside by six to seven cross-bars. The sound hole or "rose" had beautiful and complicated patterns.

Note the manner in which the strings are fastened to the lower end and to the upper peg box. The position of the latter shortened the total length of the lute somewhat. Again, the neck was broad but thin. The ideal number of frets, at first made of gut or twisted silk and later of metal, was nine. The strings were grouped in pairs with the exception of the two highest treble strings. There were

Figure 203
Enlarged Detail of Charles Montan's Lute Player Showing Correct Playing Position
Courtesy Museum of Fine Arts, Boston

six bass strings, each string having a "partner" one octave higher, thus securing a fuller and more resonant tone. All told there were two single strings and nine pairs, producing a total number of eleven tones. A pair of strings tuned in unison was known as a *course.*

The manner of playing is illustrated in Figure 203. One look at the player's left hand will convince you that this hand in no way supported the lute in the playing position, but was entirely free for fingering the strings. Note how the player presses against the lute with his chest, and how he uses his right arm for support and holds the lute firmly against his right hip. Learning to hold the lute properly was the first task set the budding lutist. The right hand was employed in the following manner: the little finger rested on the sound board close to the bridge; the thumb rested on a bass string, ready for action; and the other three fingers produced the melody, the fleshy part of the fingertips (not the nails) plucking the treble strings.

During the fifteenth to seventeenth centuries the lute was the instrument par excellence. It was used for solo, accompaniment, and ensemble work. It was as fashionable as the piano of the first quarter of our century. So esteemed was the lute that even today instrument makers are called "lutenists."

After 1850 the lute was abandoned. Today we again have lutists trying to revive the art of lute playing, but so far without too much success.

So much for the lute in general. Now to the members of the family, for being such a respected instrument it is bound to have one. And here it is.

These lutes are the *archlutes,* known as the *chitarrone* and the *theorbo* respectively. Both are greatly enlarged models of the ordinary lute. They provide the deep bass for orchestral accompaniment. As you see, these instruments have double peg boxes.

In the second half of the sixteenth century more and more bass strings were added to the lute. Naturally there was a limit to the reach of the left hand, so that the finger board could not exceed a certain width. Consequently the lower strings were arranged as open strings or drones with a separate peg box. (To introduce a new term here, a term very familiar to organists, these drones were also known as *diapasons.*) The drones were outside the finger board.

The chitarrone was the Italian instrument, the oldest of the three bass lutes (the third type was not of great importance, and is not included here). It represents the largest form of the lute, with a neck of enormous length to provide additional sonority to the deep bass strings. The sound box and the finger board are elaborately inlaid with pearl and engraved ivory. It is man-size and better, some six feet four inches long.

Figure 204. Theorbo

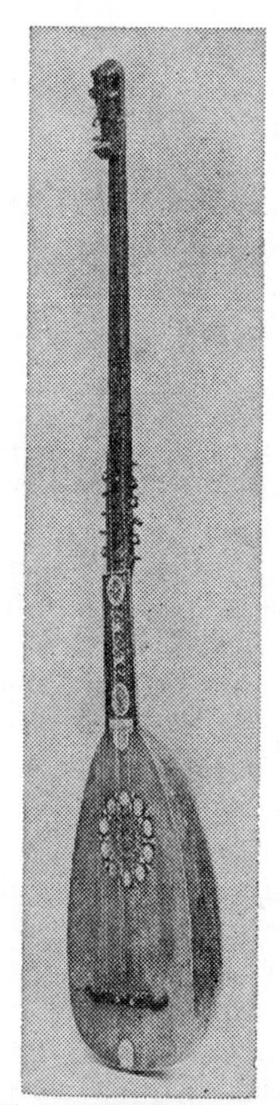

Figure 205. Chitarrone

The theorbo is somewhat smaller. Our particular model measures three feet six inches in length. You notice that the arrangement of the peg box differs somewhat from that of the chitarrone, for it is not straight, but placed slightly to the side by means of an S-shaped neck.

Archlutes gained their importance with the introduction of opera and oratorio, in other words, at a time when pure chamber music was giving way to large-scale auditorium entertainments, and harpsichords, pianos, and other string instruments had not been devised for orchestral use. The archlutes could and did provide chord playing and powerful bass accompaniment.

Up to the end of the seventeenth century the lute strings were of gut; later silver-spun bass strings were introduced.

A typical lute family (in addition to the above) consisted of seven members in descending order of pitch. They were:

1. the small octave lute
2. the small treble lute
3. the treble lute
4. the alto lute (the standard instrument of the family)
5. the tenor lute
6. the bass lute
7. the great octave bass

These seven members formed a *consort,* a name given to a family of instruments. It is clear that a consort of lutes could provide orchestral music.

If the lutes were such excellent instruments, you will wonder why they have disappeared. The answer is found in the advance of more perfect instruments. Furthermore, it was rather troublesome to keep the lute in playing order, for there were certain mechanical defects in its construction. The large number of strings required constant attention; the instrument was difficult to keep in tune. One writer of those times is said to have remarked that if a lutenist succeeded in living eighty years, at least sixty were spent in tuning. In addition, the tension of the strings was comparatively great, and once or twice a year the belly would have to be replaced, as it would sink underneath the constant pressure. Finally, the lute was expensive, as was its upkeep. In Paris, for instance, the cost of having a lute and keeping a horse was about the same.

With the disappearance of the lute its musical literature has also vanished. There is little hope that the latter will ever be restored, for composers for the lute used a system of notation different from our staff notation, the so-called *tablature system.* Instead of having staves of five lines each wherein each note is given its own place, this system had a separate line for each of the strings. To make things more complicated, not the notes but the frets were noted down, either by letters, as in the English and French tablatures, or by numbers, as in the Italian and Spanish tablatures. Since there was no one standard way of tuning the lutes, it is next to impossible to decipher the lute notations.

Some of the most famous composers wrote for the lute. Handel used the lute as an orchestral instrument up to 1741. Bach wrote three sets of pieces for the lute.

We may assume that if the lute should return to favor our modern mechanical proficiency could be applied to developing an efficient tuning mechanism without sacrificing the essential aesthetic features and balance of the instrument. But that would be "crawfishing" (with due apologies to Huckleberry Finn), a course history abhors.

*Instruments of the Lute Type*

At a time when harp and lyre, lute and guitar, psaltery, dulcimer, and fiddle had been accepted, there appeared also a superfluous little "lute," the *mandola.* The mandola was popular with the jongleurs of the twelfth and thirteenth centuries. It was club-shaped, similar to the lute, but the peg box was slightly curved, terminating in a little square head. The lower ends of the strings were fastened to the bottom of the body. It appears that at first the mandola was a rival to the lute, obstructing its improvement, but during the fifteenth century it declined in favor and became more or less an imitation of the lute. During the sixteenth century the mandola became a beggar's instrument. A miniature form of the mandola—the *mandorichen* or *pandurina*—was so small that it could be conveniently carried under the performer's cloak.

The survivor of the mandorichen is the *mandolin,* a beautifully

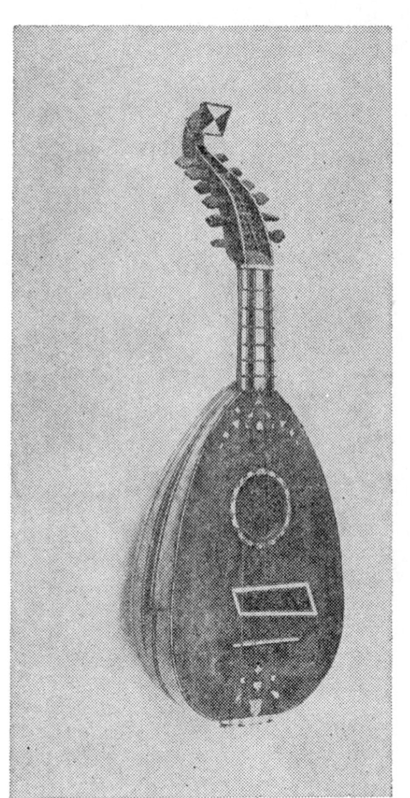

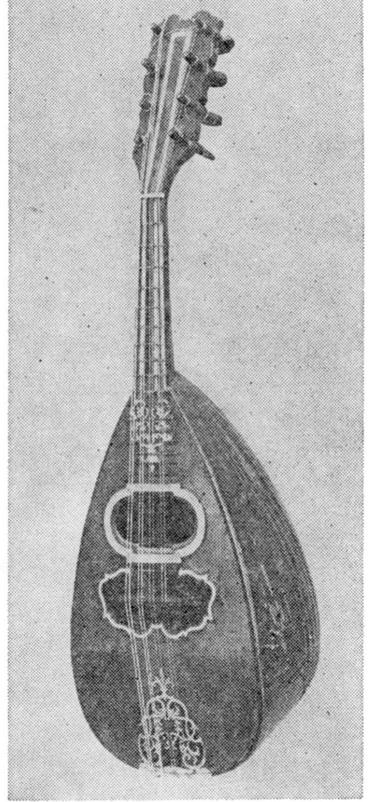

Figure 206. Italian Mandola and Mandolin
Courtesy, Museum of Fine Arts, Boston

framed instrument. Its body is deeper than that of the lute. The Neapolitan mandolin has four courses (pairs) of strings tuned like those of the violin. It is played with a plectrum.

The mandolin enjoyed more respect than the mandola, for we find that Mozart wrote a serenade for mandolin accompaniment and Beethoven accommodated a friend of his (Krumpholz, a virtuoso on the mandolin) with a special piece for this instrument. The mandolin is still popular for folk-song singing and for amateur use. It is fairly easy to learn and is not without its charms.

The search for new instruments apparently is deep-rooted. Figure 207 shows a graceful but old specimen hard to classify. It bears the

Figure 207
Harp-Lute
Courtesy Museum of Fine Arts, Boston

name of *harp-lute*. Actually it is a hybrid, for it combines in its make features of both the harp and the lute; it has a finger board and free strings. The tuning of the strings was totally different from that of either lutes or harps. Note the three nuts on the finger board. The instrument resembles the harp-lute-guitar (Figure 193).

CHAPTER XII

# THE EARLY VIOLIN FAMILY

Our present-day violin family has shrunk from almost innumerable more or less clumsy and imperfect contraptions to only four members: the violin, the viola, the violincello or cello, and the double bass. The history of these instruments constitutes one of the most brilliant achievements of musicianship. It begins with the bow, for all of these instruments are made to vibrate by friction caused by the hair of the bow.

## *The Bow*

The origin of the bow is one of the most controversial topics in our study. Theories have been advanced and discarded again. The most plausible theory has it that the bow originated in Asia (India).

It is altogether probable that the first bows used no hair at all. Among the natives of India, for instance, there is to the present day a kind of musical bow which may be regarded as the first step in its evolution. The bow is arched, and on the inner side, that is, on the side facing the string, are cut little notches. If a small stick is passed rapidly backward and forward over these notches, the bowstring vibrates and produces a musical sound without having been touched.

Figure 208. The Bumbase Bow
Courtesy Museum of Fine Arts, Boston

Later on the stick itself would be notched and rubbed against the now smooth inner side of the bow, producing the same effect. Finally, the string itself was rubbed.

The Chinese used a slip of bamboo for rubbing the strings, which they later exchanged for a stick. In medieval Europe a strip of wood notched like a saw was used. In the first hair-strung bows the hair was probably passed between the strings, as is still the custom in eastern Asia. In such a case the bow is of course an integral part of the instrument and cannot be removed from it without disassembling.

The first real bows were made of rattan, a kind of East India palm tree with long, pliant stems. How it reached Europe is uncertain, but it probably came via Arabia and Persia and thence by commercial routes to Byzantium in the eighth and ninth centuries. Somewhat later it was diffused throughout Europe by the Moorish occupation of Spain. Most likely there was yet another way to reach northern Europe. At any rate, by the thirteenth century the bow was well established.

European bows were made of wood. The very first bows bore a marked resemblance to the hunter's bow, hence the name. The stick was much bent and a chord of strings was tied from one end to the other. Gradually it lost the actual bow shape. A device to keep the hair away from the stick was invented, and the bow was on the road to real improvement.

The first straight "bows" were made of one piece of wood. The first bow shown, for instance, was made of lemon wood; it had a special peg for tightening the hair. This was the *lyra bow*. The second bow is of spruce. It shows some improvements over the lyra bow. The emergence of separate parts such as the nut and the head is already indicated. A stick with the stump of a branch to which

Figure 209
A Primitive Bow

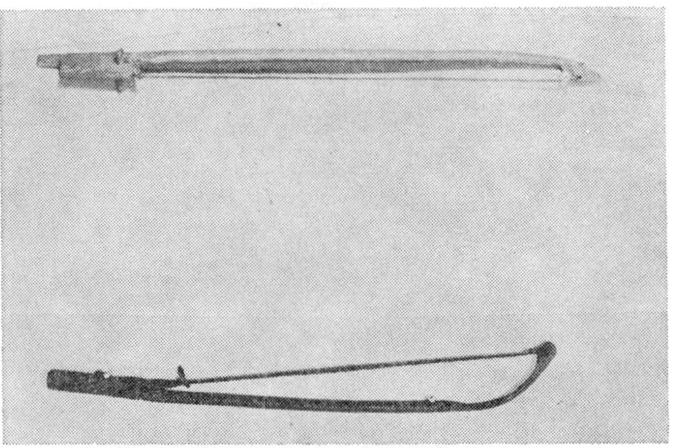

Figure 210. The Lyra and Myckelharpa Bows
Courtesy Museum of Fine Arts, Boston

the hair could have been fastened must have stood godfather to these bows.

To get away from the idea of constructing the bow from a single piece of wood, musicians began to wedge a piece of wood between the stick and the hair at the lower end. This piece of wood evolved during the twelfth century into the *nut,* an essential part of the modern bow. This nut must not be confused with the nut at the end of the finger board of string instruments. One side of the nut is fastened to the top of the bow and the other provides a place to attach the hair.

The head of the bow is really just a device for attaching the strings and varying the tension. Its movable part is technically known as *frog,* which is mostly made of ebony. The first device for tension control consisted of a narrow piece of indented iron on top of the bow that provided a hook for a piece of wire by which in turn the tension of the hair could be regulated at will. Such a mechanism, of course, was not too satisfactory, and it was replaced by a screw. The screw remained one of the characteristics of the modern bow.

The crowning success of all the experimentation with the bow came to the Frenchman François Tourte in Paris toward the end of

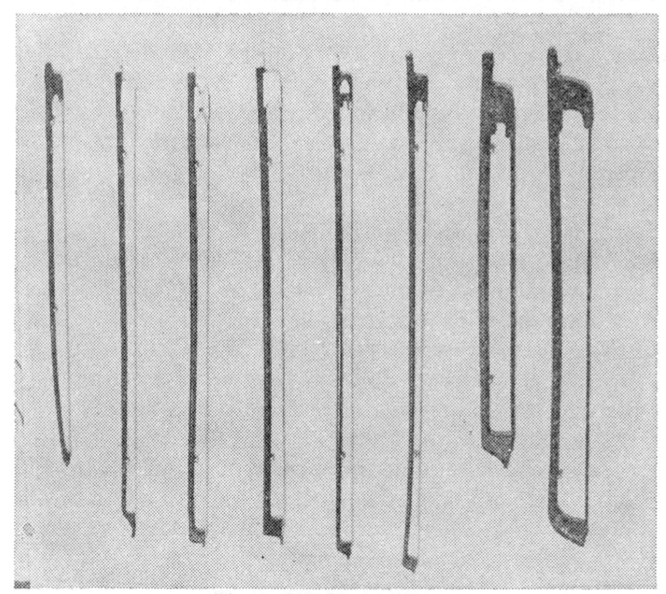

Figure 211. Various Bows

Left to Right: Early Bow, Movable Frog Held by Wire Loop; Viol Bow (ca. 1740); Viol Bow (ca. 1800); Bass Viol Bow (ca. 1800); Viola D'Amore Bow (Late 19th Century); Tourte Type Violin Bow (Late 19th Century); Tromba Marimba Bow (Late 19th Century); Double Bass Bow (Late 19th Century)

Courtesy Museum of Fine Arts, Boston

the eighteenth century. What Böhm did to the flute, Tourte did to the violin bow—and just as it is customary to speak of the Böhm flute so it is to speak of Tourte bows. Here is a brief description of a Tourte bow.

The head is at right angles to the stick, which has a reversed curve for elasticity. A screw inserted into the end of the stick operates the frog to which the hair of the bow is fastened. The head of the screw is made of ebony, ivory, or tortoise shell, and the bow of Brazilian lance or snake wood. It is cut straight following the grain of the wood and afterward slightly bent by exposure to heat.

The hair of the bow is horsehair, used because it has numerous indentations; viewed under a lense it looks somewhat like a saw. Once the "hooks" are gone, the bow must be restrung. The hair lasts some 100 to 120 playing hours. To increase the friction, the hair of the bow is rosined.

Tourte spent years experimenting with the bow. Finally he established a standard which has not been surpassed to the present day.

A Tourte bow is distinguished by its exquisite form and excellent workmanship. It is evident perfection, and has made possible the modern virtuoso violin technique with its many types of bow articulation.

For the sake of completeness, it may be said that Germany has recently produced a special bow for chord playing. This "polyphonic" bow permits the player to strike all four strings simultaneously instead of in rapid succession. The response of violin players to this invention has yet to crystallize.

### *Primitive Bowed Instruments*

In tracing the evolution of the bow we have already encountered some primitive attempts to make "music" by friction. Notched bows, notched sticks, bamboo sticks, and other such implements constituted the original bowed instruments. They had no place in art music, but they did pave the way for those instruments which eventually became the parents of the modern violin.

The Persian *spike fiddle,* found all over the Islamic world, is the earliest bowed instrument in the annals of musical history (tenth century A.D.) The body is only a coconut shell covered with skin. The shell is pierced with a long stick which protrudes at the lower end. The stick is either of wood, as in the East, or of iron as in Western countries.

As primitive as the spike fiddle is, it embodies two features characteristic of the modern violin: the pegs are parallel to the sound board (the technical word here is *lateral*), just as in all our violins; and the protruding stick at the lower end is similar to the spike of a cello and double-bass.

Malayan and Egyptian fiddles had only one or two strings.

The Arabs had a related fiddle, the *rebab* or *rabab*. In this type of fiddle the cocount shell was replaced by a quadrilateral frame forming a flat, shallow box; both sides of the box were closed in by skins, forming a kind of frame drum. The one-string rebab was used to accompany public speakers, while the two-string fiddle, on the other hand, was the singer's instrument.

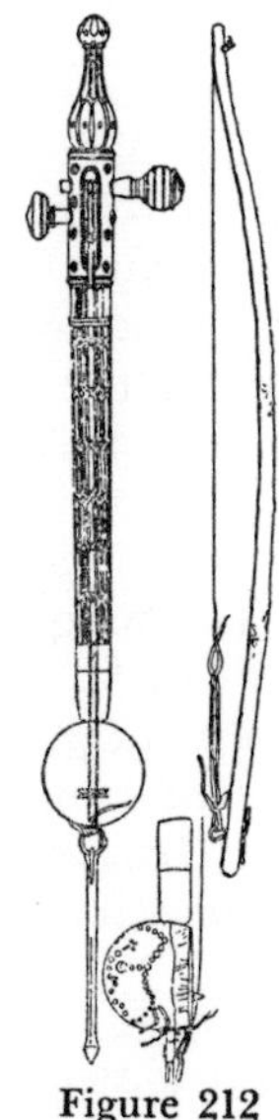

Figure 212
Two-stringed Spike Fiddle

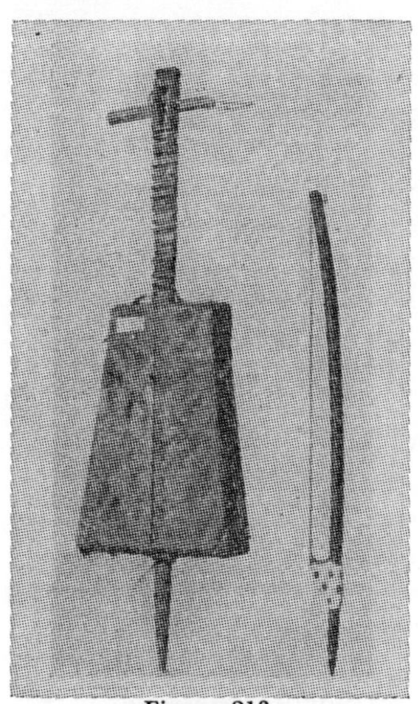

Figure 213
Arabian Rebab

The next question is how and under what guise these bowed instruments entered Europe. Classical Greece and Rome knew no bowed instruments. To the places of entry of the bow, which of course coincide with those of the instruments, themselves, we now add a fourth place, the Caucasus and the southern plains of Russia.

Different types of instruments evolved in different sections of Europe. In northern Europe it was the crwth, already described in Chapter X. However, as a rule the crwth is classified as a bowed harp, not a violin. Between Constantinople and western Europe there was the *lira* (not to be confused with the *lyre,* although some writers like to spell it *lyra*). We shall hear about liras shortly. This group of instruments influenced the development of the *lira da braccio.* From the lira and the rebab developed the *rebec,* the French name for the instrument that in England became the *gigue,* in Germany the *Geige,* a name still popular in that country. Thus, the rebec is greatly responsible for the emergence of the violin. In outline the rebec was similar to the mandolin of which, according

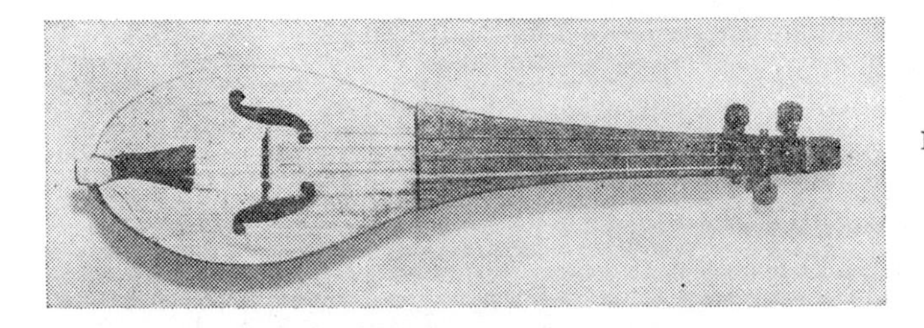

Figure 214
Rebec

to some writers, it was probably the parent. As other scholars have it, it was the bowed equivalent of the lute and the mandola.

As seen from the illustration, the rebec does resemble a lute. Note the position of the peg box and the pear-shaped body. The whole instrument is made of one solid piece of wood with the exception of the peg box. The resonator consists of the scooped-out lower portion, the cavity thus formed being covered by a short pine table.

Note the sound holes. Aren't they just about those of the modern violin? Next take a look at the tail piece for fastening the strings. Again, it does remind you of our violin, doesn't it? So you see that gradually certain features of the modern violin begin to appear long before our time. (By and by you will realize that the violin is actually a combination of the most desired characteristics of a number of bowed instruments, and that no *one* instrument can claim the honor of being its parent.)

During the Middle Ages the rebec was played like a violin, the instrument being held between the chin and the collarbone. It was also bowed like the violin.

At one time the rebec was a rather popular instrument. Representations of it in sculpture, painting, and manuscripts are abundant. In the fifteenth century rebecs were made in sets to correspond to the treble, alto, tenor, and bass voice. At the beginning of the sixteenth century, however, the rebec was classified as a useless instrument, but within two decades it was restored to favor again. Henry VIII, for instance, employed a rebec in his state orchestra, and Shakespeare's musicians in *Romeo and Juliet* are rebec players—Hugh Rebeck, Simon Catling (catgut), and James Soundpost.

The tone of the rebec was loud and harsh, and the instrument was therefore chiefly used to accompany dancing.

Finally the rebec degenerated into the *pochette* or *pocket violin*. The pochette is boat-shaped and narrow. But again, the violin is foreshadowed in its peg box, bridge, and tail piece. It has four strings instead of the three of the rebec. Its total length was from fifteen to twenty inches only, the vibrating length of the strings being about twelve inches. Hence the name *pocket violin*. It was used extensively in teaching children to dance, for it was also known as the *dance master's fiddle* (*Tanzmeisters Geige*), because it could conveniently be carried in the pockets of the coat tails.

Pochettes were often beautifully embellished with inlaid ivory or tortoise shell, carvings, and other adornments. The bows were sometimes entirely of ivory or else inlaid to match the pochette. Why their makers lavished so much fancy upon them can perhaps be explained by the fact that dance masters catered to the fashionable society of the rococo period. Goethe recalls in his memoirs how he learned to dance the minuet to the strains of the pocket fiddle.

A variety of the pochette was the *kit,* supposedly of a little later origin. It looks almost like a miniature violin, except that the neck is long and broad, making it seem out of proportion. The average

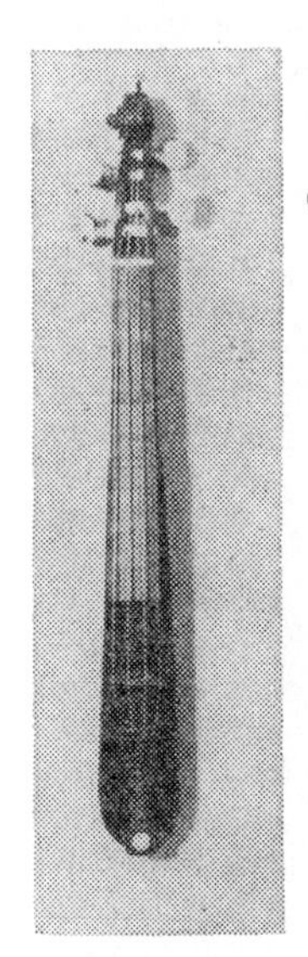

Figure 215
Pochette or Pocket Violin
Courtesy Museum of Fine Arts, Boston

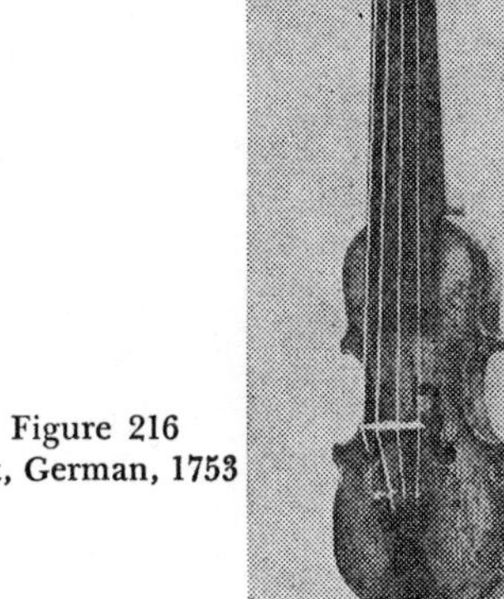

Figure 216
Kit, German, 1753

size of the kit was about sixteen inches. The name is probably derived from *kithara,* and it is also known as the *rebec kit.* It served the same purpose as the pochette, and it is not surprising that both names, *pochette* and *kit,* were used interchangeably. The accession of the piano made them superfluous, and they fell into oblivion. Today the kit is a museum piece.

Neither the pochette nor the kit was a forerunner of our violin; it will be shown later that the violin proper started in the sixteenth century. Further, the pocket violin existed side by side with the violin for nearly two centuries!

One of the rarest and perhaps strangest of all instruments, yet considered by some authorities as the archetype of all bowed instruments, is the *tromba marina*. The tromba marina somehow made its appearance on the Continent in the twelfth century or sooner. Judging by its name, *trumscheit*—a "trumpet out of a piece of wood" (which name prevailed for several centuries)—it was probably of German origin. The most primitive trumscheits were monochords.

The tromba marina or trumscheit was a long, narrow, triangular box with the top made into a sound board. The string is played with a bow close to the upper end, i.e., between the fingering left hand and the head of the instrument. It was made in sizes ranging from four to six feet, or in some cases even longer. The smaller and lighter models were played in an upright position. The number of

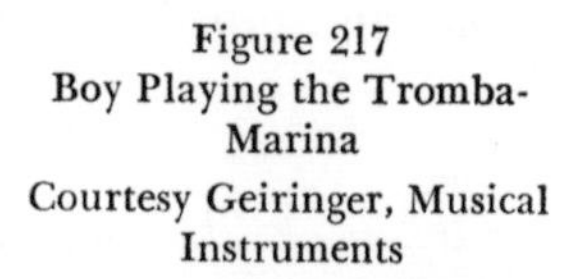

Figure 217
Boy Playing the Tromba-Marina
Courtesy Geiringer, Musical Instruments

Figure 218
Tromba Marina
Courtesy Museum of Fine Arts, Boston

strings was not necessarily restricted to one. After the fifteenth century the downward position of playing became usual.

The bottom end of the tromba marina was open. The left hand was used for stopping the strings. In ordinary playing the thumb would just touch the string in stopping and could also be used for plucking it. Herein we find the first two contributions of the tromba marina to the later violin family. (1) By pressing the string only slightly and not all the way down to the finger board, the string vibrates in sections without producing the fundamental tone, thus creating harmonics. (2) The thumb technique has been adopted by cello players. Oddly enough, if the string were pressed down completely the tone of the tromba was less melodious than the braying of an ass.

The third contribution of the tromba to the violin family is found in the peg mechanism. The peg was equipped with a ratchet wheel, a device consisting of a set of teeth on the edge of a wheel with a catch so that any motion in an undesired direction was ruled out; in other words, once a string was tuned, it would be held securely at that tension. This mechanism was later adapted not only to guitars and mandolins but also to the double-basses of the violin family.

A remarkable feature of the tromba marina will be discovered by a close scrutiny of the illustration to the right. The sound hole at the upper end, reminding one of the "roses" of the lute, is actually a rectangular cover which can be lifted at will. Now, why should this lid be removable? Because below it were the tuning pegs to tune the fifty strings hidden in the hollow of the box! These were the sympathetic strings of the tromba. It is said that some French players caused a listener to hear "a whole concert of chords together at the end of a pause" (seventeenth century). A skillful player could even produce echo effects. During the late seventeenth century serious music was quite within reach of the tromba, for sonatas were composed for it, and there is a record of a concert of four tromba marinas in London (1674).

A careful examination of the last illustration reveals yet another peculiarity of the instrument, which may account at least for the first part of its name. You note that the bridge is lopsided, the string passing over its left side. This end of the bridge is fixed firmly to the sound board. But the other end is so adjusted that it barely touches it, forming a trembling contact with the sound board. Consequently, when the string is attacked by the bow it produces a rattling noise by striking against the sound board. If the string and bridge are properly adjusted, the sound becomes surprisingly clear and loud with a penetrating, almost brassy timbre similar to that of the trumpet. Hence the name *tromba.* It is, however, also possible to rattle the bridge in such a way as to produce snare-drum effects (some writers have indeed confused the tromba with a drum).

The term *marina* has not yet been accounted for. Some scholars contend that it is derived from the Virgin Mary's name. In some parts of Germany this instrument actually was known as "the nun's fiddle" (*Nonnengeige*). Others think that it was probably named after a famous French trumpeter, Marin, because the name *tromba marina* appears about at that period (around 1600; up to then it was simply known as *trumscheit*). There are still other theories concerning the derivation of the *marina,* but they are not worth mentioning.

Like the rebec and the kit, the tromba marina helped to create the violin and then passed into oblivion. Although it possessed only on string (not counting the invisible sympathetic strings) and some writers therefore refer to it as a monochord, it must not be confused with the real monochord we shall discuss later.

Another primitive member of the violin family, also regarded as the prototype of the violin, now claims our attention: the medieval *fiddle,* also known as *Byzantine fiddle, fiedel, vielle, viella, lira, lyra,* and *viola.*

The fiddle is also of Asiatic origin. It came to Europe via the Balkan Peninsula in the ninth century. The first fiddle had a spade-shaped body and measured about two feet in length (Figure 219a).

Figure 219
Early European Fiddles
From "Alte Musikinst." —
Bayerisches Nationalmuseum

A second type of fiddle is found in the *Caucasian fiddle* with three strings (Figure 219c). The original instrument was tall, about a man's height. The outline resembles a bottle with a cork. Note the the two C-shaped sound holes and the numerous small circular holes in the belly. This fiddle is still in use in Georgia.

The fiddle with the eight strings shown in the same illustration is a later model. Four of the strings were melody strings, the remaining four the sympathetic strings. Unfortunately our illustration does not show the strings clearly, and there appear to be only seven pegs instead of eight. A most significant feature of this deep-boated fiddle is the *finger board without frets.* The lower end has a tail piece for fastening the strings similar to that of our violin except that it is like a "floating" tail.

The third type of fiddle is the *Byzantine lira.* Its pear-shaped body is made of a solid piece of wood. The body is shallow and slightly bulging. The peg box is disklike, and there is no distinct

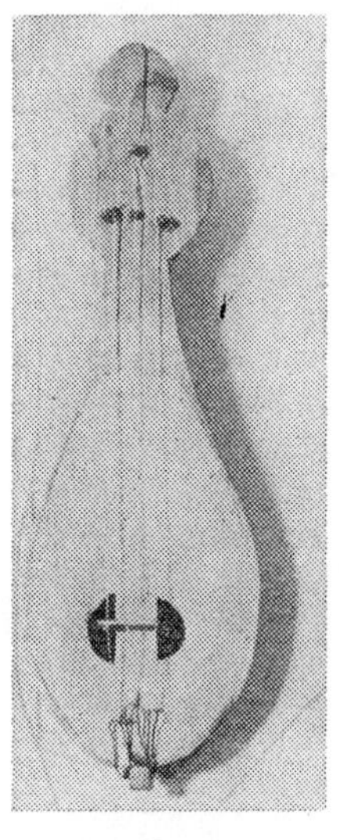

Figure 220. Byzantine Lira
Courtesy Museum of Fine Arts, Boston

neck. Above all, there is no nut between the neck and the peg box, which suggests that the strings are played in harmonics only.

The *Byzantine lira* is derived from the Islamic rebab we encountered earlier. It became the principle bowed instrument of Europe in the Middle Ages. The number of strings varied from one to five. Three was the number of the Oriental lira, five the classic number of the medieval fiddle. One of these strings was a drone, plucked with the thumb. Later this drone was dropped and the four remaining strings were tuned in almost the same way as the tenor violin of the seventeenth and eighteenth centuries.

Gradually the shape of the fiddle was altered to approach the modern form. The body was enlarged, the form became that of a flat, oval box, and the whole instrument was made of separate pieces. Furthermore, it was "waisted." The classical form evolved only gradually; for many a year numerous forms were intermingled.

The medieval fiddle has by no means given up its struggle for existence. To prove the point you need but look at the accompanying illustration. Here we see the *husli,* a roughly made peasant

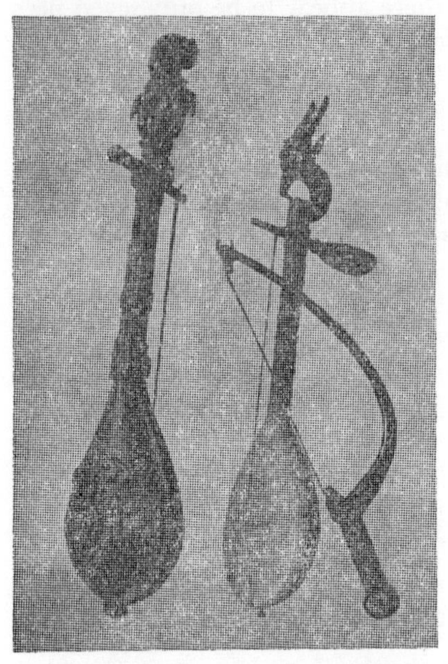

Figure 221
Husli, 19th Century
From "Alte Musikinstrumente",
Bayerisches Nationalmuseum

instrument. Up to the middle of the nineteenth century it was rather popular among Slavonic peoples, although it came from a district in Prussia. Russian folk poems make much of it.

## *The Liras*

The name *lira* was commonly applied to the smaller bowed instruments such as the rebec and the hurdy-gurdy (Chapter XIV). In Italy the fiddle was also called *lira.* From the fifteenth century on, however, *lira* designated a special type of bowed instrument particularly popular in Italy. As will be seen from the next illustrations, liras had free vibrating strings just like the theorbos.

The two principal forms of the lira were the *lira da braccio* (Figure 222) and the *lira da gamba* (Figure 223), or in plain English, the shoulder or arm lira and the lira held between the knees while playing. As will be seen, this distinction also obtains with viols.

Figure 222
Lira da Braccio,
Verona, 1511
Courtesy
Kunsthistorisches
Museum,
Vienna

Figure 223
Lira da Gamba, ca. 1590

The *lira da braccio* had seven strings, five for the finger board and two drones. Certain of its features foreshadow those of the violin. Note the curved shoulders, the shallow body, and the tail piece holding the strings below the bridge. The peg box, on the other hand, is markedly different.

During the Renaissance Italian artists and musicians held the lira in high esteem. In Raphael's paintings, for instance, we find Apollo with a lira; madonnas with angels and saints play it; Homer, the Greek poet, is portrayed with it, and women are pictured playing it.

Leonardo da Vinci learned to play the lira and gained high honors with his self-made instrument. Leonardo's instrument was a highly unusual specimen, for it was made in the shape of a horse's head, and mostly of silver at that! It is recorded that at a festival at the court of the Duke of Milan Leonardo outdid all the other musicians.

Up to 1600 the lira held its own at the most splendid festivities. Ferdinand IV, King of Naples, the Medicis, and Henry IV of France were among the noted patrons of the lira. Haydn wrote seven nocturns and five concertos for the lira da braccio.

The *lira da gamba* was the larger type with twelve, fourteen, or sixteen strings in pairs. The finger board had frets. This instrument was a late bass model of the lira da braccio, more or less a musical hybrid. There is even a rose sound hole copied from the lute. The bridge is rather flat, which indicates that the instrument's chief function was that of chord, not melody playing. The strings were so thin that the highest of them could be tuned an octave above the highest string of our cello, although they are of equal length.

It is generally conceded that both forms of the lira disappeared with the ascent of the violin, that is, during the seventeenth century or somewhat later, for it was not a sudden step from one instrument to another. Haydn is said to have played it still. The lira, too, has made important contributions to the violin.

## *The Viols*

The Italian *viola,* also applied to some fiddles, designates a class of instruments similar to our present violin. The English name for this large group of instruments is *viol.* Of all the bowed instruments of the pre-violin period, the viol is the closest approach to our modern violin.

Before the Industrial Revolution and the days of modern communication and transportation, there was little tendency toward standardization and mass production. Hence, viols showed great diversity in size, shape, and details. It would have been quite inconceivable for instrument makers in widely separated countries to turn out identical instruments or to have a tacit agreement concerning certain standards of instruments. So we find that once Europe embarked upon the construction of instruments, she showed no end of variety in kinds. This applies to practically all types of instruments—harps, lyres, lutes, guitars, fiddles, rebecs, liras, and viols.

Again, the just-mentioned instruments comprise only those that either survived or gave rise to the more refined modern types, since scores of others, now obsolete, are mentioned in books on the history of instruments. Generally a new type would evolve from the older one gradually, and usually the old and the new ran parallel courses until the one would definitely prove its superiority, a process which sometimes required centuries.

This fact accounts for the extreme difficulty we have in tracing the origin and evolution of so many instruments, especially the strings. So far there are no answers to such pertinent questions as: who invented the fiddle, the rebec, the lira, the viol, the violin; when; and which is the first of these instruments or their prototypes? These instrument evidently just grew from insignificant beginnings; we hardly know which is the parent of which.

Notwithstanding their differences, viols had certain features in common. Broadly speaking, the *viola da gamba* had sloping shoulders, deep ribs, and a flat back; the neck was broad and thin and the finger board was fitted, at least partially, with movable frets.

The viol class evolved during the fifteenth century from the types of bowed instruments already discussed. By the end of the century a certain screening had taken place, and the following emerged as the fittest to survive: the bass viol, the tenor viol, the treble or descant viol, the double-bass viol, the viola bastarda, and the viola d'amore. All of them were gradually supplanted by the violins and disappeared during the eighteenth century to emerge as worth-while curiosities with probably a fair future in our own century.

For our study we shall follow the convenient method of grouping them into *braccio* and *gamba,* with the same connotation as with the liras, namely, "arm" and "leg" viols respectively according to the position in which the instrument was held for playing.

The most important member of the viol family is the *bass viol,* a typical gamba viol. This is the instrument most used for solo work; furthermore, it came next to the lute as the instrument for accompaniment and was the foundation of an ensemble. England produced many excellent viol makers.

The bass viol measured about four feet in length and had six single strings. The strings were tuned like those of the lute. The

Figure 224. Bass Viol, London, 1713
Courtesy Museum of Fine Arts, Boston

Figure 225
Double-Bass Gamba, 1585
Courtesy Kunsthistorisches Museum, Vienna

method of bowing is described as "underhand," meaning that the bow was held with the palm of the hand turned upwards.

Bach wrote three sonatas for clavier and viola da gamba and included it in several other compositions, showing us that this instrument was held in high esteem and that it certainly had musical charms. Today the cello holds its place.

The *double-bass viol* or *violone* in Italian was to the above instrument what the double-bass of today is to the cello. Being larger in size, its range was an octave lower. The double-bass viol was popular in Italy and Germany. It was finally supplanted by the double-bass of the violin family.

In addition to the two bass viols just described, there were viols for every range of the human voice, so that, following the vogues of the time, viols formed families capable of playing complete chord music. Such families, as we have said, were known as *consorts*. The smallest viol of the consort was approximately twenty-eight inches long, whereas the deepest bass instrument measured seven feet.

From the beginning of their existence viols were regarded as noble instruments, and they never lost their standing in the esteem of the upper classes. In many cases viols were lavishly decorated. A perusal of the ornaments and decorations of the illustration, Figure 226, will be a worth-while study. Beginning at the top, there is a head crowning the peg box.[1]

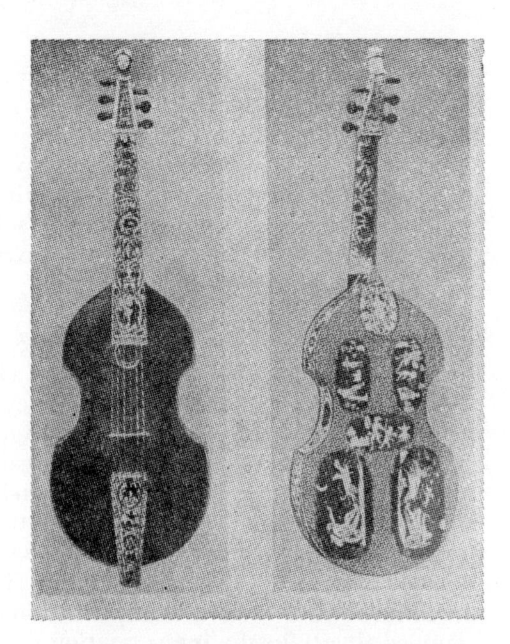

Figure 226
Tenor-Viola da Gamba,
Hamburg, 1679
Courtesy Nef, Geschichte
unserer Musikinstrumente

Scrolls, flowers, ornaments on the finger board, tail piece, and on the back—these figures alone tell a story—and even on the ribs must have made the owner proud of his treasure. Most viols lacked such

[1] This is evidently just a head of an ordinary human. Ages ago it would have been a representation of some deity, and then some symbolic figure; still later in history the head would belong to some historic personage, and finally to a mere mortal. Thus we see once more that the original symbolism gradually loses its significance and the plain ornament remains.

artistry, of course, for few people were rich enough to afford the price, and musically it would in no way enhance the value of the instrument.

Henry VIII possessed twenty-five viols in his collection of musical instruments. He also composed some fine pieces for viol consorts. At home, at church, and at court functions viols held their place. They were used as solo instruments, for voice accompaniment, and in different combinations of their own type—the *whole consort*—as well as in combination with other instruments—the *broken consort.* Skill in the playing of the viol was regarded as an accomplishment as necessary as the possession of good manners. What is more, the viol was the instrument of the amateur, so that everyone interested could learn to play it. (It was easier to play than our violin, because the true viol had fretted fingerboards.) The music, in the words of Mace, a seventeenth-century writer, was

> .... so suitable and agreeing to inward, secret, and intellectual faculties of the soul and mind, . . . that to set them forth according to their praise, there are no words sufficient in language. . . . They have been to myself (and many others) as divine rapture, powerfully captivating all our unruly faculties and affections and disposing us to solidity, gravity and a good temper, making us capable of heavenly and divine influence.

Viols, precious as they were, were kept in specially constructed pieces of furniture, *the chest of viols.* A chest of viols was a shallow vertical press with double doors and several partitions and apartments. Each partition was lined with green bags to keep the instrument from being injured by the weather. "Chest of viols" also designated a set of six viols, properly matched so as to form a consort. The ordinary consort consisted of two trebles, two tenors, and two basses; sometimes a tenor would take the place of one of the basses.

The art of viol playing throws an interesting sidelight upon the fashions of the times. The performing artist enjoyed almost unbounded liberty in the interpretation of the written score. Furthermore, improvisations, i.e., a manner of playing without score, making up the music as you go, and giving room to flights of fancy, was common practice. Thus, the musician had ample opportunity to express his individuality.

Such freedom was extended to practically all performers, not only the viol players. Haydn's and Mozart's scores are often woefully deficient in dynamic signs. Opera composers would let their prima donnas improvise their own arias—for instance, Rossini in his

*Barber of Seville,* and even Brahms left the cadenza of his violin concerto to the discretion of his violinist, Joachim. Early independent conductors of orchestras—in the nineteenth century—used to be the plague of composers by taking too many liberties with their scores. (The champion of the "back-to-the-composer's-score" movement was Toscanini of our times.) Evidently not only the instruments but the performance too lacked standardization.

One type of viol was equipped with sympathetic strings. The principal representatives of this class are the *viola d'amore* (*viole d'amour*) and the *baryton.*

The viola d'amore is halfway between the alto and the bass viol, played in the same manner as the violin. Note the free strings beneath the melody strings. The name suggests a "love" instrument, but this interpretation is somewhat misleading. Its tone is not loving but metallic. The carved figurehead represents the blindfolded Cupid. But this god of love is also found on other instruments.

Up to Bach and Handel the viola d'amore had no sympathetic strings. Later on the strings were tuned to our diatonic scale and responded to overtones which set them in vibration. Since there was

Figure 227
Viola d'Amore, Hamburg, 1670
Courtesy Museum of Fine Arts, Boston

no way of stopping them, they would continue to vibrate after the fundamental tone, affecting the tone in a rather peculiar way. The number of sympathetic strings ranged from seven to fourteen.

The viola d'amore was fashionable during the eighteenth century. For a time it seemed doomed to fall into oblivion, but it actually never became quite obsolete, for composers have continued to take a fancy to it to the present day. Vivaldi wrote a concerto for it; Bach, too, composed for it. In our own times we encounter it in Charpentier's *Louise,* in Puccini's *Madama Butterfly,* and in Richard Strauss's *Domestic Symphony;* Loeffler (1861–1935) composed a work for orchestra and viola d'amore and Paul Hindemith (1895– ) also wrote a concerto for it.

The *baryton* developed from the viola bastarda, an instrument similar to the viola d'amore but larger. It never gained popularity in England but became important in Germany. Haydn wrote 175 (!) compositions for the baryton, for his employer, Prince Esterházy,

Figure 228
Baryton, a Bass Viol with Sympathetic Strings, Germany, 19th Century
Courtesy Museum of Fine Arts, Boston

was a skillful baryton performer. Mozart also composed solos for it.

How many strings does the illustrated baryton have? Note the small blocks or pegs right on the sound board for attaching them. Some of them run below the fingerboard, others to the right of it. There are still some frets on the neck. The sound holes are somewhat peculiar, and there is our old familiar "rose" of the lute. The figurehead at the top of the peg box is identified by the wing on the scroll as a cherub's head. The instrument was a little over four feet in height.

Figure 229
Lira Viol, London, 1665
Courtesy Museum of Fine Arts, Boston

The *lira viol* is a small-sized bass viol, supposedly a later invention in imitation of the old English lute. Like the lute, it was played from a tablature instead of from staff notation. The finger board is fretted throughout. The sound holes are more violinlike than those of the baryton, and there are no sympathetic strings. The blindfolded Cupid calmly looks down from his elevated position, watching the performance. The sound board has ink-lined edges. The length of the viol is about three feet four inches.

The *cither viol* or sultana, two feet high, is another form of the lira viol. It has five pairs of wire strings and is played with a bow.

The tuning pegs are of metal, and the finger board and the tail piece are veneered with ivory. A most significant difference between the cither and lira viols is the absence of frets in the former.

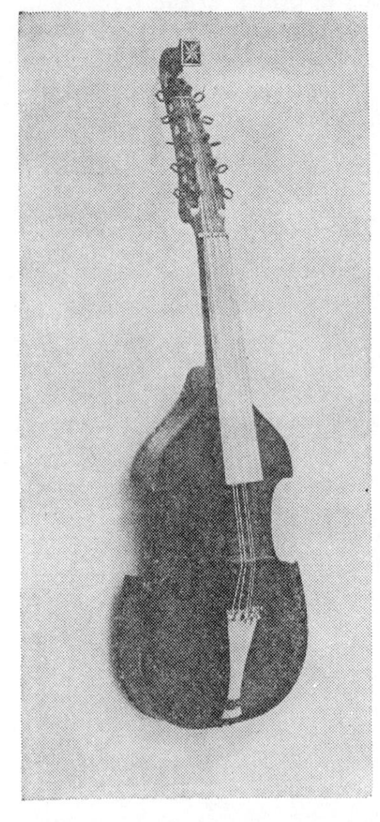

Figure 230
Cither Viol, Irish, 1794
Courtesy Museum of Fine Arts, Boston

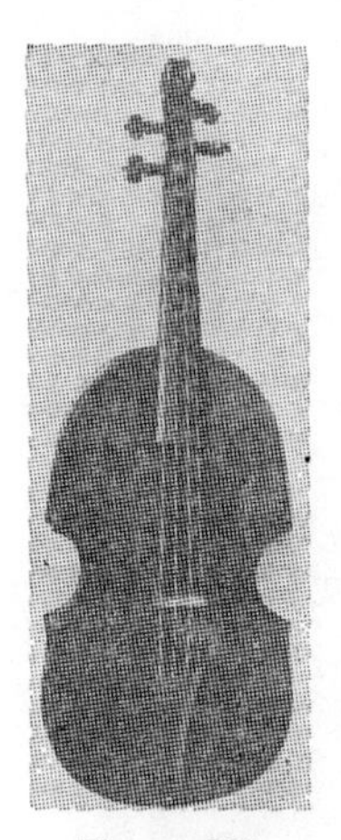

Figure 231
Viola da Braccio

The *viola da braccio* is a little later type and smaller than the viola da gamba. It, too, gave rise to a family of instruments. The smallest was the violino piccolo, a small viola only fifteen to nineteen inches long; then there was the violino, followed by the violoncello, which corresponded to the bass viola da braccio. (This violoncello is not yet the true cello of our day.)

The "da braccia" instruments were, as was stated earlier, the "arm" instruments, that is, they were not held between the knees while playing. They were evidently of far less immediate importance than the gambas, but still they were most important for the future of music, for they already embodied so many violin features that we find in them the immediate forerunners of the violin.

CHAPTER XIII

# THE MODERN VIOLIN FAMILY

Attempts have been made to ascertain the exact time of the invention of the violin and to discover the inventor and the place of origin. So far all such endeavors have been futile. What is more, they are bound to remain so unless scholars make some startling discoveries in the future, for as far as we know today the violin never was properly invented by one particular person in one particular country at one particular time, because *the violin is the happy combination of all the best features found in the earlier instruments.* If one must assign parentage to it, one may say that the rebec and the lira da braccio come closest to it. The contention that viols led directly to violins is refuted by the fact that violins and viols coexisted for several centuries, and only after a bitter struggle between them did the violin gain supremacy.

This much, however, is known: the violin emerged in the early years of the sixteenth century, or about two centuries before viols reached the peak of their popularity. Violins assumed their final form about fifteen years later than did viols. It is further assumed that violins appeared first in Italy, where they were called *liras,* upholding the contention that the lira da braccio is the mother of the violin.

Where, then, and how did the violin acquire its characteristic features?

Suppose you turn back a few pages and look for special violin features in the illustrations given. You will find that the ancient rebec possesses the same type of pegs and box as the modern violin, so we see that *the head of the violin comes from the Arabian rebec* and therefore can be traced to the Arabian influence in Sicily and the Moorish in Spain. Next you will note that *pochettes* and *bass viols* have the typical *scroll* at the head. Members of the violin family are *fretless,* a feature bequeathed to them also from the *rebec.*

The typical *sound holes in f-form* are evident in the *lira da braccio.* The *shoulders of the lira* are nearly perpendicular to the neck, not sloping to a tangent as in the viol, thus showing the close relationship between liras and violins. Liras also had a shallow, violinlike *sound box* (the body of the viols, on the other hand, was deep). The shape of the inside space of the violin sound box is like that of the guitar. Now, the guitar-shaped form can already be found on ancient Hittite monuments dated 1000 B.C. (And please don't start the argument all over again that this means the origin of the violin.) In Europe this guitar form appeared on bowed instruments of the twelfth century. The *back of the lira,* an important feature *embodied in the violin,* was arched, thus foreshadowing the shallow sound box. The *table* or belly was slightly curved and molded back, which gave the violin its brilliance of tone without the harshness of the rebec and the heaviness of the viol.

Finally, concerning the *tuning* of the open strings, we find that the violin is tuned in fifths just like the rebec. Similarly to the rebec, some of the first violins also had only three strings.

The first and basic instrument of the violin family was the *viola* and not the violin. The contention that the treble viola da braccio became the violin, the alto braccio the viola, and the tenor viola da gamba the violoncello, although still upheld by some authorities, is definitely erroneous. The viola da braccio gave way to our viola, still called *Bratsche* in German. The other three members of the family evolved only gradually, and only after years of experimentation were they firmly established.

For instance, in addition to the four regular members of the family, *Grove's Dictionary* lists fifteen subsidiary instruments of particular interest, now mostly discarded. But even these fifteen "violins" do not include all the specimens turned out, so there must have been a real mania for innovations. Here is one of the more im-

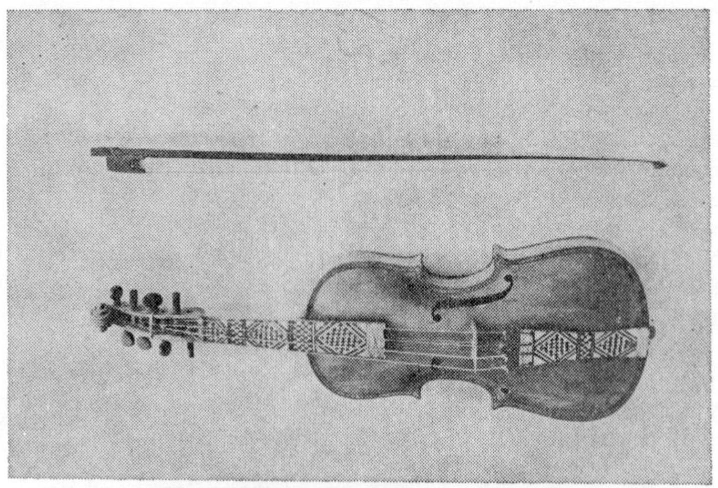

Figure 232. Hardanger Violin, Norway, 1833
Courtesy Museum of Fine Arts, Boston

portant strange violins (Figure 232). The *Hardanger violin,* also called *viol,* has four sympathetic strings of steel. It is a nineteenth-century model still found in Norway. It reminds one of the eighteenth-century lira viol, baryton, and viola d'amore.

Another odd violin was the *violone* or *octobasse,* manufactured in Paris in 1849. It stood *thirteen* feet high and had three strings. Well, how on earth could any mortal handle such a monster? The answer is provided by a special mechanism consisting of eight (perhaps seven) pedals for fingering the strings, and the strings were tuned from the tail piece.

Attempts to construct string basses for the orchestra date back to the seventeenth century. So for two hundred years the search for *the* violin bass continued. In 1889 an American constructed a fifteen-foot violone! Surprisingly, these giants had a weak tone and were soon discarded one after the other. Today the double-bass rules the field. Generally modern basses do not exceed six feet in length.

As stated before, the *viola* was the first permanent member of the modern violin group. A smaller model was made from it, the *little viola* or *violin.* A larger-model viola became the *violoncello.* Although held between the knees for playing, the violoncello—commonly called just *cello*—had for its starting point the bass viola da braccio, not the gamba. The double-bass was constructed either in the gamba fashion (in Germany) or the braccio (in Italy).

The introduction of the violin encountered strong resistance, notably in England and France. Compared to the then-popular viols with their soft and mellow but somewhat pale tone, violins were characterized by a round, full, brilliant sound. The Italians, on the other hand, regarded the violin as the queen of instruments and treated it accordingly. (They are even today generally considered the best violinists.)

Not so in England and France. Here the violin was used as a dance instrument, but not admitted for chamber music. In France this opposition persisted into the eighteenth century. Not before famous violinists had proved its merits would "decent folk" condescend to cultivate it. Following are some quotations by noted opponents of the violin: "The violin is not noble, everyone agrees on this." The cello was "a miserable, hated and pitiful wretch, whose lot was to starve to death for lack of a free meal." Dreadful were "the thick strings." The violin and cello were not able "to dispute the delicate touch of the viol"—and this some two hundred years after the famous Italian violin makers!

What circumstance then finally gave the violin its victory over the viols and its present status as queen of instruments? The glory of the violins began to shine with the shift of society's interest from small rooms and chambers to opera houses and concert halls. This shift involved a change not only in musical instruments but also in style, favoring the dramatic, overpowering music of the violins and dislodging the viols. Violins became the leading instruments in the orchestra and, once established, in the chamber as well.

### *Violin Makers*

The triumph of the violin is in no small measure due to its famous makers. By the end of the sixteenth century the violin had attained its classic form. Now violin makers began to devote their efforts to details without altering the fundamentals.

The center of the industry was northern Italy, at first Brescia and later Cremona. Violin making became an art and a most respected profession. The craftsmen were born into it and grew up with it; they thought of nothing else. To become a great violin maker was the ambition of every boy in the village. Apprentices underwent long years of exacting training. Only after rigid tests were passed did journeymen graduate to become masters of the craft. The neverfailing ambition of Cremona craftsmen was to achieve still greater things and to make each violin a masterpiece worthy of the name and a bit better than the former one.

To realize the enormity of the task confronting a violin maker, one needs to know that the instrument has up to seventy component parts under thirty-six names. (Remember the primitive rebec of one solid piece?) Every one of these parts could conceivably be altered somewhat in length, width, thickness, material, and polish.

It is customary to construct the back, neck, ribs, and bridge of sycamore; the belly, bass bar, blocks, linings, and sound post of pine or spruce, and the finger board, tail piece, nuts, and pegs of ebony. Formerly boxwood, rosewood, pear wood, and ivory were used. The varnish has far less significance to the tone of the violin than is commonly assumed.[1]

The Italian school of violin makers produced instruments that never have been surpassed, if ever quite equaled. The German school came a close second. Later on English, French, and other schools were founded, each producing good violins after the Italian models.

For the sake of completeness, the most distinguished names are included in the following list.

1. *Gasparo di Bertolotti da Salò* (1540–1609) and his pupil, *Giovanni Paolo Maggini* (1581–1628). Their violins were somewhat old fashioned in detail.

---

[1] As a matter of fact, no varnish can improve the resonance or tone: it enhances the appearance of the violin and preserves the wood. Actually it interferes with the resonance; hence the problem is to find a varnish which will do so the least. The secret of the violin does not lie in the varnish.

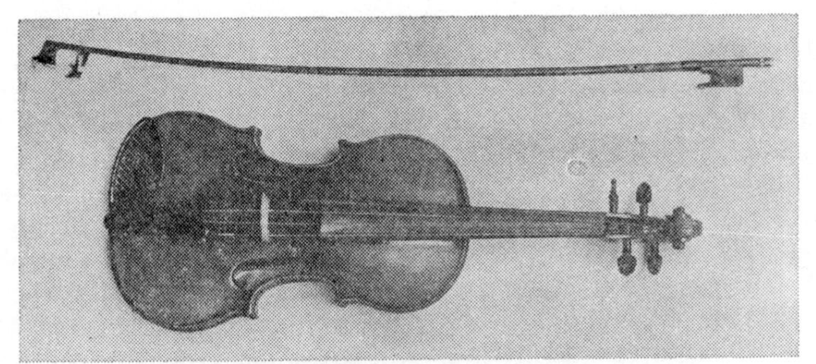

Figure 233. A Stradivarius Violin
Courtesy Metropolitan Museum of Art, New York

2. *Andrea Amati* (1530?–?1611), the *founder of the Cremona School* and first of the celebrated family. His grandson *Nicolò,* the most eminent member of the family, was the teacher of Stradivarius. The Amati violins are noted for their astonishingly sweet and soft tone and beauty of voice, considered unsurpassable in the seventeenth and eighteenth centuries.

3. *Antonio Stradivari* (*Antonius Stradivarius*) (1644–1737), the *master of masters.* The house in which he spent the most successful years of his life and where he died now bears the inscription: "Brought the violin to perfection and left Cremona an imperishable name as master of his craft."

Apprenticed to Nicolò Amati's shop, he showed remarkable skill in his work. At the age of twenty-two he turned out his first violin with his own label containing his full name, the date, the Maltese cross, and the initials A.S. enclosed within a double circle. Compared to his later models his first violins were of poor material, covered with thick yellow varnish, of solid build, and small.

Up to 1684 Stradivari adhered to Amati's smaller pattern, but after that date he definitely turned his attention to building larger instruments. In 1690 he brought forth his "Long Strad" with a new set of proportions, a strongly toned instrument suggested by a Maggini violin which had come under his notice. Finally he constructed a larger, flatter type which exceeds the Amati violins in volume and fullness of tone and yet is just as tender.

Added to their musical qualities, the precise and careful workmanship of these instruments makes them truly magnificent art pieces. The Stradivarius violin has remained the unrivaled ideal of tonal and aesthetic perfection, commanding a price today well into the five figures.

Stradivarius also made some violoncellos. At his time cellos were not too well understood, and he did not devote himself to them wholeheartedly. His violas again bear the stamp of the true genius. He is also credited with a viola da gamba, a kit, and two handsome guitars. In all he had 1116 instruments to his credit. His methods have been preserved from century to century until they have become the foundation of the art of violin making. Today there are 540 violins, 12 violas, and 50 cellos in existence known to be made by Stradivarius.

4. *Giuseppe Guarnieri* (1683–1745), the most important member of a large family of violin makers. While his violins are less regularly built, they do have a particularly beautiful tone. Jascha Heifetz and Fritz Kreisler, two of the most illustrious names among violinists, use Guarnieri instruments.

5. *Jakob Steiner* (1621–1683), the leader of the German school. His instruments had an unusually sweet, tender, and flutelike tone. For a time Steiner rivaled the Italian school. It is of interest to note that this is the only school that lasted at least to World War II.

After a century and a half the art of violin making declined. Instead of deteriorating with age violins gain by it, and the demand for the instrument had been met.

The modern violin is not a creation of the classic masters just mentioned; it is modified in its outer aspects and changed in its internal construction. For one thing, the old neck has been replaced by the modern longer form of more uniform thickness and inclined toward the back. Several other changes have affected the tonal qualities of the violin and changed its character. The tone has become more brilliant, more assertive, better adapted to larger halls. At the same time, the violin has lost some of its mellowness and warmth. Still, the modern violin is a marvel of perfection. World-renowned concert violinists no longer depend on the old classic models.

### *The Present-Day Violin Family*

A "family" of instruments corresponds roughly to the range of the human voice: soprano, alto, tenor, and bass. In the violin family we have only three instruments for these parts, the first violin for the soprano, the second violin for the alto and part tenor, and the cello for the lower tenor and bass. There is no tenor violin.[2] But since the range of the strings can extend far below the human voice, a large double-bass has been added to the family.

[2] There seems to have been a tenor violin, used by Handel and Bach, up to the middle of the eighteenth century, but for some reason or other it became obsolete.

Figure 234. The Four Members of the Violin Family Showing Relative Sizes

With the exception of the double-bass, the instruments look alike and have generally the same proportions. The violin and the viola have the same fingering technique so that a transition from one to another is possible. The cello, however, being held between the knees while played and differing in size, requires an altogether different technique of playing. Consequently, no interchange is possible from the cello to either the violin or the viola, and vice versa. The double-bass has the strings tuned in fourths, not in fifths as have the other instruments, and therefore has a playing technique all of its own.

### *The Violin*

The *violin* is the queen of instruments and the most important member of the orchestra. There is no other instrument that approaches the ideal of perfection to such a degree. Its tone quality is rich and varied, the range of emotional expression surpasses that of the human voice, and it has tremendous flexibility and agility of performance. It is a strictly melodic instrument. The four strings are spanned over an arched bridge; consequently, only two strings can be played simultaneously, although it is possible to play four-part chords so as not to make the *arpeggio* effect too noticeable.

As was stated previously, the Tourte bow is the basis of modern violin technique. The following are the most important ways of playing the violin (not that all these Latin names are all-important or to be memorized):

1. *Legato—smoothly,* without breaks.
2. *Staccato*—played in an abrupt, sharply detached manner, the opposite to *legato.* There are at least three ways to produce different *staccatos.* For instance, a staccato is obtained if the whole length of the bow is skipping as it were over the string; then again, the performer may bounce the bow heavily and abruptly against the string for a moment and let the string continue to vibrate; finally, there is the crisp and "short-hammered" bowing.
3. *Pizzicato*—plucking the strings with the fingers of the right hand.
4. *Spiccato*—obtaining a number of short detached notes by a single upward sweep of the bow.
5. *Saltando*—"jumping bow"; the player lets the bow fall and rebound on the strings. This method of playing was introduced by Paganini.
6. *Col legno*—tapping the strings with the wooden back of the bow.
7. *Tremolo*—trembling, quivering, a much-used effect obtained by rapidly repeating the same note by a quick up-and-down movement of the bow. Both *col legno* and *tremolo* are effective only in group playing.
8. *Harmonics*—producing an ethereal, flutelike effect by not pressing the string down all the way, but just touching it.
9. *Vibrato*—a highly emotional effect caused by vibrating the finger upon the string while pressing it down against the finger board, producing a slight wavering of the tone, particularly common in slow movements. The *vibrato* gives the tone the singing quality that makes the violin such an eloquent instrument.
10. *Glissando*—made by sliding the finger along the finger board while bowing. A technique borrowed from the gypsies and made possible due to the absence of frets on the fingerboard. The tone produced glides from note to note without definite intervals.
11. *Sul ponticello*—playing near the bridge, producing a curious quality of tone with strange coloring.
12. *Con sordino*—muting the strings by placing a mute (or

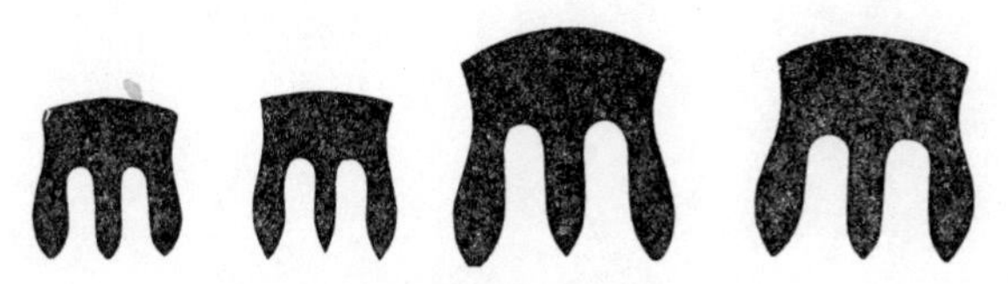

Figure 235. Mutes
Violin, Viola, Cello, Bass

*sordino*), a sort of wooden or metal clamp, over the bridge, which subdues the vibrations and creates a mournful, mysterious effect.

No wonder the violin has so many possibilities. Actually there are even more, due to the bowing and fingering of the individual player. A violin is like a human being, a personality; no two are identical. A violinist always uses his own violin. A concert pianist on tour, on the other hand, as a rule performs on the instrument provided, but a violinist and his violin are inseparable.

The range of the violin is about four and a half octaves. Beginning with the *g* below middle *c* on the piano, it extends approximately to the highest key. As there are no frets on the finger board, the player can produce any tone whatsoever within this compass—not only the diatonic scale, but any semitone or any shade between the tones. The amateur player is apt to play slightly out of tune by not stopping the string in the right place, thus sharping or flatting the tone somewhat. Even the skillful performer occasionally sins in this respect. Frets would make the correct intonation easier, of course, but they would also make the violin a much less sensitive instrument, robbing it of a great deal of its expressiveness.

The four strings are tuned in fifths, there being five tones between each two successive strings, including the lower and upper notes. The strings are turned to *g, d′, a′,* and *e″*. They need frequent tuning, as you will notice when you observe a violinist not only before the opening of a performance but also during a break in the music.

The strings of the violin are made of sheepgut (erroneously called catgut; see page 188). The *e*-string is often of steel, although gut strings are more easily tuned and have a more constant wave of vibration. The *d* and *a* are sometimes overspun with aluminum and the *g*-string with either pure silver or silver-plated copper, a practice which dates back to 1675.

*Famous Performers*

The history of violins playing is inseparably linked not only with the illustrious names of the violin makers but also with those of the

Figure 236
Niccolo Paganini
Courtesy Nef, Geschichte unserer Musikinstrumente

violin players. The princie of the violinists is *Nicolò Paganini* (1782–1840). His biography reads like a fairy-tale of triumphs.

Paganini was a bravura player. His brilliancy in rapid work was matchless. He played with deep pathos and matchless beauty of tone. His technique was so stunning that he was supposed to be in league with the devil, and in London he created such a sensation that the people once actually felt him to see if he really were flesh and blood.

Paganini inaugurated the epoch of virtuosity (daring flights, brilliant technique, etc.); he explored the harmonics, which he developed to a remarkable degree. In short, modern violin playing started with Paganini. His influence extended to composers, too. Music schools in all countries reveal his influence in every point. Berlioz, Schumann, Liszt, Brahms, and others produced works based on themes by Paganini.

Other violinists who greatly influenced players and composers alike were Spohr in Germany, Baillot in France, and Joachim in Hungary. Beethoven composed his *Kreutzer Sonata* for Rodolphe Kreutzer; Mendelssohn sought the aid of Ferdinand David in writing his *Violin Concerto in E Minor;* Brahms collaborated with Joachim, and Tchaikovsky with Joachim's pupil, Kotek, in working on their famous violin concertos. The greatest works for violin would never have been written had it not been for these geniuses of violin players.

Figure 237. First Violin Players, BBC Symphony Orchestra
Courtesy BBC, Broadcasting House

Our own time has seen the rise of a veritable galaxy of first-rate violinists of world renown. Radio, phonograph records, TV and the press will quickly bring their names to your attention.

*The Viola*

In appearance and manner of playing, the *viola* is essentially the same as the violin, but in size it is one-seventh larger. The size of the viola has not yet been standardized for the reason that no satisfactory size has been found. Admittedly the viola is the only "not perfect" instrument of the family.

Even though the viola is the oldest member of the family, it was relegated to the position of a Cinderella during the eighteenth century. The reason for this was probably that it was given to second-rate violinists who played the "second fiddle." These mediocre players were unwilling to adjust themselves to the larger size and had it reduced. As a result, the viola is not so well-proportioned an instrument as the violin.

The range of the viola is a fifth below the violin, the strings being tuned *c-g-d′-a′*, the three upper strings corresponding to the three lower strings of the violin. The strings are too heavy and thick for their size, and the tone is therefore slightly veiled and reedy and rather nasal but of a sympathetic and penetrating quality. It lacks the emotional warmth of the violin, and some refer to it as cold, mournful, and dull.

The subordinate position of the viola is also explained by the fact that for a long time it was employed as a "filler-in," helping out either the bass or the second violins. Even today it loses much of its individual character, since it usually blends with its neighbors or is absorbed by them.

Bach and Handel saw greater possibilities in the viola and gave it greater prominence. Under Haydn and Mozart it became an integral part of the string quartet and developed distinct individuality. Carl Stamitz, the son of the famous Stamitz who was the forerunner of Mozart, was a famous viola player, and he elevated the instrument to the dignity of a solo instrument. In our own times the Briton Lionel Tertius, an exceptionally fine viola player for whom the greatest contemporary composers have written special works, has done much to give the viola a dignified place in the orchestra.

Today the viola is indispensable for orchestral coloring. It holds its own as a tenor in the string quartet. Frequently it is given important melodic passages with the orchestra, and it is used more freely as an independent voice in the harmonic texture.

### *The Violoncello*

The name *violoncello* is a derivative of the Italian *violone,* meaning *double-bass,* and *cello,* meaning small; *violoncello* therefore means a small double-bass.

The origin of the violoncello, commonly called just *cello,* is even more obscure than that of the violin. The most popular theory has it that the cello was fashioned after the violin to replace the tenor viola da gamba. Beginning with the seventeenth century, it struggled for existence for over a hundred years, until by the middle of the eighteenth century it had definitely ousted the viola da gamba. During these years the cello had to be content with accompanying bass parts in the orchestra.

One of the first musicians to recognize the possibilities of the cello was Karl Philipp Emanuel Bach, one of the sons of Johann Sebastian. Haydn firmly established the instrument in the orchestra and gave it solo parts. Since then the cello has proved itself to be a most useful and beautiful instrument. If the violin is known as the queen of instruments, the cello may be called the crown prince or king consort.

The cello has a range of nearly four octaves. Its lowest string is C, one octave below the viola. Like the violin, it is tuned in fifths.

Figure 238. Piatigorsky Playing His $96,000 Stradivarius Cello
Courtesy Wide World Photo

Figure 239. Cello Players, BBC Symphony Orchestra
Courtesy BBC, Broadcasting House

The cello in its lowest range plays bass, in the middle register tenor, and in the highest position alto and occasionally even soprano.

In appearance the cello is fashioned after the violin, but it has slightly different proportions. The neck is shorter and the ribs are broader. Whereas the ratio of length of body to height of ribs is 11:1 and 10:1 in the violin and viola respectively, the cello's ratio is 6¼:1. The bow is shorter, heavier, and more rigid than the violin bow. Still, nearly all the bowing effects of the violin are possible on the cello. In playing position the cello rests on a peg on the floor. Since 1927 the peg has often been made hollow to aid in resonance for the lowest notes.

As we have seen, cello technique differs from that of the violin. A violin player therefore cannot substitute for a cello player, and vice versa.

The cello is, one is tempted to say, more of a masculine instrument than the violin with its feminine brilliancy. There is more strength in its mellow, sonorous tones. Romantic feelings, reverent worship, dreamy melancholy, pleading love—are all well-expressed by the cello.

### *The Double-Bass*

The *double-bass* or *contra-bass* supplies the very deep bass of the orchestra. Since its range extends far below the human voice, it is seldom used as a solo instrument but usually in company with cellos, bassoons, tubas, and kettledrums. In appearance and proportions it differs from the violin; the neck is shorter, the shoulders are sloping, the back is nearly flat, the ribs are even wider proportionately than those of the cello, and the peg box has metal gears.

The bow is shorter and sturdier, and not as elastic and springy. Consequently the bow effects are more limited. *Pizzicato,* however, is very effective. The *fortissimo* passages may portray savage fury, the *pianissimo* passages almost gentle droning. It can also portray gloom, brutality, or the distant mutterings of a thunderstorm. The very lowest notes resemble the pedal tone of the organ.

The range of the double bass is nearly three octaves, extending from *EE* to *a*. Since the music played is generally of low register, it is written an octave higher than it sounds, which makes it a transposing instrument. Some instruments have a fifth string to extend the compass to CC. One of the BBC players (Figure 240), for instance, plays a five-stringed instrument. (Can you find him?)

A rather interesting sidelight is thrown on bass playing by the following reflection. The low bass player must have an acutely sensitive ear. A violinist playing a melody in the higher register has over a hundred vibrations-per-second difference between the notes

Figure 240. Bass Players, BBB Symphony Orchestra
Courtesy BBC, Broadcasting House

*a''* and *b''*, and over fifty vibrations' range between *a'* and *b'*; but the double-bass player has only seven vibrations to distinguish between *AA* and *BB* notes, because the bass notes vibrate so much more slowly than the treble notes. The lower you descend the scale, the smaller the difference in the frequency of vibrations. Hence, all bass players (like double-bassoon, tuba, or kettledrum players) must have a sharp sense of hearing.

The double-bass was more easily established than its fellow-instruments. Beethoven utilized it in his symphonies. With his cello and double-bass *pizzicatos* he creates a drumlike effect, as for instance in the second movement of the *Fourth Symphony*. In the *Scherzo* of his *Fifth Symphony* Beethoven succeeds in extracting a bit of musical humor by assigning the basses a passage resembling "the gambols of a playful elephant" (Berlioz).

There is hardly a symphonic work which does not rely on the double-bass for timbre. The double-bass effectively completes the total range of the violin family.

Summing up, we see that the violin famliy comprises the most important section of the symphony orchestra. Indeed, without the strings there is no symphony orchestra, but merely a band. The string department of a large orchestra usually includes the following instruments (although there are variations as to numbers, of course):

| | | |
|---|---|---|
| first violins | — | 16 |
| second violins | — | 14 |
| violas | — | 10 |
| cellos | — | 10 |
| double-basses | — | 8 |

*The String Quartet*

The string quartet consists of a first violin, a second violin, a viola, and a cello. In contrast to a full orchestra its volume is naturally not so imposing, but since modern violins have enough brilliance and sonority even for a concert hall, string quartets do appear before large audiences. But the name for such performances has been retained from the preconcert era—*chamber music.* Chamber music is rapidly gaining in favor today. It is one of the most refined forms of musical entertainment. The four musicians must be just about perfect each in his own way.

Figure 241 shows the Armin String Quartet made up of four members of the J. J. Armin family, Windsor, Ontario. They are Otto, first violin; Adele, second violin; Richard, cello and Paul, viola.

Organizations like the Budapest, Busch, Paganini, or Stuttgart String Quartets are world-famous, each member being a first-rate artist of wide renown.

**Figure 241. The Armin String Quartet**
**From Left to Right: Otto, First Violin; Adele, Second Violin; Richard, Cello and Paul, Viola**
**Courtesy Armin, Yanamoto Studio, Windsor**

# *Part Five: Non-Orchestral Instruments*

*From*

*To*

CHAPTER XIV

# THE PIANO FAMILY

The piano is a modern instrument. It embodies so many principles and cumulative experiences of musicians that a fairly high degree of civilization and culture was its prerequisite.

The piano family includes the clavichord, the virginal, the spinet, the harpsichord, and the piano proper. Before turning our attention to the individual members, let us take a look at their forerunners. We shall see that in spite of its short span of life the piano has a respectable history.

## *The Predecessors*

Some writers contend that the prehistoric stone chimes (see page 42) must be regarded as the first piano. This is too farfetched. The mere fact that the stone slabs were struck with a mallet and piano strings are excited in a similar manner does not make the contention valid. The most widely accepted theory attributes the origin of keyed string instruments to the *monochord.* The most recent theory, however, has the *organistrum* as their godfather. Both these instruments, therefore, merit a discussion at this point.

The word *monochord* means a one-stringed instrument (mono=one, *chord*=string). It is most closely associated with the Greek

Figure 244
Monochord, Early Middle Ages

philosopher Pythagoras of the sixth century B.C., familiar to us for his theory about the squares of right-angled triangles. Since no musical instrument originated in Greece, it is assumed that Pythagoras obtained his knowledge from the Egyptians. He used the monochord not so much as a musical instrument as a scientific or experimental device (both terms were rather unfamiliar at that age) to develop an acoustical (sound) theory. He was so successful that his findings have remained the basis of all musical theory to the present day! His monochord consisted of a single string stretched between two end-bridges over a sounding board, similar to the device used nowadays in physics laboratories to demonstrate the relation between pitch and length of string. By varying the length of the vibrating portion, Pythagoras established the relationship of certain intervals. He found, for instance, that one-half the length of a string produces the octave, a tone of exactly double the frequency of the fundamental. Similarly, he established the ratio of sound waves between a fourth (from *do* to *fa* or from high *do* to lower *sol*) and a fifth (from *do* to *sol* or from high *do* to lower *fa*). So the monochord gave us the beginning of our scale.

With the decline of Greek civilization, the monochord fell into oblivion. As long as the church was content with plainsong, or one-part singing of "unmeasured" music without bars and time signatures, there was no need for a strictly regulated scale. But in the ninth century attempts at harmony were made, and from then on there was a definite need for exactitude in pitch and intervals. Polyphonic music (*poly* means *many*) must have a definite basis embodied by rules and a system of regular intervals. Once more the standardization of the scale assumed pre-eminence.

Already in the sixth century Boethius, consul under Theodoric ruler of Rome, had made a summary and condensation of the Greek theory. Later the medieval monks revived the monochord based upon this theory to teach singers the correct intervals. A string, it was found, could be divided with such skill that it could not lie (tenth century), and was consequently more reliable than the human voice. The monochord became a testing instrument.

After 1100 the monochord gradually became a musical instrument. The sounding board beneath the string was calibrated and a movable bridge was used for stopping the strings. Simple melodies were now within the musician's reach. To improve the effectiveness of the monochord more strings were added, giving rise to the *polychordic monochord.* At this stage the name *monochord* should have been discarded, for there is no such thing as a "many-stringed one-string" instrument; but the name stuck, for even the first clavichords were often called monochords.

The transformation from a mono- to a polychord was accom-

Figure 245
The Beginning of Polychordic Monochord

plished rather slowly, the one string surviving up to the sixteenth century. The first multiple-string monochords probably had only two strings, only later increased to four or more. A monochord of nineteen strings must already have been a clavichord.

As the number of strings on the monochord increased, the manner of playing it was altered. The movable bridges were fixed at the correct places for the desired intervals, and rods or keys were attached for striking the strings. These innovations are responsible for the emergence of the clavichord. The idea of mechanical keys was by no means a new one; they had been applied to various instruments already.

The second theory, as we have seen, attributes the origin of the clavichord to the *organistrum* or symphonia. This is a type of fiddle with mechanical keys. The bow is replaced by a disklike wheel

Figure 246
Organistrum Players, 12th Century
Courtesy Nef, Geschichte unserer Musikinstrumente

resined for friction. It is turned by a small crank at the lower end of the instrument. When the wheel turns it scrapes the strings much as a violin bow does. As is seen from the illustration it required two players, one for operating the wheel and the other for manipulating the keys. The keys were provided with rods, each of which had a small bit that stopped the strings when the key was turned like a latchkey.

The first organistrum had three strings. The two on the sides were tuned in unison, the middle one being tuned to the interval of a fourth or fifth. Students of harmony will recall that singing in fourth and fifths—parallel singing—was the first attempt at harmony, such singing being known as *organum*. "Organistrum" therefore suggests an instrument to accompany singing. The mechanism stopped all three strings simultaneously, and consequently the parallels of fourths and fifths were easily produced.

The organistrum was a purely mechanical instrument, of course, incapable of any personal touch or expression of feeling on the part of the player. Still it was held in high esteem as proved by our illustration, which is from a carving of the Archduke of Santiago.

The organistrum too underwent several changes. The first of these was a reduction in size. (Is it not remarkable that so many instruments started out on a prodigious scale? Just recall as examples the giant slit drums and the ten-foot-long musical bows. Similarly, small radios and small pianos succeeded the original larger ones.) This made it a one-man instrument. Next, the number of strings was increased and the drones (see page 187) equipped with a special mechanism so that they could be operated independently. Furthermore, the bridge was constructed in such a way that tromba marina effects could also be obtained. This was during the twelfth and thirteenth centuries. Now the organistrum became known as the *hurdy-gurdy* in England, and in Germany as the *old woman's* or *peasant's lyre*. In the late Middle Ages the hurdy-gurdy

Figure 247. Hurdy-gurdy
Courtesy Museum of Fine Arts, Boston

degenerated into the stock-in-trade of the peddler and the blind beggar. Hence the later name—beggar's lyre (fifteenth century).

Curiously enough, this instrument became briefly popular again in the eighteenth century when composers saw in it and the bagpipe a means of expressing the new pastoral mood in music. Also during the eighteenth century the hurdy-gurdy was equipped with a little organ attachment and sympathetic strings. Today's barrel organ of peddlers is no doubt a descendant of the hurdy-gurdy.

During the reign of Louis XV of France the hurdy-gurdy became the favorite instrument of the nobility for a while, undoubtedly due to the fact that the queen consort had taken a fancy to it and was a proficient player in it. The vogue, however, was short-lived. Today the hurdy-gurdy survives in southern France and in rural districts of other European countries. Schubert's song *Der Leiermann* features a beggarly hurdy-gurdy player.

As most other instruments, the hurdy-gurdy offers some riddles to scholars. The method of stopping the strings shows the influence of the monochord. The key mechanism, on the other hand, must have influenced the clavichord. Further, there is good reason to assume that the instrument is derived from the fiddle. But again, there is no evidence that any bowed instrument came to Western Europe prior to the hurdy-gurdy. So until further light is shed on the subject, the real ancestry of this instrument remains an unsolved mystery.

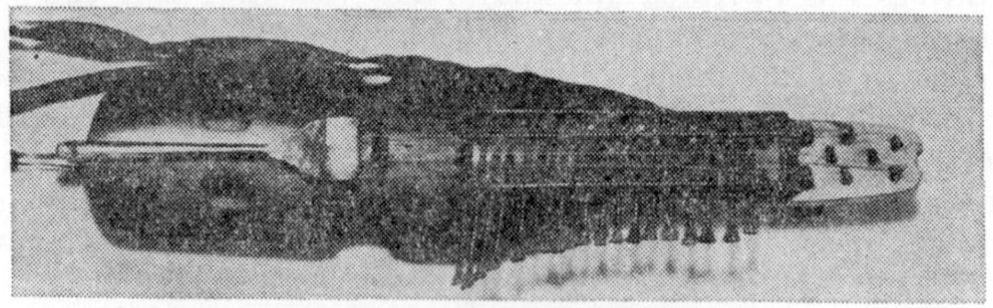

Figure 248. Nyckelharpa
Courtesy Museum of Fine Arts, Boston

The hurdy-gurdy and the monochord were by no means the only instruments with mechanical playing devices. Quite a few ingenious contraptions appeared—in fact, over fifty! Most of these, however, never rose to a place of prominence. A few survived. The *nyckelharpa,* a keyed viol, is a folk fiddle still found in Sweden. These facts point out once more that most of our instruments owe their existence not to brilliant inventions but rather to a slow process of evolution.

*The Clavichord*

The *clavichord* (*clavis*=a key) is the first real member of the piano family. Of all the keyboard instruments it was the simplest, smallest, and most delicate. It consisted of an oblong case four to five feet by two feet and five to seven inches deep; a series of keys at the front end of the case comprised the keyboard. The keys were simple levers mounted on a keyshaft and weighted with lead. Inserted at the rear end of each key was a slender blade of brass, flattened at the top. By depressing the front end of the key this so-called tangent struck the string and elicited the required vibrations. The important difference betwen this mechanism and that of the piano is that the tangent did not rebound after striking the string as is the case with the hammers of the piano, but stayed in that position pressed against the string till the key was released. The sound produced was consequently rather weak but delicate.

The tangent pressing against the string acted as a bridge dividing the string into a vibrating and a nonvibrating section. The section to the left of the tanget was damped by a piece of cotton or cloth woven into the string and known as *listing*. Thus, only the section to the right of the tangent vibrated. The right end of the string passed over a fixed bridge and was fastened to the tuning pegs mounted at the extreme end of the box in the wrest plank, a piece of hardwood. (A wrest plank is therefore that section of the sound board or frame which contains the tuning pegs. It is also known as pin block.) Our diagram should make this arrangement clear.

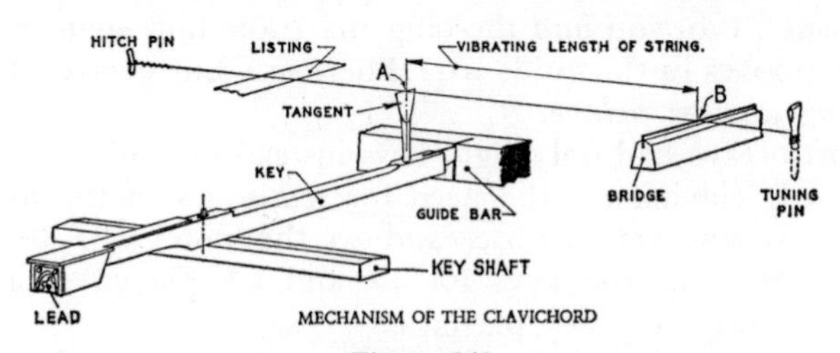


MECHANISM OF THE CLAVICHORD

**Figure 249**
Courtesy Museum of Fine Arts, Boston

To prevent the keys from rattling against each other, a small piece of whalebone projected from each key and was sheathed in a groove of the guide bar. The keys were much shorter than the ordinary piano keys, the lower keys projecting only three centimeters beyond the upper ones. Oddly enough, the natural keys were usually black and the upper ones white, except in the Italian and Dutch makes.

Figure 250. Clavichord, Genoa, 1568
Courtesy Museum of Fine Arts, Boston

The illustration above shows one of the earliest clavichords. Its case is elaborately painted, the central landscape showing Orpheus and Eurydice. You can even see Orpheu's flute in the lower right-hand corner. Can you find the tangents (note how slender they are) and the grooves in the guide bar? There are four octaves, the lowest one being a *short octave.*

A short octave had only eight keys instead of twelve. At the time of the early clavichords the need for semitones in the lowest bass register was not very accute, and so the notes *c#, d#, f#,* and *g#* were left out, the keys for *f#* and *g#* played *d* and *e* respectively, and the *e* key played *c.*

The next illustration shows a later-model clavichord. It is some-

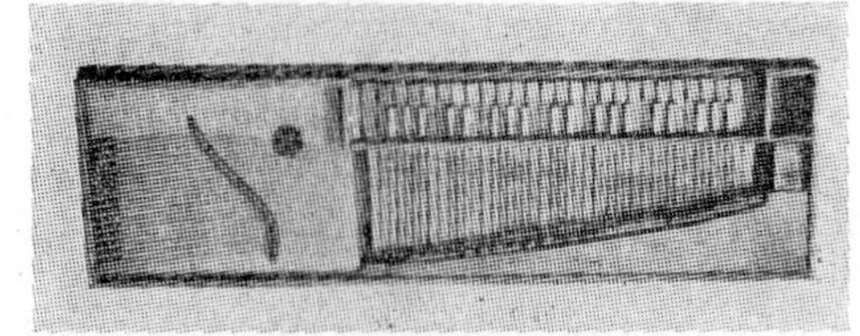

Figure 251
Clavichord, Germany, 1750
Courtesy Nef, Geschichte unserer Musikinstrumente

what simpler in construction and has only one bridge. Not the "rose" in the sounding board. In common with all keyboard instruments built prior to 1750, it had no legs and rested on a table or a special stand. If you can count the number of strings, you will note that there are more keys than strings. This is an important characteristic of the clavichord.

As we have seen, the length of the string itself is not responsible for the pitch of the tone. The tangent divided the string into a vibrating and a nonvibrating section. The pitch was therefore determined by the place at which the tangent struck the string. Neighboring notes could thus be produced on the same string, and the keys for such notes as *b, c,* and *c#* all operated the same string. A closer inspection of the first clavichord illustration shows the keys grouped in pairs and threes, each group using but one string.

Such an arrangement had the disadvantage of making close intervals impossible, but in those days such intervals were simply unknown, the third *(do-mi)* being the closest accepted. On the other hand, this simplified the construction and the tuning of the instrument, and one of the greatest charms of the clavichord was its simplicity. One of the earlier clavichords had only nine double strings but thirty-five keys, which meant three to four notes to each pair of strings. Such clavichords were known as *fretted,* from the German *gebunden,* meaning tied up.

The clavichord is a European invention. In the first quarter of the eighteenth century it became "unfretted." Now each key had its own string, thus permitting every conceivable interval within our diatonic scale. This made the instrument not only larger and heavier, but also more expensive and more difficult to tune. Hence, it encountered some opposition and the earlier models were not ousted.

The home of the clavichord was Germany, where it attained its greatest popularity and was in general use up to the beginning of the nineteenth century. It consequently existed side by side with the piano for about a whole century. It was a favorite instrument with J. S. Bach, who preferred it to the piano. K. P. E. Bach, Mozart, Beethoven, and many others lauded this instrument. It was the fundament of all keyboard stringed instruments. Musicians mastered the skill of playing the clavichord so that they could play the spinet and harpsichord properly. Wherein, then, lies the charm of the clavichord, and why has it become almost obsolete?

The charm of the clavichord is conditioned by its very simplicity of structure. There was only one mechanical link acting between the finger and the string; hence, the slightest feeling of the finger communicated itself to the vibrating string. The keys required but a gentle touch; an unduly heavy string pressure tightened the vibrating part of the string and made the note slightly sharp in pitch. A trembling pressure on the key gave warmth and passion to the note, producing an effect similar to the *vibrato* of the violin. (In this respect it had no equals.)

Although the tone was weak, it was clear and delicate, charmingly hesitating and tremulous. In short, it was the ideal thing for sweet melancholy, quiet meditation, and pensive, dreamy love reflections. (Today we probably would call it "moody" music.) James IV of Scotland is known to have courted Margaret of England on a clavichord. The string sang the melody; each tone was animated. Grace notes could be executed with greater tenderness than on any other keyboard instrument.

During the second half of the eighteenth century, the "period of sentimentality," the clavichord was the "comfort of the sufferer and the sympathising friend of cheerfulness," the perfect instrument for anyone who disliked noise, raging, and fuming. (Any wonder it is not coveted by modern jazz orchestras?)

All told, the clavichord was a charming little instrument of noble simplicity. It held its own for about four hundred years. Just the same, the other members of the piano family rivaled it in popularity and finally gained supremacy over it.

### *The Virginal and the Spinet*

Virginals and spinets, as well as harpsichords, are keyboard instruments similar to the clavichord. The fundamental difference in their build lies in the manner of exciting the strings. Whereas in the last the strings are struck by a hammer, the strings in the others are plucked by a plectrum.

The parent of the plucked keyboard instruments is the *clavicytherium* or *upright virginal* or *spinet.* It is a modification of the psaltery which, as we have seen, was plucked either with the fingers or with a small plectrum of bone or metal. Our illustration shows a trapeze-shaped case with a decorated sound board. The upper keys are black but inlaid with ivory. It also has a short octave (Figure 252).

Using a plectrum for plucking strings is an age-old device. We have seen how the ancient lute player used a plectrum (Figure 202). A plectrum was also used on lyres and other instruments. All that was needed for plucked keyboard instruments was a mechanical device for plucking. This was accomplished in the following manner.

On the back end of the key-lever (Figure 253) rests a thin, rectangular strip of wood enclosed in a suitable framework to keep it in the proper upright position. This is the *jack.* The diagram to the left shows the upper part of the jack. A tongue mounted on a

Figure 252
Clavicytherium, Italy, ca. 1600
Courtesy Museum of
Fine Arts, Boston

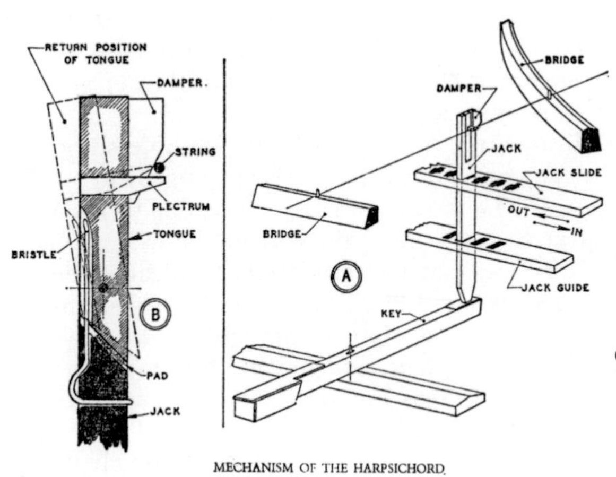


MECHANISM OF THE HARPSICHORD

Figure 253
Courtesy Museum of
Fine Arts, Boston

thin wire axis operates the plectrum. When the jack is raised, the tongue swings out of its normal position. The plectrum, being inserted in the tongue, plucks the string each time the tongue swings out. Above the plectrum is a special damper to silence the string when the key is released. The string is between the damper and the quill. The tongue is held in place by a stiff boar's bristle or a metal spring.

Surprisingly enough, the action of the jack mechanism is very rapid. Trills and embellishments are therefore readily executed. Still, it remains a mechanical way of producing the tone—there is no personal touch to it as with the clavichord, and the dynamics cannot be very well controlled. In other words, the intensity of tone, which in itself is very pleasing, is rather uniform and inflexible and therefore becomes monotonous after a while, even though the instrument sounds charming at first. The material of the plectrum is somewhat responsible for the tone quality. Crow quills give a more brilliant and less harsh tone than leather, but leather quills produce a more powerful tone.

Virginals and spinets made their appearance about the same time as the clavichords, the beginning of the fifteenth century. As to the names given these instruments, there was and still is some confusion. From the reign of King Henry VII (1485-1509) to that of Queen Anne (1702–1714) the name virginal was in general use, frequently applied to any plucked keyboard instrument, even to harpsichords. After Anne *spinet* replaced *virginal.* The term *virginal* has been popularly applied to the square-shaped instrument resembling the clavichord. The contention that the instrument was named in honor of Queen Elizabeth must be dismissed, for the name was popular at least a few decades before the birth of the royal person. However, it was a maiden's instrument (just as the lute was a man's). Many writers still associate the virginal with virgins. Dr. Sachs, however, has advanced the valid explanation that *virginal* is derived from the Italian *virgo,* a jack.

The instruments illustrated (page 266) both resemble the clavichord not only in appearance but also in the arrangement of the strings and tuning pegs. The strings run perpendicular to the keys, and the tuning pegs at the extreme right end of the case. Broadly speaking, these characteristics may be considered as typical of the virginal. Both instruments are lavishly decorated with scrolls, flowers, and fruit. The second one has a plainer case and shows a typical scene of Flemish town life. Their makers are the most famous craftsmen of the period: Andreas and Hans Rucker respectively. Handel possessed a virginal made by Andreas Rucker. The inscriptions on these virginals bear testimony to the then prevalent conviction concerning the function of music: music is divinely inspired

Figure 254. Virginal, Antwerp, 1610
Courtesy Museum of Fine Arts, Boston

Figure 255. Double Virginal, Flemish, 1581
Courtesy Metropolitan Museum of Art, New York

and must be dedicated to the service of God. Thus, the first inscription means, "All spirits praise the Lord;" the second, "Music sweetens the labor of men."

Figure 256. English Spinet, 1684
Courtesy Metropolitan Museum of Art, New York

Spinets generally had an oblong triangular form. The name may have been derived from the Italian *spina,* a thorn which served as the plectrum. Again, the instrument may have received its name from the Venetian instrument maker Giovanni Spinetti. In these instruments the strings run parallel (or nearly so) to the keys, and the jack mechanism is close to the front, just behind the keyboard.

These instruments are not as large as would be judged by their appearance. The Baker Harris spinet measures only approximately forty-four by twenty-seven inches, so that it could easily be carried to a performance by the musician himself. It has an inlaid walnut case and brass trimmings. The other specimen has still the upper white keys. It is said that such spinets could be purchased for five pounds sterling, but the triangular three-legged stands were extra.

### *The Harpsichord*

The harpsichord (*harp* plus *chord*) was the first answer to the quest for an instrument capable of dynamic modulations. It soon became the most important of the keyboard instruments, and from the sixteenth to the eighteenth century it held a place analogous to that now held by the grand piano. (Incidentally, until 1750 none of the keyboard instruments stood on its own legs, but invariably had to rest on a table or a special stand.)

Figure 257. Italian Harpsichord, 1656
Courtesy Metropolitan Museum of Art, New York

The harpsichord is fundamentally a combination of several spinets of different sizes in that as it has more than one set of strings. A set of strings in the harpsichord is known as a *stop* or *register.* The registers are referred to as four-, eight-, twelve-, or sixteen-foot stops respectively. They are arranged in such a way that a single key can pluck one or more strings simultaneously. At the back end of the key-lever there are several jacks instead of one only, one jack for each of the strings of the separate stops. By means of special levers operated by buttons placed within easy reach of the performer, more than one stop can be operated at will. Each stop in operation would add to the loudness of the music, of course, and thus dynamic variations were within reach of the musician, and the monotony of the spinet could be relieved. (As we shall see later, such a method of varying the dynamics was not wholly satisfactory.)

The fact that the buttons themselves are often referred to as stops need not worry us. If a harpsichord had, let us say, six stops, it meant that it had six sets of strings, each operated by a knob, and that each key had six jacks. The principle of the stops is on somewhat the same line as on the organ.

Six jacks to a key naturally made the construction as well as the operation somewhat cumbersome. Hence, such harpsichords were equipped with two manuals or keyboards. Up to the seventeenth century the manuals were different in pitch, but later on they were identical. Such instruments were called double harpsichords.

Figure 258
Double Harpsichord, England, 1798
Courtesy Museum of Fine Arts, Boston

The most common stops included the cymbal, the lute, the buff, the unison, the octave, and the machine. The machine stop was controlled by the footpedal. It was used to regulate the volume of the sound. These stops afforded such splendid combinations for the production of sound and such rich tonal and dynamic resources that the instrument became known as the "lordly harpsichord." Naturally, a great deal of skill was essential for lordly playing.

Up to the time of Haydn the harpsichord was not only a solo instrument but also the backbone of the symphony orchestra. At the opening of the nineteenth century, however, it practically disappeared to reappear again at the close of the century. Today it is fairly popular again.

We may well ask why such a change—why should a "lordly" instrument fade from the scene only to be revived about a century later? The answer is found in the advent of the piano. This instrument quickly became so popular that it simply pushed the harpsichord into the background. When the first enthusiasm began to fade, however, musicians started to draw comparisons, with the result that a desire for the restoration of the harpsichord became more and more pronounced. The French philosopher Voltaire, for instance, is said to have remarked that compared to the harpsichord the piano was so crude that it seemed the work of a blacksmith. As we shall see later, he was badly mistaken.

The very disadvantages of the harpsichord now became recognized as merits, among them one of its outstanding characteristics, evenness of tone. The instrument therefore is not used to produce subtle dynamic changes, for each tone is clear, crisp, and of the same loudness. Although by means of the various stops dynamic shades can be effected, compared to our modern piano effects the harpsichord nuances in loudness spell monotony. Actually herein lies the charm of the harpsichord. Before this fact was generally accepted, composers unscrupulously transcribed harpsichord music for the piano, with somewhat disappointing results.

Scholars contend that such works as Domenico Scarlatti's sonatas for harpsichord or Bach's fugues or his *Well-Tempered Clavier* cannot be properly executed on the piano. For one thing, there is too much resonance in the piano, and the bass notes, which often lie close together, are apt to become muddled. Today musicians no longer pose the question, piano or harpsichord, for both are recognized as instruments in their own right. It is generally conceded that Scarlatti's sonatas and Bach's and Handel's fugues belong to the harpsichord. It is interesting to note that Bach evidently never had a piano of his own, and even Mozart was at heart a harpsichordist, not a pianist.

Today the harpsichord is on the road to glory again. In 1913 the Berlin Conservatory established a harpsichord class, and other conservatories followed suit. At the present time harpsichord courses are offered also in New York at the Juilliard School of Music. Harpsichord music is featured over the radio and harpsichordists appear on television.

It must be admitted, however, that harpsichord playing is not a paying proposition. In the first place, a harpsichord costs anywhere between three and seven thousand dollars. Then the harpsichordist on concert tours must transport his own instrument from place to place, tuning must be frequent and is difficult and expensive, repair parts are not easy to procure, teachers are hard to find—in short, today's harpsichordist must find compensation in his passion for the instrument.

Fortunately there are such artists. Wanda Landowska reigned like a queen among harpsichordists. Her name is almost a legend. She had her own instrument, a seven-pedal harpsichord manufactured by Pleyel. She had the whole world at her feet after a concert tour. She had been heard in America since 1923.

Harpsichord music is also available on phonograph records. It is surprising how this music grows on you with repeated hearing. One realizes that the harpsichord is not merely a piano with a cold, but that it has a beauty all its own.

Modern harpsichord makers naturally take full advantage of all modern devices at their disposal and use metals like aluminum and even plastics, materials unknown a century ago. Thus, these instruments are made with more precision and are more durable in construction; they are sturdier and probably more practical, and boast a louder tone. There is no question that the harpsichord will ever supplant the piano or even offer it competition, but it has its own charms, and for special effects not obtainable on the piano it remains indispensable.

CHAPTER XV

# THE MODERN PIANO

The piano is truly an invention of Western civilization. It is a complicated instrument and yet easy to play, at least to play *at;* that is to say, almost any child can learn to play delightful tunes on it, but it taxes the greatest skill of the virtuoso and is the delight of the true musician. The great pianists of our day are actually geniuses of world fame. In fact, our civilization is hardly conceivable without the piano.

The piano is the final answer to the search for an instrument capable of graduating tone from soft to loud. As we have seen, neither the clavichord nor the virginal or spinet could satisfy the music lover in this respect. The harpsichord was an improvement in this regard, but still the stops always and invariably changed the volume abruptly, there being no gradual shading off or building up of tone intensity. The outstanding feature of the piano is that it can be played at any desired loudness at any moment. In fact, the original name for the instrument embodied this characteristic—the Italians called it a "harpsichord with [the ability of playing] soft and loud." Its common English name during the eighteenth century was *forte piano.* Today's *piano* is merely an abbreviation of that name.

The invention of the piano is now commonly attributed to the Italian harpsichord maker Bartolommeo Cristofori. Cristofori's first piano (*c.* 1710) not only antedated that of his rivals—notably Marius of Paris and Schröter of Germany—but was so superior in construction that it is the real prototype of the modern piano. The piano is therefore of Italian origin.

Two of Cristofori's pianos have been preserved; one, shown in the illustration (Fig. 259), is now in the Metropolitan Museum of New York, and the other is in the Leipzig Collection of Musical Instruments (at least, it was there up to World War II). As you note, this early-model piano looks like a harpsichord, except that it has no stops or pedals and only one manual. The keyboard is still indented and forms part of the total box. There are no longer lavish decorations; the case is almost streamlined.

Cristofori's invention was so perfect that there is reason to assume that his was not the first conception of such an instrument. Indeed, there is evidence that as early as 1598 a pianoforte instru-

Figure 259
Cristofori's Piano
Courtesy
Metropolitan
Museum of Art,
New York

ment existed. It stands to reason that musicians generally toyed with the idea of a soft-loud instrument during the seventeenth century, until finally several music makers almost simultaneously and in different countries came forth with the invention.

Some authorities derive the piano from the dulcimer, since the dulcimer, too, had hammers, for striking the strings. This theory is not necessarily valid. The contention that the clavichord is the parent of the piano must also be accepted with certain reservations. The truth of the matter is that Cristofori substituted hammers for quills in a harpsichord and retained the name *harpsichord* for it.

In form and arrangement of parts, early pianos were nearly identical with harpsichords. Indeed, during the eighteenth century many a harpsichord was remodeled into a "piano." Such a change did away with the tedious job of requilling the harpsichord, a task that had to be done at frequent intervals. Some of these piano-harpsichords had both jacks and hammers. The substitution of hammers for quills was only a logical step in the evolution of the instrument.

The main difference between the old and new instrument was an ingenious hammer mechanism which converted the harpsichord into the cherished *forte piano.* Christofori made his hammers so flexible that they responded to the *force of the touch on the key and transmitted this impact to the string.* The loudness of the tone accordingly depended upon the player's touch on the keys.

We have seen that the hammer action of a clavichord was rather rigid but uniform. Cristofori solved this problem by adopting several free-swinging levers with attached hammers. The accompanying

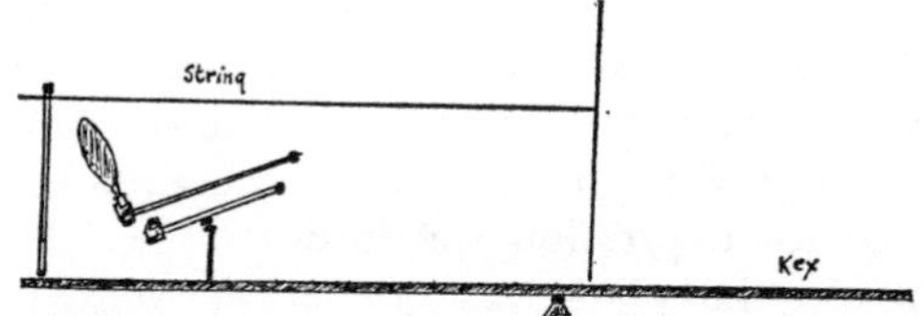


**Figure 260**
Skeleton Diagram of
Cristofori's Action

diagram represents this action as found in the Leipzig specimen. When the key is struck, the hopper bounds upward and strikes the middle hammer; this in turn activates the upper hammer, which strikes the string. You note that both hammers swing freely so that they rebound instantly, leaving the string free to vibrate. The rebounding of the hammer is known as *escapement.* To stop the string from vibrating, there is a special damper at the rear end of the keys. In neutral position the damper rests upon the string; when the key is depressed the damper is lifted a moment before the string is struck, thus setting it free. When the player releases the key, the damper falls back and stops the vibrations.

Cristofori had no followers for some reason, and the Italians abandoned the piano. Now the Germans took it up. For several decades following they excelled in their work and experiments toward perfection of the instrument. Several famous piano makers supplied pianos to Bach and Mozart. After the Seven Years' War, that is, in the 1760's, some of these piano makers became jobless, and a dozen craftsmen settled in England. Their leader was Johannes Zumpe, and they soon were nicknamed "the twelve apostles." They established a school of piano makers and were enthusiastically received by the British. This school was so successful that we owe to them not only the special key-action known as the *English action,* but also the modern form of the piano. At the same time German manufacturers started their work also in Austria and before long developed the so-called *Viennese action mechanism.*

The details of both these actions need not concern us here, nor is the inclusion of a dozen or so names of famous piano innovators all-important. But since it is such a far cry from the piano of the eighteenth century to current models, let us touch briefly upon the milestones in the development of this instrument.

Before engaging upon this task, it may be said that the piano almost immediately became very popular. By the end of the eighteenth century it had supplanted the harpsichord. It received a great impetus from Johann Christian Bach, the youngest son of the great Johann Sebastian. He gave the world's first piano recital in London in 1768.

The conversion of the first piano to the grand instrument of today involved a good many problems. One of the first problems to solve was the operation of the keys. Since a whole mechanism was required to strike the string, more strength was needed to depress the keys in playing. When J. S. Bach was shown a piano made by the famous maker Gottfried Silbermann, he complained that the keys required too much strength for playing. Just how much weight a key of those early pianos needed for depression we do not know. Undoubtedly Bach was right. So the piano makers set to work to accommodate Bach and future generations of pianists.

After nearly two hundred years of experimentation and perfection, we find that the most desired average weight of touch for middle *c* is two and a half ounces, slightly more for the bass notes, and somewhat less for the higher keys. Even at that a pianist expends a tremendous amount of energy in playing. You would get almost astronomical figures if you were to count all the notes a pianist plays during a ninety-minute recital allowing two and a half ounces times a half-inch for each (force times distance) to compute the foot-pounds of work accomplished. No wonder a pianist has to have a strong physique.

Another problem was to improve the mechanism of the key in such a way as to permit rapid repeats by the same key. In early pianos the hammer, after striking the string, rebounded instantly and returned to its original position regardless of the position of the key. As we have seen, this was known as simple escapement. About a century after Cristofori's first piano a French piano maker, Erard, invented the *double escapement,* still in use. The double escapement prevents the hammer from falling back into its original position as long as the key is depressed; the hammer resumes its neutral position only upon the release of the key. The advantage of such an arrangement is that one can play a series of notes on the same key much faster than if the hammer had to return all the way to its original position. You can easily clarify this for yourself by removing the front panel of a piano and watching the key and hammer in action.

The first pianos were delicate and fragile. In the words of Bach, they were deficient in volume of tone. Today's pianos, on the other hand, are so strong and sturdy and have such powerful resonance that one single piano can hold its own against a full symphony orchestra. How then was such a change effected? Briefly, through *larger hammers, heavier wires, sturdier frames, better sound boards, and cross-wiring*. Let us consider each of these in turn.

Cristofori employed small hammers of leather. About a century later a Parisian maker, Pape, introduced the felt hammer. He used rabbit's hair for the felt. Later sheep's wool was substituted by Broadwood. Felt hammers give the instrument both a softer impact and a louder tone. So important is this part of the mechanism that Paderewski had the felt hammers on his own concert piano made to his specifications!

*The wires* of early pianos lacked the tensile strength to produce a tone loud enough for the modern concert hall. They could not be made much heavier as long as no proper frame was supplied. The problem of heavy wires and sturdy frames was not satisfactorily solved till the middle of the last century. Today the wires are made so strong that they can bear great tension and withstand the heaviest impact of the hammers. In some modern pianos the tension on a string is nearly 200 pounds, the ideal or most common tension being 175 pounds per string. This adds up to 25 to 30 tons of tension on the frame, considering all the strings of a grand piano. Naturally, such tension cannot be sustained without an extra-heavy frame and a sturdy case.[1]

This problem baffled piano makers for nearly 150 years. In early pianos the pin block was identical with that of the harpsichord: the tuning pegs were inserted at the upper end of the sound board. As long as instrument makers adhered to this method, no appreciable progress could be made. Then the idea was conceived to construct a special wrest plank (or pin block) outside the sound board. Thus, in 1806 iron bars were applied to a grand piano as reinforcements to the frame. Then metal tubes and plates were introduced for the same purpose, and next bolts, until an American manufacturer, Babcock, came out with a cast-iron frame in 1825. After about three more decades of experimenting the American Steinways (originally Steinweg from Germany) turned out the first pianos with a successful iron frame. Thus, the iron frame is America's contribution to the piano.

With these innovations the fragile instrument of the early days was gradually changed into a majestic tone carrier capable of producing all dynamic nuances from a *pianissimo* to a *fortissimo* and of filling a large concert hall either as a solo instrument or against an orchestral background.

A great deal of research and skill finally produced the proper *sound board,* the basis for resonance and reinforcement of tone. Today's sound boards are made of small pieces of spruce glued together and fitted into the back of the piano diagonally, or of laminated wood which has a hard surface veneer on either side like maple or birch. The size of the sound board is determined by the size of the piano, a grand piano naturally having a larger sound board than the bungalow type and—it stands to reason—more resonance. Generally the sound board is the full width of the piano inside the back and most of the height of the back. The pin block is glued to the back of the sound board, above it in the vertical and

[1] Parenthetically, a piano does not improve with age. The mechanism is so complicated it is bound to deteriorate, albeit over a long period of time. Metals also "age," but not to their advantage.

behind it in the horizontal piano. It is made of rock maple and fitted into the iron frame.

*The pedals* as found in our pianos are likewise the fruit of years of experimentation. Like the harpsichord, the first pianos were supplied with stops for special effects. To set the hands free, these stops were later operated first by the knees and then by special foot levers or pedals. By means of these pedals the acoustical possibilities were greatly enriched.

The original grand pianos had no stops. These are found first on the square pianos. The two principal stops were the *forte* or damper pedal and the soft pedal, both invented about 1783. They are still found on modern pianos.

The forte pedal takes the dampers away from the strings and leaves them free to vibrate even after the keys are released. This not only prolongs the sound but also augments it due to sympathetic vibrations, thus enhancing the beauty of the tone.

The original soft or *piano* pedal interposed a piece of cloth between the hammers and the strings, a device still found on some pianos with three pedals. The hammers then strike the strings through the cloth, thus muting them. Somewhat later a similar effect was achieved by shifting the keys sideways in such a way that the hammer would strike only one or two of the three strings. (Just open the front panel of a piano and you will see that there are two or three strings for each of the keys.)

The effect of this shifting is to reduce the volume of tone produced. Furthermore, the unused strings are excited from the sound board, giving the tone an aeolian charm and imparting to the instrument a most delicate beauty of tone. The shifting of hammers to eliminate one or two strings from the direct hammre blow has been discarded lately.

Beethoven, however, made frequent use of this device; to him it must have been reminiscent of the clavichord. In case you should find the expression *una corda* in a Beethoven score, know that he meant that particular passage to be played on one string only. You may find such remarks as "gradually more strings" or *"tutte le corde"* —meaning all strings or full register.

The most common soft-pedal mechanism of today consists of a lever operated by the left pedal which moves all the hammers out of the original position closer to the strings, thereby shortening the striking distance and giving the hammers a softer impact.

In addition to the pedals already mentioned, several other stops merit our attention. A harp register, obviously for harp effects, used a brush applied to the strings from above; a padded slat pressed against the strings from below provided a lute register. Some pianos had a sort of drum attachment at the time when Turkish military music was in vogue, consisting of a triangle, cymbals, and a drum-stick hitting the sound board. Also, a small enclosed organ attachment and a "swell" pedal enjoyed brief periods of popularity. Again, the bassoon pedal pressed a strip of wood lined with tissue paper against the bass strings, making them rattle. But as the piano gained in brilliance and resonance, all these special effects became superfluous.

So far nothing has been said about the outer appearance of the piano. It is only natural to assume that the outer shape has undergone various transformations. Such is indeed the case.

When the first harpsichord-shaped piano appeared on the market, the clavichord was still a popular instrument. Consequently, there was a constant demand for a simplified and small piano. Shortly after the middle of the eighteenth century such an instrument, the square piano, was constructed.

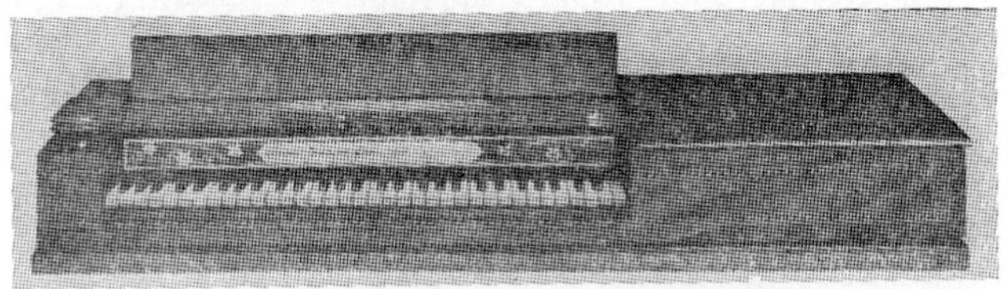

Figure 261. Square Piano, London, 1774

In its outer shape the square piano resembled the clavichord. It, too, could be set on a table, wherefore it was also known as the *table* piano (*Tafelklavier* in German). The square piano held its own for some forty years. Then the upright piano became briefly

Figure 262
"Upright "Giraffe" Piano, Early 19th Century, Vienna
Courtesy Nef, Geschichte unserer Musikinstrumente

popular. The first attempts at constructing such a piano can be traced to the beginning of the eighteenth century. The instruments were merely grand pianos turned up with slight modifications. Among the several types of upright piano were the "giraffe" piano and the "lyre" piano. None of these types has survived. They were not strongly built and had but a dull tone.

The real upright or cabinet piano belongs to the nineteenth century. At the beginning of the century inventors extended the strings of the upright piano to the very floor. At the same time the wrest plank, which up to then had been close to the keys, was moved up to the top of the frame. In this form the upright has survived to the present day, although it is no longer much in demand, the bungalow or cottage type being preferred.

The "piccolo" or low upright also deserves mention. It was introduced in 1829. The height of this piano did not exceed forty inches, although the strings were placed vertically. The small piano, the bungalow type of today, is evidently the most popular type for the home; with its wires overstrung, it is a rather pleasing instrument. So far, however, it has not invaded the concert stage, and there seems little likelihood that it will take the place of the grand piano.

A few sentences above the term "overstrung" was used. Overstringing was introduced by Babcock of England about 1830. The strings were no longer arranged in straight lines along the sound board but strung across the board diagonally from left to right and from right to left so that they overlapped. The treble strings were spread over the larger part of the sound board and the bass strings crossed over them at a slightly higher level. An inspection of any piano will make this arrangement clear. Not only does such an arrangement economize on space, but it brings the strings closer together and closer to the center of the sound board, which is more resonant than the edges. Because the bass strings are placed in proximity to the treble strings, sympathetic vibrations are increased, thus greatly augmenting the resonance of the instrument.

The grand piano still reigns supreme among all pianos. The first pianos adhered rather closely to the harpsichord form. When the "twelve apostles" resumed their work in England, they turned again to the harpsichord form since the British were not so fond of the clavichord. But now they abandoned the tradition of the harpsichord by making the piano much heavier and giving it the two pedals. Moreover, the keyboard no longer remained recessed between the walls of the case but was projected forward.

Mozart's piano has no pedals whereas Beethoven's has the lyre-shaped pedal supports. (I wonder how much a person should credit the contention that since Mozart never used pedals, his music should be played strictly without pedals).

Figure 263. Mozart's Piano
Courtesy Mozarteum, Salzburg

Figure 264. Beethoven's Piano
Courtesy Historisches Bildarchiv, Handke - Bad Berneck

It was stated at the beginning of this chapter that the piano has become an integral part of our civilization. Let us briefly sum up its merits.

The keyboard itself has such a marvelously simple outlay of notes that almost any musician can pick out a tune and learn to play a melody. You strike a key and you have a correct note. Compare this with a violin, guitar, or any brass or woodwind. How difficult it is to produce the desired tone on some of those instruments! Furthermore, on the piano keyboard you have the bass-to-treble outlay of tones and semitones in a simple pattern of white and black keys. So the beginning is very inviting; still, the challenge is there.

And now consider the importance of the piano for the student of harmony and especially for the composer. The piano supplies not only the melody but the harmony as well. Here, then, the musician finds his perfect writing desk. At his keyboard he can combine tones, test resolutions and progressions, experiment with new chords. Whatever ideas a composer works out in his mind, he can put them to a test on the piano. The piano is his working tool he can consult time and again. And what would a choir leader do without his piano?

From our discussion of special pedals and stops, it is evident that the style of playing has had its variations. Modern composers evidently are not always satisfied with the traditional way of playing the piano. In their search for novel effects, they resort even to bizarre methods. Henry Cowell composed music which he wants the performer to play with his elbow instead of fingers! Percy Grainger employs fists, and Charles Ives directs the player to use a 14¾-inch board for striking the keys!

But let not our hearts be troubled over such a fantastic style (to say the least), and don't you start using elbows and fists instead of fingers before your teacher demands it of you. In the meantime, do not forget that the piano remains an instrument of sublime nobility, and when you speak of musical instruments you might almost give it the same position you give the earth when speaking of planets.

CHAPTER XVI

# THE PIPE ORGAN

The modern pipe organ is the most magnificent instrument human genius has yet devised and the most majestic of all tone-producing media.

The origin of the pipe organ may be found in the combination of open-reed pipes into a syrinx (Figure 116), for, after all, the organ is a combination of pipes. The evolution of the organ has been extremely slow, for even to date the search for improvement is going on.

If you were to compare the primitive Panpipes with the modern pipe organ and ask yourself how you could transform the one into the other, you would no doubt find the task beyond you. Your life would be too short to arrive at anything tangible, especially if you had never seen a real pipe organ. Yet this is what the human race has accomplished, except that nobody ever had any idea about the finished product; musicians were just trying to improve whatever was at their disposal at the given time. How, then, were primitive pipes assembled and how did they evolve into an organ?

The first step was taken when it was conceived that *the wind for blowing the pipes could be supplied by some source outside the mouth of the player himself.* In time a wind chest was inserted between the pipes and the source of the wind. The primitive wind chest was simply a box perforated at the top in such a way as to provide a hole for each pipe. The pipes were then fitted into these holes. To sound the pipes air was blown into the chest by two men, usually slaves, using their lungs as the source of power and pliable tubes to convey the air current into the box. To provide a steady stream of air they blew alternately. Unless some of the pipes were stopped by the fingers of the players, all the pipes would sound. Such an antique organ is shown in Figure 265. The carving shows the back of the instrument.

Figure 265
Antique Organ
Courtesy Grove's Dictionary

The second achievement was the *introduction of slides for closing the holes,* so that the pipes no longer needed to be stopped by the player's fingers. A slide was placed beneath each hole leading to the pipe and perforated so that when it was drawn in or out it would either admit or exclude the wind. As before, the wind was supplied through a tube projecting from one side of the wind chest. The tube was still mouth-blown.

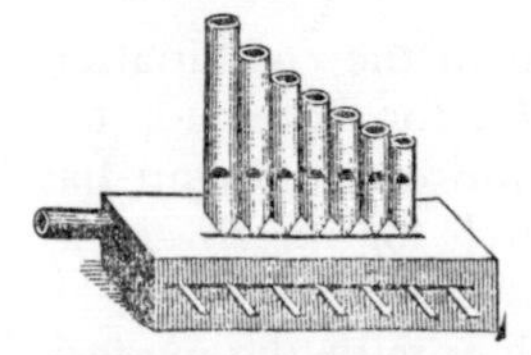

Figure 266
First Improvement: Slides
Courtesy Grove's Dictionary

The third step is obvious: by supplying *hand bellows* a more efficient, reliable, and powerful source of wind was obtained. Still, a tube operated by one set of bellows could at best supply only an intermittent current, so two tubes and a pair of bellows were introduced. As a result of this innovation more and larger pipes could be added and the wind increased; the slides were altered correspondingly. In short, they were in for "bigger and better things," and the road was paved toward the growth of the pipe organ conforming to our conception of it.

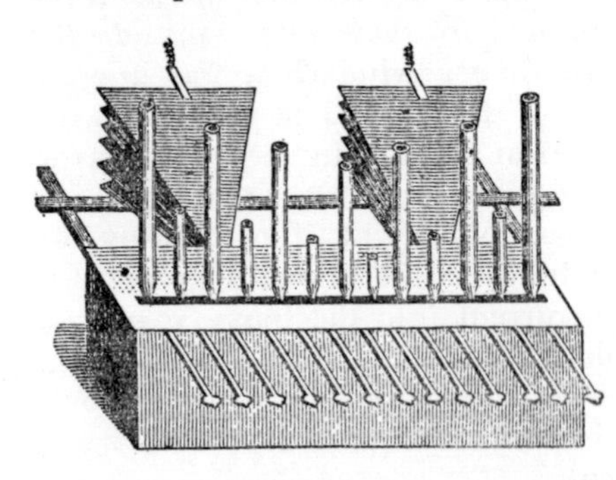

Figure 267
Hand Bellows Added to Organ
Courtesy Grove's Dictionary

The three characteristics just described—*bellows, wind chest* and *slides,* the germ of the most important features of the pipe organ—are from pre-Christian times.

The earliest authentic reproduction of an antique organ with bellows is found on an obelisk at Constantinople erected by Theodosius (346?-395). According to this sculpture two treaders give pressure to the bellows by their weight, a method of operating bellows which became more widespread some centuries afterward. There must have been two sets of bellows with a boy standing on each one who then shifted his weight back and forth from one set

Figure 268
Antique Organ with Bellows
Courtesy Grove's Dictionary

to the other. It is doubtful whether the sculptor has reproduced the work in its true proportions, for there is too little variation in the size of the pipes to permit the playing of a scale or a tune.

We are justified in concluding that in the fourth century A.D. wind or pneumatic organs as shown above were well-known instruments. Representations of small organs are found on coins of the Roman period, and remains of such organs have been excavated at Pompeii.

Before pursuing the development of the pneumatic organ further, we must retrace our steps and examine the *water organ* or *hydraulis.* By the third century B.C. Alexandria had become the center of technical art and engineering skill. It was here that Ctesibius[1] invented his famous water organ. His invention was the technical application of already existing principles of organ playing. Instead of bellows he employed pistons and water compressors. The compressor was a dome-shaped reservoir. The air pressure above it forced the water into the chambers at the sides, and the rise and

**Figure 269**
**Water Organ, 120 A.D.**

[1] Barnes (see Bibliography) disputes this. According to him, the hydraulis was invented about the fourth century B.C., and the name of the inventor is uncertain.

fall of the water level resulted in a steady flow of air into the wind chests. As in other organs, the pipes were closed and opened by slides.

An innovation on the water organ were *stops*. A stop is a mechanism connecting a number of pipes to the same wind channel, meaning that two, three, or more pipes, and in some cases as many as ten, sound simultaneously when one key is depressed or, as in antique organs, one slide is drawn. The stops of the organ are accordingly similar in function to the stops of the harpsichord. (We must of course remember that the organ stops are of a much earlier origin, and that consequently the harpsichord must be the borrower here.)

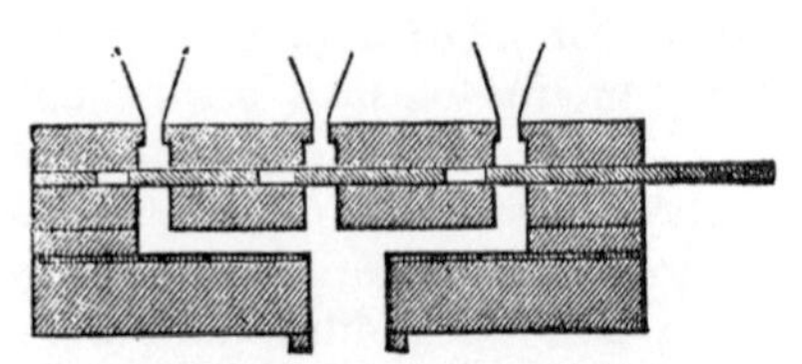

Figure 270. Stop Action of Early Organs
Courtesy Grove's Dictionary

The diagram to the left makes the operation of stops clear. Air enters the wind chest from the bottom. When the slide is closed the current is interrupted, and hence no pipes sound. When the slide is opened the unshaded portions of it correspond with those above and below, and the playing position is reached. Our illustration shows stops with three sets of pipes, that is, one slide operates three pipes; pull the slide and three pipes play instead of one. It would be interesting to know what intervals these pipes rendered. Inasmuch as in those days our diatonic scale had not yet evolved, it is proper to assume that the pipes either played in unison or in intervals that suited the then-prevalent Greek modes (ancient scales).

By means of stops the tone of the organ could be greatly augmented. The hydraulis had a loud, penetrating tone, appropriate as accompaniment for the robust entertainment of the Roman circus and for pagan rites. The early Christians looked upon the organ as a strictly heathen instrument of sinful entertainments, and for centuries the organ—today's embodiment of church music—was not admitted into the church. (The Greek Orthodox Church will not tolerate the organ to the present day. Lately, however, the Greek Orthodox Cathedral of Boston has installed a small organ as an accompaniment instrument, a miniature work.)

No ancient organ had any provisions for dynamic variations or for tone coloring. The tone was invariably and consistenly loud and uniform. The "keys" of the hydraulis were connected to the slides by means of levers. When a key was depressed the slide was pushed in; when released, sometimes by means of a spring, the slide was pulled back to the neutral position. But whenever the slide was opened, the pipes resounded to their full capacity.

The hydraulis gave way to the pneumatic organ in the fourth century A.D. It should be kept in mind that in the water organ the water itself was just a means of regulating the air current and was in no way responsible for tone production.

By the end of the sixth century pagan rites had disappeared. Now the West began to use the organ as an addition to the human voice —the organ accompanied the singer. Naturally, such organs had to be small or they would drown out the voice. But these small organs of the first millennium of the Christian era, contrary to common belief, were neither slow nor clumsy in spite of their primitiveness.

The center of organ making was Byzantium. Organ makers and players were exclusively ecclesiastics. From Byzantium the organ found its way into Italy (seventh century, when the Pope of Rome introduced it to improve the singing), France (Pepin, the father of Charlemagne, imported one from Constantinople in 757), Germany (imported by Charlemagne about 812), and England (where the organ became common during the ninth century).

Hre we see an amusing illustration of an early organ.

The picture below is typical of a Charlemagne organ. We can see

Figure 271
9th Century Organ Playing

that working such an organ must have been a real chore.

But now look at some later models.

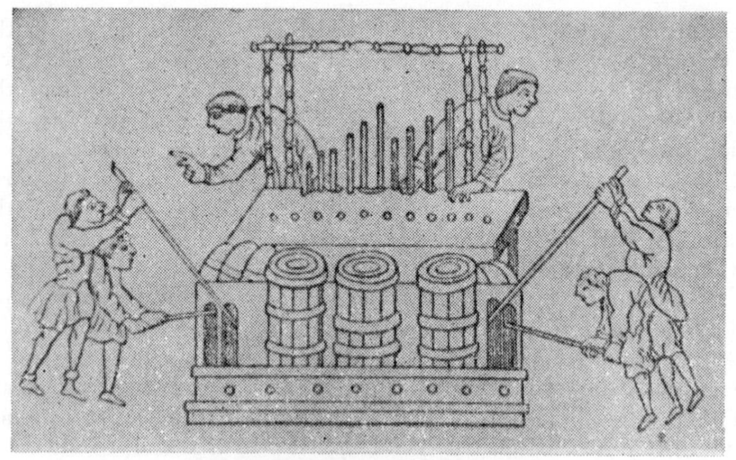

Figure 272. Organ of the 11th Century

Figure 273
Thirteenth Century Organ

There is vast difference between the two illustrations above. In the first one the two players are evidently unable to concentrate on their music and are admonishing the four hard-working blowers, who it seems are sweating desperately to get up the wind supply. In the second the player is already able to devote himself to the music. Whereas the older model still uses hand levers for working the bellows as in the ancient hydraulis, the wind supply in the second is obtained by employing one's weight for operating the bellows, a system that survived well into our century.

The pipes in Figure 272 are not clearly seen, but they must have been small, judging by the player's fingers placed between them on the table. Only one row of pipes is shown, the second row being indicated by the slits in the front of the table. The bellows do not lead the wind directly into the pipes, but keep up the supply in the chests, which in turn feed the pipes.

The second organ appears to have a sort of keyboard. If the scale of the drawing is at all accurate, the pipes must have been rather small. The function of the bells is nowhere stated. Did they tinkle in rhythm with the pumping of the bellows or were they merely ornamental? Or were they supposed to keep the evil spirits at bay? (see page 37).

Up to the year 1400 the evolution of the pipe organ was extremely slow. Even so, certain improvements were made earlier. In the eleventh century organ makers already knew how to produce a fuller or a more delicate tone by varying the proportions of the mouth of the pipe. In the fourteenth century the pedal keyboard was invented, either in Germany or in Flanders.

The pipe work itself underwent some drastic changes. We have already referred to the organ stops. In the early Middle Age all organs played in stops. The combinations of tones obtained were mostly octaves, thirds, and fifths. At the end of the fourteenth century came a great innovation: *solo stops* were added. A solo stop was a row of pipes imitating the tone color of certain woodwind instruments. The first solo stop was the flute. Thus, it was possible to obtain contrast to the principal pipes. *The combination and contrast of timbres became one of the distinctive features of the organ.*

With the advent of polyphonic music, the organ became firmly established. Large church organs came into being, and each one of them assumed an importance worthy of historic record. Almost any book on the history of music will enumerate them with date of construction, builder, number of stops, pipes, and other details. Of all these early gigantic organs we shall mention only two.

The first truly big church organ was the one erected in 980 in the monastery at Winchester in England. This organ had twenty-six bellows and two keyboards. Each keyboard had twenty slides and each slide operated ten pipes at once, making a total of four hundred pipes. A player could operate two slides at a time at the most, and two-part harmony was all that could be expected from a single keyboard. But at that time nobody expected anything more than such simple harmony.

The organ employed two organists, one for each keyboard. The keyboards were probably on opposite sides of the organ. The wind supply for operating all the pipes was so great that it required seventy men to work the bellows! And what was the result of this monstrosity's performance? Chroniclers speak of "the awful roar of bellows," which they compare with the rumble of a thunderstorm, of "the poor crowd inside trembling and covering up their ears."

Such was the instrument "with a thousand blasts." The Winchester organ was the largest of the so-called antique organs.

The Halberstadt organ (Germany), not completed till nearly 1500, already embodied some features of our modern organ, such as solo stops. It is the earliest organ with a chromatic keyboard.[2] It had two middle keyboards, designed for the usual two-part playing, and two outer ones, a descant manual and a pedal board. Some of its keys sounded as many as fifty-six pipes!

During the late Middle Ages two types of small organs were perfected: the *positive* and the *portative.* The term *positive* was applied not only to domestic organs but also to reed organs (see Chapter XVII). It was the larger instrument of the two, the portative of course being a portable model.

Portative organs (twelfth-sixteenth centuries) had keyboards and one pipe per key. The left hand worked the bellows while the right hand manipulated the keys. The instrument was held in such a position that the keyboard ran perpendicular to the body of the player. The player therefore used only two fingers, because he could not very well use his whole hand in such a position. (This custom of playing the keyboard with two fingers remained general for all keyboard instruments, and until the eighteenth century players practiced their scales with two fingers only!)

The portative was a flutelike instrument with a clear, pure, mellow tone. The instrument never became standardized. Thus, the number of pipes varied from six to thirty, with one, two, or three ranks; the keys were either press-buttons or levers; the semitones had no fixed places; some notes were entirely left out; and in many cases the instrument was made to the specifications of the performer. Pipes could even be changed for the performance of different compositions.

Portatives were used by laymen for secular music.

The *keyboard* as we know it today took several hundred years to reach its modern look. The first keyboards appeared in the thirteenth century, when the slides which controlled the openings of the pipes were operated by levers. The first levers were inside the organ and worked from the outside by means of button-rod connections, similar to those of a typewriter. Later the levers were made to project and were operated directly by hand. They were from three to five inches wide and from a foot to a yard long, and required the full strength of the arm for depression; hence they were often played with the fist. "To beat the organ" was a common saying in German.

Chromatic keys (sharps or flats) were only gradually introduced.

---

[2] For that matter, *the organ is the first instrument with a complete diatonic chromatic scale.*

Figure 274
Organ Bellows,
Halberstadt Cathedral, 1618

Figure 275
Positive Organ, 14th Century

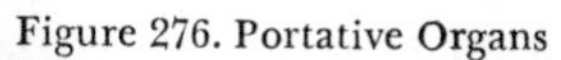

Figure 276. Portative Organs

At first they were not given any special position on the keyboard, but merely labeled as all the other keys with plain large capitals to guide the player. There were no distinguishing black and white keys, and what is more, the keys were not arranged according to a set pattern. During the fourteenth century black and white keys gradually were arranged into the modern pattern, but the black color was by no means indicative of semitones.

By 1500 the modern keyboard had become a reality. This, however, does not mean that from that year on all organs had chromatic keyboards, for organs of the older type remained popular many a year afterwards.

No noted improvements on the organ are recorded during the seventeenth and eighteenth centuries. Late medieval organs, although simple and somewhat primitive of construction, already had a beauty of their own. Bach certainly achieved amazing results on his organs. Organ makers of the last and present century, however, have exploited all scientific avenues to the fullest to create a pipe organ which in its construction truly baffles the imagination of the uninitiated. Still, Bach's organ and his style of playing keeps dominating the art of organ playing.

Although a detailed study of all the component parts of the modern organ is beyond the scope of this book, a short discussion of the principal features merits an inclusion. They are summed up under the headings: wind supply, pipes, divisions of the organ, expressive playing, and the console.

### *The Wind Supply*

Let us begin with the simple reminder that the pipe organ is primarily a wind instrument. Hence the *wind supply* is of first importance. The pipes must be supplied with an *adequate amount*

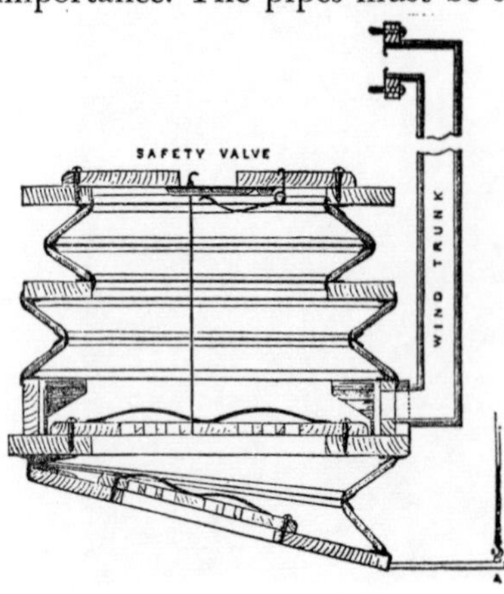


Figure 277
Cross Section of an Organ Bellows, Showing Reservoir with Double Folds and Feeder Below
Courtesy Barnes, The Contemporary American Organ

of wind at a *steady pressure.* It is easily understood that the pressure required to voice the pipes varies with the number of pipes in action. The more notes the player strikes, the greater the supply of wind must be. And this supply must be at his fingertips for any changes from a solo pipe to full organ.

We have already seen that a direct passage from bellows to pipes was found inadequate even by ancient organ builders. The answer, therefore, was the interpolation of a special *wind reservoir* between bellows and pipes. The first organs had one reservoir only. To meet the requirements, such a chest had to be of prodigious proportions, often eight by fifteen feet or even larger. Today's organs have a number of wind reservoirs, so that not too many pipes are fed from the same source.

Each reservoir has its own rotary *electric fan blower.* These blowers fill the reservoirs with up to fifty inches of *compressed air*[3] so that a high enough pressure is maintained at all times regardless of the number or size of pipes sounded.

The air pressure per pipe has been standardized for moderate-sized organs as six to seven and a half inches per pipe; indeed, except in large buildings pipes seldom require more than four to five inches of pressure. Furthermore, there is no direct relation between an increase in pressure and volume of sound, that is, the volume is not necessarily determined by the pressure. Modern organ builders therefore tend to minimize the air pressure. Thus, the Aeolian-Skinner Organ Company uses a chest so efficient that it is possible to operate the organ on a wind pressure as light as one inch. Light wind has several distinct advantages, the chief of which is tonal beauty; flexibility and speed of articulation are also increased, and the power requirements are decreased.

The next problem is to lead the wind from the high-pressure compartment into the pipes. The wind chest of old as shown in Figure 265 is still the answer. Between the wind chest and the reservoir there are either rectangular wooden conveyances or round galvanized sheet-iron pipes and a system of valves to control the flow of air into the pipes. The slide, however, is no longer operated by hand or keys of the keyboard but by means of knobs on the panel of the console (Figure 286). The pipes are sounded by means of a *tracker action* explained by the following two diagrams.

---

[3] The air pressure is measured by means of a wind gauge, a glass tube in the form of a widened S. One end of the gauge is connected with the wind supply of the organ, the lower curve of the tube being filled with water. When no pressure is exerted, the water level is even in both arms of the tube; pressure against the water column forces the water down one side and up the other. The difference in levels thus created is measured in inches and is indicative of the wind pressure.

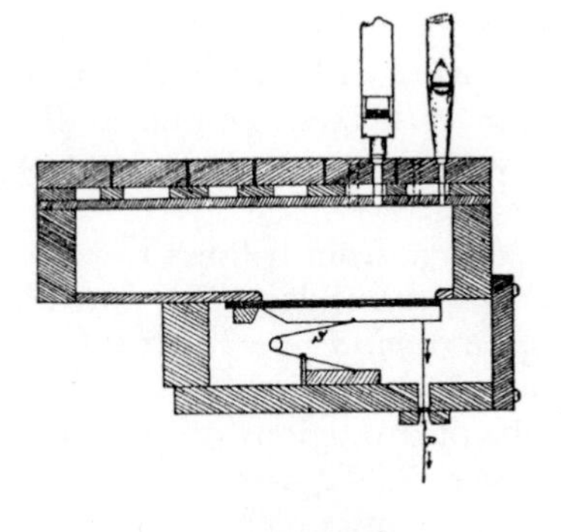

Sectional View of the Pallet and Slider Windchest

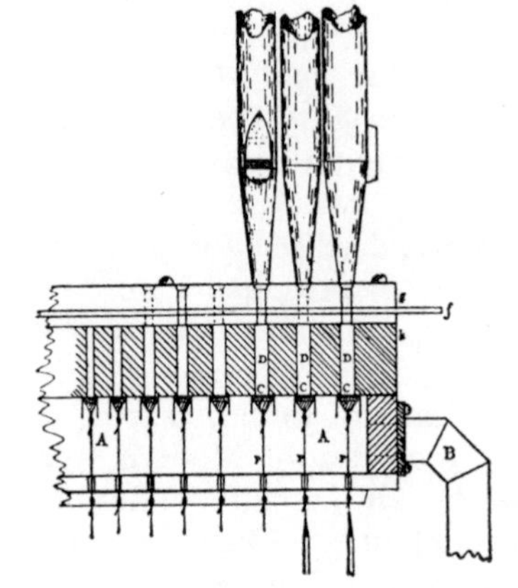


Figure 278
Courtesy Barnes, The Contemporary American Organ

Sectional Front View of the Same Windchest

The above action seems to be simple and satisfactory enough. As a matter of fact, it isn't. Here is the reason: B fills A with enough air pressure to make the operation of the pallets difficult; whenever valve C has to be opened the pressure in A against it must be overcome, which requires considerable force, the more so as one pallet may admit the wind to more than one pipe. The pressure on the key of the keyboard in such tracker action is therefore too great for smooth performance of rapid passages and too uncomfortable even for slow playing. How to overcome this resistance posed a serious problem to organ makers. Finally, in 1832 Charles Barker of England invented the *pneumatic lever*. So revolutionary was his invention that it was like erecting a milestone in the history of organ making.

The pneumatic lever uses special bellows operated by the organ wind itself to overcome the resistance to the pallets. This device has become so popular that it is generally known as the *Barker lever*. (Evidently "a prophet is not without honor, save in his own country," for English organ builders not only ignored Barker's invention but they also opposed it, so that Barker had to go to France to win recognition!) After some modifications of the first model, the Barker lever won universal favor. The organ touch is now comparable to that of the piano.

In short order it was found that even the modified Barker lever was not entirely ideal, especially in large organs. Further experimenting led first to tubular pneumatic action in which a series of tubes for the passage of the wind connected the end of the key to the Barker lever and then to the *electropneumatic* action.

The electropneumatic action consists of an *electromagnet* which operates the small bellows which in turn work the pallets. When the player at the console depresses a key, an electric current energizes the electromagnet; the magnet then opens a valve which in turn operates the Barker lever. After the initial problems were overcome, electropneumatic action became an integral part of the modern organ.

Electricity is also used elsewhere in the organ. An electromagnet is placed wherever an action is desired. Some wind chests even have individual valves for each pipe. The electromagnet transforms an electric impulse into a pneumatic one.

The advantages of a reliable electric mechanism are obvious: (1) it operates instantaneously—as soon as a key makes the contact action follows; (2) it eliminates a number of levers; and (3) it makes for ease of performance. It must be kept in mind that the wiring of the organ is a problem that can be solved only by the expert. Questions like the following—and I dare say many more—must be solved: where to place the magnet, the size of the magnet, the material, the source and strength of the current, keeping contact points free of corrosion or oxidization and dust; connecting the hundreds of magnets. (As many as thirty-six contacts may be made by one key!)

Since the organ is such an exceedingly complicated machine, there is little standardization. Organ builders will employ differently constructed reservoirs, bellows, chests, magnets, motors, tubes, etc. In many cases organ builders have contributed inventions which today bear their names as does the Barker level, for example, the Moller magnet, the Austin air chest, and the Pitman chest, which has been in use for at least forty years.

All told, the wind supply in the modern organ is adequate and steady and literally at the fingertips of the player; the lightest touch on the key evokes the desired tone. The organist consequently is in position to play runs as on a piano, but he may also prolong a tone at will.

### *The Pipes*

Figure 279 shows parts of the interior of a pipe organ. You note at once that there are far more pipes than you had expected and that they vary greatly in appearance.

In *size* the pipes vary from three-eighths of an inch speaking length to thirty-two feet and a yard or more in diameter. (The largest metal pipe ever made is found in the Atlantic City Auditorium organ; it weighs 2200 pounds. According to their sizes the pipes are grouped into registers, such as the two- four- eight- and sixteen-foot registers, plus the pedal pipe with a thirty-two-foot register.

The meaning of the length of the register is this. In the eight-foot register the standard pipe, the longest in the series, is eight feet long. (It sounds *CC,* the lowest *c* on the piano.) In the four-foot register the standard pipe is four feet long, and so on. Suppose now you play middle *c* on the eight-foot register; it will have the same pitch as middle *c* on the piano. This register therefore corresponds to the piano, and any notes played in it will be of standard pitch. The four-foot register has pipes only half the size of the eight-foot; consequently, they will play any note an octave higher. The two-foot will raise the pitch an octave more, while the sixteen-foot register will make a note sound an octave lower than the eight-foot.

The beauty of the whole thing is that one can sound as many registers simultaneously as one wishes. If the organist wants to play a simple tune, he will likely use the eight-foot register; if he wants to enrich the tone, he can couple one, two, three, or four of the registers by means of the stop knobs on the panel of the console. In other words, by depressing one key only he can play not only five different pitches but any and all of these five pitches together. The registers thus increase the range of the organ. If the manual keyboard of a console shows a range of five octaves, the actual compass of the organ extends above and below it.

*Pipes are made either of metal or wood.*[4] Two considerations determine the choice of the material: the desired strength and durability of the pipe and the quality of tone to be produced. For metal pipes the best material is pure tin. When lead is mixed with the tin a differently colored tone is produced. Generally, therefore, the pipes are made of an alloy of tin and lead. The percentage of tin varies from twenty to ninety, depending upon the tone quality desired. Occasionally some antimony may be added for stiffness.[5]

---

[4] Review the importance of material as a sound producer as explained on page 93.

[5] The shiny brass pipes seen in churches are as a rule only ornamental. The pipes proper are concealed in the organ chamber, part of which is shown in Figure 279. Brass pipes would sound rather disagreeable.

Figure 279. Pipe Work of the Great Division, with the Positive in the Foreground and the Choir Swell Box in the Rear

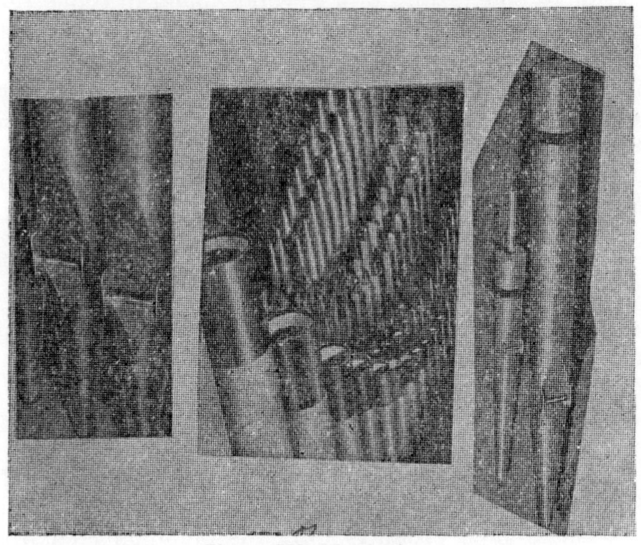

Figure 280. Metal Pipes

As is shown in Figure 280, the metal pipes vary not only in size (for different pitches, of course) but also in shape and proportions of the parts as well as in structure of upper parts. These variations account for the timbre of pipes.

Wooden pipes are usually made from spruce or white pine, although they may be made from maple, mahogany, oak or almost any wood. Whereas metal pipes are generally round, wood pipes are square in shape. They are simpler to make than metal pipes, and their characteristic tone is some type of flute tone. As you can see from the diagram, Figure 282, the various parts have rather interesting names.

If one wanted to list all the parts of the wooden pipe one would have to compile a goodly list of technical names. Suffice it therefore to point out that the lower end has *lips, ears,* a *tongue,* and a *beard as* well as a *mouth.* The whole pipe consists of *three divisions:* the *foot,* the *languid,* and the *body.* The foot rests on top of the wind chest and admits the air into the pipe. The languid is a partition across the bottom of the pipe directing the air stream to the narrow opening lip, known as the flue. Languids come in different shapes, forming different openings as the occasion may warrant. A typical languid is shown in part one of Figure 282. The body of the pipe is above the sound mechanism.

The principle of tone production is the same as that of woodwind instruments and need not be explained again. A study of the diagram above should make it clear.

Wood pipes pose certain problems not found in connection with metal ones. If, for instance, their joints become loose or open, the tone is ruined. Furthermore, wood is affected by the humidity of the air. Hence these pipes must be made waterproof and watertight.

Pipes are further divided into *closed* and *open* pipes, depending on whether the top of the pipe is closed or open. Both openings are found in the following illustration. (The differently shaped openings are for variations in timbre.)

Without advancing the scientific reason for it (textbooks on physics are concerned with that), the open pipe generates a tone exactly one octave higher in pitch than the closed pipe. A thirty-two foot open pipe consequently has the same pitch as a sixteen-foot closed pipe.

Immediately the question comes to mind, why not have all the pipes closed and half the size of the open ones? One could certainly economize on material and space. Theoretically there is no need for large open bass pipes, but the question of timbre must be considered here. As it is, open pipes produce more overtones than closed ones. A closed pipe produces only the odd-numbered overtones, which of course is good for clarinet effects. So depending upon the

Figure 281
The 32′ Pedal-Diapason. The Largest Pipe Is 31-13/16″ x 28-1/16″ x 33′ Long, Made of Sugar Pine 3″ Thick
Courtesy Barnes, The Contemporary American Organ

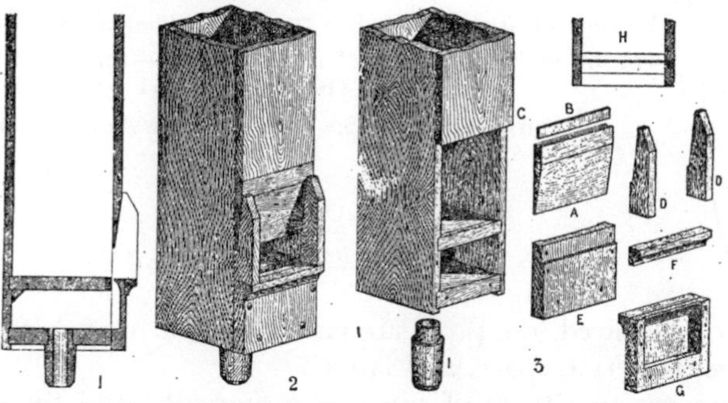


Figure 282. Parts of a Pedal Bourdon. 1, Cross Section; 2, Completed Pipe; 3, Separate Parts of the Pipe, as for Example at A the Upper Lip with B the Tongue Grooving the Lip to the Body of the Pipe at C; DD Represent the Two Ears; F the Beard; E and G Are Front and Back Views of the Cap or Lower Lip

Figure 283. View of Top Openings of Organ Pipes

Figure 284

Portion of Reed Pipe: E —the Reed Tongue; F — Wedge; G — Portion of Pipe; H — the Tuning Wire; I — the Reed Boot or Foot That Fits into the Block A

Courtesy Barnes, The Contemporary American Organ

tone color desired, the pipes are either open or closed, regardless of expense, material, space, and labor.

There are two types of pipes: the *flue pipe* and the *reed pipe*. The principle of the flue pipe has already been accounted for (Figure 282). The reed pipe employs a reed for tone production similar to reed wind instruments instead of the open flue. An important feature of the reed pipe is the tuning device. The lever marked H as shown in the above illustration serves this purpose. To raise the pitch, the lever is lowered, thereby shortening the free vibrating portion of the reed. By raising H the pitch, of course, will be lowered. Reed E must have a certain elasticity and is not supposed to strike against the reed block but rather "roll down," else the tone will be harsh and blatant. Any particle of dust interferes with the action of the reed; hence, dust is the greatest enemy of reed pipes.

It stands to reason that in a pipe all the parts must bear the right proportion to the pipe as a whole. This is known as the *scale of the pipe*. For a given length the pipe must have a certain width, a certain embouchure (mouth opening), languid, etc. The pitch of a pipe depends on the volume of air vibrating in the pipe. A short, wide pipe will generate a mellower tone than a narrow pipe; a thin, narrow pipe will produce a penetrating tone. These and many more considerations are taken into account by organ makers in building their instruments of many tone colors. Small wonder the successful organ builder is always famous in his own right.

Figure 285
Tone Finishing

"*Tone finishing* is the element of greatest subtlety in the whole organ-building process." [6] Certain problems confront the organ maker here. First of all, each pipe—and remember, there may be thousands of them—must not only be tuned to a certain pitch but it must be voiced so as to "speak" with the tone for which it was designed. Secondly, all the pipes of one stop must be coordinated so that they will blend and be of equal strength and tone quality. Thirdly, the divisions (sets of stops) must harmonize. Fourthly, the pipes must be distributed in the organ chamber to the best advantage. Finally, the pipes must be placed in the most advantageous places in the building.

The last statement merits a closer inspection. The point is that just as a resonator can make or unmake a string instrument, so the environment of the organ determines its fate. Even the best-made organ would perform poorly in improper surroundings. To solve this mystery we must now say a word about *acoustics.*

Acoustics refers to the science of hearing, but the word is generally taken to include the physical basis of sound. In simple terminology it amounts to this. As the sound waves of the organ fill the church building, the walls, the ceiling, the pillars, the furniture, the balcony, the cornices, the arches, in brief, all the interior architecture and contents of the building will partly absorb and partly reflect them.

[6] Quoted from a pamphlet by the Aeolian-Skinner Organ Company, Boston.

The reflected sound may interfere favorably or otherwise with the original sound, causing reverberations or echo effects or obstructions. The absorption of sound waves, on the other hand, deadens the original source. (Choir singers usually find that it is "easier" to sing in certain buildings than in others.) If the total effect of reflection and absorption in a building makes for ease of performance and well-balanced tone reception, we say the acoustics of the building is good, and vice versa. The best concert halls are built strictly in accordance with the laws of acoustics.

When, therefore, an organization decides to install an organ in their building, they cannot simply order the organ from the manufacturer. The organ builder will first of all "size up" the building, and then he will build the organ to suit that particular building. This explains why some churches are famous for their organs, for the "wedding of planning and environment" has been most successful. An ideal case, especially for recording and taping, is the Great Organ in the Methuen Memorial Music Hall, shown in Figure 289.

### *The Divisions of the Organ*

A division of an organ embraces all the pipes of a certain tone color. Within a division the pipes are arranged in stops which are controlled by the stop-knobs of the console. The grouping into stops is necessitated by the large number of pipes in one division, which may reach or even exceed a thousand. Some organs have only one or two divisions, while the larger ones have as many as ten or more. As in a good orchestra every instrument has to blend with the others and fit into the whole pattern, so each division of the organ must be a harmonious part of the whole.

The *flue pipes* are divided into four divisions: (1) the diapasons, (2) the flutes, (3) the strings, and (4) the echoes.

The diapasons produce the foundation tone of the organ and are consequently of the utmost importance.

The flute division pipes produce the characteristic flute tone (marked by a deficiency of upper overtones), which is obtained from stopped pipes, from open wood pipes with square blocks, or from metal pipes with very high mouths; it can also be gotten from "overblowing." The organ thus possesses several kinds of "flutes," even those with two mouths known as *Doppelflöte* (double flute).

The string pipes offer a sharp contrast to the flutes inasmuch as they produce an abundance of upper harmonics, if necessary at the expense of the fundamental tone. Usually of metal, they are made to a special scale. A large organ has a whole family of strings with about a dozen members, the more familiar ones being the violone and the violoncello. Each stop of strings has a different timbre, of course.

The echoes are miniatures of the above three groups employed to create music in a quieter mood. The name *echo* is obviously very appropriate.

The reed pipes are indispensable for contrast and enrichment of tone color. The main categories of reed pipes are *chorus* and *solo.* Over two dozen reed stops are in use today, such as the clarinet, bassoon, oboe, English horn, and French horn. Some organs incorporate even obsolete types, such as the krummhorn and shawm. And finally, some chorus reeds are given names of brass instruments, no doubt on account of their timbre—the trumpet, trombone, ophicleide, tuba, and others. The names of the stops are often non-English and cannot very well be translated. They have been contributed by the leading organ-making countries—Germany, England, France, Italy, Spain, Holland, and America. To the organist each name has its correct connotation.

### *Expressive Playing*

One of the marvels in organ building is the fact that in spite of the organ's being a purely mechanical instrument the playing itself can be highly individualistic.

It is obvious that a single pipe of the organ is incapable of dynamic shading, nor can it be played similarly to a string where the violinist can impart to it a beautiful lifelike *vibrato* or *tremolo.* Yet both the *vibrato* and *tremolo* are within the reach of the organist.

There are several devices to aid the organist in expressive playing. One of these is the *tremulant,* a device which causes a disturbance in the wind supply in such a manner that the *vibrato* effect is imitated. Used judiciously, this adds beauty and warmth to the fundamental tone; overdone, it becomes loathsome (as, for instance, in radio commercials). Used with the stop *vox humana* (human voice) the tremulant can be lovely. Incidentally, the tremulant is not a modern invention, for Bach already had it.

Another *vibrato* effect may be caused by *pitch beats.* Beats are caused by small difference in the frequency of two adjacent tones. Suppose the fundamental pipe is tuned to 256 vibrations per second and another pipe to either 252 or 260. Then the second pipe will sound the fundamental middle *c* but slightly out of tune. When sounded together the two pipes will produce four beats per second, because the combined sound will no longer be of uniform intensity. The total effect is that of a *vibrato,* and the tone will be "warmer" and more vibrant than the "straight" tone obtained from one pipe only.[7]

---

[7] Some piano tuners adopt a similar method in tuning their instruments; by tuning one of the three strings of a key slightly out of pitch they also obtain a *vibrato.*

Several devices for *special effects* are in use. Percussions like bells, chimes, jingles, and drums used to be and still are popular. The harp register is still used frequently. As long as these devices are used with discretion and judgment they have their places. Time and again their usefulness has been dulled by overuse. Just for your amusement, let me tell you that there was an organ built around 1500 with the figure of a monk in the lower part of the organ case, falling out of the window and jumping back again. In the seventeenth century an organ in Magdeburg had forty-two "figures," among them a crowing cock. Bells and jingles on rotating wheels were frequent up to the nineteenth century. Naturally, such queer additions rob the organ of its dignity; hence true musicians shun them. Unfortunately, there is no saying to what oddities people might resort to suit a "rock 'n' roll" craze.

For *dynamic effects* the *swell* has been universally adopted. There are two kinds of swells: the *Venetian swell,* seen in the background of Figure 279, and the Rollschweller. The Venetian swell was first invented for the harpsichord in England in the eighteenth century. It works on the principle of Venetian window blinds. A division of the organ is enclosed in a special chamber, the swell forming one partition. By means of a special pedal the swell can be partially or wholly opened as the organ is played. The wider the shutters open the louder the music of course.

The rollschweller, known as the *register crescendo,* was invented in Germany in the nineteenth century. Its name indicates a rolling swelling device. It functions by bringing more and more stops into action through a cylinder with ledges on its surface. In other words, the player can bring a number of stops, even the full organ, into play without touching any knobs on the console. If he begins to play with one stop open, he can gradually open more stops till the full organ is in play. Rapid crescendos can be obtained in this way. Conversely decrescendos are equally well executed. Some noted organists, however, do not take kindly to the register crescendo and consider it an undignified way of achieving dynamic variations; it is true that by opening more stops not only the volume but also the tone color is changed.

The *sforzando* or *full-organ pedal* is a sudden forte pedal which enables the player to throw all the stops into immediate action without using any stop knobs. Thus, sudden outbursts are effected with ease, aiding expressive playing. Both the register crescendo and the sforzando pedal are provided with warning signals to remind the player that they are in action, because they nullify the action of the stops he has drawn.

All the pedals mentioned may be duplicated or tripled; a pedal may be used for certain sections of the organ or for the whole organ.

## *The Console*

Figure 286. A Pipe Organ Console
Photo Davis Studio, Boston

In contrast to the piano keyboard, the keyboard of the organ is in itself a most complicated affair. It is known as the *console.*

The console of the organ is detached from the organ itself and is generally placed in some convenient spot from which the organist can overlook the choir and hear both the singers and the organ music. There are no standardized consoles, each manufacturer turning out his own makes according to his ideas. Consoles vary in size, number of manuals, and arrangement and number of stop knobs and pedals. The organist is often put at a disadvantage when playing other than his own organ. Certain important features of the console, such as the size of keys and distances between the manuals, are of course standardized.

As you note from the illustration, the console has two types of keyboards. The upper type is played with the hand and is known as the *manual;* the lower is played with the feet and comprises the *pedal* keyboard. The pedal usually operates the large bass tubes. This keyboard is just about as old as the manual, for it was started during the fourteenth century. Not until the last half-century, however, did it assume the shape shown above. The four shutters above the pedal keyboard are for dynamic effects.

Let us now briefly consider some of the tonal combinations within the reach of the console player. Each manual controls a different division of the organ. By shifting hands from one manual to the other the organist varies the timbre, thereby producing tone contrasts. There are also *couplers* by means of which the manuals can be "tied" together: with the help of couplers one or more manuals are made to function simultaneously, even though only one is played. The pedals, too, may be coupled to the manuals.

Next, by means of certain stop knobs, a note played may be reinforced by its octave or its most important and pleasing overtones (such combinations being called *mutations*), or mixed octaves and overtones may be produced (called *mixtures*). The number of possible combinations at the disposal of the organist is legion. How much diligent study and how many hours of practice do you think the successful organist will need?

Today there are special organ courses given at various music schools. Some of these schools have special "practice organs" at the disposal of their students.

Organ making and playing has been subject to the whims of time. As the times changed the demands made on the organ varied. From the ancient circus and theater the organ slowly wound its way into the church, until with the advance of polyphonic music it became the ideal church instrument, dignified and of unified solemn tone.

The art of organ playing culminated in Bach, the greatest composer of organ music. As we have seen, certain crazes were indulged in occasionally. Beginning with the nineteenth century there was a tendency for larger organs with all kinds of extras. The number of pipes and stops was constantly increased. By 1917 the world's greatest organ (in Philadelphia) had 5 manuals, 232 stops, and 18,000 pipes. In 1932 the organ in Convention Hall at Atlantic City, New Jersey, took the lead in size with 32,882 pipes with 1,233 stops and 7 manuals. All this was in keeping with the spirit of the time when composers tried to overwhelm the listener with size, volume, and novel effects.

Today the tendency is back to Bach and Silbermann. Most modern organs are built of moderate size. Novel effects, special devices, and all sorts of extras have fallen out of favor with competent organists. Tone efficiency and dignity of tone quality are the passwords today.

And here you see E. Power Biggs, one of the eminent organists of our time, at the console of his portable organ, made to his own specifications.

It may be said that the great organs of today are like celebrities,

Figure 287. A Practice Organ,
New England Conservatory

Figure 288. E. Power Biggs at His Portable Organ
Photo Wittkowsky Studio, North Tonawanda, N. Y.

each being famous in its own way. The Great Organ in the Methuen Memorial Music Hall, Massachusetts, is such an organ. Originally it was built in Germany according to specifications given by the Boston Music Hall Association. The cost was not to exceed $25,000. When, however, the organ arrived in Boston in 1863 (it had been ordered in 1856), the final cost was $60,000. Since then the organ has had its ups and downs. It was rebuilt, remodeled, and modernized until in 1947 it assumed its final form. The acoustics of the Hall are so perfect that the organ-hall combination is considered ideal for recording on tape and phonograph records.

A church choir accompanied by a pipe organ makes a imposing picture.

Lately the pipe organ has been introduced into the concert hall.

The history of the evolution of the organ from the mouth-blown reed pipe to the present stage is so large that one is almost inclined to compare it to the evolution of the wheel to a modern Cadillac. Naturally, the music is much better, too. And having studied this part on the organ, you will probably delight in studying organ music. If you do not have access to a real organist and his music, the next best approach is to study fine recordings played on proper high fidelity equipment. You will be amazed how the music will grow on you with repeated hearings, for truly the pipe organ is the king of instruments.

Figure 289
The Great Organ, Methuen
Photo King Covell,
Newport, R. I.

## CHAPTER XVII

# FREE-REED INSTRUMENTS

The pipe organ we have just discussed is king among instruments also in the sense that it is not available to the common man, or in other words it is not an instrument which can be used in homes and for social entertainment. What was needed was something simple and inexpensive, something for domestic use. The answer was provided by free-reed instruments.

The principal members of today's free-reed instrument family are harmonicas, accordions, and harmoniums or reed organs. Although they date back only to about 1800, they have some prototypes of great antiquity.

Free reeds, in contrast to the clarinet and pipe-organ type (which are called *beating reeds*), do not strike against any surface but vibrate freely within a metal frame or other hole. The vibrations set up a pulsating air stream resulting in sound waves. The tone is determined by the size, thickness, elasticity, and material of the reed. Pipes are superfluous, although they are sometimes used for timbre and resonance. The reeds are excited either by blowing or by suction.

The oldest of the free-reed instruments is the Chinese *sheng*, which according to tradition was invented in the third millennium B.C. The earliest picture of it dates from the sixth century A.D.

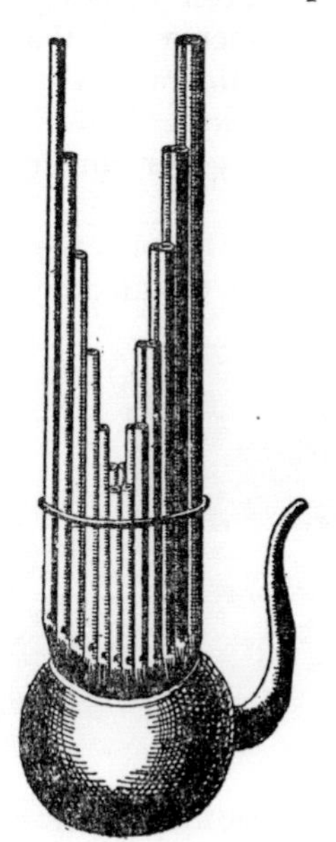

Figure 290
Chinese Sheng, a Mouth Organ,
Two Forms

The wind chest of the sheng was originally a gourd. The gourd was later replaced by a wooden box with a neck which served as a mouthpiece and air conduit. Into the box a number of bamboo canes was inserted in a circular arrangement, the number and size varying with time and place. Thirteen was a usual number. Each pipe had two holes; the lower one was inside the chest and covered by a reed, usually a thin metal tongue, while the upper hole provided the fingerhole above the box. To sound any particular pipe the upper hole was closed and the air drawn in. Thus the sheng was a suction-type reed organ. The sound was delicate and sweet.

The sheng is today widely distributed throughout south and east Asia. Some of these instruments have pipes up to twelve feet in length. Even so they are light, being of bamboo canes, and are therefore portable. Several shengs played together produce agreeable harmony. We can picture young fellows serenading their sweethearts with these instruments.

In the second half of the eighteenth century the sheng was carried westward. European instrument makers were delighted with the "lovely organ of the Chinese," and after various musicians had toyed with the idea awhile, a whole family of free-reed organs fashioned after the sheng appeared on the scene, some small, some large. The most outstanding member of this family is the *mouth organ,* also called the *harmonica.*

The mouth organ was invented in 1821 by Buschmann in Berlin. The first harmonica had a length of two and a quarter inches. A series of free reeds were fitted into a metal frame in such a way that one tone was produced by blowing and another by suction. Today the harmonica comes in many varieties, either as a sort of toy in primitive form or as a more elaborate and expensive instrument. The latter, like the pipe organ, also have mutations.

However, the mouth organ has failed to gain the approval of serious musicians and has remained the instrument of the amateur.

Figure 291
Typical Modern Moth Organs, Priced at 20c, $10.00 and $150.00, Respectively

Its place among the instruments is probably analogous to that of a comic strip in a newspaper.

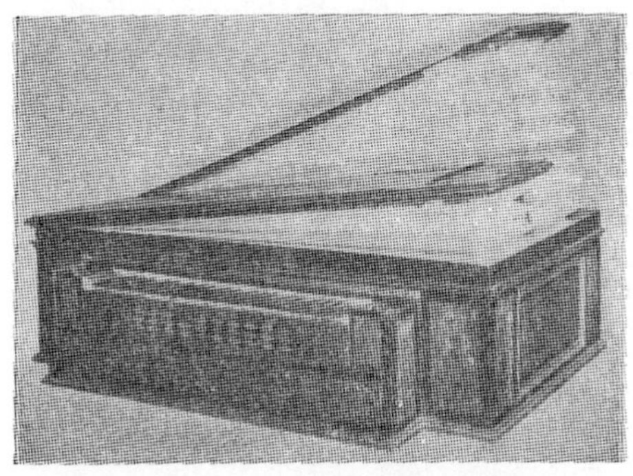

Figure 292
Regal

The first portable reed organs, however, antedate mouth organs by centuries, for they were known as early as the second half of the fifteenth century under the name of *regals*. The name suggests that the instrument was employed to regulate the plain chant of the monks. In the course of time the regal also became a secular instrument used for entertainment.

At one time the regal was rather popular. King Henry VIII had seventeen regals in his collection of instruments, both *double* (eight-foot register) and *single* (four-foot register). The tone of the regal was, as some writers have it, "good and lovable," but in Bach's time the instrument was abandoned on account of its "hateful and repugnant" tone! Still, it must have been held in some esteem, for up to 1773 (Bach died in 1750) there was a special post at the Court of England for a regal maker, and the tuner of regals at that time received £56 per annum.

During the sixteenth century the regal was constructed with a detachable keyboard which could be packed into the bellows when not in use. The whole instrument thus assumed the shape of a large book and was know as the *bible regal*. Subsequently the regal has

Figure 293
Bible Regal

been supplanted by the pipe organ and the free-reed organ proper.

The interplay between pipe and reed organs is quite obvious. The pipe organ borrowed reeds for its own enrichment, and the regals were, at least occasionally, equipped with pipes. Hence, there is some confusion in the naming of the positives and portatives encountered previously. Generally, both types relied on pipes only, but some of these organs also had reeds so that the name "portative" or "positive" could refer to either type, pipe or reed. After all, "portative" means something portable and "positive" in this case something more substantial or larger. The following two illustrations bear out the case.

Figure 294. Positive Organ or Regal

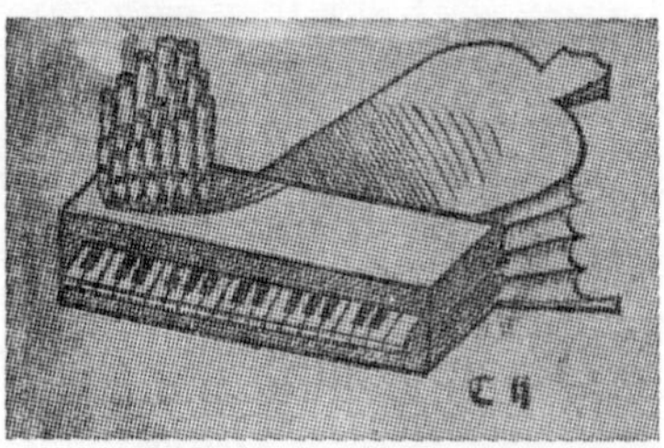

Figure 295. Portative

The first organ shown, constructed in 1650, was known as *positive* or *regal.* Some of the pipes were used as resonators, while others had reeds. The second, known as *portatyff* (sixteenth century), has pipes for the bass section only.

The nineteenth century saw numerous other specimens of free-reed organs. Most of these were portable and paved the way for the now common harmonium. Among others there was the *American rocking melodeon;* the *Apollo lyra,* which resembled the classical lyre in shape; the *harmoniflute,* where the wind was supplied by the mouth through a tube to the air reservoir; the *melophone,* modeled after the guitar; the *melophone-harpe,* made in the shape of a harp; the *cecilium,* constructed like a cello, and finally the *séraphine* in England (around 1840), which attained great popularity in spite of its harsh tone. All these experiments culminated in the *reed organ* or *harmonium,* the "noblest Roman of them all."

The immediate predecessor of the reed organ was the *physharmonica,* a little reed organ invented in Vienna in 1818. Its original function was to sustain the tone of the piano strings, for which purpose it was placed under the piano keyboard. Other inventors came forth with improvements and enlargements until in 1840

Figure 296. Seraphine, ca. 1840

Figure 297. Harmonium, 19th Century
Courtesy Metropolitan Museum of Art, New York

Debain of Paris brought forth the *harmonium,* a reed organ almost identical with the present-day models. Debain had his instrument patented and the name *harmonium* reserved exclusively for France. Hence the same instrument became known in other countries as *reed organ, phisharmonium* in Germany, and *American organ* in America.

The harmonium is closely related to the pipe organ. In fact, the resemblance is so pronounced that many look upon the reed organ

Figure 298. Modern Reed Organ

as a substitute for the pipe organ. This is a mistake, for the reed organ certainly has a claim to individual existence. Its evolution is similar to that of the pipe organ. Debain had four stops in his instrument. By and by more stops were added, so that today we have in the harmonium a highly expressive instrument for domestic (and church, for that matter) use.

Some of the most common stops of the reed organ are the following.

1. An *expression stop* enables the player to cut out the wind chest and lead the air stream directly from the bellows to the sound board (which contains the reeds). Thus, the player can vary the intensity of the sound by his feet which work the bellows and produce sudden and gradual dynamic nuances at will.

2. The *percussion stop* uses a device similar to the escapement hammer of the piano. With the depression of a key a hammer strikes the tip of the reed while the air stream sets it into vibration. This invention has given the harmonium "quicker speech."

3. The *prolongement* is similar again to the sustaining pedal of the piano; it prolongs certain notes after the fingers have released the keys. There is a special hand-operated stop knob for it, but it can be disengaged with a little heel movement.

4. The *melody attachment* accents the melody in the highest parts.

5. The *pedal substitute* makes the lowest predominant.

6. The *double-touch,* an important invention, permits the player to emphasize tones by greater depression of the keys. This gives the harmonium almost the piano touch.

7. The *pneumatic balance* is achieved by certain valves in the wind reservoir which equalize the pressure.

In addition to the above mechanical devices for expressive playing, harmoniums have a variety of stops similar to pipe-organ stops, so that colorful sound combinations are within the reach of the skillful player. The *full organ* and the *swell* stops are similar to those of the pipe organ.

The harmonium is quite capable of rendering first-rate music with great expression, and there is no reason why there should not be a school of composers and skillful players competent to realize and develop the beauties of this organ.

The *American organ,* as was stated before, is also a free-reed instrument. It differs from the European type in that the reed operates by suction instead of by pressure. Suction bellows were first employed by Buschmann, the inventor of the mouth organ, as early as 1836 in his phisharmonica. Independently of Buschmnan, a French workman discovered the same principle. Disillusioned in France, he went to America, carrying his invention with him.

The first suction-bellows organs in America were known as *melodeons*. However, it was not until 1860 that Mason and Hamlin of Boston turned out the first reliable organs.

The tone of the American organ is more "pipe-organ-like" and softer than that of the harmonium, but the organ itself is not so expressive an instrument as the European type. It, too, has many stops, and like its prototype it sometimes has two manuals.

### *The Accordion*

The *accordian* is also an invention of Buschmann (1822). The name implies that the instrument can play chords.

The accordion owes its recent popularity to the simplicity of its operation and ease of playing. The tone has elements of the bassoon, horn, organ, violin, oboe, clarinet, and piccolo in it. Such a conglomeration of tones has great popular appeal but has failed to interest professional musicians. Still, the accordion occasionally functions with a symphony orchestra. Tchaikovsky and Prokofiev both employ it once in a while, and modern composers use it freely in their search for novel effects. Indeed, the accordion is sometimes heard in major concert halls in programs of the masters.

In 1950 at least 150,000 accordions were sold in the U.S. alone. In the same year the International Conference of Accordionists held their Fifth World Congress in Paris.

The accordion works on the following principle. At each end of the bellows free reeds are fitted into a head board in such a way that one tone is produced by the opening—*expiration*—and another on the closing—*aspiration*—of the bellows. In other words, the reeds have "pushed-out" and "drawn-in" tongues. The left hand works the bellows and the studs on the board, while the right hand plays the melody on a keyboard fashioned after the piano keyboard (hence the often used name *piano accordion*). The range of the keyboard is nearly three and a half chromatic octaves.

The left-hand board has up to 120 studs or push-buttons for the bass notes and the chords. A stud releases not just one tone but several at a time, as many as eight. Each chord is therefore prefabricated. In addition, the modern accordion has a series of switches, operated by tabs, similar to stops. The effect total is a range of over seven octaves and a variation in timbre.

The accordion is a mechanical instrument not capable of subtle personal expressions. Whereas the violin, organ, and most other instruments require endless effort and years of study, the accordion can be mastered with comparative sease by the amateur. It is true, of course, that some players rise to a "professional" status and take their instruments seriously.

### *The Concertina*

The *concertina,* invented by Sir Charles Wheatstone in 1829, is a hexagonal portable instrument which works on the same principle as the accordion. But unlike the accordion it has only a push

Figure 299. Concertina, England, 19th Century.

action, the reeds not being excited by suction. The blowing, however, works both ways on the reeds, producing the same tone. Imitations of the violin, flute, and oboe can be performed with great expression. The melody concertina has been supplemented by tenor, bass, and double-bass models, so that the four of them can form an ensemble. Nineteenth-century literature frequently features the village musician with the concertina. The name *concertina,* incidentally, suggests that the instrument was used for giving concerts.

### *Bagpipes*

The bagpipe is a unique instrument. It has such peculiar characteristics that we may say there is nothing like it on the face of the earth.

The history of the bagpipe is rather controversial, and it is difficult to arrive at a clear picture of its evolution. We know practically nothing of its origin except that it is supposedly Asiatic. The immediate forerunner of the bagpipe was probably a bladder pipe, an instrument which had an elastic bag inserted between the mouthpiece and the playing portion of the pipe to assist the player in equalizing the wind pressure. Such bagpipes were known as the *chorus,* the name, according to Dr. Sachs, owing its derivation most likely from *chorion,* a hide. The hide-type of bagpipe was well known during the Middle Ages.

The name *bagpipe* can be traced back to the first century A.D. Nero is known to have played it, and Roman coins display citizens playing it. The ancient Greeks are supposed to have had some kind of bagpipe as early as the fifth century B.C., but there were no bagpipes at the court of Nebuchadnezzar, nor did the Hebrews of the Old Testament know them. In Europe bagpipes appear in the ninth century, although it is quite possible that the Romans carried them to Britain centuries earlier. The Irish bagpipe, for instance, is mentioned as early as the fifth century.

The bagpipe has had its ups and downs. Until the fourteenth century it was not fully developed and was mainly a herdsman's instrument. No musical value was attached to it. With the addition of more parts, the bagpipe penetrated higher society, for even princes are known to have played it. Chaucer's miller performed on it—"A bagpipe well couth he blowe and sowne." The pilgrims of the same tale set out from Canterbury to the music of bagpipes. Shakespeare frequently alludes to it. He speaks of the "drone of the Lincolnshire bagpipe," and we gather that already in those days some people abhorred it, while others laughed "like parrots" at the players. Henry VIII had five bagpipes in his collection of musical instruments.

By and large, however, the aristocracy of the sixteenth century abandoned it, and the bagpipe once more became the instrument of shepherds and of dancing peasants and the military as well. During the eighteenth century the demand for pastoral music restored it to favor. Today it is mostly associated with Scotland, and the Highland bagpipe is like a legendary epic, embodying far more than a mere instrument. Nevertheless, we should keep in mind that the bagpipe is common to many countries, and that the Irish still hotly dispute any country's claim to priority.

The bagpipe is a simple instrument. Fundamentally it consists of a flexible wind chest of leather with pipes fitted into it for blowing

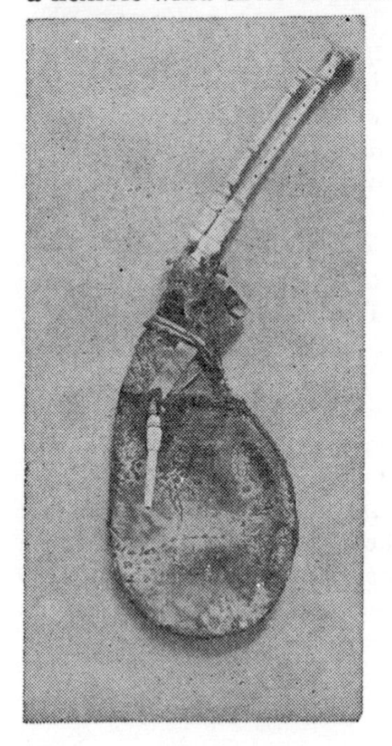

Figure 300
Cornemuse, France, 1700
Courtesy Museum of Fine Arts, Boston

and sounding. Early bagpipes had only two playing pipes, the chanter, a flutelike pipe with holes for playing the melody, and the drone, a pipe without holes sounding one note only as accompaniment for the melody. Both pipes are fitted into the same opening and lie alongside one another.

The reeds of early pipes were of the beating type, meaning that the pipes were clarinets. The present-day *cornemuse* embodies the same principles. The leather bag is covered with brocaded silk and gilt braid. The pipes are of ivory, the lower one being the *blow pipe,* the upper left one the *drone* and the longest the melody pipe, the *chanter.* Notice from the illustration that the holes of the chanter are spaced symmetrically, so the intonation is probably faulty.

After the thirteenth century improvements to the bagpipe were made, such as the adoption of a double reed (the oboe type) for the chanter, and somewhat later the chanter and the drone were separated. Next more drones were added.

According to their reeds, bagpipes are either of the clarinet or the oboe type, or both combined. Eastern bagpipes use oboes only.

Bagpipes are further classified according to the method of wind supply. The earlier types were supplied from the breath of the player, the later models from a small pair of bellows placed under one arm and a bag or wind chest under the other. Both the bellows and the bag are shown in Figure 301. In each case the bag is worked by the elbows to force the wind from it into the pipes. There are special valves to prevent the air from rushing back.

To the mouth-blown pipes belong the *cornemuse* (Figure 300), the German *sackpfeife,* the old *Irish bagpipe,* the *Highland bagpipe,* and others. Pipes blown from bellows include the *musette* (Figure 303), the *Lowland,* the *Northumbrian bagpipe,* and the *Spanish bagpipe.* The villean bagpipe from Iceland has both, the bellows for the five smaller pipes and the mouth-blown pipe. The special bellows came into use in Europe about the sixteenth century.

The French *musette* is an interesting example of the bellows-type bagpipe. The bag is covered with light green velvet richly ornamented with silver braid and fringe. The pipes are of ebony and ivory. There are two chanters and one drone. The longest chanter has nine holes in the front and two in the back, just like the cornemuse, the shorter one being fitted with silver keys.

The drone looks somewhat like a flashlight. It is a remnant of the rackett (page 164), the bore of the pipe running up and down a dozen or more times. There are eight grooves in the side of the drone with ivory slides running in them. The slides regulate the pitch of the drone. The hole in the right of the drone corresponds to the hole in the bellows for proper connection of the two. All pipes have oboe-type reeds.

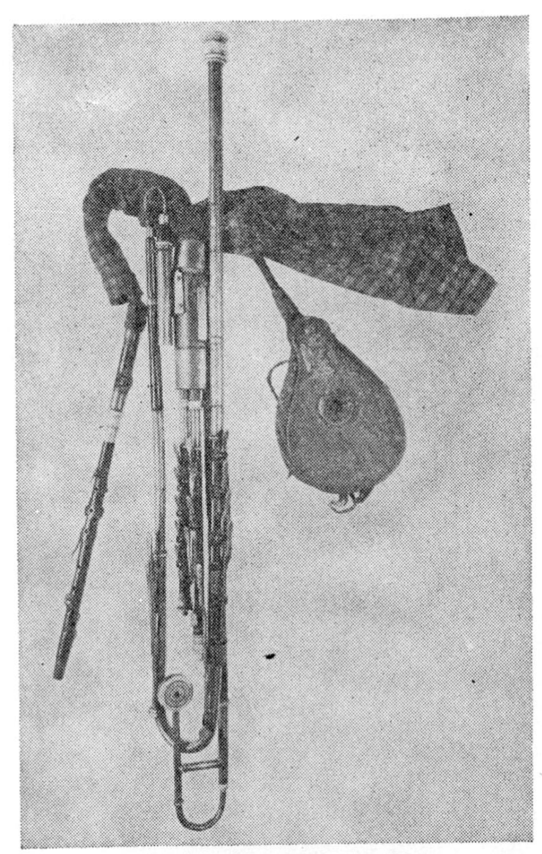

Figure 301
Irish Bagpipe, Parts Assembled
Courtesy Museum of Fine Arts, Boston

Figure 302
Early Bagpipes

At one time the musette was so popular that Lully, a famous French composer of the seventeenth century, used it in his operatic orchestra.

The Highland bagpipe has three drones of the clarinet type and an oboe chanter. The longest drone measures about three feet.

Bagpipes seem to have a profound impact on the listener, for people either love the music or loath it. It is definitely an open-air instrument, unfit for chamber music or lullabies. Nor does it mix with the piano or string instruments. It defies dynamic shading and personal expression. Associated with open-air functions, such as military parades, festivals, or field days, it has charms in spite of its steady, incessant drone. To those who love it, it remains a favorite instrument.

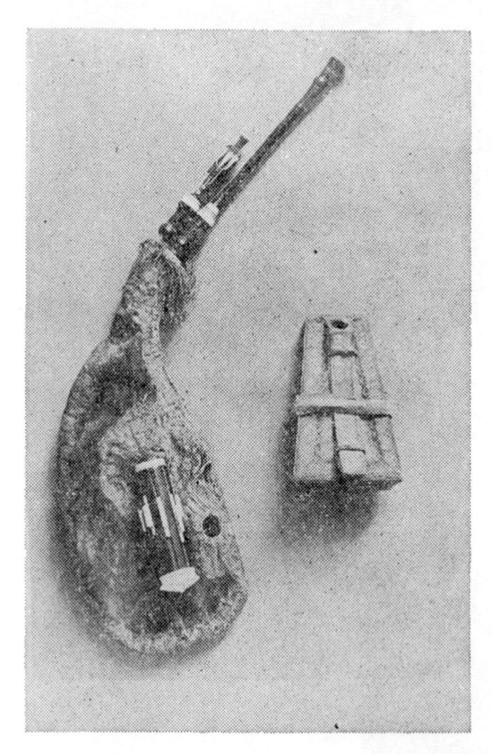

Figure 303. French Musette
Courtesy Museum of Fine Arts, Boston

CHAPTER XVIII

# ELECTRONIC INSTRUMENTS

All the instruments discussed so far are conveniently classified into three groups according to the method of sound production, regardless of their number and diversity. The group known as *idiophones* depends for sound on a sonorous substance; it includes most of the percussion instruments. The second group, the *chordophones,* uses strings, whether plucked, struck, or sounded by friction. The third group, the *aerophones,* needs a pulsating air column for sound production; it embraces wind and brass instruments as well as organs. *Membranophones* use membranes for sound production, as kettledrums, but the method of sound production is embodied in the above three principles.

It is rather significant that all three methods of sound production were discovered in prehistoric days. By the time man became conscious of them, it was too late to answer the question about the inventors or the place or time of origin. Up to the twentieth century all music makers relied on these three methods of sound production, and nothing new in this respect could be discovered. Lately, however, an entirely new method is becoming prominent, namely, *electronic sound production.*

Broadly speaking, electronic devices are of three types: mechanical, amplifiers, and true electronics devices. It is not always possible to distinguish them sharply.

Before turning our attention to electronic instruments proper, let us pause to consider in what ways electricity has aided the musician mechanically. Radio receiving sets, television, public address systems, and sound film projectors in the cinema and school are all part and parcel of our daily fare. Yet none of these devices are music instruments in a true sense, for they do not create music but merely reproduce music made by the usual instruments. We have also seen already how over a century ago organ makers began to use electrical equipment in their organs, and how greatly indebted is the organ of today to electricity for the organ's ease of function and perfection in execution.

What role does electricity play in the above devices? Briefly, it is this: electrical equipment speeds up the function of certain parts, such as levers and valves, or amplifies sound impulses, that is, makes them audible by increasing their volume. In many cases the electric circuit includes microphones, tubes, and other devices to change sound impulses to electromagnetic waves, transmits these waves over distances without loss of time, and then changes them back to sound waves again in your home. This is the principle of the radio. Common as these devices are, they are exceedingly complicated, and the most brilliant minds of the world have worked together to give us today's high fidelity equipment.

Many attempts have been made to employ electric current for *amplification* of musical sound. It will be worth our while to consider several of them.

One of the first electric instruments was the *Boston chordocelo* (1909), a piano without the striking hammers but with electromagnets for setting the strings in vibration.

Then in Germany there appeared the electric violin and cello. Instead of using a sound chest, these instruments employ microphones, amplifiers, and loudspeakers. A special pedal or foot-switch enables the performer to increase even a whisper to a *fortissimo* without any effort on his part. Today electric violins usually rely simply on amplification.

Figure 304
An Electric Violin

In 1936 Americans developed the electric zither and guitar. Both of them have discarded the hitherto indispensable sound board, although some of the latest models again use simple amplification from the sound board.

As we have seen earlier in the book, without a sound board on ordinary instruments the strings can produce only a feeble sound even at their best. On the other hand, the electric current passing through a magnet, amplifier, and loudspeaker makes the sound powerful. Indeed, the electric guitar will hold its own against a background of a 120-piece military band.

There are other illustrations of "applied" electricity. They are all more or less concerned with transmission and amplification of impulses. It is clear that some of the impulses undergo certain modification or even deterioration due to loss of certain overtones and wave characteristics during the process. The best available systems cannot yet reproduce music faultlessly, which means of course that even the best hi-fi sets are inferior to live music. You might find it amusing to compare a phonograph recording of forty years ago with a modern LP recording. RCA Victor has a special series called *Collector's Items* on which one can hear excerpts recorded as early as 1910. One hearing of such a recording is sufficient to realize how far we have traveled toward perfection on the road of mechanized music.

Electronic instruments proper are not concerned with the mechanical aspects of music but with the creation of sound itself. A detailed description of the principles involved would far exceed the scope of this book. Actually it takes a physicist to grasp them. A much-simplified generalization will therefore serve our purpose.

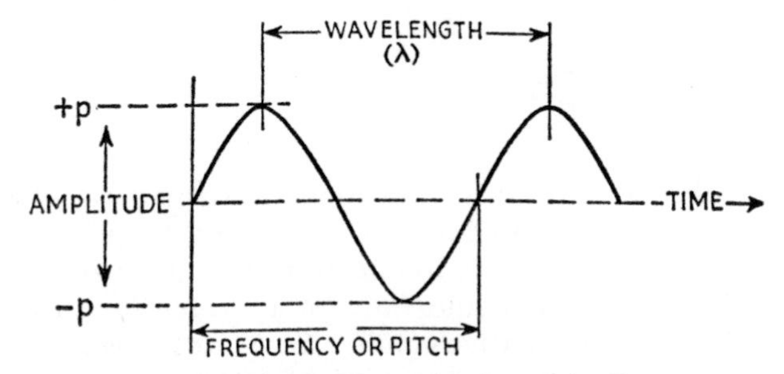


Figure 305. Simple Wave with Quantities Shown

Let us begin with a brief analysis of a sound wave. A regular sound wave can be represented by a symmetrical curve. An irregular wave does not conform to any pattern, and we call it noise. We have learned already that the beauty of a musical tone is determined by its overtones, caused by sectional vibrations of a string or air column. As long as the frequencies of the sectional vibrations bear a simple multiple ratio to the fundamental tone, such as 1:2:3:4 or 1:3:5 or 2:4:6, we find the combination agreeable to our hearing and call it music; if there is no such relation between the frequencies of tones produced, we dislike it and call it noise.

The presence of overtones naturally changes the pattern of the waves. The dotted curves in the following diagrams show the regular curves of the fundamental and some harmonics, while the heavy line represents the resultant wave of fundamental and overtones combined.

What we hear, of course, is represented by the resultant, a more complicated wave pattern than either the fundamental or the harmonics.

Another example of a complex wave pattern represents a combination of two widely divergent frequencies. The more harmonics

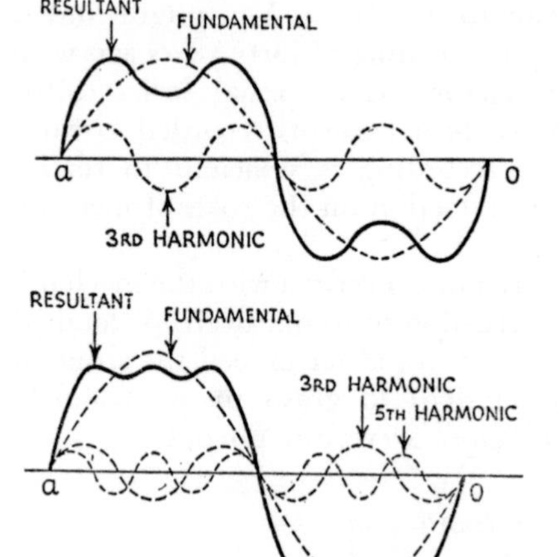


Figure 306
Fundamental and Harmonics Combined
Courtesy Douglas, The Electronic Musical Instrument Manual, Pitman

there are, the more complex the sound-wave pattern. Depending on the number and kind of harmonics present, the wave may be a *simple* one, i.e., practically without overtones; a *square* one, made up of odd-numbered harmonics only; or a *saw-tooth,* which is made up of both odd and even harmonics. *Each instrument has its own characteristic wave pattern, and this is the starting point in generating new sounds.*

The electronics engineer now endeavors to set up oscillations (electrical vibrations) which, when translated into sound, will form the desired wave pattern. To do so he needs various pieces of equipment, chief of which are certain tubes somewhat resembling radio tubes. In practice this means that if he knows the wave pattern of, let us say, the clarinet, he reconstructs it electronically and thus

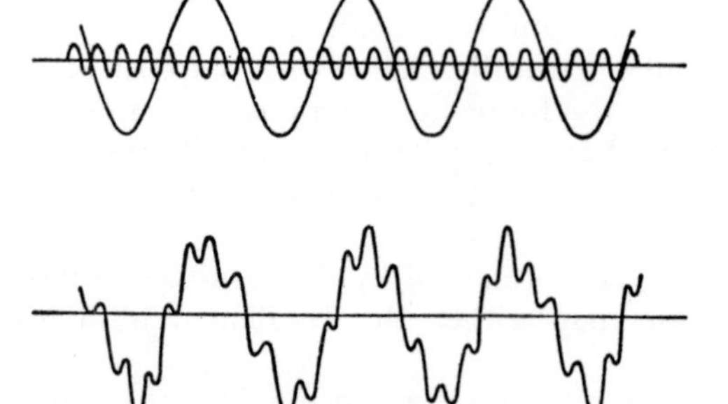

Figure 307
Two Waves of Widely Differing Frequencies and Their Resultant
Courtesy Douglas, The Electronic Musical Instrumental Manual, Pitman

imitates the clarinet without using a clarinet. Thus, an intimate knowledge of wave patterns set up by the individual instruments—and there are tools to discern and study them—is the first essential for the electronics engineer.

The second step leads to the construction of equipment capable of producing the desired wave pattern. This includes setting up oscillations, connecting sound generators, mixing harmonics, filtering complex tones, setting up interferences and so forth. After the sound has been generated and "shaped" it is properly amplified and fed into loudspeakers.

Mere imitation is never satisfying, and naturally engineers realized right at the outset the enormous possibilities of *creating new sound electronically.* Makers of electronic instruments are emphatic in this: their instruments are not just imitators, but instruments in their own rights. The Hammond organ is not an imitation of the pipe organ, but a new instrument with altogether new tone colors. So great is the possibility of the new sound medium that one is inclined to look upon it as a revolution in music.

In 1929 Leopold Stokowski predicted that within a few years a new era in music would begin, during which the new electronic technique of tone production would entirely replace the well-known ones. This prediction was evidently too optimistic, for it has not yet materialized. Since the first enthusiasm has given way to more objective reflection, musicians have become more reserved in their outlook on the future of electronic instruments. While some musicians have sided with Stokowski, a great many, possibly the majority, refuse to accept electronic music as real music. The case is analogous to modern photography; the real artist will always prefer his palette and canvas to a photographic camera.

There are several reasons why electronic instruments have little prospect of supplanting traditional instruments. In the first place, electronic sound waves are too regular and therefore too pure, the effect in many cases being the same as that of overeating sweets. The fact is that although musical sound waves have regular sound patterns, as seen in the preceding illustrations, a sound wave has a "build-up" and "die-out" period, the *attack* and *decay* respectively. Both the attack and the decay are shown (Figure 308).

In listening to musical sound we are so used to this build-up and decay of a tone that we never realize their existence. But a simple, yet highly instructive experiment can prove the point to your satisfaction. Record a few notes played slowly and in a sustained manner on the piano on a tape; then play the same notes from the tape till you are thoroughly familiar with them; and finally, play the tape backwards! Now you will hear the attack as the decay and the decay as the attack. You will be amazed at the difference.

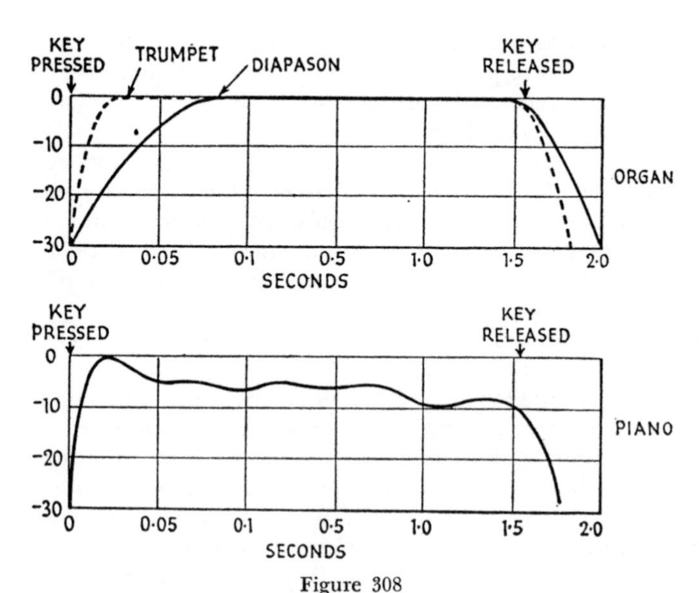


Figure 308
Average Rate of Attack and Decay of Sound in Pipe Organs and Grand Piano
Courtesy Douglas, The Electronic Musical Instrument Manual, Pitman

So each instrument has not only its characteristic sound waves, but also its peculiar attack and decay curve.

Now let us pose this question: what would a certain tone be like if the build-up and decay phases could be eliminated? In other words, what is the "steady-state" tone of an instrument like? Researchers have the answer. In January 1955 K. A. MacFadyen demonstrated that the steady-state sound of a trumpet and a flute are actually difficult to distinguish. Based upon this demonstration, Dr. LeCaine (see Bibliography) concludes rightly "that the way a tone begins in a trumpet or a flute is more characteristic of the instrument than the harmonic spectrum of the steady-state tone." As long as electronic instruments are unable to recapture the characteristic attacks of conventional instruments, a violin stop on an electronic device will sound artificial. The same applies, of course, to any other electronic sound combinations. On the other hand, the elimination of the initial stages of sound may be advantageous for certain other tones, such as the electric vibraphone, celesta, and glockenspiel, all of which yield clear, bell-like tones of great purity.

A second reason why the common instruments need not fear too much competition from the electronics is that it is next to impossible to set up the customary harmonic patterns. As we have seen, instruments are characterized by certain harmonic structures, technically called *spectra*. The harmonics differ in intensity, however, some are louder, others softer. To quote Dr. LeCaine again, "there is . . . little hope of imitating exactly orchestral or even pipe organ sounds." So the designers of electronic instruments are more concerned with the production of new sound than with supplanting traditional instruments.

The first attempt at producing new sound by means of electricity dates back to 1897, when Professor Thaddeus Cahill devised a generator with a rotating electromagnetic mechanism. This mechanism produced the fundamental pitch frequencies and anticipated the requirements of harmonic mixing. Since amplification by means of vacuum tubes was impossible in those days, further development was delayed until 1907, when DeForest launched his patents and gave rise to scientific electronics. In 1917 DeForest published a popular article on an electronic instrument.

The *superpiano* of Spielmann (1927), and the American *rangertone* work on the principle of the photoelectric cell, similar to the device used to change the sound track of a film strip to sound. The keys of the keyboard excite a lamp the light rays of which fall through a perforated rotating disk on the photocell. Thus, a fluctuating current is set up in the electric circuit which in turn is changed to sound waves.

The *Neo-Bechstein piano* of 1931 designed by a group of scientists and made by Bechstein of Berlin employs electromagnetic action. There is neither an iron frame nor a sound board and there is only one string per key. The fundamental tone, therefore, is rather soft but of great purity. Eighteen microphones pick up the vibrations and amplify them through a system of loudspeakers. There are two pedals, the one on the right acting as the ordinary sustaining pedal of the piano and the other one working like the organ swell pedal. The touch on the key requires only a twentieth of the force needed for the piano. A great variety of timbres can be produced. Yet the instrument is smaller and lighter than a grand piano.

The *electric vibraphone,* mentioned earlier, is fundamentally a xylophone, but is equipped with disklike vibrators in the resonators that impart a pleasant *vibrato* to the tone.

Although the above-mentioned instruments embody new principles of sound production, they are still imitators of conventional instruments. We now turn our attention toward instruments producing *new* tones.

One of the earlier examples (1924) is the *theremin* or *thereminvox* of Professor Leo Theremin, also known as the *etherophone.* The essential features of the theremin are the two bars, the vertical and the horizonntal. The player's hands are held in free space before them, playing the instrument without touching it. The right hand plays the upright rod by approaching and withdrawing; thereby raising and lowering the pitch; the nearer the hand approaches the rod, the higher the pitch becomes. In a similar way the left hand controls the volume of the tone producer by the right hand.

The standard type of theremin has a range of four octaves. One of its major drawbacks is the inability to separate tones from each other sharply. Hence the differentiation between individual tones is not clear. Some models are therefore equipped with interrupters, worked by the left hand, and a pedal for regulating the volume. By means of a wire, which is substituted for the hand, the player can control the pitch of each note with greater accuracy. In addition, more than one tone can be produced simultaneously, rendering the theremin a polyphonic instrument, although it is generally used just as a melody instrument.

The theremin has already made an inroad into symphonic music. Modern composers of eminence have given it some attention. A quartet of theremins has played with the Philharmonic Orchestra of New York; on another occasion a dozen theremin players staged a concert at Carnegie Hall; the Cleveland and Philadelphia Symphony have also used the theremin, and other organizations are to follow suit in the near future.

The tone color of the theremin is similar to that of the strings, with the higher tones like those of the violin and the lower resembling the cello's. Some of the deeper bass notes are reminiscent of the low pipe organ and are therefore effective in symphonic music.

Another drawback of the theremin is the lack of a guide for the player's hands which compels him to "feel" his position. To remedy such defect, Martenot of Paris (1928) and Trautwein of Berlin (1930) put forth their *ondes musicales* and the *trautonium* respectively. Both instruments use a sort of keyboard which indicates to the player the exact place for his hand for the correct scale. For the French instrument the player wears on his finger a ring fastened to a cord, while in the German specimen a metal string is placed over a metal rail with added marks simulating a keyboard. Trautwein used a neon tube for oscillation production. Both instruments are not only excellent imitators of conventional instruments, but are capable of producing an indefinite number of timbres. Their range, however, is somewhat limited.

The American *emicon* (1930–1931) is a relative of the trautonium, but is equipped with a proper keyboard.

The *solovox* is a device which can be attached to a piano. It has a shallow keyboard with a number of stops just below it. Some of the stops can be used in combination, thus producing not only string tones but also those of woodwinds and brasses. The keyboard has three octaves of keys with a pitch range of five octaves. By using

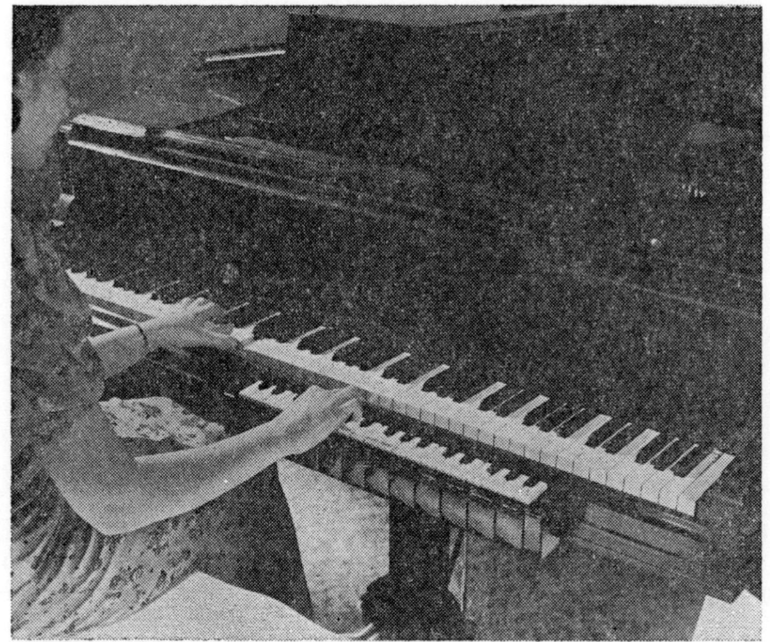

Figure 309. Solovox

"frequency dividers" the output from the oscillator can be divided into a series of notes from one to five octaves lower than the original oscillator pitch. The tone is enriched by the application of the *vibrato* mechanism. The solovox is a melodic instrument.

Of the numerous chord-playing electronic instruments only a few need be mentioned here. They have the conventional keyboard in common. The temptation to divide them into piano and organ-type instruments is really not too great since they are not mere imitations of either the piano or the organ, regardless of their appearance.

The *electrochord* has the same number and arrangement of strings as the piano. The sound is heard through loudspeakers. By means of stops, the harmonic content of the string can be varied. Likewise, the attack and decay may be varied. Each set of strings is provided with a series of electrostatic pick-up plates which enable the player to bring forth any number of overtones desired. The electrochord can produce either piano or organ tones. The general effect of the music is richer and mellower than the ordinary piano's.

Another versatile instrument is the *novachord,* producing both percussion and sustained tones. There are no strings, but there are 144 valves in the tone-generating circuits and 14 controls. The playing technique is difficult to acquire.

The most commonly known electronic instruments are the pipe-

Figure 310
Novachord
Courtesy Douglas,
The Electronic Musical
Instrument Manual,
Pitman

less "pipe organs" of today. One of the first notable achievements in this field is the *Givelet-couplex organ* constructed in 1932 in Paris. This organ provides a separate tuning valve for each note. There are three manuals, one pedal, and thirty-four stops.

A modern version of this organ is the *consanata*. The *Wurlitzer organ* is a reed organ. The reeds are set in motion by wind pressure and controlled by pallets as in the pipe organ.

The *Hammond organ,* introduced by Laurens Hammond in 1935,

Figure 311. Concert Model Hammond Organ
Courtesy Hammond Instrument Company

is the most widely known example of an electric organ. Let it be remembered, however, that there are other firms putting out such instruments. The Hammond organ is a complete organ but uses no strings, pipes, reeds, or any other conventional sounding device. The tone is generated electrically by tone wheels.

The typical tone wheel may be visualized as a small disk the size of a silver dollar with teeth somewhat like a gear. The disk revolves at constant speed in front of a coil-wound magnet, thereby inducing (creating) a tiny fluctuating current in the coil. The fluctuations in the current depend on the number of teeth and the speed of rotation. If, for example, the high spots of the tone wheel pass the magnet at the rate of 440 per second (8 teeth at 55 revolutions per second), a current is set up which, when its fluctuations are transmitted into sound, will have a tone of 440 vibrations per second, i.e., middle *a* on the international scale.

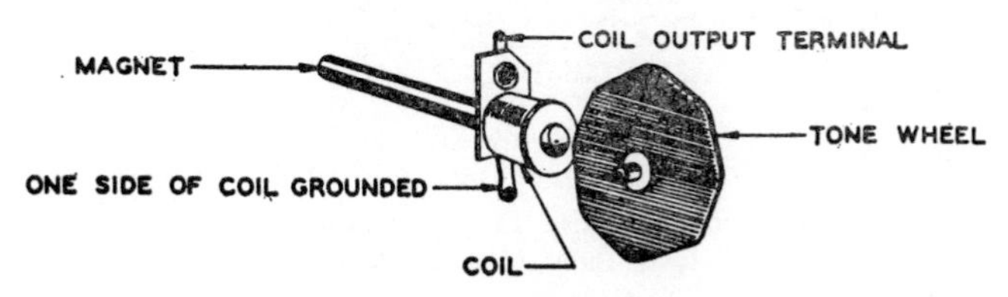


Figure 312. Tone Generator
Courtesy Hammond Instrument Company

There is a separate tone wheel for each note of the complete range of the organ. Each wheel produces the fundamental note. Because the tone wheels are driven at constant speed, the Hammond organ is always in tune.

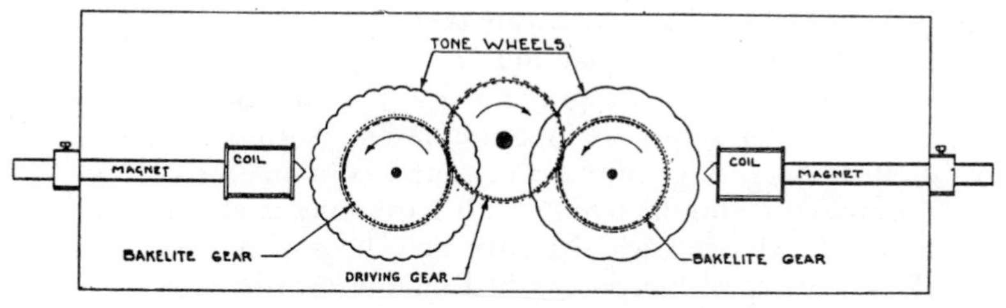


Figure 313. Double Tone Generator
Courtesy Hammond Instrument Company

To enrich the fundamental tones, there are the double tone wheels and an assortment of wheels for mixing harmonics.

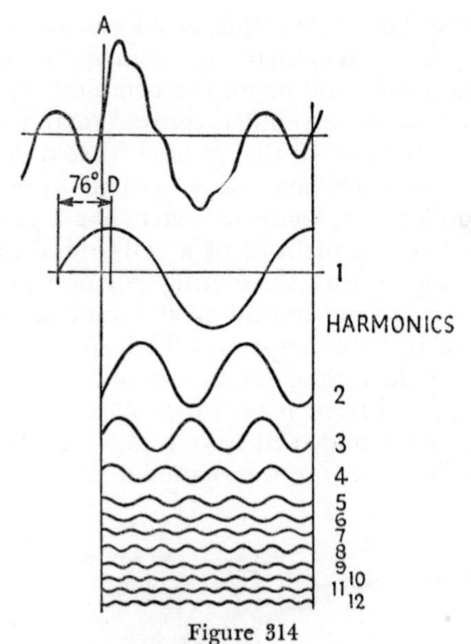


Figure 314
Analysis of Organ Tone
Courtesy Douglas, The Electronic Musical Instrument Manual, Pitman

To grasp the meaning of "mixing" sounds, let us look at Figure 314. The top curve shows the wave pattern of the whole tone, i.e., the resultant of the fundamental and harmonics. Curve 1 represents the fundamental wave (the attack and decay sections are left out); the other curves, 2 to 12 respectively, show the curves of the different harmonics. The Hammond tone wheels, as we have seen, produce straight tones only. But visualize a separate tone wheel for each of the harmonics, which can thereby be selected and played at will. This is exactly what the organ player can do. By means of special mechanisms the player has any of the harmonics at his finger tips, either singly or in combination. Such an arrangement truly offers staggering numbers of sound combinations.

The mixing of fundamentals with harmonics is accomplished by means of drawbars. Each drawbar may be set in eight different positions; each position, as marked on the drawbars, represents a different degree of intensity of the harmonic controlled. When drawn out to position 0, the harmonic is altogether eliminated; position 1 will render the harmonic with minimum intensity, position 2 will yield a little more volume, and so on up to position 8, when the harmonic will be loudest.

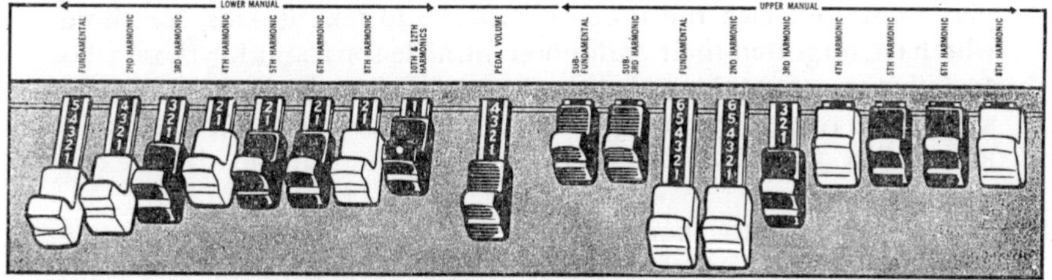


Figure 315. Complete System of Drawbars
Courtesy Hammond Instrument Company

A complete system of drawbars is shown above.

The first eight bars control the lower manual, the single drawbar in the center controls the volume of the pedals, and the next nine drawbars control the upper manual. It has been estimated that by mixing and combining all the possibilities about twenty five million sound colors can be produced! In other words, the player is confronted with an endless challenge to discover new timbres. To avoid confusion, the manufacturers recommend certain patterns of drawbar positions for various effects.

Thus, the drawbars in Figure 315 read on the left side, 54322221, and on the right side, 006630000. Strings, reeds, flutes—all have their own number pattern.

The drawbar pattern may be prearranged; the player may set them before he begins his playing and manipulate them by the keys to the left of the keyboard. For the player's ease, here the upper keys are white, the lower ones black.

In addition to the drawbars there are special "stops" and pedals to provide a number of useful effects. These stop-knobs control volume, the timing of the attack for *staccato* and *legato,* the *vibrato* and *tremolo,* etc.

Today Hammond organs come in different models, such as the spinet, the church model, the home model, and the concert model. They all have common features, such as two manuals and a certain number of keys, pedals, and controls. Generally, the larger the model, the greater the possibilities. All but the spinet model have special tone cabinets.

*Tone cabinets* are by no means standardized. They vary in design and size depending upon the room in which the organ is to be placed. Each cabinet has a series of loudspeakers. A typical tone cabinet, for instance, has two twelve-inch treble speakers and eight ten-inch bass speakers. In large churches and concert halls any number of tone cabinets may be placed in the most advantageous places acoustically. The music then does not seem to come from one particular spot as with a radio set, but is diffused through the room.

The *Hammond chord organ* is designed for those "who yearn to play music but lack the time or patience to take lessons, for those who have forgotten their childhood music lessons, and for those who feel they are too old to learn to play an instrument."[1] We may safely add that such an organ is also for those who lack the skill and ability to master the real instrument and are loath to exert themselves.

At the left of the keyboard there is a panel with studs for releasing chords. Every chord, of course, is prefabricated. The right hand plays a one-tone melody on the keyboard proper, while the left hand presses the studs as indicated on special notation sheets. We find here the same principle of music making as on the accordion.

The manufacturers of the Hammond organ claim that their organs are not merely imitative instruments. Yet their chief merit seems to lie in the fact that they are just that, for they imitate practically every orchestral instrument as well as the orchestra itself and the pipe organ. Judging by the claims of the company itself, Hammond organs are used in thousands of churches of every denomination, in countless homes, in schools, in mortuaries, and in many other places ranging from battleships to tiny chapels in far-off tropical islands.

The cost of a Hammond organ compared to that of a grand pipe organ is negligible. The most famous pipe organs cost well over $100,000, and even the smaller ones run into five figures. The price of a Hammond organ, on the other hand, compares favorably with that of a grand piano. Its easy installation, permanence of all parts, light weight and portability, adaptability to practically any room, its negligible operating and maintenance cost, the fact that it never gets out of tune—all these features make it an appealing instrument to the masses.

This, of course, is keeping in line with the Zeitgeist, where effortless music is the slogan and where any music lover, although he be no musician, can enjoy comparatively good music by radio and hi-fi reproductions. Many of the truly great musicians of our day scorn the instrument and the true artist of the pipe organ still claims that the electric organ is "no food for *serious* thought."

The Hammond organ is by no means the only instrument of this type. The *Jennings electronic organ* (Kent, England) appears to be an elegant little organ with supposedly a "wealth of orchestral effects with many thrilling novelty effects".

The *Compton electronic* organ approximates a pipe organ tonally. Its console, too, is almost identical with that of the pipe organ. The tone generator is similar to that of the Hammon organ, inas-

---

[1] Taken from an advertisement.

much as it also consists of disk units. The actual sound comes from the speaker.

While some present-day electronic instruments, especially the electric organs, are being turned out commercially, others are still in the experimental stage. Scientists the world over quietly but ceaselessly work in their laboratories to enrich the world of music. Who knows how many top-ranking electronic engineers are engaged at this very moment in creating new sound-producing media? Who can tell how many years of head-splitting research work will go into some new instrument before we will be entertained by it?

Figure 316. Electronic Sackbut
Courtesy LeCaine

Take, for instance, the case of LeCaine's sackbut.[2] On July 11, 1954, Dr. Hugh LeCaine of the Microgroove Section of the National Research Council, Canada, demonstrated over the CBC his remarkable *electronic sackbut,* which in the words of the *CBC Times* "is capable of producing all musical sounds—and then some—from the most delicate tones of the violin to the robust notes of

[2] There is no connection between the ancient, now obsolete sackbutt (page 135) and the electronic sackbut.

the post-horn." However, according to Dr. LeCaine himself, his sackbut cannot be played "in such a way as to be indistinguishable from an instrument of long established musical value." The above press quotation is therefore aimed at public consumption and somewhat deceptive.

The first thing to note from the illustration is that the sackbut is homemade. In other words, it is not being manufactured on a large scale and not available commercially. Dr. LeCaine started his project in 1945. The following information is supplied to the author by Dr. LeCaine himself:

> The keyboard facilitates rapid execution of scales and arpeggios. In distinction to the conventional keyboard, the "sackbut" keys are constructed in such a way, that by applying a lateral (side) pressure to the key such subtleties of pitch control as a smooth slide from one not to another, the vibrato or wavering pitch which a violinist produces by rocking his finger back and forth on the string, and the occasional use for musical purposes of sounds which are not on the musical scale or are off the pitch can be produced. The extent of the pitch change in any direction produced by this lateral pressure may be made as much as an octave either way. To produce long slides and other special effects a continuous pitch control is placed behind the keyboard in such a way that when the finger is moved along the control the pitch varies gradually over the range of the keyboard.
>
> To control the loudness of a note the player controls the vertical pressure on the key. Not only gradual crescendi and diminuendi but changes in attack may be produced in this way. If the player uses the gradual pressure a violin-like attack results. If he strikes the key a blow, a sharp attack is produced. Since it is all too easy for the electronic instrument to have a tone of monotonous purity, means of introducing irregularity have been included. One device produces an effect similar to a rasp in the voice or the buzzing produced by a trumpeter. Another mechanism produces breath tone as sometimes heard in the flute. These effects of course are introduced in only small amount and only occasionally, but they add to the expressive power of the instrument and avoid the monotonous purity of the "electronic tone".

Dr. LeCaine is by no means certain that all the extra new effects of his sackbut (or any other electronic instrument, for that matter) will have lasting musical value. But neither was Columbus sure to discover America.

Figure 317
Electronic "Melochord"

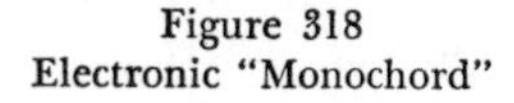

Figure 318
Electronic "Monochord"

The Studio of Electronic Music at Cologne, Germany, has lately put out two electronic instruments which are not only improvements on the solovox and the trautonium but are also important for further research.

## *Mechanically Performed Music*

Mechanical music, technically known as *synthetic music,* probably began about 1000 A.D. with the invention of clockwork. Some mechanically operated sound devices were known even earlier. Ever since, mechanical instruments have had a certain fascination for music makers. Henry VIII owned a "player-virginal." Johann Maelzel (1772–1838), constructed a mechanical orchestra of over forty pieces. Handel composed music for the mechanical barrel organ, and Stravinsky and other modern composers have written music to be punched directly onto player piano rolls.

Perforated disks and rolls for clocks, music boxes, and player pianos have been familiar fare to many for years. With the advent of electronics, designers gave synthetic music some attention also. At first they took over perforated disks and used monophonic electronic oscillators (Paris, 1929); then came needles in grooves, optical wedges, photoelectric cells, "conductive ink" with brushes, a "sound library," and many other things. All these devices are still in the experimental stage and rather difficult to explain.

### *New Musical Horizons?*

It is possible that we are on the threshold of a new era in music. Until now the world has depended on music made up of the three elements of pitch, amplitude (loudness), and timbre. Music makers of the future are working on the idea of combining the three elements into one. The *new sound* is the watchword. By means of electronic equipment, tape recorders, photoelectric cells, and so on, they are in position to analyze practically any sound, break it up, and then put it together in hitherto undreamed-of proportions.

Consider a symphony orchestra. Its total sound may be condensed into a narrow track on sound film, so that in reproducing the performance we get audio-visual effects. The question now arises: cannot a sound track be handmade without musicians? In other words, is it not possible to make a sound track by means of pen and ink, needles and brushes, or direct photography of differently shaded areas?

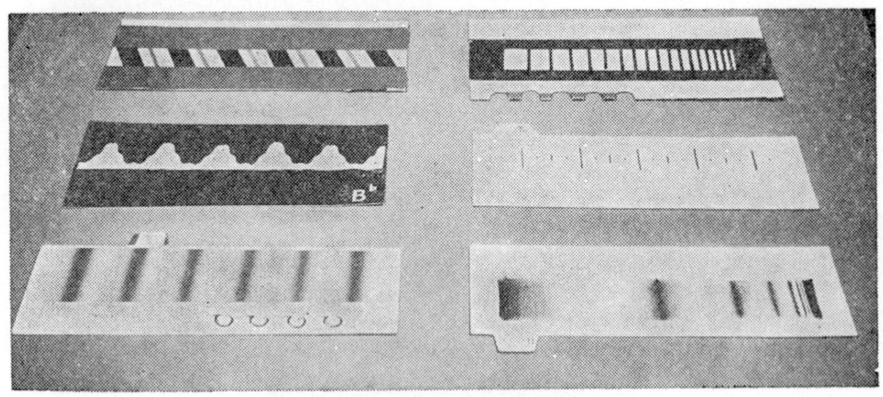

Figure 319. Variable Density Patterns
Courtesy National Film Board, Ottawa

Such is indeed the case. Norman McLaren,[3] a film craftsman of international reputation and one of the most unique artists in the film world, has since 1939 made a special study of such a method of producing sound. In his *card system* he uses drawings representing sound waves and dispenses with traditional musical instruments

[3] At present employed with the National Film Board of Canada.

or noise-making devices; neither does he use any microphones or sound-recording devices. A series of variable density patterns are photographed through an adjustable mask. The final result is a track on the film strip comparable to the ordinary sound track of the movies. The patterns shown above were made in different ways —drawn with a pencil, cut out of paper, or applied with strips of adhesive tape. The top and bottom right-hand cards have rising-falling pitch; all the others have an evenly sustained pitch. Not only is it possible to create musical tone in such a manner, but even tone coloring and dynamics are within the reach of the composer or performing technician.

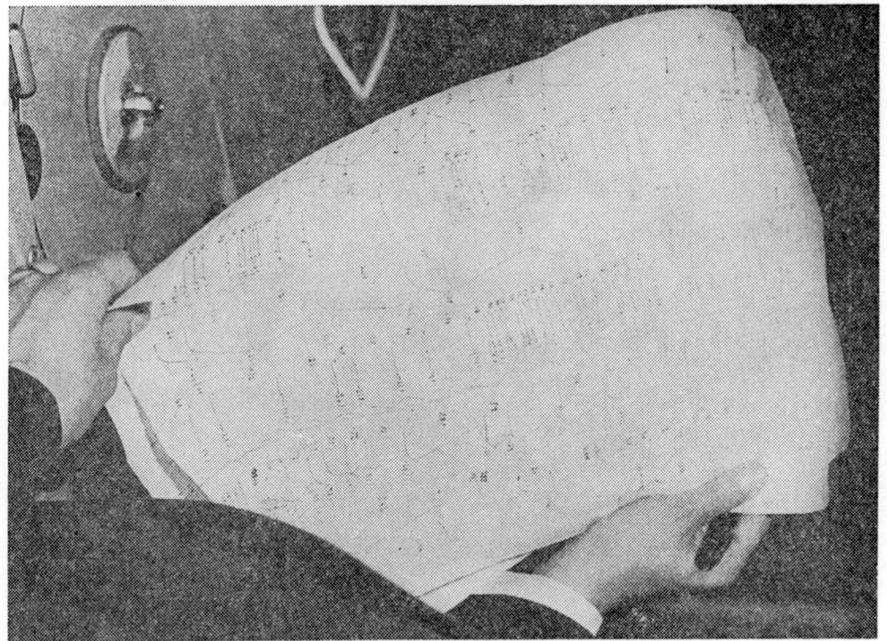

Figure 320. A Score Sheet for Electronic Instruments
Courtesy WDE, Photo Rudi Gemmecke, Cologne

The latest trend in the creation of new sound does away with even the artificially drawn sound track. Pioneering this newest venture is the West German Radio, Westdeutscher Rundfunk, (WDR), Cologne. Highly trained technicians operate sound generators according to score sheets as shown in Figure 320. Ancient Egyptian hieroglyphs could hardly be more mystifying to us than such a score. The horizontal lines indicate duration and pitch of notes, while the vertical curves give the dynamic pattern and combine the individual tones into musical phrases. Just how such a score is "played" is shown by the following two photos.

Figure 321
Heinz Schuetz Making Music Following Directions from a Score Similar to the One Shown in Figure 320
Courtesy WDE, Photo Heinz Karnine, Leverkusen

Figure 322
Studio Director Eimert and Composer Stockhausen (Seated) Trying a New Composition
Courtesy WDE, Photo Heinz Karnine, Leverkusen

**Figure 323. Music Without Musicians, Premiere Concert, Cologne, May, 1956**
Courtesy WDE, Photo Rudi Gemmecke

*Music without musicians* has become a reality. The following illustration shows the first concert of this type, given at Cologne on May 30, 1956. The packed hall would indicate that there is public interest in this field. On the stage you see two tone cabinets, each embracing a system of loudspeakers. The white rectangle on the right is part of another system. Five other systems of loudspeakers were installed in the hall. It is to be hoped that phonograph records of electronic music will soon be available on the market. Already the Deutsche Grammophon company of Hamburg has released a few records.[4]

In addition to the WDE (West German Electronics), there are two other schools, the French and the American. It would be premature to venture a characterization and differentiation at this point, but they both rely more on tape recording. One cannot help wondering to what extent mankind will eventually benefit from the efforts of these highly trained scientists in the field of music. Is

[4] Since these lines were written, the author has obtained a recording of electronic music. The sound is indeed a novelty, to say the least.

new music research actually to be delegated to the field of engineering?

But this is not yet the whole story. Just listen to this.

Another possibility of new sound production is found in the variable speed recorder. If a phonograph record is played at the incorrect speed, the music sounds altogether different. I wonder if you ever heard the Columbia network broadcast bird calls at various speeds from a record prepared by the Cornell University. Suppose you try to play 33⅓ r.p.m. record at 78 r.p.m. or vice versa. You realize that sound may be changed to something quite different by varying the speed of reproduction. Naturally, such a procedure is a great temptation to electronic engineers.

The *phonogène* of the Musique Concrète Group of the French Radio and Television System in Paris is a tape recorder with twelve spools, each of which revolves at a different speed. The twelve spools correspond to the twelve semitones of our chromatic scale. Each spool can revolve at two speeds, so that the total combination of speeds is twenty-four. Suppose now the twelve spools record one and the same note at their individual speeds. Each section of the tape will now have a different tone, and only one will reproduce this tone in its correct pitch. Next, all the twelve tones from the tape are played at once, producing *one* tone only. I am sure you have never heard the like of it. But here is your "new" sound.

It is quite possible to change an ordinary piano tone somewhat in this manner: A key is struck, and within a second the tone is screwed up to five octaves above the fundamental and down again; if recorded, this may be combined with any other sound.

The sound made by a drop of falling water may be analyzed and put together in a fantastic number of ways. So *new* sound is a possibility. One cannot help wondering, however, how agreeable this new sound is going to be to the untrained ear of the conventional music lover and how long it will take him to become accustomed to it.

According to convention, a work of art presupposes the idea for that work. A dictionary will, of course, contain the complete vocabulary of a Shakespeare; yet no amount of fishing out words from it will create a drama. Will the creation of new sounds, bizarre or otherwise, give us new music? The time may come when the new musician, having learned to handle the new sound, will also learn to put it together according to a creative idea. So far, at least, the creators of new sound seem to be concerned with the technical aspects of music, and these are, let us freely admit it, tremendous.

# *Part Six: Ancient to Modern Music*

*From*

*To*

CHAPTER XIX

# ORCHESTRATION AND TENDENCIES IN MUSIC

To round off our discussion of the evolution of individual instruments, this chapter will attempt to give the reader an over-all picture of the musical situation throughout the centuries. Our discussion will center mainly around the following questions: What is the meaning of the words *orchestra* and *orchestration?* How did man learn to group and coordinate instruments into ensembles? What were the first groups of instruments like? What instruments were popular at particular periods of history, and why? What attitude did people take toward music in various epochs? Why were some instruments discarded while others were preferred? What were the tendencies in music throughout the ages? And what is modern music? In short, let us endeavor to obtain a bird's-eye view of the field of music.

## *Ancient Orchestras*

In today's terminology an *orchestra* embodies a group of musicians playing different instruments in such a way that all the tones produced blend into one harmonious whole. *Orchestration,* therefore, means the art of instrumentation, of combining different instruments in such a way as to obtain contrast of color, individuality, and balance of tone.

Originally the word *orchestra* meant a dancing pit, that portion of the Greek theater between the semicircular seats of the auditorium and the stage buildings, designed to accommodate the singers and musicians. The idea of such an arrangement was to give the audience an unobstructed view of the stage. In Roman times the orchestra or pit was used as the arena for gladiatorial contests. Later it was absorbed into the auditorium, and the chorus performed on the stage. Just when and why the word assumed its present-day meaning of a group of musicians playing together has yet to be explained; during the Middle Ages the word *consort* was more commonly used.

Figure 324 shows an ancient orchestra of Nineveh, Assyria. One is hardly inclined to call such a group an orchestra, for it was composed of only four men. Still, the principle of the thing is embodied even here: different instruments are being played together. In this case there are three harpists and one drummer, or strings accompanied by percussion.

With the Greeks assemblies of aulos and kithara players would occasionally assume prodigious proportions. The function of such music was to glorify or appease the gods and to accompany the plays on the stage.

The Egyptians evidently believed in structure on a grand scale. Witness their monstrous pyramids, sphinxes, temples, and obelisks. Their art also displays such grandeur. No wonder they used large orchestras. We read, for instance, of King Ptolemy Stoe II staging a performance with a chorus of twelve hundred voices accompanied by three hundred Greek kitharas and many flutes. Their temple music had to be on a large scale, embodying as many as six hundred players of harps, lyres, lutes, and sistra. In one procession (third century B.C. in Alexandria) there were three hundred musicians playing golden lyres. (The golden lyres no doubt impressed the audience as a spectacle of opulence, for as we saw earlier silver and gold have but poor resonating qualities.) Processional music for the entries of kings, however, was generally on a much smaller scale.

The Israelites of the Old Testament period had under King David four thousand male singers, organized into ten divisions of four hundred singers each, one division performing at a time.

The Romans, too, united considerable numbers of instruments into fantastic assemblies. We read of orchestras made up of cymbals, gongs, castanets—at that time the motor impulse was still strong, and hence percussions predominated—flutes, bagpipes, and gigantic lyres the size of a chariot. Roman theaters often had a seating capacity of from seven to twelve thousand spectators, so the number of singers and musicians had to be correspondingly great. They would be distributed throughout the auditorium, and auoli and organs would be placed on the stage.

Large-scale performances then, were familiar to peoples of antiquity. But let us not be misled by mere numbers. The instruments employed were primitive and crude and the sound obtained far from aesthetic. We are also certain that no attempts at harmonization were made, and that part singing and part playing were unknown—if more than one kind of instrument were played, like lyres and flutes, they nonetheless played the same music. Furthermore, it is extremely doubtful whether harps, lyres, lutes, flutes, trumpets, tibias, and possibly other instruments were sounded simultaneously. It is far more likely that they played the instruments in turn. *Orchestration in the modern sense was unknown to the ancients.* Group playing and mass productions were known, true enough, but orchestras conforming to our concepts did not exist.

### *The Music of the Early Christian Era*

The first three centuries of the Christian era were practically barren of music. The Christians fought for survival, leading a more or less underground existence. Naturally, they had no places in which to indulge in music, no churches or halls. In addition, the early Christians shunned all pagan music. So the pagan organ, aulos, kithara, and possibly even the lute and lyre were frowned upon. In fact, musical instruments were actually feared as temptations of the devil. In the course of the centuries, though, some of the old instruments were reinstated.

The invasion of Western Europe and Italy by the Goths put an end to one phase of civilization, and mankind took a plunge downward. As far as musical instruments went it meant a new beginning, for the connection with ancient Rome and classical Greece was severed. Byzantium was in a more favorable position, and it now laid the foundation for the music of eastern Christendom, transmitting its influence later to Western Europe. Rome had ceased to be the center of culture.

Our knowledge of musical instruments of the period following the invasion by the Goths is rather meager, and whatever dates are given by the authorities are as a rule contradictory, at least up to 1300. This much, however, is certain: *all musical instruments were subservient to the voice,* and the voice was to be employed in the service of the church. Pure instrumental music as such did not exist.

In the field of singing the church made some remarkable advances. All singing was based on *plainsong,* that is, songs without key, time signatures, bars or phrases, harmony, in simple monophony. It was introduced from the East. Singing was inseparably linked with religion, and was definitely an integral part of religious services. We also know that dances figured in the service of worship in early Christendom, and that hand clapping accompanied hymn singing.

Gradually liturgical services evolved and built the edifice upon which the Roman Catholic Church stands to the present day. The hymns of Bishop Ambrose of Milan are still found in the hymn books of practically all churches. Pope Gregory the Great established church music on a firm basis. It is still correct to speak of *Gregorian music* as the greatest force in the evolution of church music.

So firmly did the church dominate all music that the terms "sacred" and "secular" did not even exist, for no other but sacred music was tolerated. Whatever music there was outside the church was looked upon as strictly pagan and hence lascivious and pernicious.

The "worldly" influence of music was felt on such occasions as the Feast of Martyrs, which assumed the character of a fair. Instruments banned by the church were used by the populace. Up to the sixth and seventh centuries tambourines and castanets were used at funerals. In the theaters professional singers were employed with "pleasing tunes of the heretics," and to the consternation of the church fathers even women entertained the large crowds. The church declared that anyone feasting his eyes and ears on women singers was committing adultery. In spite of this anathema and other endeavors to ban musical activities, the church has never been able to suppress the urge of the people to make music. Thus, since the dawn of Western history, we encounter two streams in music: the one dominated by the pagan priests and later the Christian church, and the other the people's music—in short, the sacred and the profane.

Finally the church banned all worldly music, putting a severe restraint on all the musical enterprises of the people and suppressing their musical instinct. This oppression was particularly felt in northern Europe, where the plainsong of the church was alien to the people.

With the sixth century organs entered the church, first in Spain and then in other countries. The early organs were rather awe-inspiring, but soon they became instruments for the accompaniment of the voice.

The ninth century saw the beginning of harmony (some writers trace it back as far as the seventh century). The first harmony was *organum,* a kind of harmony developed by the monks wherein a second part followed the melody in parallel intervals as either fourths or fifths. The *organistrum* (hurdy-gurdy) was well-suited to such harmony.

## *Music in the Early Middle Ages*

The early Middle Ages found church music with its liturgy and masses far too complicated for the people. Music had reached a stage where it was within the reach of only specially trained singers. Consequently people looked for something simpler, and we come to the *beginning of folk songs and folk music.* The keystone of folk music was, and still is, simplicity. Thus, a simple snatch from a difficult work would be taken up and sung time and again, giving rise to strophic singing cadences (ending of phrases in *do* or *sol,* for instance). Or somebody would compose a simple tune, somebody else would take it up and improve on it, and so on.

In a time of illiteracy the composer's name would easily be forgotten, which has led some people to the conclusion that folk songs never were composed, that they just appeared spontaneously. So strong, however, was the influence of the church that no folk song could escape it, and even though folk songs originated in divers countries, they bore a close resemblance to each other. It is also significant that all folk music received its polish and final form from the upper strata of society, and so the folk songs in time came to represent the civilizations of the countries in which they originated.

As before, all instruments were subordinated to the voice, and the division between vocal and instrumental music had not yet been made. Generally speaking, the period up to 1300 was the time of importation of instruments from Aisa. With the fourteenth century began a period of improving on imported instruments and adapting them to European needs; gradually they were so well transformed that their Asiatic character was hardly recognizable.

Mention has been made of the fact that harmony dates back to the ninth century and that some writers go farther back than that. Polyphony may indeed be much older than it was thought till recently. We know, for instance, that bagpipes existed as early as the first century A.D. But bagpipes sound more than one tone, the drones providing a steady accompaniment of one note. If we consider the monotonous chant of the drone pipe we realize that two-tone music had its beginning prior to the ninth or even the seventh century. So let us be content with the statement that about that time the organum, two-part harmony in the form of parallel parts, took its roots. Not without a struggle, for with the ascendancy of the Christian church plainsong was firmly established, and the addition of extra parts was strictly forbidden.

In regions remote from the influence of the church many-voiced music obviously had better chances. It has been established that the oldest developed examples of polyphony originated in Britain. By the tenth century such music was well-known there and universally practiced. Both forms of music—monophony and polyphony—existed side by side for some time. Finally harmony entered the church, too. Once taken up it blossomed, finally culminating in the marvelous structures of counterpoint polyphony by Bach.

Wales and northern England had polyphonic singing long before other European countries. The early form of this music was round songs or canons, where each singer had his own independent part to sing. In other words, there was no division into soprano and alto. Often one would hear as many parts as there were singers. There is a theory that this form of music was taken over from the Danes, who in turn might have imported it from Iceland before or around the seventh century.

The rounds were not necessarily restricted to two-part singing. Singers would improvise their own parts. Just how harmonious such an effort would sound is anybody's guess. Some of the rounds have been preserved. The oldest and most famous is "sumer is icumen in" of the fourteenth century. It is a masterpiece of melody and harmony—at least, the way it is rendered today. So common was the practice of round singing that in Wales even children were able to participate.

## *The Late Middle Ages*

With the growth of polyphonic singing more and more instruments were brought into the foreground. In the fourteenth century musical instruments seemed to have gained equal status with the voice, although the concept of pure instrumental music was still lacking. But it was permissible to perform ballads just on instruments without the voice.

The most frequent instruments encountered at this time were viols, harps, psalteries, lutes, hurdy-gurdies, trumpets, chimes, cymbals, bagpipes, reeds, horns, and flutes. They were classified as "loud" or "soft" instruments. They still had an Oriental touch about them. The loud instruments were used for outdoor entertainment, festivities, and dances. Their tone was sharp and penetrating and of a flat and dry quality. Judging by our standards, even the soft instruments were anything but soft, because sharp sonority was expected of them, according to the spirit of the times.

With us it is customary to associate the grouping of instruments with the aim of obtaining harmony and blend of tone. The fourteenth century evidently had different ideas about orchestration. Instruments were grouped together for the sake of contrast in color production. Musicians just "dabbed" in tone colors, pairing instruments together in a rather primitive fashion. There was no lack of timbre, but each instrument strictly maintained its independence. You may get an idea about it if you put dabs of oil paints on the palette straight from the tube in any fashion whatsoever as long as you strive for sharp contrasts of bright and flashy color. Ensembles of from two to twelve singers and players were most common.

Among the instruments of the fourteenth century the organ soon took the lead. The organist had to be an experienced musician. He had to fill in missing parts, hold performing groups together, enrich and embellish the music, and plan interludes between parts of songs. Besides the church organ, the positive and the portative were common, the latter being convenient enough for social gatherings in and out of doors.

Slowly music freed itself of the dominance of the church, laying the foundation of mundane music. People learned to express themselves musically following their innate instincts. Before long their music had to be considered by church musicians, who profited immensely thereby. Here again music followed the other artistic endeavors of man, for philosophy, literature, and art in general had started on the road to emancipation. Music began to be enjoyed on festive occasions as well as in hours of leisure and during daily work. On their way to the grave of Thomas à Becket the pilgrims sang and played. Mystery plays were replete with music. Music became an integral part of children's education, religion, and amusement. Reading and singing was of greater importance than writing. Song schools sprang up. Chaucer's *Prologue* makes frequent references to singing and playing.

As in days of old, trumpets and percussion instruments were used by the military, even during battle. Flourishes of trumpets opened tournaments and preceded the announcement of the winners.

Wealthy people fond of music, especially the nobility and reigning royalty, engaged musicians for their private entertainment, starting a practice which prevailed to the eighteenth century. Musicians would be attached to the courts. To show their allegiance, they would carry the crests of their masters on their instruments in the manner of knights carrying the ensigns of their ladies; small flags embroidered with the coat of arms were hung on trumpets and bagpipes. In spite of their evident importance, these musicians were relegated to a status of servitude and did not enjoy any social prestige—again, this is a practice which was kept up well into the eighteenth century.

Companies of musicians attached to courts were occasionally allowed to play in different parts of the country, in which case they were supplied with letters of introduction.

Wandering minstrels came into their own. Festivities without minstrels, whether public or private, soon became unthinkable. The favorite instrument of minstrels was the harp.

As the number of minstrels and musicians increased, it became necessary for them to organize. At the beginning of the thirteenth century guilds originated. Guilds were analogous to present-day trade unions. Their rules were severe and their disciplinary powers extensive. Thus, guild members had their districts assigned to them, and musicians not belonging to their particular guild were banned from the territory. Every member had to receive compensation for services rendered.[1] By and large the guilds protected their members, and these enjoyed a considerable amount of freedom.

Before long disciplinary measures were extended into the realm of composition. Certain rules of writing and composing were introduced. As is usual in such cases, the rules were initially a help and guidance to guild members, but in time they fettered all artistic endeavor and put budding artists in strait jackets (cf. Wagner's *Meistersinger von Nürnberg*). In time musicians began to abuse their status, encouraging social and political revolt under the guise of singing, so that they were finally forcibly disbanded. (This applies mostly to wandering minstrels. Queen Elizabeth is said to have stamped out the last minstrels altogether.)

In addition to music guilds, there were official musical positions. One of the first official positions was that of the town shepherd in a German town, for he received his horn from the town council. The role of the medieval watchman is familiar. Then there were such positions as that of the town trumpeter, the king's instrument maker, and the tuner, among others.

The place of music in the lives of people was, it seems, not well defined. While music was enjoyed and numerous instruments were in common use, the all-powerful church curbed all worldly endeavors. For about a thousand years St. Augustine's concepts about the enjoyment of music were upheld. Here is part of the quotation from St. Augustine's *Confessions* which had such a profound influence upon the authorities concerned: "Whenever the music [song] delights me more than does the sentence which is sung, then I confess that I sin grievously." Wycliffe, the English religious reformer of the fourteenth century, lamented the fact that "the songs of his time encouraged jollity and pride and did not lead to mourning and dwelling on the words of God's Law, that vain tricks, such as descant [two-part singing], many voices, and organum were employed which stimulated men more to dancing than to mourning."

The further development of music was inseparably linked with the development of *counterpoint*. Since this term is part and parcel of any musician's vocabulary, it will bear closer inspection.

We have already seen that organum is generally considered the

---

[1] Musicians' unions of today have similar rules. Thus, members of a professional orchestra must be paid not only for rehearsals but for every minute the conductor oversteps the set time for practice. Regulations govern the activities of union members, such as giving concerts, recording, servicing theatre groups, and so on.

beginning of harmony. The period between 900 and 1200 is often referred to as the age of organum. Now, let us recall from our history that the Middle Ages were characterized by scholasticism. Scholars, therefore, were responsible for the development of harmony, for it was mathematicians who laid the foundation. Together with musicians, scholars worked out different relations between notes, introducing other intervals such as thirds and sixths; brought form into rhythm, and evolved a system of notation. By 1050 the notation staff had crystallized, which enabled musicians to write down musical ideas with accuracy and thus insure growth in music. Without written notation there could have been no progress, no more than literature could thrive on oral tradition only.

A little later, around 1100, came the invention of a notation to express fixed time values. Gradually the principles of fixed rhythm found practical application. "Sumer is icumen in" already embodied rhythmic principles akin to our own. So much work was done on rhythm by scholars and musicians—the musicians practicing, the scholars codifying—that the period between 1200 and 1400 is known as the *age of rhythmic forms.*

The principle of counterpoint evolved around 1300. The word itself is derived from the fact that a note was represented on the staves by a point or dot, the Latin *punctum.* When dots were set against dots not in the form of parallel intervals as done in organum harmony but each having its own melodic line i.e., one melody running counter to the other, the composition was known as *counterpoint.* Counterpoint made horizontal harmony, also known as polyphony. The theory of counterpoint took over a century to crystallize. In 1425 we definitely find the *independent entry,* that is, the fugal kind, and soon after the *golden age of polyphony* was ushered in. Now every voice became part of an organism with an individuality of its own. Instruments began to work *interdependently* for the creation of a harmonious whole.

### *The Renaissance* (*1400–1600*)

The fifteenth century is the time of the *birth and development of free composition.* Musicians freed themselves of the influence of mathematicians. At first musicians took over dancing songs, adapting them to the peculiar techniques of their instruments. Then in some countries (at first in Germany and then in Italy) vocal works were transcribed for instrumental use, which practice ultimately produced an independent instrumental style.

It is only natural that instruments should undergo certain

changes during such a transformation. For one thing, the early medieval drone was no longer appealing, hence, the hurdy-gurdy had to go and the bagpipes lost their significance. Woodwind instruments were modified to sound less shrill. The oboe gained ascendancy over the clarinet. Shawms and pommers were paired with trumpets and percussions. Flutes became very popular, especially the recorder, the pipe and tabor and the fife being used as military instruments. Trumpets became prominent as solo instruments.

Stringed instruments, such as the vielle (fiddle), were built with "waists" so as to permit individual approach to all strings with the bow, again eliminating the drone. Percussion instruments also became more prominent. Kettledrums, the companions to trumpets, grew larger; snare drums, on the other hand, were not particularly loud and were therefore fit accompaniment for the flute. All told, the grouping of individual instruments into orchestral ensembles was just being started. Like all other arts, the music of the fifteenth century was dominated by the spirit of the Renaissance, and thus "worldly" music took ascendancy.

The sixteenth century saw some important and far-reaching changes made. A new era was approaching, an era emphasizing the deepening of the harmonic sense. Already existing instruments were being transformed and new designs appearing. Lutes, harps, clavichords, spinets, harpsichords, and above all the pipe organ—*instruments capable of chord playing*—became all-important. Single-voice instruments, like flutes and recorders, emphasized the melodic line with a view to realizing harmonic effects.

Tone coloring during the sixteenth century followed a different trend from that of the Middle Ages—toward the creation of related shadings. This tendency gave rise to "families" of instruments, known as *consorts*. The purpose of consorts was to create effects similar to those obtained from keyboard and many-stringed instruments. Consorts thus constituted choirs of instruments which did not tolerate the intrusion of any alien instrument. To obtain a desired shading, more than one consort could be grouped together. Such grouping led to orchestration (mid-sixteenth century) the way we understand it today. Not that the sixteenth century saw it completed, far from it; but at least the beginning of modern orchestration was established.

We are accustomed to considering flutes, oboes, and the like as single instruments of one size each. A consort of flutes, however, included several flutes of different sizes, even the great bass flute; bassoons were not only bass instruments, for a consort of bassoons included a high-pitched *octave bassoon,* twelve tones higher than the standard one. The first consorts (still of the fifteenth century) had three members, but later they grew up to seven sizes. Consorts of one kind of instrument were known as *whole,* while mixed consorts were known as *broken* consorts. A three-choir performance might include a consort of flutes playing all four parts, a choir of singers also in polyphony, and a family of viols in four-part harmony.

Now, let us recall that the Renaissance was great in art. A disposition to visual enjoyment was therefore also manifest in musical instruments. An instrument was there not only to delight the ear but also to please the eye. People took a fancy to instruments as objects in art. They took pleasure in the elegance of a viol's curves, were enthralled by its harmonious proportions, delighted by the gleam of the varnish, and charmed with the inlaid mosaic of ivory, tortoise shell, or gems. First-rate painters were commissioned to adorn instruments, and precious materials were used in their construction. It was held that a voice of beauty could not possibly emanate from an ugly or unpretentious instrument. Never before or since had the beauty of instruments been so much appreciated.

The instruments of this period had such charms that kings and people of the higher ranks of society made it a hobby to collect them for their own libraries. Henry VIII possessed a collection of 381 instruments; the Duke of Tyrol near Innsbruck had about 240; and a certain count in Augsburg had 400, to give you but a few examples. Naturally, the lavishly decorated instruments were prized also by art collectors. Fortunately for posterity, some marvelous specimens have been preserved in museums.

An inspection of the instruments of such collections reveals the importance of wind instruments in the sixteenth century. Henry VIII's collection was made up of seventy-two percent wind instruments and only twenty-eight percent strings. An orchestra in Berlin (1582) was composed of eighty-five and fifteen percent respectively of wind and string instruments. Wind instruments reflect the pastoral mood; we may recall that one of the slogans of the Renaissance was "Truth to Nature," hence the strong prevalence of the wind instruments.

Chord playing not only necessitated the refashioning of some instruments, but also tended to increase loudness and fullness of tone and extend the range. Hence, such instruments as the portative organ, the rebec, the mandola, the psaltery, and the tromba marina lost favor with the public and fell into oblivion. The most popular instrument of the Renaissance was the lute.

The grouping of consorts, as we have seen, paved the way to proper orchestration. But in one way this orchestration differed radically from our own, for people had an altogether different concept of dynamic changes. The music was rendered in uniform loudness, *crescendi* and *diminuendi* being unknown at that time. Whatever dynamics there were, were more or less "terraced," that is, as long as one choir or consort performed, the intensity of loudness had one level; two choirs would increase the volume, but again the music would stay at a monotonously uniform strength. We recall that the harpsichords too produced similar effects with their stops.

We must now trace the penetration of music into the masses of common people. One factor which greatly contributed toward popularization was Gutenberg's invention of the printing press (1455). Prior to this invention, people had little incentive to learn to read, for the simple reason that there were only expensive handwritten scrolls to read. Music scores were written mostly by monks, and only the wealthy could afford to own them. But now people awakened to books, and their minds were sharpened. Books and treatises on musical theories, design, harmony, and instruments appeared.

By 1501 the first musical scores began to appear in print. The first printed sheets of music were still somewhat primitive, of course, and in many respects differed from our own. For instance, the notes were rectangular or square. But just the same, the chaotic condition of handwritten manuscripts was ended. (It has been said that many of such manuscripts could be likened to jigsaw puzzles, which could be solved only by those familiar with the music. One can conjecture what happened to the performance in the hands of the uninitiated.) From now on composers were at least reasonably sure that their music would be played according to their ideas and would represent a more or less accurate rendition of their compositions.

### *Music of the Reformation*

To complete the picture of the sixteenth-century music trends, we must now consider the greatest force to move the human spirit of that century: the Reformation, brought on by Martin Luther. Under the impact of the Reformation, the cheerful and eager but worldly generation of the fifteenth century gave way to a more serious and dignified race of men. Naturally, the new music also reflected such tendencies.

Fortunately for the world to the present day, Luther was a profound musician and a first-rate composer, well versed in musical theory, harmony, and counterpoint. His ideal was to recruit music for the service of the church. To achieve his ideal he *introduced congregational singing* first of all. Next he harmonized and composed hymns, creating that most wonderful vehicle for expressing religious thought, the *chorale*. He went back to the earliest source of Christian music, the psalter, and gave us, among other chorales, "A Mighty Fortress is Our God." He rescued the loveliest melodies of Ambrosian and Gregorian music, and last, but not least, explored the store of folk music and remodeled some of the folk songs into chorales. He spiritualized music and once more made it church-dominant. The school of thought which he thereby established was to blossom in succeeding years and bring forth such fruit as Schütz, Handel, and Bach!

In the meantime the mother church was not standing by idly watching the growth of the new music. Church music of the fifteenth century had been permeated with profane music, probably lovely melodies but otherwise shallow and not conducive to true worship. Now the church set to work to purify its own music and church services. The Council of Trent (1542–1562) decided that all popular music should be banned from the church. Popular airs and words not approved by the church fathers were to be excluded from the mass and liturgy. Again, fortunately for the world, they found a man to champion their cause in the Italian musician Palestrina. (His real name was Giovanni Pierluigi, Palestrina being the name of his birthplace, a suburb of Rome.) Palestrina wrote many excellent masses, motets, hymns, and so forth before his death in 1594 in such masterly fashion that he profoundly influenced not only church music but all contemporary and succeeding composers and musicians. He was the crowning master of choral music before the days of instrumental achievements. Palestrina has gone down in history as the Prince of Music.

So the Roman Catholic Church had freed its portals once more from profane and vulgar music and has ever since kept them pure and in line with a religious atmosphere, very much more so than most other churches.

Looking back upon the musical trends of this period, here is a summary of music in general.

There was boundless enthusiasm for all the arts including music, for letters, and for science. Musical compositions reflected sincere and devout religious feeling unknown by our musicians of today. A well-rounded musical education was indispensable in the proper upbringing of any well-bred person, and peasants as well could be seen with lutes in their hands. Court musicians and chapel choirs were considered an essential part of a king's retinue. Rich merchants had their share in the artistic life. Amateur composers numbered legion, offering keen competition to the professionals.

Having permeated the arts, beauty and enjoyment became the function of music. Every person of culture was expected to be able to participate, for instance, in madrigal singing. Thus, music had a social aspect. Women, who had been elevated by the courtliness of the knights and belittled by the theology of the monks, were reinstated in human society and became ardent patrons of the finer arts and skilled musicians. The feminine influence greatly benefited music. Women entertained brilliant salons, from which gatherings poets, artists, and musicians gained inspiration and encouragement.

Boys' voices were cherished for soprano and alto parts, and men's falsetto voices were highly prized. In the second half of the sixteenth century a new type of voice appeared whose art was admired for two centuries, the emasculated male soprano. These singers possessed voices of high pitch and great beauty but which were much more powerful than a boy's voice, and they had the advantage of years of continuous training not interrupted by the mutation of the voice.

Musicians were almost invariably men of high culture and education, well-grounded in the classics, philosophy, and literature, something which can hardly be said of the musicians of today.

Not in vain is it claimed that the sixteenth century was a great one even for music. We note that from early times each succeeding century became more interesting musically. What have the remaining three and a half centuries to offer? Is interest going to be kept up or have they nothing to say? Far from it, for we are just ready to enter the wonderland of miracles.

## *The Baroque and Rococo (1600–1750)*

The seventeenth century differs from the sixteenth in some remarkable aspects. The advent of the year 1600, of course did not mark a decisive change; forces at work before that date came gradually to the fore. Now we find an ever-greater emphasis placed on emotion. Music began to appeal to the hearts, the passions of men. Composers expressed human feelings and played upon the emotions of the audience, moving them to tears and laughter so that they felt themselves personally involved. Consequently, instruments capable of expressing such feelings were sought.

*The answer was the violin family, and strings replaced the woodwinds.* We enter the golden age of violin making. String ensembles became far more important than the hitherto popular consorts. The dignified and majestic but impersonal music of the late Renaissance gave way to the genuine language of the heart. Furthermore, there was definite striving for picturesqueness, important words were underlined by impressive melodic and harmonic passages, and dissonance and chromaticism were introduced. So the style in music changed once more.

The all-important instrumental form of the century was the *fugue,* a form of counterpoint composition where melodies entering in turn "chased" each other, forming complicated horizontal patterns of harmony. It is erroneous to assert that Bach invented the fugue or that Bach was its father; but he brought the art of fugue writing to perfection. The Italian Gabrieli, for instance, still of the sixteenth century, was a great benefactor in that he transmitted the principles of choral writing to instrumental music, so later fugue writers are indebted to him. Gabrieli's aim was purposeful grouping of instruments and the use of special orchestral coloring. In this way he among so many others helped to pave the way for Bach, Haydn, and Beethoven.

Another epochal event of the seventeenth century was the emergence of the *opera.* The opera did not mushroom suddenly into the open. Let us remember that we are discussing the age of Shakespeare, in which the cry was literature and drama. The Renaissance went back to the classics, the drama of the ancient Greeks. As we recall, the drama of those cultured Greeks depended for maximum effect on a musical accompaniment for their choruses. It is only natural that the rebirth of classicism called for a revival of the classic music drama. The medieval mystic plays—Bible stories enacted in the open, a custom which has survived to the present, for instance, in Oberammergau in Bavaria—may in a vague sense be regarded as the forerunners of the opera. The pageants and masques featured in Shakespearean plays and elsewhere were important social events of "kings and beggars alike" in merry England. But the birthplace of the real opera was Italy.

The history of the opera is a fascinating study, but of course does not merit an inclusion in this text. But its influence upon instrumental music cannot be disregarded. For one thing, due to the opera, *melody became conditioned by harmony,* i.e., the melody was given a harmonious foundation, a custom never since discarded. *The opera also changed the concept of dynamics.* Terraced dynamics gave way to graduated dynamics.

Furthermore, in the hands of Monteverdi, that master composer of operas, the orchestra was given a "new look." It was adapted more and more to the expression of the whole scale of human emotions. The large number of musical instruments was greatly curtailed. The double reeds enclosed in wind chambers, such as in the rackett, being mechanical instruments, disappeared, the shawm bowed to the oboe, but the bassoon survived. Already existing instruments had their range enlarged, especially downwards, to provide the deeper basses. The orchestra was made to blend with the singing. Out of *this spirit of the opera evolved the symphony,* the greatest utterance of the ideal orchestra.

The eighteenth century was strenuously engaged in perfecting the above trends. The violinist was expected to vary the tone intensity on his own instrument, and the harpsichord and the organ were provided with swells. By 1740 the Italians were practicing orchestral *crescendi.* But the most important group of musicians of the century belonged to the *Mannheim school* of Germany. It was here that much pioneering in the new symphonic idiom was done. Johann Stamitz, also of the Mannheim school, the great forerunner of Mozart (who unjustly seldom is given credit for his achievements), established the new design and idiom of symphonic orchestration.

Another feature of this period was the *ground bass.* When the harmonic-melodic line became the vogue, the fundamental support to it was provided by the bass parts, the middle parts, considered of less importance, being left out in the written score to be supplied by the performer. The musicians consequently had to know how to harmonize the superstructure on the bass part. So important was the bass part that it became known as the *thorough-bass* or *basso continuo.* Each player had to be able to improvise the missing parts on the spur of the moment, and the demands on the leader were accordingly severe. Such improvisation soon led to ornamentation, wherein a player had a chance to display his own ingenuity. Instruments were now divided into *fundamentals* and *ornamentals.* Once printed music had assumed the modern look, composers began to lay more stress on details, but the custom of improvising parts was slow to die out. Rossini, a great nineteenth-century composer, still permitted his prima donnas to improvise their own arias in some of his operas, and even Brahms had his violinist, Joachim, supply the cadenza for the first movement of his violin concerto (1879).

Instrumental music became so important that it began to influence choral composition. In its truest sense absolute instrumental music was still lacking. But so much experimenting was carried on and such a degree of perfection was reached that the stage was now ready for the classic masters.

## *The Classical Period (1750–1825)*

To many people the term *classical music* means serious, highbrow, difficult music as compared to *popular* music. Of course, classical music is first-class but the word *classical* has a different connotation. Classical music embraces the period of the eighteenth century during which the German genius revived the antique as a creative force in a hitherto unknown intensity, not only in the field of music but in all cultural endeavors. In music the greatest exponents of this art are Haydn (1732–1809), Mozart (1756–1791), and the early Beethoven (1770–1827).

The classical period is the culmination of sixteenth- and seventeenth-century tendencies. In other words, whatever was started during those years was brought to perfection by Haydn and Mozart. The countless claims that Haydn is the father of the symphony, the father of string music, the founder of the modern orchestra, or the inventor of various musical forms, or that he and Mozart added the clarinet to the orchestra are popular misconceptions.

Symphonic form in all its complexity evolved but slowly. Haydn and Mozart summed up the achievements of the Italian, French, and German schools of composers and gave the world music of such pure beauty and perfection in melody, harmony, rhythm, phrasing, and design that it delights the heart of the most untutored listener and challenges the ambition of the most profound musician. Haydn's music is crystal clear, and Mozart is a world in himself. *Absolute music reached its peak* and *pure instrumental music of celestial beauty became a reality.* (As usual, their successors lost no time in "laying down the law," codifying their works into theories and rules for the nourishment of common mortals.)

The tendency of the classical period was to restrict the number of types of instruments to those most capable of individualized treatment. The composers of this period—naturally, there were far more than just Haydn and Mozart—strove for lucidity and precision, and hence each instrument demanded perfection of execution and a maximum of individual expression. Consequently the instruments themselves had to be perfected technically. Improvements were particularly noticeable in the wind and brass instruments.

Precision of execution and exactness of reproduction made the classicists fill in every note in their composition, thus avoiding the thorough-bass and doing away with wanton embellishments and ornamentations by the performer. The characteristics of each instrument were emphasized as clearly as possible. The practice of transferring passages of, let us say, string music to the harpsichord could no longer be upheld. A string quartet by Haydn, a horn concerto by Mozart, or a piano concerto by Beethoven are simply inconceivable on any but the prescribed instruments, because each instrument speaks exactly the language envisioned by the composer.

The classical orchestra confined itself mostly to strings, oboes, and horns. To these were gradually added the flute, clarinet, bassoon, trumpet, and kettledrums. It was not uncommon to find the number of Haydn's orchestra restricted to sixteen players. Occasionally, but sparingly, other instruments were added for special effects, thus foreshadowing the marvelous orchestration of the romantic composers.

Classical music has remained the purest form of absolute music to the present day. It charms by its tonal beauty, and it has no other motives; it is aesthetic in the truest meaning of the word.

### *The "Isms" in Music (1810–1925)*

The nineteenth century is the most active and brilliant period in the history of music. It brought with it new schools of thought which may conveniently be referred to as "isms" in music: romanticism, impressionism, expressionism, and neoclassicism.

Beethoven, the colossus among musicians, is generally considered as marking the turning point from classical to modern music. The young Beethoven followed in the footsteps of Haydn and Mozart, but the mature genius opened the field to new ventures. All his life he experimented with the symphonic form of music. Briefly, we may say that Beethoven introduced literature into instrumental music. It is also said that Beethoven found music a science and left it an art. He opened the door for personal impressions in instrumental music. His orchestrations and compositions have remained models to the present day and the foundation of all present-day orchestral activities.

The romanticists strove for an enriched color palette. New instruments appeared, sixteenth-century instruments were revived, and existing instruments were made technically so perfect (for instance, the flute, trumpet, and horn) that the whole chromatic scale was at the fingertips of the performer. Special attention was paid to the percussions; the xylophone, celesta, tubular bells, castanets, and rattle found their way into the orchestra in addition to the piano, organ, and harmonium. The style of orchestration once more underwent a radical change.

The size of the orchestra was augmented in an unbelievable manner. Only ten years after Beethoven, Berlioz demanded an orchestra of over 450 instruments! It was felt that the greater the number and variety of instruments the richer the timbre. Likewise, chamber music gave way to public performances.

Public concerts assumed an ever more important function. Haydn and Mozart performed mostly for their "patron saints" and the elite society. The end of the eighteenth century saw the bird of democracy in Europe, Beethoven championing its cause in the field of music. So royal courts were replaced by concert halls. Consequently instruments had to have more sonoirty and brilliance. Witness the changes made: clarinets and oboes were given a conical tube of large bore, which made them approximate trumpets and horns;

flutes received the modern cylindrical form, which made their voices harder and sharper; the piano of the eighteenth century with its weak and thin though pure tone became the powerful and brilliant grand piano of today.

With the classicists form in music was all-important; accordingly they developed it to perfection. The romanticists, on the other hand, made the form subservient to their themes. While by no means discarding the classic form of composition, they took certain liberties to put their ideas of expressing feeling, longing, dreaming, in short, sentiment into the focal point. Hence the change in style and orchestration.

The romanticists brought forth some delightful fruit. Just think of Schumann, Mendelssohn, Weber, Chopin, and the incomparable Schubert.

Romanticism opened the door for the orchestration of the impressionists.

Both impressionism and expressionism are no longer absolute music (romantic music still at least verges on it) but *program music.* It would be a mistake to assume that program music, so prominent today, originated in the middle of the nineteenth century. The oldest example of program music is found in the composition of the Greeks, 586 B.C., called *Pythic nome,* which depicts Apollo's fight with a dragon. Throughout the ages composers delighted in portraying certain events in music. Bach's forerunner—J. Kuhlau— definitely composed program music. Beethoven's *Pastoral Symphony* in a way is along this line, too. But it remained to the second half of the nineteenth century to make a cult of it.

Witness, for instance, Berlioz's *Symphonie Fantastique,* in which he pictures the unhappy course of unrequited love. Liszt came forth with his *Symphonic Preludes* and other *tone poems.* Richard Strauss's *Ein Heldenleben* (*A Hero's Life*), *Don Juan, Death and Transfiguration;* Saint Saëns's *Danse Macabre;* and Sibelius's *Finlandia* and *Swan of Tuonela,* to mention only a few tone poems, clearly demonstrate a new style of composition. Utilizing a gigantic orchestra capable of all shades of loudness from a mere whisper to a thundering fortissimo and of gradual and sudden changes not only in dynamics but also in timbre, orchestras perfectly blended and trained to perfection, composers now draw tone pictures like artists draw their canvases. This much, however, may be said to the credit of these composers, that they did not discard the conventional means of expressing their musical ideas, i.e., they employed conventional harmony, phrasing, orchestration, timbre, and balance although they were rather daring innovators compared to their forerunners. The total effect of these tone poems is sublime music.

The impressionists proper went a step further: they did discard a great deal of convention and introduced such daring innovations that their music for a while was considered next to impossible. The greatest of the impressionists is Claude Debussy (1862–1918), also the first great master of the new music of the twentieth century.

The impressionists in music followed the trend of impressionism in art: instead of painting an object or a scene, they painted the idea of things. This art flourished particularly in France. Debussy was surrounded by such artists. No wonder musicians in their turn became obsessed with expressing ideas for things. Debussy developed a new harmony based on a whole-tone scale. Being a genius, he succeeded marvelously.

Yet he not only discarded the conventional form in music, but also repudiated any melodic design. His musical pictures are far more daring than any that had appeared till then. He painted pictures as *nuages* (clouds) and *la mer* (the sea) with an intense, warm, and sensitive musical temperament and created a harmony of feeling and intellect. His works were inspired by true genius and absolute originality. He found new forms, new tones, and new expressions for the symphonic poem, chamber music, and even the song. His opera *Pelléas et Mélisande,* written in the new idiom, has become a classic.

Once audiences became used to Debussy, they took him to their hearts.

The expressionists arose in answer to the impressionists. Whereas the latter strove to impress the listener by creating certain moods and giving him the idea of the thing, the expressionists approached music from the opposite pole. Their idea was to express, not to impress. They emphasized man's solitude and isolation, his seeking of the truth. Impressionism voiced the influence of the external world; expressionism, on the other hand, concentrated on the inner self. The former is coloristic, the latter abstract.

What concerns us at this point again is the orchestration, the means composers adopted to achieve their ends. They were, of course, ultra modern in their orchestration and treatment of musical idioms. We will hear more about this later.

Another "ism" that flourished briefly in the second half of the nineteenth century was *nationalism.* Today it is generally conceded that music is an international language. Time was when certain composers felt they should bring forth the "spirit of their nation" and immortalize their nationalities in music. Glinka in Russia, Grieg in Norway, and Smetana in Bohemia, to mention only a few, are sometimes spoken of as "fathers" of the music of their countries. Regardless of how much they contributed to bring their countries into the limelight musically, they are cherished today not so much on account of their nationality but for their merits as composers.

Grieg's *Piano Concerto* actually will not remind the listener of Norway, and his incidental music to *Peer Gynt* certainly can be enjoyed by itself.

Still another "ism" merits mention at this point: *Neoclassicism*. A group of composers tried to revive classicism. They represent one of the countercurrents of the new trends in music.

To which category the greatest symphonist of the second half of the nineteenth century belongs need not concern us unduly, but by claiming the heritage of Beethoven he has left us magnificent works second to none. Johannes Brahms (1833–1897) is the last in the line of great German symphonists. At heart he was a romantic; intellectually he tried to re-establish the form of the classics.

### *The Music of Our Own Times*

For lack of perspective no attempt is being made here to arrive at an objective analysis of the present-day situation. We are merely endeavoring to note certain trends.

One of the most characteristic tendencies of our century is that we try to *get away from convention to create something new*. "Novel effects" it is called. In itself it is a creditable thing, but we have reached the stage of "novelty for novelty's sake." Here are some of the reasons and ways we have reached such a stage.

In no other field of cultural activity is the artist in the same difficult position as the composer of music. When a new piece of sculpture or a new oil painting is exhibited, no one stops to compare it with the statue of Colleoni in Venice or with a Raphael or a Rembrandt. If you write a novel or a poem or a drama, chances are that your work will be judged on its own merits; you won't have to compete against Dickens or Tolstoi, Milton or Tennyson, Shakespeare or Shaw. But as soon as a new musical composition appears, people invariably summon Bach, Mozart, Beethoven, and the whole galaxy of the nineteenth-century composers and expect the new work to hold its own against the greatest masterpieces ever produced. Small wonder that composers no longer are interested in adhering to the ideals of their predecessors.

The rock of music up to the turn of our century was composed of melody, harmony, rhythm, form or design, balance in phrasing and structure, and blend of tonal colors—all based on the diatonic scale with its major-minor tonality. We have seen how one generation bequeathed their achievements to the next and how each generation built upon its inheritance. Not so today. The new experimenters have discarded the whole edifice erected before them.

Music was looked upon as organized sound aimed at the creation of beauty. Apparently beauty of sound and expression is no longer the goal. To arrive at the new slogan, throw overboard everything that you have held in high esteem. Write melodies which will be entirely "different," so that nobody will recognize them as such in a hurry; throw harmony overboard and write music without it; forget about phrases and cadences; abandon regular rhythm with its time signatures; overlook regular scales and keys (be "atonal"); avoid blend of timbre—in short use every device you can think of (and then some) to create something new, but make sure nobody else will have thought of the same thing. It need not be beautiful or harmonious, but it must be different! So what kind of instruments are you going to use?

Deems Taylor sums up the situation with the following analogy: Suppose the new cook prepares a dish. The first thing you know he discards the conventional ingredients such as flour, butter, milk, honey, and salt in favor of sand, ground glass, lubricating oil, kerosene, and sawdust. If you don't find the dish tasty or nourishing or appetizing, the cook will say, "Ah, but it is not supposed to be nourishing! We don't want you to relish it! But admit, kind sir, it is something new, for we are the new generation, we are modern!" If you find this picture exaggerated, remember it is put forth by one of the leading musicians of our day!

The craze for new effects makes pianists, for instance, play the piano with the elbow or a plank of wood. In its nobler aspects it is producing the "new sound" we discussed in the preceding chapter under electronics. And since no master thought of utilizing noise for its own sake, noise-making instruments are precious in the eyes of the modern entertainer. In addition, *glissando* and *vibrato* effects on trumpets and saxophones (heaven shield us), whimpering saws, hammered xylophones—any device to create a novelty is welcome. Symphonic music is "jazzified." George Gershwin (1898–1937), the American composer, succeeded even in this, but more often than not the best classical music is vulgarized thereby. The most beautiful melodic lines of the great masters are "popularized." Tape recorders compile sounds like crowd noises, trains, bells, and anything else that is likely to strike the listener as something he has not yet heard. (Staples credits the crooners with using the sound of a cow bellowing in pain!)

A certain amount of noise and certainly discords are essential for harmony, just as shades are necessary for light. But today disharmony and noise are an end in themselves; no longer are spices used to flavor the food, but are used for food itself.

In *Grove's Dictionary* we find this judgment passed on some of the present-day church music: ". . . it is difficult to describe the emptiness and vulgarity of much that has been produced in England

and America for revival services, and even for use in regular Sunday worship." [2]

The "hit tunes" of our century are so terribly shallow that their average span of life is only several weeks. Jazz has an unusually strong sensual appeal only, and the "rock 'n' roll" craze unloosens savage instincts in the crowd.

It is also amazing that most people nowadays dismiss the terms "good" and "bad" in music. Whatever appeals to them personally, no matter how vulgar, profane, or shallow, is good.

The twentieth century has yet to produce a work of such dimensions as *The Messiah* or *The Creation,* not to speak of Bach's all-powerful and immortal masses and passions. (The last great work of church music is probably Brahms's *Requiem.*) In church music nothing worth while is being produced today.

Such are the symptoms of our present musical life. On the surface it appears we are sick to the core of our hearts. The underlying cause for the disease is found in the world outlook of our generation, conditioned no doubt by two world wars. All writers on contemporary music agree in this respect. To make a long story short, let me quote you just one sentence from Lang's book: "Our century shows a lack of spiritual ideals, submission to materialism and technicalism, and a resultant hunger for sensation and bluff." [3]

The serious composers are quite sincere and honest in their efforts to create something worth while. But they too, instead of enlarging the inherited edifice and modernizing it, are striving for something radically new. The total effect, according to Deems Taylor, is "woefully monotonous." [4] There are exceptions, of course.

Some modern works, even ultramodern ones, are here to stay.

Fortunately there is another side to the gloomy picture just painted: the reaction of the music-loving public, the efforts of music teachers and countless organizations, and the activity of orchestra leaders and their musicians.

In the first place, music-lovers do not endorse the efforts of the ultramodern composers. Dr. Furtwängler throws an interesting light on this attitude of the public. He shows that for over forty

[2] 3rd ed, vol. II, p. 396.

[3] H. P. Lang, *Music in Western Civilization,* page 1025.

[4] The author tried the following experiment on one of his Grade 11 classes: without telling the students the title of the composition to be played, he played a recording of a classical symphony they had never heard before and later a modern symphony. In each case the students were told to let the instructor know when they had had enough. In the first case the record was stopped after five and a half minutes of quiet listening due to time pressure; the second record was stopped on demand after fifty seconds!

years the public has refused to take modern music (the serious or real music, mind you) to their hearts or to give composers their support. Never has recognition of new works been so slow in coming.

Yet music critics and musical societies do their best to promote modern works. Organizations stage competitions and offer scholarships to promising composers. Conductors of world fame champion the cause of the new music. Orchestras and soloists are willing to perform it. But what usually happens to the modern composer is that he gets a première of his work and is then forgotten—forgotten for the simple reason that the public does not want to hear him again.

The argument that all new music had to fight for recognition and that our century is no exception in this respect, although usually put forth with great force, is not valid. We read of fiascos of first performances of great operas or symphonies, but the public—in the final analysis the supreme judge—would always in short order recognize the intrinsic values of great works in spite of the critics. Why do they so stubbornly refuse to endorse ultramodern music? And yet it must have something in it that makes it stay, or else it would have died out in four or five decades.

Another feature of modern musical activity is public performances. Democracy has succeeded in shifting the performance from the courts and the chambers of the aristocracy to public music halls. Musicians, composers, and performers alike used to depend on the graces of patrons, but today they depend on the support of the public. Concerts in large auditoriums have become the backbone of musical organizations. Concert music has become a million-dollar industry. As a rule orchestras are sponsored by boards of directors, and their activities must return tangible financial results or else. (All too often the financial position of a symphony orchestra is rather precarious.) Consequently they play what the public demands.

And what do they demand? They demand the great masters. A Beethoven concert, a Wagner or Verdi opera will always command a full house; in fact, the house will be sold out months in advance. Substitute modern composers and be prepared to face a serious deficit. People have stormed against a Beethoven, a Berlioz, or a Bizet to no avail; a meritorious work always comes out victorious. Where does that leave the ultramodern?

The tremendous expense of concert activities and the dire necessity to attract large crowds has brought highly skilled players, high-rate specialists, and well-trained conductors to the foreground. Consequently there is a never-ending quest for better instruments. Musicians of today have a higher level of proficiency than their forerunners. A few illustrations will bear out the point.

Wagner's opera *Tristan and Isolde,* now in the repertoire of all standard orchestras, had to be abandoned as unplayable in 1862 after fifty-four rehearsals. Furthermore, the chief tenor could not learn the role of Tristan. In 1861 Tchaikovsky's violin concerto was turned down by Auer, one of the greatest violin virtuosos and teachers, on the grounds that it could not be played! Paganini's violin music was considered so difficult that nobody could duplicate his feats, and he had to endure the flattering nickname of "devil on the violin." Today any concert violinist plays not only Paganini and Tchaikovsky but any concerto ever written. The same holds true with other instrumentalists. One needs only to consider the improvements made in flutes, oboes, clarinets, bassoons, trumpets, and horns to realize the tremendous advantages musicians have today.

Orchestras owe their proficiency and perfection in no small measure to the skill of professional leaders. So important have the leaders become that one is tempted to call the present age the *age of the conductor.*

Conducting as a profession is comparatively new. In former days the conductor used to lead his orchestra from the harpsichord, or the piano or he was "playing the first fiddle" standing in front of the orchestra. If he played the violin he would stamp his feet to indicate time. (We still use the expression "to beat time.") Little importance was attached to the conductor as such.

The situation changed radically with the appearance of Baron Hans Guido von Bülow (1830–1894), who is given the credit of laying down the working methods of the modern concert conductor. He was a brilliant pianist and orchestra leader. Under his conductorship the German orchestras soon became the envy of the world. Whatever he did with his orchestra was much admired and naturally imitated. He interpreted another composer's works in his own way and as often as not would ignore given instructions. In his hands the results were laudable, but in the hands of his followers all too frequently lamentable. Drawing one's inspiration not from the printed score of the composer but from his own interpretation is always risky, to say the least. Yet this became fashionable, and conducting became an art in itself. Not without reason did Berlioz warn his fellow composers that their most dangerous interpreter was the conductor.

Toward the end of the last century a new trend in conducting was established: the faithful reproduction of the written scores. The new genius to champion the cause was Arturo Toscanini (died 1957). Mercilessly he opposed any arbitrary changes in the composer's score. His maxim was that Mozart must be played as

Mozart saw it and not the way Toscanini felt about him. So the conductor must know the score to a T (Toscanini knew every score by heart, just as Bülow did), submerge himself in the work, and then recreate it. Toscanini had a profound influence upon the conductors of the world; by and large the conductors of today are faithful to the composers.

So important have conductors become that they make world news headlines, and the destiny of orchestras is in their hands. Under the leadership of brilliant conductors the performance of orchestras has reached such a state of perfection that last century's performances would pale in comparison. Not that those musicians did not strive for perfection—Gluck, for instance, is said to have been more exacting in his demands on the players than Toscanini, and one hardly pictures Mozart being satisfied with mediocre performances—but the players did not have the training and the perfect instruments of our time, nor true conductors to lead them.

Still, Furtwängler (1886–1954), also one of the truly great conductors, claims that the symphonies of the masters are no longer played the way they were played fifty years ago, for the spirit to enter the ideas of those times is lacking in our musicians. After all, music is more than the rendering of the notes written down. Technical perfection is not the only requirement for perfect music. In the main, however, the symphony orchestra of the twentieth century is the most marvelous instrument mankind has ever seen.

Orchestras and bands have been fairly stabilized by now. The classicists employed delicate orchestras of small numbers, while the romanticists increased the size of the orchestra tremendously. Berlioz, Wagner, Richard Strauss, and Stravinsky made almost impossible demands on the orchestra. Mahler (1860–1911) went so far as to write his *Eighth Symphony* for such a large ensemble of players and singers that it became known as the "symphony of the thousand." He required a great organ, a large choir of children, several hundred male singers, two ladies' choirs, an enlarged orchestra plus a piano, harmonium, mandolins, bells, glockenspiel, a wide variety of unusual percussions, and finally a special brass choir. The sum total was rather disillusioning, of course, for the output was in no way proportional to the input. Who, after all, is in position to sponsor the performance of such a monstrosity?

But note the evolution from the dozen or so of Haydn's performers to the hundreds of the modern composer. Mahler had no imitators, for the whole idea was neither economical nor practical. The orchestra began to shrink again. Today a typical symphony orchestra is made up in the following manner (with slight modifications, of course):

| | |
|---|---|
| 58 strings | 16 first violins |
| | 14 second violins |
| | 10 violas |
| | 10 cellos |
| | 8 double-basses |
| 12 woodwinds | 2 flutes |
| | 1 piccolo (or third flute) |
| | 2 oboes |
| | 1 English horn (or third oboe) |
| | 2 clarinets |
| | 1 bass clarinet |
| | 2 bassoons |
| | 1 double bassoon (or third bassoon) |
| 10 brasses | 2 trumpets |
| | 4 French horns (or simply horns) |
| | 2 tenor trombones |
| | 1 bass trombone |
| | 1 tuba |
| Percussions | 1 timpani |
| | 1-2 players for the rest of percussion instruments |
| | 1-2 harps |
| | occasionally: celeste, piano, pipe organ |

To secure a blend of the various instruments certain seating plans have been adopted. The following diagram shows one of the typical arrangements of the modern orchestra.

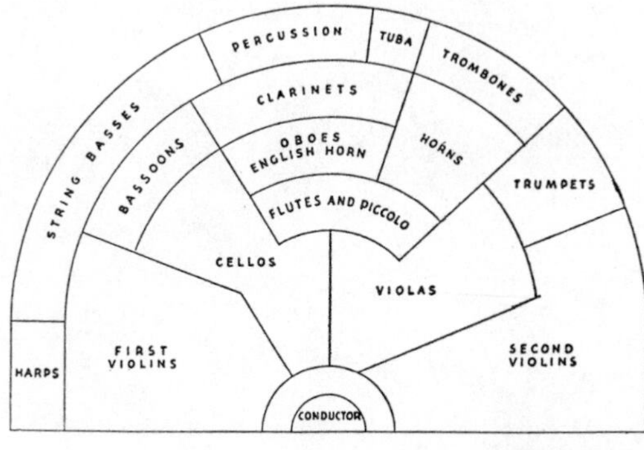


**Figure 326**
**Seating Plan of a Symphony Orchestra**
**Courtesy C. G. Conn Ltd., Elkhart, Indiana**

Bands differ from symphonic orchestras in not having the string section. A typical band seating plan is shown on page 378.

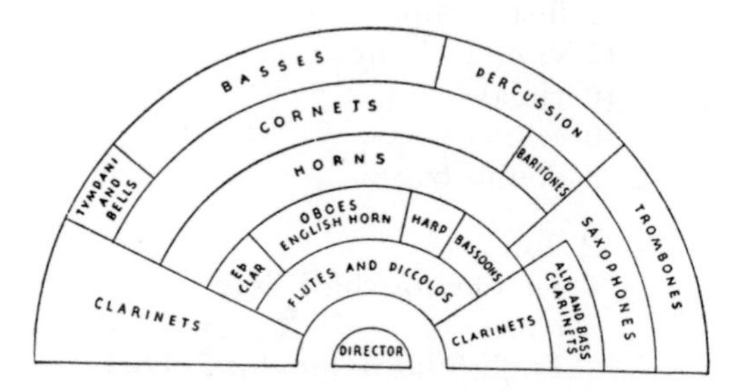


Figure 327
Seating Plan of a Band
Courtesy C. G. Conn Ltd.,
Elkhart, Indiana

During the second quarter of our century the number of symphony orchestras literally mushroomed. Thus, in 1932 Canada had five symphony orchestras, in 1938 eight, in 1947 ten, and in 1956 sixteen. The situation in the United States is just as encouraging. These numbers do not include school and university bands and orchestras.

In many places the teaching of music in elementary and high schools has assumed large-scale proportions. Bands, being made up of instruments easier to play than the symphonic instruments, are popular even in smaller centers. Girls, too, are being organized into orchestral ensembles.

Mention must also be made of and credit given to musical organizations which bring live music to the younger generation by special

Figure 328. Spokane, Washington, Clinic

concerts for high-school students and children. Furthermore, touring artists, choirs, and orchestras of world renown have brought first-rate concerts within the reach of people even in small towns.

Never before has so much music been available to so many. Not only is the number of active musicians greater than ever but people barred from attending actual performances have recourse to high-fidelity long-playing phonograph records and lately to stereophonic music.

As common as "high fidelity" has become, few people are aware of the full meaning of the term. Literally it means "high faithfulness", presumably referring to accurate reproduction of the recorded sound. One frequently finds the manufacturer advertising his product as reproducing all sound waves from 20 to 20,000 vibrations per second. How much music there is in sounds of let us say, 10,000 or more vibrations per seconds can be conjectured if we stop to consider that the highest note on the ordinary piano is of some 5,000 vibrations per second. Suppose pianos had two more octaves added to their highest range; would that be of any advantage? In fact, it requires keen perception to hear sounds above 15,000 vibrations, so why emphasize the highest frequencies?

More correctly, "hi-fi" aims at reproducing the complex wave patterns set up by the overtones of the instruments or voice. In such a way instruments are sharply delineated and the characteristics of individual instruments are more or less faithfully maintained. In this way the illusion of nearly perfect reproduction is created. For their effectiveness, hi-fi recordings depend on expensive equipment. Far too many cheap record players parade under the trade mark of "hi-fi".

Stereophonic music is analogous to three-dimensional pictures as shown on stereoscopic viewmasters. Briefly, it works on the following principles. In stereoscopic pictures one picture is taken from the position of the left eye, and the other from that of the right eye. The sound entering our ears from a live source also does so at slight intervals of time, giving us a sense of perspective and enabling us to locate the source of the sound or place or origin.

In stereophonic music, therefore, the sound is taken up by a double-track tape from two microphones, each track recording from is own microphone. The two microphones are placed a certain distance apart so that the sound for the tape emanates from two sources. In playing such tapes, each tape has its own "head," amplifying and loudspeaker system, where each loudspeaker reproduces exactly what its corresponding microphone picked up. The loudspeakers are spaced the same distance apart as the original microphones. In this way the illusion of depth and directionality is created.

Stereophonic sound is the nearest approach to live music. True, it is expensive, but even the discerning music lover may be misled into taking it for the real thing, other factors being equal. *Time* magazine reports that during a performance of Mozart's *Marriage of Figaro* in San Francisco engineers had put concealed speakers on the stage; the orchestra went through the motions of playing while the engineers ran off a stereo tape of the overture. Few of the listeners knew that they were listening to recorded music.

To date we have witnessed the transfer of stereophonic sound from double-track tapes to double-track phonograph records. The groove of such records contains both tracks, one on each side. Special stereo needles, cartridges, and pick-up arms, two amplifiers, and at least two loudspeaker systems properly spaced are essential equipment for stereo music. The acoustics of the home must also be considered. By and large most stereo is badly handled. But there is no denying that true stereo is really great, by far the best illusion of perfect reproduction.

It appears that 1961 is going to inaugurate *reverb,* a technical device which can change the apparent acoustics of your room. It is supposed to change your room into a concert hall! Just how this is accomplished is still a riddle to the author. It is possible that by the time this book is published the reader will be able to find the answer to this problem in some of the current hi-fi or stereo magazines.

All told, we are justified in dividing the musical activity of our day into two classes: the popular and the serious. The former embraces the majority of the listeners and includes those who take their music effortlessly. "Serious" music must not be taken literally, for it refers to the music of the masters and their like, in short, music which is more than a mere expression of the motor impulse and which has more than a sentimental or emotional value, although these aspects are not necessarily excluded. Time was when music was divided into sacred and secular. This distinction hardly holds today, inasmuch as a great deal of so-called church music is rather profane.

It is possible that the historian of the future will call our century (or at least the first half of it) the period of consolidation and/or experimentation in search of a new musical idiom. After all, such a tremendous amount of music has already been written that much of it is never performed. No wonder musicians are reviving the contemporaries of Bach, Mozart, Vivaldi and company.

At the same time the human race is groping for new horizons. Technically our age has wrought miracles. Ideologically too? The reader must draw his own conclusions. But it is my belief that as always the best will survive, and something worth while is going to emerge in the long run.

Abbreviations for Staff Notation

Each sequence begins on the note C and embraces twelve semitones

## BIBLIOGRAPHY

(Books consulted by the author in compiling his manuscript)

M. Bauer & E. Peyser. *Music Through the Ages.* New York and London: G. P. Putnam's Sons.

*How Music Grew.* New York and London: G. P. Putnam's Sons.

A. L. Bacharach. *Lives of Great Composers,* 3 vol. Baltimore: Pelican Books.

W. J. Baltzell. *History of Music.* Philadelphia: Theodore Presser Co.

W. H. Barnes. *The Contemporary American Organ.* New York: J. Fischer & Bro.

Bessaraboff. *Ancient European Musical Instruments.* Boston: Harvard University Press.

F. K. Buchanan. *How Music Grew.*

R. Donington. *The Instruments of Music.* London: Methuen & Co., Ltd.

Douglas. *The Electronic Musical Manual.* London: Pitman & Sons.

Eastman School of Music, *Milestones in the History of Music.* Rochester.

A. Elson. *The Book of Musical Knowledge.* Boston & New York: Houghton Mifflin Co.

C. H. Farnsworth. *How To Study Music.* New York: Macmillan.

Faulkner. *What We Hear In Music.* New Jersey: R. C. A. Manufacturing Co.

Fryberger. *Listening Lessons in Music.* New York: Silver, Burdette & Co.

Furtwängler, Wilhelm. *Gespräche über Musik.* Zürich: Atlantis Verlag.

F. W. Galpin. *Old English Instruments of Music, Their History and Character.* London: Methuen & Co., Ltd.

*A Textbook of European Musical Instruments.* London: Williams & Norgate Ltd.

I. H. Graham. *Music Appreciation for Schools.* Edmonton: Institute of Applied Art.

C. Gray. *A Survey of Contemporary Music.* London: Oxford University Press.

K. Geiringer. *Musical Instruments.* London: G. Allen & Unwin.

*Grove's Dictionary of Music and Musicians.* New York & London: Macmillan.

J. Hallstrom. *Relax and Listen.* New York & Toronto: Rinehart & Co.

W. Heinitz. *Instrumentenkunde.* New York: Musurgia Publishers.

R. Hill. *Music 1950.* Baltimore: Pelican Books.

A. J. Hipkins. *Musical Instruments, Historic, Rare and Unique.* London: A. & C. Black, Ltd.

H. E. Huntington. *Tune Up, The Instruments of the Orchestra and* Their Players. Garden City, New York: Doubleday & Co.

J. H. Howard. *The Modern Music.* New York: Thomas Y. Crowell Co.

G. Jacob. *Orchestral Technique.* London: Oxford University Press.

F. Joede. *Elementarlehre der Musik.* Berlin: Kallmeyer Verlag.

A. E. Johnstone. *Instruments of the Modern Symphony Orchstra.* New York: C. Fischer.

E. S. Kelly. *Musical Instruments.* Boston: O. Ditson Co.

G. Kinsky. *Geschichte der Musik in Bildern.* Leipzig: Breitkopf & Haertel.

Lachmann. *Die Musik der aussereuropäischen Völker.* New York: Musurgia Publisher.

La Prade. *Alice in Orchestralia.* Garden City: Doubleday & Co.

P. H. Lang. *Music in Western Civilization.* London: W. W. Norton & Co., Inc.

H. LeCaine. *Electronic Music.* From *Proceedings of the I. R. E.*

W. R. Maclaurin. *Invention and Innovation in the Radio Industry.* New York and London: Macmillan.

C. Morse. *Music and Music Makers.* London: G. Allen & Unwin Ltd.

H. J. Moser. *Musikgeschichte in 100 Lebensbildern.* Reclam.

National Film Board. *The Life and Work of Norman McLaren.* Ottawa.

K. Nef. *Geschichte unserer Musikinstrumente.* Basel: Amerhard Verlag.

K. Pahlen. *Music of the World, A History.* New York: Crown Publishers.

P.Panoff. *Die Altslavische Volk und Kirchenmusik.* New York: Musurgia Publishers.

C. Huebert and H. Parry. *The Evolution of the Art of Music.* New York: Appleton & Co.

A. Robertson. *Music 1952.* Baltimore: Pelican Books.

Curt Sachs. *The History of Musical Instruments.* New York: W. W. Norton & Co.

*Die Musik der Antike.* New York: Musurgia Publishers.

H. W. Schwartz. *The Story of Musical Instruments.* Elkhart, Ina.: C. G. Conn.

Th. Seder. *Old World Overtones.* Philadelphia: University Museum.

Dinn and Sharp. *Music, The Observer's Book.* London & New York: F. Warne & Co., Ltd.

R. Staples. *Exploring the World of Music.* New York & London: Macmillan.

*Music Manual for the Classroom Teacher.* New York & London: Macmillan.

Stoddard. *From These Comes Music* New York: Thomas Y. Crowell Co.

Steiner. *Music of the Bible.*

Deems Taylor. *Of Music and Men.* New York: Simon & Schuster Inc.

*R.C.A. Victor Instruments of the Orchestra, Handbook.* Philadelphia: J. W. Pepper & Sons.

*Elektronische Musik.* Die Reihe I. Wien: Universal Edition.

J. Weakly. *Music and Its Makers.* London: Harrap & Co., Ltd.

M. Wegner. *Die Musikinstrumente des alten Orient.* Münster in Westfalen: Aschendorffsche Verlagsbuchhandlung.

J. H. Yocom. *Music Enjoyment and Appreciation,* 2 vol. Toronto: Reyerson, Toronto.

Bayerische Nationalmuseum. *Alte Musik, Instrumente.* München.

# INDEX

Note: Figures in italic refer to illustrations.